Green & Sustainable Finance
From vision to market practice

綠色及可持續金融
從願景到市場實踐

VOLUME 2

下冊

Edited by HKEX

香港交易所　主編

商務印書館
THE COMMERCIAL PRESS

Green & Sustainable Finance: From vision to market practice (Volume 2)

Executive editor: Chris CHEUNG

Publisher: The Commercial Press (H.K) Ltd.,
8/F, Eastern Central Plaza, 3 Yiu Hing Road,
Shau Kei Wan, Hong Kong

Distributor: The SUP Publishing Logistics (H.K.) Ltd.,
16/F, Tsuen Wan Industrial Building,
220-248 Texaco Road, Tsuen Wan, New Territories, Hong Kong

Printer: Elegance Printing and Book Binding Co. Ltd.
Block A, 4th Floor, Hoi Bun Building
6 Wing Yip Street, Kwun Tong, Kowloon, Hong Kong

© 2022 Hong Kong Exchanges and Clearing Limited
First edition, First printing, February 2022

ISBN: 978 962 07 6678 7
Printed in Hong Kong

綠色及可持續金融 : 從願景到市場實踐（下冊）

責任編輯：張宇程

出　　版：商務印書館（香港）有限公司
　　　　　香港筲箕灣耀興道 3 號東滙廣場 8 樓
　　　　　http://www.commercialpress.com.hk

發　　行：香港聯合書刊物流有限公司
　　　　　香港新界荃灣德士古道 220-248 號荃灣工業中心 16 樓

印　　刷：美雅印刷製本有限公司
　　　　　九龍觀塘榮業街 6 號海濱工業大廈 4 樓 A 室

版　　次：2022 年 2 月第 1 版第 1 次印刷
　　　　　© 2022 香港交易及結算所有限公司

　　　　　ISBN 978 962 07 6678 7
　　　　　香港印刷

Contents

Volume 2

目錄

下冊

3   The role of exchanges in green and sustainable finance

3　交易所在綠色及可持續金融中的角色

Risk statements and disclaimer

Risks of securities trading

Trading in securities carries risks. The prices of securities fluctuate, sometimes dramatically. The price of a security may move up or down, and may become valueless. It is as likely that losses will be incurred rather than profit made as a result of buying and selling securities.

Risks of trading futures and options

Futures and options involve a high degree of risk. Losses from futures and options trading can exceed initial margin funds and investors may be required to pay additional margin funds on short notice. Failure to do so may result in the position being liquidated and the investor being liable for any resulting deficit. Investors must therefore understand the risks of trading in futures and options and should assess whether they are suitable for them. Investors are encouraged to consult a broker or financial adviser on their suitability for futures and options trading in light of their financial position and investment objectives before trading.

Disclaimer

All information and views contained in this book are for informational purposes only and do not constitute an offer, solicitation, invitation or recommendation to buy or sell any securities, futures contracts or other products or to provide any advice or service of any kind. The views expressed in this book do not necessarily represent the position of Hong Kong Exchanges and Clearing Limited ("HKEX") or the other institutions to which the authors of this book belong ("Relevant Institutions"). Nothing in this book constitutes or should be regarded as investment or professional advice. While information contained in this book is obtained or compiled from sources believed to be reliable, the authors of this book, HKEX, the Relevant Institutions or any of HKEX's or the Relevant Institutions' subsidiaries, directors or employees will neither guarantee its accuracy, timeliness or completeness for any particular purpose, nor be responsible for any loss or damage arising from the use of, or reliance upon, any information contained in this book.

風險與免責聲明

買賣證券的風險

證券買賣涉及風險。證券價格有時可能會非常波動。證券價格可升可跌,甚至變成毫無價值。買賣證券未必一定能夠賺取利潤,反而可能會招致損失。

買賣期貨及期權的風險

期貨及期權涉及高風險,買賣期貨及期權所招致的損失有可能超過開倉時繳付的按金,令投資者或須在短時間內繳付額外按金。若未能繳付,投資者的持倉或須平倉,任何虧損概要自行承擔。因此,投資者務須清楚明白買賣期貨及期權的風險,並衡量是否適合自己。投資者進行交易前,宜根據本身財務狀況及投資目標,向經紀或財務顧問查詢是否適合買賣期貨及期權合約。

免責聲明

本書所載資料及分析只屬資訊性質,概不構成要約、招攬、邀請或推薦買賣任何證券、期貨合約或其他產品,亦不構成提供任何形式的建議或服務。書中表達的意見不一定代表香港交易及結算所有限公司(「香港交易所」)或本書其他作者所屬的機構(「有關機構」)的立場。書中內容概不構成亦不得被視為投資或專業建議。儘管本書所載資料均取自認為是可靠的來源或按當中內容編備而成,但本書各作者、香港交易所和有關機構及其各自的附屬公司、董事及僱員概不就有關資料(就任何特定目的而言)的準確性、適時性或完整性作任何保證。本書各作者、香港交易所和有關機構及其各自的附屬公司、董事及僱員對使用或依賴本書所載的任何資料而引致任何損失或損害概不負責。

2

Market practice and infrastructure

市場實踐與基礎設施

Chapter 10

Understanding your options in the burgeoning global ESG investment landscape

AXA Investment Managers

Summary

As green and sustainable finance is gaining more traction due to its increasingly important role in an overall green and sustainable world, the investment options in the market are also drastically growing.

In this chapter, we will go through what options investors have and how can they better understand these options when considering investing in the sustainable space to meet their goals.

We will first look at the existing main approaches that are adopted by key market players when designing Responsible Investment (RI) products. These include Exclusion, Environmental, Social and Governance (ESG) Integration, Sustainable Focus and Impact Investing, each of them with a different level of RI goals.

We will also walk through how RI investing is implemented in different asset classes, including equities, fixed income, alternatives and real estate. Each asset class will have its own unique offering in the RI front and it is important for investors to understand what to expect and how they work.

Once we have established a general view of the RI world, it's time for investors to put it into practice and make the decisions based on their own responsible investing goals. This is easier said than done. Multiple challenges remain for investors when they try to overlay an ESG lens, ranging from how they practically integrate ESG factors into their portfolios, to how their approach can be consistent and repeatable to align with their sustainability goals. We will go through a list of key questions to carve a clear path for investors to follow with their options.

In the end we will zoom into the green bond market — an area in the RI space of great growth potential — and specifically take a closer look at China's green bond market by examining both the opportunities and unique risks associated.

A considerable range of responsible investment (RI) options

Over time, as investor appetite for sustainable investment continues to grow, the number of environmental, social and governance (ESG) tools and products on the market is also quickly expanding to meet a variety of needs. The development of the RI universe offers different levels of approach, from simple exclusion of the worst sustainability risks, through to ESG integration and, ultimately, impact investing. When deciding which approach to select, investors need to clearly understand their individual expectations — for financial performance and in terms of ESG criteria and outcomes.

Main RI approaches

There are typically four main RI approaches available to investors:

Exclusion: the aim here is to eliminate exposure to the companies and sectors that bring the most significant risks in terms of sustainability. This might include the coal sector, which is now often excluded by financial institutions, or companies which face severe controversies. Some investors also look to exclude sectors, such as gambling or alcohol, that conflict with their particular ethical principles.

ESG Integration: this type of approach relies on ESG analysis, such as ESG scores and other indicators, to inform and influence investment decision making. ESG-integrated strategies are increasingly popular with investors because they can reveal more clearly the risks and opportunities at hand, as well as providing evidence of expected impact more clearly than exclusion strategies. For example, ESG-integrated strategies can target specific ESG scores and position themselves further up the scale in the investment universe.

Sustainable Focus approach (such as Best-in-Class): this approach is typically more selective and seeks greater impact than ESG-integrated strategies. Products in this category might remove the "worst" issuers from the investment universe, helping portfolio managers to focus on stronger ESG players and avoid major ESG risks. Further, some sustainable focus approaches have a target to materially outperform based on an ESG indicator such as ESG score or carbon intensity. Investors may deem this a more meaningful approach than seen in ESG integration, demonstrating greater intentionality.

Impact Investing: the goal in this final category is to deliver verifiable, positive change based on agreed ESG outcome targets. Impact investing could help investors tap into key financial markets megatrends while addressing some of the most important sustainability challenges. The sector was initially built on powerful private market foundations, but a growing roster of large, listed companies are now providing products and services that can deliver positive and demonstrable effects for our society and the planet. The evolving impact investing universe is offering investors an important choice.

Other than the above four approaches, **stewardship strategies** are often applied as an important complement, combining the integration of ESG criteria and voting at annual general meetings, based on an on-going engagement with investee companies. The engagement dialogue with companies enables investors to actively monitor their investments and press for improvements that will ultimately protect the long-term interests of investors, investee companies, and financial players. The relationship with investee firms can continue for many years — decades in some cases. This RI technique has met a growing interest over the past years, and is an essential tool for investors to help support the "transition" to a more sustainable world, helping companies to adapt to tackle challenges and to contribute to the ambitious goals on climate change.

RI approaches and options across different asset classes

Investors now have more choices than ever before in terms of investing responsibly — and growing demand is only increasing the abundance of ESG products and funds on offer. Previously, responsible investing was largely about excluding certain companies, or so-called "sin stocks", from portfolios. These typically included businesses engaged in weapons manufacturing, gambling, alcohol, or tobacco production. Corporations deemed a threat to environmental well-being, such as oil and gas companies, were also often barred from responsible investment strategies.

But simply divesting from companies, such as those polluting the environment, is a blunt tool that can fail to drive positive change. The good news is that there are plenty of assets and investments in the market available to investors which proactively aim to deliver measurable and beneficial outcomes for both society and the planet. This is the "impact investing" approach introduced above.

Investors seeking out impact strategies look to companies and funds which can potentially generate not just long-term returns, but also a positive — and quantifiable

— environmental or social impact. Transparency around such investments is vital, so investors can ensure their holdings align with their values.

We believe this can be achieved by investing in the shares and bonds of companies which vigorously aim to deliver on ESG standards. Figure 1 outlines the main asset classes and choices available to investors.

Figure 1. Responsible investment options across different asset classes

Equities	Fixed Income	**Alternatives and Real Estate**
• Environmental-focused, e.g. electric vehicles	• Green bonds	• Mostly private investment
• Social-focused, e.g. diversity, education	• Social bonds	• Allows greater influence over the holdings
• Governance-focused	• Transition bonds	

Equities

Equity investing has been given a powerful boost through the increasing effectiveness of ESG scoring for both screening and integration approaches. Ultimately, ESG scoring provides material information on risk and opportunity required for long-term investment decisions — something that is particularly important for active investment managers.

Delivering specific, intentional and positive societal outcomes — above what would have ordinarily taken place — is more difficult to prove when buying a stock in the secondary market. However, we believe there are certainly ways that impact investing can be applied in public equities, provided careful analysis is conducted to identify and record the genuine and intentional impact outcomes.

Environmental

Industries like low-carbon transport, and the supply chains around electric vehicles, for example, are likely to benefit from the increasing adoption rates in the coming years. Smart energy sectors represent another opportunity — the digitalisation of buildings and industries, and smart grid technology, is opening new possibilities for energy efficiency and renewable sources. In the agricultural sector, companies are exploring new ways to meet demand from growing populations while limiting the use of scarce land. This creates opportunities to invest in companies that are developing food and agricultural technologies and solutions to address food waste.

Social

The scale of unmet social needs also creates opportunities for companies, and investors, to improve outcomes for underserved people in developing and developed countries. For instance, one can look for businesses which improve access to essential services, increasing inclusion for underserved populations and helping to address large unmet needs. Businesses looking to improve access to and affordability of healthcare, or that support medical innovation, represent another opportunity, as do companies which foster diversity, entrepreneurship and education. Such firms can create more opportunities for people around the world and sustain development within disadvantaged communities.

Governance

Ultimately, public opinion is shifting and putting pressure on companies. Responsible asset managers have a duty to monitor and engage with companies whose shares they own. Fundamentally, if a corporation wants to be truly sustainable it needs to have robust governance structures in place, which proactively aim to tackle societal issues to deliver a better future for people and the planet. For example, businesses which mitigate environmental damage should, in our view, yield large net gains to the global economy. History shows that well-governed companies outperform in the long term and are better positioned to take advantage of new opportunities[1]. If they are not, it can have a potentially significant and negative impact.

Fixed income

When it comes to fixed income, RI issues contain material financial information which affects the credit quality of an issuer. ESG criteria effectively add a layer of additional qualitative information. Fund managers can incorporate this information into their decisions, taking account of risks and opportunities, and apply them to their fixed-income portfolios.

---

1   Source: Deloitte, "Good governance driving corporate performance? — A meta-analysis of academic research & invitation to engage in the dialogue", December 2016.

Green bonds

One of the most powerful demonstrations of RI in the bond space has been the rapidly growing green bond market, which set a record for issuance at US$269.5 billion in 2020[2]. The proceeds from green bonds are dedicated to financing new and existing projects which aim to have a positive impact on the environment. When it comes to investing in green bonds, there are two main approaches. One is to allocate green bonds into an existing fixed-income portfolio and the other is to invest in dedicated green bond strategies. At AXA IM, we do both and a key ingredient to selecting the right issuers is our green bond "go/no go" framework. There are four key criteria on which we believe investors should base their analysis of each green bond: ESG quality of the issuer; the merits of the project; the use of proceeds; and, how the issuer will monitor and report on the project.

Social bonds

Social bonds are very similar in terms of concept to green bonds but are designed to finance social projects. These range from social housing, microfinance, access to education, improvements in gender equality, support for employment in underserved regions and more. In 2020, social bond issuance jumped sevenfold to US$147.7 billion, as businesses and governments borrowed for relief from the pandemic in the wake of significant investor demand[3]. We expect to see this strong growth continues. We believe that social bonds should be measured against a set of principles like green bonds, including a clear definition of the issuer's environmental strategy and commitments. We also expect social bond issuers to apply relevant and robust criteria to define the target populations and areas that they aim to support through funded projects, and to provide reports on the use of the bond's proceeds and its impact. This is very important to ensure that we will finance social projects that really do make a difference.

Transition bonds

While green bonds are intended to finance environmentally friendly projects, there is a significant gap where investors could step in and deliver real impact for companies which are not yet at this stage. There is an opportunity to provide finance to companies which

---

2   Source: Jones, L., "Record $269.5bn green issuance for 2020: Late surge sees pandemic year pip 2019 total by $3bn", published on the website of Climate Bonds Initiative, 24 January 2021.

3   Source: Mutua, D. C., "Social bonds propel ESG issuance to record $732 billion in 2020", *Bloomberg*, 11 January 2021.

are "brown" today but have the ambition to transition to "green" in the future, including firms that are not yet able to issue green bonds due to a lack of sufficiently green projects for which they can use the proceeds. Transition bonds are intended to provide financing for such companies, i.e. most businesses in the world today. We firmly believe this new form of financing can play a potentially vital role in supporting the transition to a low-carbon society.

But for investors their transparency is critical. For example, investors need to be comfortable, that proceeds raised are used to finance projects within pre-defined climate-transition-related activities. As such, transition bond issuers should give investors a clear description of the eligible assets, their eligibility criteria, and the asset selection process. Issuers should also have guarantees in place to ensure the proceeds are effectively allocated to the eligible projects. In addition, alongside issuance-level components, there should be clear expectations for an issuer's broader environmental strategy.

Alternatives and real estate

Alternative investments have historically lagged traditional investments such as equities in terms of offering ESG or impact vehicles. However, this is changing, and alternative investments have at least one great advantage when it comes to delivering sustainable and socially responsible funds — a large part of the alternative universe (including the real estate sector) is private, i.e. not publicly listed. This allows investors a much greater influence over the holdings, and consequently a greater opportunity to steer business activities in a sustainable or socially responsible direction. In terms of private equity, one of the largest alternative asset classes, the aim is often to take a position in the target company that is significant enough to drive restructuring that can deliver improved returns. Investors may leverage this greater control to weigh in on issues such as the environmental impact of the operations, the transparency of the corporate governance and the social practices of the firm.

Alternative investments are generally more suitable for investors with a longer investment horizon compared to traditional investments. For example, insurance and pension firms — an important part of the alternatives' investor base — typically have longer expected holding periods than retail clients investing in an equity fund. This longer investment horizon, often several decades, means these investors can be in a more advantageous position to ensure the investee assets deliver sustainable returns.

Responsible investing is also of increasing importance in the real estate sector. Questions such as which building materials are to be used and what level of insulation they provide, as well as how the property will derive its energy and what the total level of carbon emissions may be, are key to ensure a property portfolio can deliver both financial and environmental returns. On the social front, key concerns can include how large a portion of affordable housing is included in a development project.

Finally, some alternatives asset classes are by nature part of the transition towards a more sustainable society and offer great opportunities for impact-seeking investors. Infrastructure investments, for example, involve assets such as electric vehicle charging points, data centres and public transport networks, all of which are essential to reach global climate change targets.

Key questions investors should ask about RI

Now that we have scanned through the RI options in different asset classes, investors can move on to the next stage of ESG investment consideration: getting specific about their ESG goals and how to achieve them.

On the product side, to match the breadth of investor expectations and to ensure transparency, the focus has increasingly been on how to measure the effectiveness of an approach. Although we continue to witness rapid growth in ESG integration, there remains no true global standard for defining the terminology, for applying ratings, or for assessing the quality of data and disclosure. This makes it difficult for investors to compare ESG offerings across different providers. Figure 2 summarises the key questions that investors should ask about RI.

Figure 2. Key questions investors should ask about responsible investing

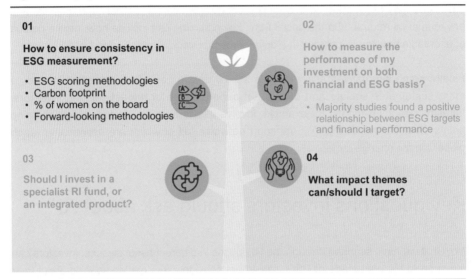

01

How to ensure consistency in ESG measurement?

- ESG scoring methodologies
- Carbon footprint
- % of women on the board
- Forward-looking methodologies

02

How to measure the performance of my investment on both financial and ESG basis?

- Majority studies found a positive relationship between ESG targets and financial performance

03

Should I invest in a specialist RI fund, or an integrated product?

04

What impact themes can/should I target?

How can I ensure consistency in ESG measurement?

Despite this challenge, we believe there is no reason that an investor cannot create an RI approach that aligns closely with their requirements by asking the right questions and unearthing valuable insights. In order to help investors kick-start this journey, we highlight four areas to consider before they make any RI decisions. Fundamentally, does the manager have a transparent and consistent ESG evaluation framework, and can they explain how it is used across the business?

Whether an investment strategy is focused on screening or integration — where a nuanced approach uses ESG scores to determine a company's long-term ability to evolve — the analysis for informing investment decisions is critical. Therefore, investors need to ask what assessment criteria lie at the heart of a scoring process, and how does that fit into the wider framework. ESG scoring methodologies, although not yet standardised, are useful tools to help investors compare and monitor the performance of their investments. ESG scoring systems are often a necessary step to synthesise all material ESG information and help portfolio managers to further differentiate between thousands of issuers. It is also the starting point to assess the ESG quality of an issuer, or of a portfolio, relative to its benchmark or peers.

Core areas for consideration when building an ESG scoring methodology include assessments of a company's business model in the context of long-term sustainability trends such as climate change, demographics and regulation. These will all influence the way companies conduct business and highlight the most material ESG risks faced by the firm.

There are likely to be key themes in each of the ESG pillars. These include resources, ecosystems and climate change (in environment), human capital and business behaviour (in social) as well as board oversight and management quality (in governance).

To make this as detailed as possible there should be sub-factors for each, so in the business behaviour category, human rights, business ethics, customer relationships and the supply chain would generally all be considered.

To ensure that the most accurate and material sectoral information is used to populate an ESG scoring framework, a thorough selection of rating agencies and criteria should be conducted.

An important point investors should note is that there is currently no consensus between market players on the framework to build these scoring methodologies. Recent studies show that the correlation between the ESG scoring of the main data providers remains below 0.5 when the correlation for credit ratings is close to 1[4].

We expect ESG scoring methodologies to converge, but before they do, investors may also look at other ESG indicators, which might have higher, although not perfect, comparability. Such indicators include the carbon footprint or the percentage of women on the board, which are not only well understood these days, but also widely reported by investee companies and relatively easy to compare.

The latest challenge is to develop forward-looking methodologies, notably to help investors assess how a company is expected to transition and to perform over time on specific sustainability matters such as climate. Those methodologies, such as the warming potential, or temperature of a company for instance, are aimed at measuring to what extent it has developed a "Paris-aligned strategy". These tools are in their infancy but may be essential for investors committed to supporting the goals of the Paris Agreement

---

4   Source: Berg, F., J. F. Kölbel and R. Rigobon, "Aggregate confusion: The divergence of ESG ratings", 17 May 2020, available at SSRN.

through their investments by implementing "net-zero" (carbon emission) approaches. They are, however, often perceived as more complex to develop and use than scoring methodologies.

How do I measure the performance of my investment on both financial and ESG basis?

Investors are naturally keen to monitor how their portfolio has performed in financial and ESG terms, and to understand the ties between the two. A growing number of academic studies demonstrate how ESG can deliver value to investors. As examples, the following two meta studies looked at the relationships between corporate and investment performance for different asset classes:

- Friede, Busch and Bassen (2015)[5] looked at more than 2,200 empirical studies on the link between ESG and corporate financial performance. The results show that approximately 90% of studies analysed found a relationship between ESG and financial performance, and a large majority of these found the relationship a positive one.

- The University of Oxford (2015)[6] looked at more than 200 academic studies, industry reports, newspaper articles and books. Among these sources, 88% indicated that companies with strong sustainability practices demonstrated better operational performance, which ultimately translated into cash flows. In addition, 80% showed that strong sustainability practices have a positive influence on investment performance.

Investors should ask what tools are available that can determine whether investments are simultaneously meeting financial and ESG targets including, among others, their carbon footprint and diversity levels.

---

5   Friede, G., T. Busch and A. Bassen. (2015) "ESG and financial performance: Aggregated evidence from more than 2000 empirical studies", *Journal of Sustainable Finance & Investment*, Vol. 5, Issue 4, pp.210-233.

6   Clark, G. L., A. Feiner and M. Viehs. *From the stockholder to the stakeholder: How sustainability can drive financial outperformance,* jointly prepared by University of Oxford and Arabesque Partners, published on Arabesque Partners' website, March 2015.

Should I invest in a specialist RI fund, or an integrated product?

Deciding on what approach should be taken will depend again on the investment profile required — whether via a specialist fund that solely concentrates on RI themes, or an integrated product that blends RI ideas with other criteria.

Investors should ask managers about the differences between products and look closely at which might be the best fit for their mandate, both now and in the future. Requirements might change as the mandate changes, especially as integrated approaches embed more ESG factors. It is also worth noting that suitability might be driven by different investment approaches such as fundamental investing — in which stock selection is based on convictions — and by a recognition that the long-term investment focus is increasingly shifting from a sectoral to a thematic approach.

Alternatively, an investor might see value in a quantitative investing approach — using advanced modelling techniques in which new technology and data is harnessed to conduct a deep analysis of company performance.

What impact themes can/should I target?

Impact investing seeks out businesses and projects designed to have intentional, positive and measurable impacts on society, while delivering financial market returns. As such, it will appeal to those wanting to achieve both these goals in tandem. It has an even greater focus on defining impact goals, assessing how every investment can contribute to these goals, and on measuring and reporting progress over time. Even so, as for ESG and climate-aware investing, measurement remains a challenge and currently relies on robust individual frameworks and verifiable, comparable data at the level of each asset.

Specific expectations can be tailored to areas such as health and well-being, agriculture and nutrition, environment and biodiversity, climate change, education, livelihoods and entrepreneurial support or sustainable housing. Take education for example, the goal might be to increase education access for an underserved population. The ideal outcome can be tailored to an investor's requirements. Critically, outcomes must be specific and measurable with targets clearly identified from the earliest stage to ensure that projects are directed effectively. Questions for managers should include what an impact measurement framework will look like, how it will be carried out, and of course, what key performance indicators will be employed.

The United Nations' Sustainable Development Goals (SDGs) — established in 2015 to address key global challenges including poverty, inequality, climate and health — have played a vital role in driving the impact agenda. They provide a very good reference for identifying areas of significant unmet demand, and with long-term secular growth opportunities. As a result, the SDGs are adopted by a wide range of stakeholders — governments, businesses, financial institutions and not-for-profits — as a framework to assess unmet societal needs.

There are 17 SDGs, with clearly defined objectives, as well as 169 underlying targets to be met by 2030 (see Figure 3). The SDGs offer useful foundations, but any successful impact strategy must also display some key features:

- A clear definition of what the strategy seeks to achieve;

- An assessment of the scale of the problem it aims to address;

- An assessment of how capital can be deployed to do that;

- A clear understanding of the route to financial returns alongside impact; and

- A path to measuring and verifying impact over time.

Figure 3. United Nations' Sustainable Development Goals

Source: United Nation's website, SDG logo presented in accordance with the United Nations' guidelines (May 2020).

A new engine driving the green bond market?

For investors considering impact investing, it is impossible to ignore the sharp growth of the green bond market. And within that sector, China's commitment to go from the world's biggest emitter to net-zero by 2060, appears to offer tremendous potential opportunities.

Development of the global green bond market

Green bonds have emerged as a unique asset class that can help tackle climate change by financing environmental solutions. These bonds can help support a myriad of different initiatives, including renewable energy, pollution prevention, energy efficiency and biodiversity preservation, among many others.

There is, in our view, a growing and powerful awareness that climate change is a threat to our economic well-being. The green bond market has emerged as an important part of addressing that threat. It is one of the most dynamic areas in our evolution towards a sustainable global economy, which we believe can reward in-depth active management as investors seek genuine financial returns, alongside genuine environmental impact.

Virtually all types of issuer — sovereign, supranational and agency (known collectively as SSA), financials and corporates — have now entered the green bond market. Since the sector first emerged in Europe, developing countries and especially China have since injected new impetus. Recent growth in the green bond market has been driven by an influx of inaugural issuers, a trend that has helped to address the concentration issue which was a concern for investors some years ago. But this is still afar from conventional universe. It remains uneven, innovative, and exciting — a place where we believe active management is needed to ensure broadly balanced issuer selection and to avoid any unwanted bias. One of the many records the green bond market sets every year is the volume of primary issuance.

In 2020, global green bonds issuance reached US$269.5 billion, making the total value of cumulative green bond issuance over US$1 trillion[7]. The market's development has been accompanied by improved governance thanks to the *Green Bond Principles of* the International Capital Market Association (ICMA) and through the work of the international non-profit organisation, the Climate Bonds Initiative (CBI), which together have helped to monitor the market and make it more credible.

China's green bond market: Driving growth

One market that has experienced tremendous expansion in recent years is China, where formally labelled green bonds did not exist until 2016. In little over five years, the country has become the world's second largest green bond market[8]. While the primary market cooled in 2020 during the COVID-19 pandemic, signs of a revival in activity are already visible in the early months of 2021[9].

---

7 Source: "$1 trillion mark reached in global cumulative green issuance: Climate Bonds Data Intelligence Reports: Latest figures", published on the website of Climate Bonds Initiative, 15 December 2020.
8 Source: "China leads global green-bond sales boom but faces headwinds", *Reuters*, 1 April 2021.
9 See, for example, CBI's website for green bonds issuance data.

We think China's green bond market can offer potential opportunities for ESG-conscious investors seeking assets with positive environmental impacts. The country has made a public commitment to reach carbon neutrality — a goal that will require trillions of dollars of new investments to revamp its carbon-intensive economy and energy system over the coming four decades[10]. Developed to mobilise private-sector resources to facilitate this green transformation, the green bond market in China is poised to benefit.

For global investors, there are several reasons that the Chinese green bond market could appear attractive. First, the market is large enough to accommodate significant foreign investor participation. China is the second largest green bond market behind the US, with a total stock of bonds at US$127 billion, accounting for almost 13% of the investable universe[11]. Building on recent growth momentum, the market is set to grow further in size, depth and liquidity to meet China's ambitious net-zero target by 2060.

Second, we think the market offers a decent level of diversification in terms of project and credit exposure. In China, green bonds finance a wide range of environmental projects, with an emphasis on pollutant reduction, ecological protection, resources conservation and mitigation of global warming. Transportation (mostly electric vehicles and railway projects) and energy (predominantly renewable fuels such as wind and solar) accounted for over 50% of green bond issuance in 2019[12]. Water conservation, waste management and efficient construction accounted for the vast majority of the rest. This market composition is broadly in line with the global aggregate, but more diverse than many smaller markets, which can be quite concentrated on clean-energy projects.

The profile of green bond issuers in China has also evolved over time. In the early years, primary activities were dominated by large financial institutions, as a support to the People's Bank of China (PBOC) initiative to jump-start the market. This was done by carving out parts of the banks' loan books, with lending to eligible projects, and repackage them into green bonds. But as the market continues to mature, non-financial issuers — corporates at the frontline of pursuing the green transformation — started to join in by tapping the market for new investments.

---

10 Source: Yao, A. and S. Shen, "China: Path to Net Zero", *Research and Strategy Insights*, AXA IM, 18 March 2020.
11 Source: "$1 trillion mark reached in global cumulative green issuance: Climate Bonds Data Intelligence Reports: Latest figures", published on the website of Climate Bonds Initiative, 15 December 2020.
12 Source: CBI, *China Green Bond Market 2019 Research Report*, June 2020.

Extra risks to be managed for investing in China's green bond market

To gain access to the positives, global investors will need to understand the unique risks of the Mainland green bond market. Navigating the partially-open capital account, a limited-convertible currency, and constantly evolving bond market — including default dynamics, regulations and market instruments — is necessary for all fixed-income investors. But for those investing in green bonds, there is an extra layer of complexity in assessing the "greenness" of bonds. This complication is further underlined by the lack of a unified global green bonds standard, with all major markets — the US, China and Europe — operating under somewhat different regulations and guidelines.

If the CBI standard is used as a yardstick, we can see that the discrepancies between China's definition of "green" and the international definition have narrowed over time. However, some differences still exist today, and prospective investors need to evaluate them carefully before making decisions. An examination of the two standards shows three categories of discrepancy:

- The first is simply a lack of information on how the bond proceeds are utilised. While this was an important driver of Chinese green bonds exclusion by the CBI in the early years, it has gradually become less of a concern as Chinese issuers have strengthened information disclosure over time.

- The second category relates to the definitions of "green". Among the most notable is the treatment of clean coal projects. While they can qualify for green bond financing in China provided the reduction in carbon dioxide emission meets a certain threshold relative to regular coal technology, no fossil fuel projects are accepted by the CBI given the presence of emissions. Fortunately, as China is moving towards net zero, less clean coal projects have broken ground in recent years, leading to progressively fewer bonds to be excluded for this reason. In addition, China has removed clean coal in its 2021 edition of Green Bonds Endorsed Project Catalogue, which is set to further align Chinese and international standards.

- Finally, the most significant discrepancy — accounting for over 70% of Chinese bonds' exclusion by the CBI in 2019[13] — is the percentage allocation of proceeds for specified green projects. While the CBI requires at least 95% of the proceeds to go to earmarked

---

13 Source: Ditto.

investments, some Chinese regulators, notably the National Development and Reform Commission, allows up to 50% of the proceeds to be used as general working capital. This difference has contributed to US$17 billion worth of Chinese green bonds being excluded from the international definition in 2019[14].

Despite the substantial convergence, the remaining differences in "green" standards still present a hurdle for global investors keen to tap this market. However, these are not insurmountable challenges and investors could potentially address these with proper research of the issuing documents and with clear green bond filters in mind. The extra costs are small in comparison to the benefits and opportunities offered by what is looking to be the world's largest, most diverse, and potentially highest-yielding green bond market. What this does highlight, however, is that further regulation changes are needed to harmonise China's local standards with those of the developed world to entice global investors to this fast-rising and soon-to-be-mainstream asset class.

Conclusion

Overall, we believe the trend of responsible and sustainable investing are here to stay. The momentum behind RI will undoubtedly continue to build, helping to contribute to a more sustainable planet. We expect greater standardisation of ESG reporting in the short to medium term, as asset managers put pressure on data providers to deliver a consistent set of metrics to allow efficient comparison between company scores or even investment portfolios.

From green bonds to impact and dedicated carbon reduction investment strategies, investors and companies alike want strategies that deliver the resilience to navigate the type of uncertain market conditions seen during COVID-19, as well as the range of social infrastructure needs that the pandemic exposed and the perils of climate change.

We believe that investors have an important role to play in the global green recovery and transition, and it is vital that they understand their options before venturing into this emerging investment area. We hope this chapter has served this purpose.

---

14 Source: Ditto.

第10章

在日益興旺的全球ESG投資
格局中準確了解您的選擇

安盛投資管理

摘要

在一個全面追求環保和可持續發展的世界，綠色及可持續金融扮演着越來越重要的角色，隨着其受歡迎程度日益增加，市場上的投資選擇亦激增。

在本章中，我們將介紹投資者在考慮投資可持續發展領域時，他們有何選擇以及如何能更了解這些選擇，以達到其目標。

首先，我們將介紹主要市場參與者在設計「責任投資」產品時採用的現行主要方法，包括剔除法、環境、社會與管治（Environment、Social、Governance，簡稱 ESG）整合、聚焦可持續發展和影響力投資等，每一種方法都有不同程度的責任投資目標。

我們亦將講解如何在不同的資產類別中實踐責任投資，這些資產類別包括股票、固定收益、另類資產和地產，每種都有其獨有的責任投資特色，投資者必須明白對其應抱持甚麼期望，以及它們的運作原理。

一旦對責任投資領域有概略認識後，投資者就是時候付諸實踐，並根據他們自己的責任投資目標作決策。但要付諸實行，卻知易行難。當投資者嘗試套用 ESG 視角時，他們眼前仍然有着重重挑戰 —— 從如何將 ESG 因素切實整合到投資組合，到如何保持一致和可重複的投資策略，以達到其可持續發展目標等。我們將詳細講解一連串關鍵問題，為投資者開闢一條明確道路，讓他們跟着作出選擇。

最後，我們將聚焦於綠色債券市場，它是責任投資中一個極具增長潛力的領域。我們將特別深入探討中國的綠色債券市場，分析其相關的機遇和獨有風險。

多種不同的責任投資選擇

隨着投資者對可持續投資的興趣不斷增加，市場上的環境、社會及管治（Environment、Social、Governance，簡稱 ESG）工具和產品的數量亦迅速擴大，務求滿足各種需要。責任投資領域的發展帶來不同程度的投資方法，從簡單地剔除最惡劣的可持續發展風險，到ESG 整合，最後是影響力投資。在決定選擇哪種投資方法時，投資者需要清楚了解他們個人對財務表現、ESG 準則和成果的期望。

主要的責任投資方式

投資者可使用的主要責任投資方式一般有四種：

剔除：目的是排除帶來重大可持續發展風險的企業和行業，可能包括現時常常遭金融機構剔除的煤炭行業，又或是面臨嚴重爭議的企業。部分投資者還希望將有違其個人道德原則的行業（例如賭博或酒類等）剔除。

ESG 整合：這個方式是以 ESG 分析為依據，例如 ESG 評分和其他指標，目的是提供資訊左右投資決策。ESG 整合策略越來越受到投資者歡迎，因為與剔除策略相比，它們能更明確地顯示即將到來的風險和機會，並提供更清晰的助證以洞悉預期的影響。例如，ESG 整合策略可以瞄準特定的 ESG 評分，並對投資範圍的更高級別作出部署。

聚焦可持續發展（例如「同類最佳」）：這種方式通常較挑剔，並追求產生比 ESG 整合策略更大的影響。這個類別的產品可能會將「最差」的發行人從投資範圍中剔除，幫助投資組合經理專注於更強的 ESG 參與者，並避開重大 ESG 風險。此外，一些聚焦可持續發展對投資方式的目標是以 ESG 指標（例如 ESG 評分或碳強度）為基準而取得大幅領先的表現。投資者或會視之為比 ESG 整合更有意義的方式，能展示出更大的意向性。

影響力投資：最後這個類別旨在根據商定的 ESG 成果目標，創造可驗證的正面改變。影響力投資可以幫助投資者把握主要的金融市場大趨勢，同時應對一些關鍵的可持續發展方面的挑戰。此領域最初以具有影響力的私人市場為基礎而建立，但越來越多大型上市公司現時提供的產品和服務，能夠為我們的社會和地球帶來明顯的正面影響。不斷演變的影響力投資範圍為投資者提供了一個重要的選擇。

除了上述四種方式外，**盡責管理策略**通常用作重要補充，它同時兼顧 ESG 準則的整合，以及根據與被投資公司的持續議合在股東週年大會上投票。與企業議合對話使投資者能夠積極監察其投資項目，並要求作出改進，最終保護投資者、被投資公司和金融業者的長期利益。與被投資公司的關係可以持續多年,有時候甚至是幾十年。這種責任投資技巧在過去幾年越來越受到關注,它是一個必不可少的工具,讓投資者可協助邁向更加可持續發展的世界,幫助企業適應和應對挑戰,並為實現應對氣候變化的遠大目標作出貢獻。

不同資產類別的責任投資方式和選擇

現在,投資者擁有比以往更多的責任投資選擇,不斷增加的需求使市場上提供的 ESG 產品和基金數量有增無減。以往,責任投資基本上是將某些公司或所謂的「罪惡股」剔除在投資組合之外,它們通常包括從事武器製造、賭博、酒精或煙草生產的企業。被認為對環境福祉構成威脅的公司,例如石油和天然氣公司等,亦常常不獲納入責任投資策略。

但是,純粹售出公司(如那些污染環境的公司)是一種笨拙的手段,無法帶來正面的改變。幸好,市場上有大量旨在為社會和地球帶來顯著效益的資產和投資可供投資者選擇,這就是以上介紹的「影響力投資」方式。

追求影響力策略的投資者,其關注的公司和基金不但有潛力產生長線回報,還有可能產生正面、可量化的環境或社會影響。此類投資必須具有透明度,投資者才能確保所持資產與其價值觀相符。

我們認為可以透過投資於積極達到 ESG 準則的公司之股票和債券,實現上述目的。圖 1 概述了可供投資者運用的主要資產類別和選擇。

圖 1:不同資產類別的責任投資選擇

股票	固定收益	另類資產和地產
• 以環境為主,例如電動車	• 綠色債券	• 大多是私人投資
• 以社會為主,例如多樣性和教育	• 社會責任債券	• 可以對所持資產有更大的影響力
• 以管治為主	• 轉型債券	

股票

ESG 評分對篩選和整合投資法的效力不斷提高，大大提振股票投資。最重要的是，ESG 評分提供長線投資決策所需的重大風險及機遇的信息，這些信息對主動型投資管理者尤其重要。

購買二級市場上的股票時，較難證明其能否創造出比平常更具體、更有意向性和更正面的社會成果。不過，我們認為只要仔細進行分析，以識別和記錄真正有意向性的影響力成果，就一定有方法可以將影響力投資應用於公開股票。

環境

未來幾年，低碳交通等行業、以電動車為中心的供應鏈等都有望受惠於其普及率的提高。智能能源業代表着另一個機會，建築和工業的數碼化，還有智能電網科技，正在為能源效益和可再生資源開創新的可能性。農業方面，企業正在探討新方法以滿足人口增長的需要，並同時限制稀缺土地的使用；這造就了投資機會，着眼發展農業糧食科技，以及研發方法以解決糧食浪費問題的公司。

社會

社會上有一定需求規模未獲滿足，這亦讓企業和投資者有機會為發展中國家及已發展國家中未獲足夠服務的人羣改善服務成果。例如，我們可以尋找致力提高基本服務可及性、增加服務不足人口共融性，以及協助解決需求龐大但未獲滿足等問題的企業。力求提高醫療服務可及性和可負擔性的企業，又或是支持醫療創新，以及促進多樣性、創業精神和教育的企業，都提供了另一個投資機會。這些企業可以為世界各地的民眾創造更多機會，並維持弱勢社區的發展。

管治

最後，公眾輿論正在轉向，並向企業施加壓力。負責任的資產管理者有義務監督和與它們持有股份的公司議合。基本上，如果一家企業想要真正做到可持續發展，它就需要有健全的管治結構，積極解決社會問題，為人類和地球締造更美好的未來。例如，在我們看來，致力減輕環境破壞的企業將會為環球經濟帶來巨大的淨增長。從歷史可見，管治良好的公司從長遠而言會表現領先，亦更能抓住新機遇[1]；若管治不佳，則會產生潛在的重大負面影響。

1　資料來源：德勤〈Good governance driving corporate performance? — A meta-analysis of academic research & invitation to engage in the dialogue〉，2016年12月。

固定收益

就固定收益而言，責任投資事項包含對發行人信貸質素有影響的重大財務資訊。ESG 準則有效地添加一層額外的質性資訊，基金經理可以將這類資訊納入他們的決策，考慮有關風險和機遇，並將它們應用到固定收益投資組合中。

綠色債券

綠色債券市場發展迅速，是責任投資在債券領域中最有力的體現之一，2020 年綠色債券發行量創下 2,695 億美元的新紀錄[2]。綠色債券的所得款項用於資助旨在對環境產生正面影響的新項目和現有項目。投資綠色債券主要有兩種方式，一種是將綠色債券配置到現有的固定收益投資組合當中，另一種是專注投資於綠色債券的策略。安盛投資管理同時採用這兩種方式，並以選擇合適的發行人為綠色債券「投資/不投資」框架的重要元素。我們認為，投資者對每種綠色債券的分析都應基於以下四個關鍵準則：發行人的 ESG 質素、項目的價值所在、發債所得款項的用途，以及發行人如何對項目作出監察和匯報。

社會責任債券

社會責任債券在概念上與綠色債券非常相似，但其目的是資助各種社會項目，從社會房屋、小額信貸、受教育機會、改善性別平等到支持服務不足地區的就業等。2020 年，社會責任債券發行量暴升 7 倍至 1,477 億美元，原因是投資者需求巨大，企業和政府藉發行此類債券來紓解疫情[3]。我們預計此強勁增長將會持續。我們認為社會責任債券應像綠色債券般以一組原則來測量，包括對發行人環境策略和承諾的明確界定。我們亦期望社會責任債券發行人運用相關健全的準則，以確立他們打算透過資助項目來支持的目標人羣和地區，並匯報發債所得款項的用途及其影響。為了確保我們資助的社會項目真的能帶來改變，這一點至關重要。

轉型債券

雖然綠色債券旨在為環保項目提供資金，但當中有着一個巨大的缺口，投資者可以介入其中，為尚未發展到這個階段的企業帶來實質影響。我們有機會為目前處於「棕色」狀態但有志在未來「轉綠」的公司提供融資，包括由於可以使用發債所得款項的綠色項目不足而尚未能夠發行綠色債券的公司。轉型債券旨在為這類公司 —— 亦即是現今世界上的大多數企業提供融資。我們堅信這種新型融資可以發揮重要作用，協助邁向低碳社會。

2　資料來源：L. Jones〈Record $269.5bn green issuance for 2020: Late surge sees pandemic year pip 2019 total by $3bn〉，載於氣候債券倡議組織（Climate Bonds Initiative，簡稱CBI）的網站，2021年1月24日。

3　資料來源：D. C. Mutua〈Social bonds propel ESG issuance to record $732 billion in 2020〉，載於《彭博》，2021年1月11日。

不過，它們的透明度對投資者來說至關重要。例如，籌集所得款項乃用於預先規定的與氣候變遷相關的活動融資項目，投資者需要對此感到安心。因此，轉型債券發行人應向投資者清楚說明其合格資產、合格標準和資產選擇流程。發行人還應提供保證，以確保發債所得款項實際上分配給合格的項目。除了債券發行層面的部分，我們還應對發行人的整體環境策略有明確的要求。

另類資產和地產

在提供 ESG 或影響力工具方面，另類投資向來落後於股票等傳統投資。然而，這種情況正在改變。就提供可持續發展及社會責任資金來說，另類投資至少有一個很大的優勢 —— 另類投資範圍（包括地產行業）主要是私人的，也就是非公開上市。這讓投資者對所持資產有更大的影響力，從而有更大的機會將業務活動引向可持續發展或對社會負責的方向。私募股權是最大的另類資產類別之一，其宗旨通常是在目標公司中持有足以推動重組的股份比例，從而創造更佳的回報。投資者可以利用更大的控制權，就業務活動對環境的影響、企業管治的透明度和公司的社會實踐等事宜發揮影響力。

與傳統投資相比，另類投資通常更適合投資期較長的投資者。例如，保險和退休金公司（另類資產投資者羣體的重要組成部分）的預計持有期通常比投資於股票基金的零售客戶長，投資期較長（通常是幾十年）意味着這些投資者能夠站在更有利的位置，確保被投資資產提供可持續的回報。

在地產領域，責任投資的重要性亦與日俱增。使用哪種建築材料？其隔熱能力如何？物業將如何獲得能源？碳排放總量是多少？諸如此類的問題是確保物業組合既能提供財務回報，又能帶來環境回報的關鍵所在。在社會方面，重點關注事項可能包括可負擔房屋佔一個發展項目的多大比例。

最後，一些另類資產類別本來就是朝着可持續發展社會轉型的一部分，為追求影響力的投資者提供巨大的機會。例如，基建投資涉及電動車充電站、數據中心和公共交通網絡等資產，它們都是實現全球氣候變化目標所必要的。

投資者應就責任投資提出的關鍵問題

既然已經粗略看過不同資產類別的責任投資選擇，投資者可以進入 ESG 投資考慮的下一個階段：明確了解他們的 ESG 目標及實現目標的方法。

在產品方面，為了滿足投資者廣泛的期望並確保透明度，市場日益將注意力放在如何測量投資方法的有效性上。儘管我們繼續看到 ESG 整合迅速增長，但仍然沒有確實的全球標準可供界定所涉的詞彙、給予評級或評估數據和信息披露的質素，以致投資者難以比較不同供應商的 ESG 產品。圖 2 總結了投資者應就責任投資提出的關鍵問題。

圖 2：投資者應就責任投資提出的關鍵問題

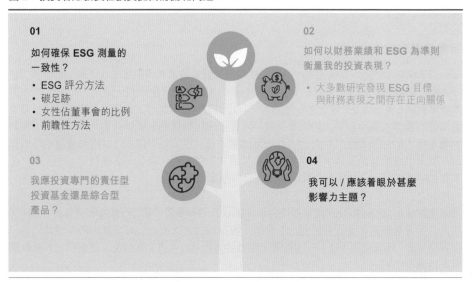

如何確保 ESG 測量的一致性？

儘管面對這樣的難題，但我們認為只要投資者提出正確的問題和發掘有價值的見解，就沒理由制定不出一個貼合其要求的責任投資方法。為了幫助投資者展開這趟旅程，我們會在他們作出責任投資決定之前，重點說明四個要考慮的方面。根本問題是，資產管理者有沒有一個具透明度和一致的 ESG 評估框架？它們能否說明如何將該框架運用於業務的不同方面？

不管投資策略的重點是篩選還是整合（縝密的投資法會使用 ESG 評分來判斷企業的長遠演化能力），為投資決策提供資訊的分析都至關重要。因此，投資者需要了解評分過程以甚麼評估準則為主，以及該準則如何融入整體框架。雖然 ESG 評分方法未有劃一標準，但它是有助投資者比較和監察投資表現的實用工具。ESG 評分系統通常是綜合所有重要的 ESG 資訊，並幫助投資組合經理進一步區分大量發行人的必要步驟。它亦是評估發行人或投資組合的 ESG 質素相對其基準或同行的着眼點。

在構建 ESG 評分方法時，需要以氣候變化、人口結構和監管等長期可持續發展趨勢作為核心考慮，來評估企業的業務模式。這些方面都將影響企業經營的方式，並凸顯企業面臨的最重大 ESG 風險所在。

每一個 ESG 支柱都可能有其重點主題，這些主題包括資源、生態系統和氣候變化等環境方面、人力資本和商業行為等社會方面，以及董事會監督和管理質素等管治方面。

為了盡可能令主題更加詳細，每一個主題之下都應該有次因素，故在商業行為類別中，人權、商業道德、客戶關係和供應鏈一般都會獲納入考慮。

如欲確保在 ESG 評分框架中使用最準確和最重要的行業資訊，則應慎選評級機構和準則。

投資者應注意的一個要點是，目前市場參與者對構建這些評分方法的框架還沒有達成共識。最近的研究顯示，當各信貸評級的相關性接近 1 時，各主要數據供應商所提供的 ESG 評分之間的相關性卻保持在 0.5 以下[4]。

我們預計 ESG 評分方法會趨同，而在此之前，投資者還可考慮其他 ESG 指標。雖然這些指標並不完善，但可比性或許較高，當中包括碳足跡或女性佔董事會的比例，它們現已廣為人知，被投資公司亦普遍有匯報，比較起來相對容易。

最新的挑戰是研擬前瞻性方法，特別是幫助投資者評估一家企業將如何轉型，以及在氣候等特定可持續發展議題上應有的長線表現。這些方法（例如升溫潛能值或企業溫度）旨在衡量企業在制定「與《巴黎協定》一致的策略」方面達到甚麼程度。這些工具尚處於起步階段，但對於承諾實施「淨零」（碳排放）策略，透過投資支持《巴黎協定》目標的投資者來說，它們不可或缺。不過，人們往往認為它們比評分方法更難制定和使用。

如何以財務業績和 ESG 為準則衡量我的投資表現？

投資者理所當然地熱衷於觀察其投資組合在財務和 ESG 方面的表現，並理解兩者之間的關係。越來越多學術研究證明 ESG 如何為投資者帶來價值，以以下兩個統合研究為例，它們考究了不同資產類別的企業表現和投資表現之間的關係：

4　資料來源：F. Berg、J. F. Kölbel 與 R. Rigobon〈Aggregate Confusion: The Divergence of ESG Ratings〉，載於 SSRN，2020年5月17日。

- Friede、Busch 和 Bassen（2015 年）[5] 審視了 2,200 多份關於 ESG 與企業財務業績關係的實證研究，結果顯示，約 90% 的研究發現 ESG 和財務業績之間存在一定的關係，其中絕大多數發現兩者之間存在正向關係。

- 牛津大學（2015 年）[6] 審視了 200 多份學術研究、行業報告、報紙文章和書籍。在這些資料來源中，有 88% 顯示堅定實踐可持續發展的企業展現出更佳的經營業績，並最終轉化為現金流。另外，有 80% 的資料顯示，堅定的可持續發展實踐對投資表現有正面影響。

投資者應查探有哪些工具可以判斷投資是否同時達到財務和 ESG 方面的目標，包括其碳足跡和多樣性水平等。

我應投資專門的責任投資基金還是綜合型產品？

同樣，採取甚麼投資方法應取決於所需的投資風格，是透過僅專注於責任投資的專門基金投資，還是透過將責任投資理念與其他投資準則相結合的綜合型產品投資？

投資者應向基金經理查詢產品之間的差異，並鑽研哪種產品最適合他們當前以至未來的委託管理。要求可能會隨着委託管理的變化而改變，尤其是當綜合投資法納入更多 ESG 因素時。還有一點值得注意，就是投資的適合性可能受不同投資方法所影響，例如根據信念選股的基本面投資；意識到長線投資焦點正日益從行業法轉向主題法亦可能會產生影響。

另外，投資者或會認為量化投資法可取，此投資法採用先進的建模技術，利用新科技和數據深入分析企業的表現。

我可以 / 應該着眼於甚麼影響力主題？

影響力投資在追求企業和項目提供金融市場回報的同時，還要求其對社會產生目標明確的顯著正面影響，故它會吸引希望同時實現這兩個目標的投資者。此投資法更加注重確立影響力目標、評估每一項投資如何有助於實現這些目標，以及持續量度和匯報進展。即使如此，就 ESG 和氣候意識投資而言，量度結果仍然是一項挑戰，現時量度乃依據不同的健全框架，以及每項資產的可驗證和可比數據進行。

5　G. Friede、T. Busch 與 A. Bassen（2015年）〈ESG and financial performance: Aggregated evidence from more than 2000 empirical studies〉，載於《Journal of Sustainable Finance & Investment》，第五卷，第四期，第210-233頁。

6　G. L. Clark、A. Feiner 與 M. Viehs《From the stockholder to the stakeholder: How sustainability can drive financial outperformance》，牛津大學與 Arabesque Partners 聯合發佈，載於Arabesque Partners的網站，2015年3月。

投資者可針對健康福祉、農業與營養、環境與生物多樣性、氣候變化、教育、民生與創業支援或可持續房屋等領域設定具體的期望。以教育為例，目標或許是為服務不足的社羣增加受教育的機會。投資的理想成果可根據投資者的要求調整。最重要的是，成果必須明確顯著，要在最初階段就清楚釐定目標，以確保項目得到有效的導引。向投資管理人提出的問題應包括：影響力的量度框架會是甚麼模樣？怎樣執行框架？當然還有，會採用甚麼關鍵績效指標？

聯合國可持續發展目標於 2015 年制定，目標提出主要的全球挑戰，包括貧困、不平等、氣候和健康等，並且在推動影響力理念方面發揮了至關重要的作用。它們具有寶貴參考價值，可供找出擁有巨大但未獲滿足的需求及存在長期增長機會的領域。因此，可持續發展目標獲廣泛的利益相關方採用（包括政府、企業、金融機構和非牟利組織），作為評估未獲滿足社會需求的框架。

可持續發展目標包含 17 項定義明確的目標以及 169 項細項目標，需要在 2030 年之前實現（見圖 3）。可持續發展目標固然提供很有用的基礎，但任何成功的影響力策略還必須顯示出一些重要特點：

- 明確界定策略追求的目標；

- 評估所提出問題的規模；

- 評估如何動用資本實現目標；

- 清楚了解在實踐影響力時同時創造財務回報的方法；以及

- 持續量度和驗證影響力的途徑。

圖 3：聯合國可持續發展目標

資料來源：聯合國網站，可持續發展目標標誌依據聯合國的指引展示（2020 年 5 月）。

推動綠色債券市場的新驅動力？

綠色債券市場急劇增長，考慮進行影響力投資的投資者不可能對此視若無睹。在這個領域，中國於 2060 年前從全球最大碳排放國走向淨零排放的承諾，似乎帶來巨大的潛在機會。

全球綠色債券市場的發展

綠色債券已崛起成為一門獨特的資產類別，能夠透過資助環境解決方案，幫助應對氣候變化。這類債券有助於支持各種不同的倡議，包括可再生能源、污染預防、能源效益和生物多樣性保育等範疇。

我們認為，越來越多人強烈意識到氣候變化對我們的經濟福祉構成威脅。綠色債券市場已成為應對該威脅的重要一環。此乃我們朝着可持續全球經濟邁進的過程中最具活力的領域之一，我們相信，隨着投資者尋求真正的財務回報和真正的環境影響，對此進行深入主動型管理可獲得回報。

幾乎所有類型的發行人 —— 主權與超國家及政府支持機構、金融機構和企業現在都已進駐綠色債券市場。該領域最先於歐洲出現，後來發展中國家（尤其是中國）為其注入了新的動力。綠色債券市場最近的增長是由首次發行人的湧入所推動，這個熱潮有助於解決幾年前投資者擔心的集中問題。不過，這個市場還是與傳統領域相差甚遠，它依然不平衡、創新且新奇有趣。我們認為需要對這個領域採取主動型管理，以確保發行人的篩選大致上達到平衡，並避免任何不必要的偏向。綠色債券市場每年都創下許多紀錄，新債發行量就是其中之一。

2020 年，全球綠色債券發行規模達到 2,695 億美元，累計綠色債券發行總額超過 1 萬億美元[7]。除了市場發展外，管治質素亦有改善，這要歸功於國際資本市場協會（International Capital Market Association）的《綠色債券原則》及國際非牟利組織《氣候債券倡議組織》（Climate Bonds Initiative，簡稱 CBI）的努力，這兩個組織同心協力監察市場，提升其可靠度。

中國綠色債券市場：推動增長

近年有一個市場經歷了空前的擴張，那就是中國，正式貼標的綠色債券直到 2016 年才出現，但在短短 5 年多，中國就已發展為全球第二大的綠色債券市場[8]。雖然一級市場在 2020 年新冠肺炎疫情期間有所降溫，但市場活動已在 2021 年首幾個月出現復甦的跡象[9]。

我們認為，中國綠色債券市場可以為具有 ESG 意識並要求資產對環境有正面影響的投資者提供潛在機遇。中國已公開承諾要實現碳中和，這個目標需要注資數萬億美元，才能在未來 40 年將其碳密集型經濟和能源體系改頭換面[10]。發展綠色債券是為了調動私營部門資源，推動綠色轉型，因此中國的綠色債券市場有望從中受惠。

對於全球投資者來說，中國綠色債券市場看起來具吸引力的原因眾多。首先，該市場規模龐大，足以容納大量外國投資者參與。中國是僅次於美國的全球第二大綠色債券市場，債券總存量為 1,270 億美元，佔可投資總額的近 13%[11]。憑藉近期的增長態勢，中國綠色債券市場有望在規模、深度和流動性方面進一步增長，以實現中國進取的 2060 年淨零目標。

7　資料來源：〈$1 trillion mark reached in global cumulative green issuance: Climate Bonds Data Intelligence Reports: Latest figures〉，載於 CBI 的網站，2020年12月15日。

8　資料來源：〈China leads global green-bond sales boom but faces headwinds〉，載於《路透社》，2021年4月1日。

9　請參閱如CBI網站的綠色債券發行數據。

10　資料來源：姚遠與沈曉瑩〈中國：邁向「淨零排放」之路〉，載於安盛投資管理的《研究及策略觀點》，2020年3月18日。

11　資料來源：〈$1 trillion mark reached in global cumulative green issuance: Climate Bonds Data Intelligence Reports: Latest figures〉，載於 CBI 的網站，2020年12月15日。

第二，我們認為中國綠色債券市場在項目和信貸風險方面的多元化程度恰到好處。在中國，綠色債券為各種環境項目提供資金，尤其是污染物減排、生態保護、資源節約和減緩全球暖化等領域。運輸（以電動車和鐵路項目為主）和能源（以風能和太陽能等可再生燃料為主）佔 2019 年綠色債券發行量的 50% 以上 [12]，其餘絕大部分為節水、廢棄物管理和高效建築工程。這樣的市場構成與全球總發行量的市場構成基本一致，但與許多頗集中於潔淨能源項目的小市場相比，則較為多元化。

中國綠色債券發行人的結構亦隨時間逐漸變化。在初期，新債發行活動由大型金融機構主導，以支持中國人民銀行啟動市場的倡議，過程是銀行從其貸款賬簿中劃出部分份額，發放給合格項目，並將其重新包裝成綠色債券。但隨着市場不斷成熟，非金融發行人（站在推行綠色轉型前線）的企業開始加入行列，利用這個市場進行新投資。

投資中國綠色債券市場需管理的額外風險

全球投資者需要了解內地綠色債券市場獨有的風險，才能從中獲益。所有固定收益投資者都必然要應對半開放的資本賬戶、有限的可兑換貨幣，以及不斷演變的債券市場（包括違約動向、監管和市場工具），但至於綠色債券投資者，他們還要面對評估債券「綠色程度」的額外複雜性。由於美國、中國和歐洲等各大主要市場的規管和指引略有不同，缺乏統一的全球綠色債券標準，進一步凸顯這種複雜性。

如果用 CBI 的標準來衡量，我們會發現，中國對「綠色」的定義與國際定義之間的差距逐漸縮小。然而，目前仍存在一些差異，潛在投資者在作出決定之前有必要謹慎評估。審視兩項標準後顯示出以下三種差異：

- 首先是缺乏如何使用發債所得的信息。信息不足是 CBI 在初期剔除中國綠色債券的一個重要因素，但隨着中國發行人加強信息披露，這個問題已逐漸沒那麼令人擔心。

- 第二個方面涉及對「綠色」的定義，當中最引人注目的是對潔淨煤炭項目的處理。假如潔淨煤炭項目相對於常規煤炭技術的二氧化碳排放量降幅達到一定的門檻，它們就可以在中國進行綠色債券融資；而化石燃料項目因為存在碳排放一律不獲 CBI 接受。可幸的是，中國朝着淨零排放邁進，近年來開闢的潔淨煤炭項目有所減少，因為前述原因被剔除的債券亦逐漸減少。此外，中國亦在其 2021 年版的《綠色債券支持項目目錄》中刪除了潔淨煤炭，使中國和國際標準進一步接軌。

---

12 資料來源：CBI《China Green Bond Market 2019 Research Report》，2020年6月。

- 最後，最顯著的差異是特定綠色項目的發債所得分配比例，2019 年遭 CBI 剔除的中國債券中，有超過 70% 是因為這個原因被剔除 [13]。CBI 要求將至少 95% 的發債所得用於指定投資，一些中國監管機構（特別是國家發展和改革委員會）則允許不多於 50% 的發債所得用作一般營運資金。此差異導致 2019 年有 170 億美元的中國綠色債券不獲納入國際定義範圍 [14]。

儘管綠色標準已顯著趨同，但餘下的差異對於渴望開拓這個市場的全球投資者來說，仍然是一個障礙。然而，這些挑戰並非無法克服，投資者可以透過徹底研究債券發行文件，以及秉持清晰的綠色債券篩選條件，來解決這些問題。與有望成為全球最大、最多元化、收益最高的綠色債券市場所帶來的好處和機遇相比，要付出的額外成本並不大。然而，這凸顯出中國還需要施行進一步的監管改革，使本地標準與發達國家的標準相一致，以吸引全球投資者投入這個迅速崛起並即將成為主流的資產類別。

總結

總括而言，我們相信責任投資和可持續投資的趨勢將持續下去。責任投資背後的動力無疑將繼續增強，協助建構更可持續發展的地球。隨着資產管理者向數據供應商施壓，要求後者提供一套一致的衡量標準，使企業評分甚至投資組合之間能作出有效的比較，我們預計中短期內 ESG 報告將進一步規範化。

從綠色債券到影響力投資和專門的碳減排投資策略，投資者和企業都希望策略能提供抗逆力，以有效處理疫情期間出現的那種不明朗市場環境，以及應對疫情揭露的各種社會基建需求和氣候變化風險。

我們認為投資者在全球綠色復甦和轉型中扮演着重要角色，在進入這個新興投資領域之前，他們必須理解自己的選擇。希望本章對此有所幫助。

註：本文原稿是英文，另以中文譯本出版。如本文的中文本的字義或詞義與英文本有所出入，概以英文本為準。

13　資料來源：同上。
14　資料來源：同上。

Chapter 11

Climate risk and financial innovation

Enrico BIFFIS
Associate Director for Development Finance
Brevan Howard Centre for Financial Analysis
Imperial College Business School

Summary

In this chapter, we provide an overview of some of the main challenges faced by market participants in dealing with climate risks, but also present examples of solutions recently developed to address them.

Challenges include mapping, quantifying, comparing and assessing climate risk disclosures, monitoring and mitigating climatic risks at a resolution sufficiently high to reap valuation and regulatory benefits.

On disclosure, we refer to recent evidence derived from natural language processing, which demonstrates how only a minority of companies exhaustively disclose the financial impact of climatic risks.

We then discuss the extent to which climatic risks and their disclosure can affect valuations, offering in turn some examples of mixed empirical evidence pertaining to different sectors, such as real estate and energy.

The chapter then considers a few representative areas of climate finance in which recent innovations are particularly promising. These include developments in climate risk analytics and climate surveillance, with applications to valuation, asset pricing, and supply chain risk management, as well as innovations in security and product design, with applications to sustainability-linked bonds, parametric insurance, and bundled finance solutions.

Climate risks and their disclosure

There are two types of risks arising from climate change[1]: **physical risks,** brought about by rises in global temperature and associated changes in weather patterns and sea level rises; **transition risks,** resulting from policy interventions and shifts in consumer demand and the broader business environment arising along the transition to a low-carbon economy. These risks cut across different sectors and value chains. A food producer, for example, may experience greater volatility in sourcing agricultural products from areas of the world more affected by severe droughts occurring at higher frequency. A logistics company may find important transportation links more frequently disrupted by excessive rainfall and floods. A real estate conglomerate may find that important assets are simultaneously threatened by sea level rise, heat stress, and wildfires. An energy company may find that a large portion of its production plants will turn into a liability as a result of asset retirement obligations brought about by curbs on emissions. The list of examples could go on *ad libitum.*

Corporates are under increasing pressure from investors and regulators to map out, quantify, and disclose their exposure to climatic risks. Climate risk disclosures are just a subset of broader Environment, Social and Governance (ESG) metrics, which have received considerable attention during the last few years. Still, there is currently no uniform set of rules to rank companies according to their "green credentials" and no uniform framework to compare companies' supply chain exposure to climate threats and opportunities.

Important initiatives are represented by the Climate Disclosure Project (CDP), the Global Reporting Initiative (GRI), and more recently the Task Force on Climate-related Financial Disclosures (TCFD). The recent strengthening of national environmental regulations has been a key factor in accelerating the development and adoption of voluntary climate disclosure mechanisms[2]. For example, the European Union (EU) regulation on Sustainability-Related Disclosures started to apply in 2021, thus broadening the requirement of incorporating sustainability risks for financial advisors.

---

1 See, for example, *Climate Risk and Response: Physical Hazards and Socioeconomic Impacts.* McKinsey & Company, 2020 (referred to as the report "McKinsey (2020a)").

2 See, for example: Zhang, Y. J. and J. Y. Liu. (2020) "Overview of research on carbon information disclosure", *Frontiers in Engineering Management,* Vol. 7(1), pp.47-52; Walker, B and D. Salt. (2006) *Resilience Thinking: Sustaining Ecosystems and People in a Changing World.* Island Press: Washington, D.C; Kolk, A. (2005) "Environmental reporting by multinationals from the triad: convergence or divergence?" *Management International Review,* Vol. 45, pp.145-166.

The market is recently attempting to converge to a unified set of standards and methodologies favouring scenario analysis and bottom-up assessment of granular climate exposures (see section on "Innovation" below)[3]. Although third-party rating and verification mechanisms are still in their infancy and need improvement[4], voluntary corporate disclosures represent an important information channel for investors. Empirical evidence suggests that the breadth and depth of climate risk disclosures differ considerably by company and jurisdiction. According to a report of the Ping An Digital Economic Research Centre (Ping An DERC)[5], among four major equity indices (including CSI 300, S&P 500, EURO STOXX 50 and NIKKEI 225), Japanese companies lead in the coverage of climate risk in company reports by both number of companies and market capitalisation (see Figure 1) — 52% of companies in NIKKEI 225, which represent 68% of market capitalisation, discussed climate risks in their company reports; 33% of S&P 500 companies (53% by market capitalisation) and 40% of EURO STOXX 50 companies (44% by market capitalisation) do so. Only 3% of companies (13% by market capitalisation) in CSI 300 discussed climate risks in their sustainability reports.

Figure 1. Percentage of companies that discuss climate risks in 2020 company reports

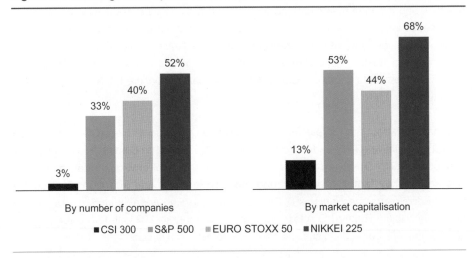

By number of companies   By market capitalisation

■ CSI 300   ■ S&P 500   ■ EURO STOXX 50   ■ NIKKEI 225

Source: "Where we stand with climate disclosures and why we need them — A textual analysis approach to company sustainability reporting", ESG Report Series, Ping An DERC, 2020 (hereinafter referred to as the report "Ping An DERC (2020b)").

---

3   In the report, "ESG investment in China", *ESG Report Series*, Ping An DERC, 2020 (hereinafter referred to as the report "Ping An DERC (2020a)"), for example, it is reported that among just the 300 Chinese companies that are part of the CSI 300 Index, a total of nine different guidelines are being followed.

4   See Berg, F., J. F. Koelbel and R. Rigobon. (2019) "Aggregate confusion: The divergence of ESG ratings", *MIT Sloan School Working Paper*, No. 5822-19, 17 May 2020. (Referred to as Berg et al. (2019) paper.)

5   Source: Ping An DERC (2020a).

Using the TCFD framework as a reference benchmark, a textual analysis study presented in the Ping An DERC (2020a) report reveals that among the companies providing climate risk disclosures, more than 90% report on metrics related to **carbon emissions** and **energy usage** (see Figure 2). On the other hand, **water** and **land use** are considerably underreported. Although disclosure of carbon emissions is high, the devil is in the detail. The standard exercise of disclosing carbon emissions from company operations becomes much more challenging when **indirect emissions** are considered. These come from sources that are not within a company's own operations, such as supply chains, and are often referred to as "Scope 3" emissions. In complex value chains, disclosure of indirect emissions requires a granular understanding of the carbon footprint of upstream and downstream transportation and distribution, as well as use of sold products and purchased goods and services. There is no doubt that this area will attract growing scrutiny by market participants in the coming years.

Figure 2. Disclosure rate of climate-related metrics by sector

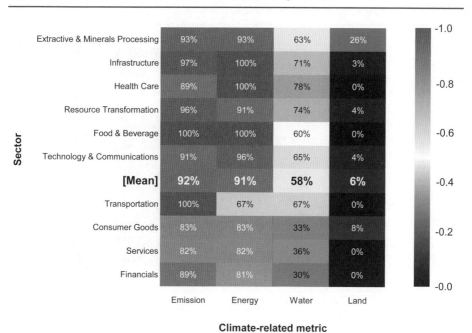

Source: Ping An DERC (2020b).

From an investor's point of view, the financial impact of climate risk is clearly of crucial importance (see section on "Valuation" below). Some reporting frameworks, such as those of TCFD[6], provide articulated guidance on specific impact dimensions that should be disclosed within each sector. Natural language processing analysis carried out in the Ping An DERC (2020b) report reveals that important dimensions of impact remain unfortunately largely undisclosed (see Figure 3). For example, very few companies disclose impact on "capital and financing" and any such disclosure is sizeably neglected by "brown" relative to "green" companies. This stands in contrast with material transition risks which are well known to affect several companies in the sample: risks include asset retirement obligations brought about by curbs on emissions and rationing of funding for assets that are becoming stranded and turning into liabilities. The flip side of undisclosed climate risk dimensions is of course the strategic bias that might drive what is actually being reported. This is more broadly related to the issue of greenwashing, which recent transparency, third-party verification, and standardisation efforts are trying to address.

Figure 3. Disclosure rates of financial impact metrics by sector

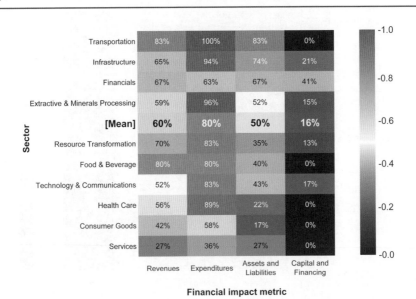

Source: Ping An DERC (2020b).

6   TCFD, *Recommendations of the Task Force on Climate-related Financial Disclosures*, June 2017 (referred to as the report "TCFD (2017a)"); TCFD, *Technical Supplement: The Use of Scenario Analysis in Disclosure of Climate-Related Risks and Opportunities*, June 2017 (referred to as the report "TCFD (2017b)").

Valuation

The evolution of climate reporting frameworks and associated efforts to improve transparency and comparability testify to the growing interest of investors in climate risk exposures. An obvious question is whether company valuations factor in climatic risks, and if so, to what extent. The empirical evidence on the matter is rather mixed. On the one hand, there is evidence that some real estate markets have started discounting the threat of sea level rise[7], and that weather derivatives price in climate projections beyond short-term weather variability information recorded by weather stations[8]. With regard to the transition risk side, some studies suggest that high-emission firms trade at a discount relative to low-emission firms, thus justifying claims of existence of a carbon risk premium[9]. On the other hand, several studies found evidence of mispricing in a number of sectors and asset classes ranging from agricultural production to real estate[10]. There are several reasons for why mispricing might be more the rule than the exception:

- Competing physical risks (e.g. drought vs. floods) and heterogeneity of exposures (e.g. in terms of geographical location or product characteristics) make the vulnerability of complex value chains difficult to understand.

- There is considerable uncertainty in climate projections informing our understanding of physical and transition risks, thus assessing their impact on firms' cash flows is highly speculative.

- The trade-offs brought about by policy responses aimed at mitigating climate change while delivering economic prosperity are complex, require considerable coordination, and are intertwined with the success of green innovation.

- Even if investors were to form correct expectations about the future impact of climate change on firms' cash flows, the appeal of particular firms/sectors may be an important driver of prices (e.g. capital flows associated with ESG investing).

---

7   See Bernstein, A., M. T. Gustafson and R. Lewis. (2019) "Disaster on the horizon: The price effect of sea level rise", *Journal of Financial Economics*, Vol. 134(2), pp.253-272.

8   See Schlenker, W. and C. A. Taylor. (2019) "Market expectations about climate change", National Bureau of Economic Research, No. w25554.

9   See Bolton, P. and M. Kacperczyk. (2020) "Carbon premium around the world", available at SSRN.

10 See, for example, Hong, H., F. W. Li and J. Xu. (2019) "Climate risks and market efficiency", *Journal of Econometrics*, Vol. 208(1), pp.265-281; Jiang, R. and C. Weng. (2019) "Climate change risk and agriculture-related stocks", available at SSRN, 15 December 2019; Ding, Y., C. Sun and J. Xu. (2020) "Climate changes and market predictability: Evidence from satellite readings of soil moisture", available at SSRN (3637698), 1 January 2020.

In the face of inconclusive evidence, one may wonder whether asset pricing theory could provide some help, but even the perspectives differ. Some market participants hold the view that climate risk metrics mainly appeal to investors with green preferences. In line with the literature on "sin stocks" (such as those related to tobacco and gambling)[11], this means that investors who are driven by green considerations leave money on the table for the benefit of those who do not constrain their investment opportunity set. Some market participants are instead in favour of recognising, where appropriate, the informative value of climate risk metrics to model firms' fundamentals (e.g. impact on cashflows) and their exposure to aggregate risk[12]. Indeed, climate change represents a major source of systematic risk, which should be priced in as per standard asset pricing theory. The two perspectives can be reconciled by noting that the first one applies in equilibrium, whereas the second one emphasises the transition to a new equilibrium, where changes in policy, regulation, and market participants' climate awareness can result in sizeable repricing across assets. The latter view is adopted by regulatory stress tests aimed at making financial institutions internalise the impact of physical and transition risk in their capital modelling exercises[13].

Understanding the link between climate risk exposure and financial performance is rather complicated due to several competing drivers of value[14] and the shortcomings of self-reported disclosures discussed in the above section. The broader issue of ESG ratings is also plagued with sizeable dispersion of scores and ranking inconsistency in rankings[15]. Use of artificial intelligence (AI)-based indicators can shed some light on some of these relationships and has recently been shown to suggest a positive relationship between

---

11 See, for example, Fama, E. F. and K. R. French. (2007) "Disagreement, tastes and asset prices", *Journal of Financial Economics*, Vol. 83(3), pp.667-689, and Hong, H., and M. Kacperczyk. (2009) "The price of sin: The effects of social norms on markets", *Journal of Financial Economics*, Vol. 93(1), pp.15-36.

12 See, for example, Benedetti, D., E. Biffis, F. Chatzimichalakis, L. L. Fedele and I. Simm. (2021) "Climate change investment risk: Optimal portfolio construction ahead of the transition to a lower-carbon economy", *Annals of Operations Research*, Vol. 299, pp.847-871.

13 See, for example, Bank of England. (2021). *Guidance for Participants of the 2021 Biennial Exploratory Scenario: Financial Risks from Climate Change*. Bank of England, London, UK (referred to as the report "Bank of England (2021)").

14 See, for example, Cornell, B. and A. Damodaran. (2020) "Valuing ESG: Doing good or sounding good?", available at SSRN (3557432), 20 March 2020.

15 See, for example, Berg et al. (2019) paper.

better disclosure of financial impact metrics and higher equity valuations, as well as lower cost of capital, after controlling for carbon emissions and other standard variables[16].

Although the discussion of climate risks and ESG ratings has predominantly focused on the equity area in the last few years, debt markets are clearly very important and there is some evidence supporting similar findings. When looking at bank loans in the United States (US), for example, a study[17] found that socially responsible firms pay between 7 and 18 basis points less than other firms, unsecured loans being the most sensitive to social responsibility concerns. There is also increasing evidence that debt investors are becoming more climate conscious and some commercial lenders have begun to peg lending rates to ESG performance[18].

To illustrate why and how climate risks (and their disclosures) could affect both equity and debt, let us consider Figure 4 below. Figure 4(a) presents the standard convex payoff faced by equity holders (the dark blue line), who have a call option on the assets of the firm, and the standard concave payoff faced by bondholders (the red line), who effectively sell a put option on the asset of the firm. In a simple one-period, two-date model, a firm raises debt of amount D at time zero. After the firm's cash flows are realised during the period, the firm's assets at time one (denoted by X) determine the payoff to shareholders and bondholders. Should the firm's assets fall below the face value of debt, equityholders would be protected by limited liability, whereas bondholders would recover whatever is left. Market participants would price equity and debt at time zero by rationally anticipating these outcomes[19]. Figure 4(b) depicts two possible probability distributions for the realisation of the firm's assets value X. The two distributions reflect different degrees of climate risk: in

16 Source: Ping An DERC, "Climate disclosures and financial performance: AI driven indicators, green washing detection, and firm characteristics", *ESG Report Series*, Issue 4, December 2020 (referred to as the report "Ping An DERC (2020c)"). In particular, large capitalisation firms that are TCFD-compliant tend to have higher valuations, whereas small and medium capitalisation firms engaging in climate disclosures may still offer considerable opportunities for appreciation.

17 Goss, A., and G. S. Roberts. (2011) "The impact of corporate social responsibility on the cost of bank loans", *Journal of Banking & Finance*, Vol 35(7), pp.1794-1810.

18 See, for example, Bae, S. C., K. Chang and H. C. Yi. (2018) "Corporate social responsibility, credit rating, and private debt contracting: New evidence from syndicated loan market", *Review of Quantitative Finance and Accounting*, Vol. 50, pp.261-299; Gatti, S., and A. Florio. (2018) "Issue spread determinants in the green bond market: The role of second party reviews and of the Green Bond Principles", *Research Handbook of Finance and Sustainability*, Edward Elgar Publishing; Barth, F., B. Hübel and H. Scholz. (2019) "ESG and corporate credit spreads", available at SSRN (3179468), 30 March 2021.

19 Companies engage in risk management to signal to investors that such issues are under control and mitigated where needed. Indeed, the risk-taking incentives induced by the convex payoff of equityholders can make agency problems such as asset substitution particularly acute. Proper risk disclosure and risk management will mitigate these frictions by aligning more closely the perspectives of bondholders and equityholders.

the particular example depicted, the "business as usual (BAU)" distribution (black curve) has a higher default probability which will result in a lower value of debt; the "climate de-risking" distribution (light blue curve) reduces downside risk by addressing physical/ transition risks, thus leading to higher valuations of debt, and may exploit climate change opportunities, thus increasing the upside payoffs to equityholders. Proper disclosure and engagement with market participants may therefore result in sizably lower financing costs and greater firm valuations[20].

Figure 4(b) provides support for the growing interest in tail risk measures for climate risk disclosures. Examples include the use of climate stress testing and the computation of climate Value-at-Risk measures attempting to quantify the impact of different global temperatures scenarios on the prospects of a firm in present value terms[21]. In addition to long-term investors, which are clearly interested in the pricing of such impacts into equity and debt holdings[22], regulators are also looking into the systemic risk implications of climate risks[23].

Figure 4. Payoff charts on equity and debt investment

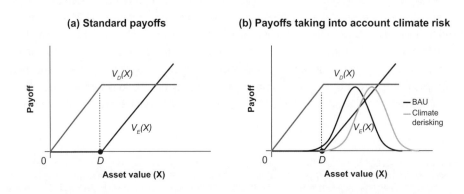

Note: The above diagrams report payoffs to different stakeholders (E for equityholder, D for debtholder) in the y-axis as a function of the terminal value X of the firm's assets in the x-axis. Figure 4b provides possible distributions for X in the case of "Business as Usual" (BAU) and climate de-risking strategies.

Source: Ping An DERC (2020b).

20 For further discussion and some empirical results, see Ping An DERC (2020c).
21 See TCFD (2017b) and *Forward-Looking Financial Sector Metrics Consultation*. TCFD, October 2020 (referred to as the report "TCFD (2020)").
22 See, for example, Gründl, H., M. Dong and J. Gal. (2016) "The evolution of insurer portfolio investment strategies for long-term investing", *OECD Journal: Financial Market Trends*, Vol. 2016(2), pp.1-55.
23 See Bank of England (2021).

Innovation

Financial innovation around climate risks provides huge opportunities for innovation in analytical tools and product innovation. We discuss here the areas of climate risk analytics, supply chain risk monitoring, insurance, and factor investing.

Climate risk analytics

Large part of the literature focuses on top-down approaches to understand the economic impact of climate change under different technological and lifestyle scenarios. Integrated Assessment Models (IAMs) are among the most popular tools in climate risk modelling. They model the potential evolution of the global energy system and other greenhouse gas (GHG) emitting sectors by making assumptions on economic and population growth, as well as other drivers of GHG emissions. They allow for the comparison between a BAU scenario with alternative pathways implementing technology and lifestyle changes aimed at curbing emissions and limiting long-term temperature increase to particular targets. These models represent a powerful tool to inform policymakers on the *cost-effectiveness* of risk mitigation measures[24]. A simplified set of models abstract away from the complexities of fully fledged IAMs and focus on *cost-benefit* analysis of emission reductions, by introducing simplified relationships between emissions and economic growth, while attempting to monetise the impact of climate change and the benefits of a reduction in temperature rises[25]. The outputs of these models are often presented in the reports of the Intergovernmental Panel on Climate Change (IPCC)[26]. A summary of the well-known DICE (Dynamic Integrated Climate-Economy) model[27] is depicted in Figure 5.

---

24 See, for example, Dessens, O., G. Anandarajah and A. Gambhir. (2016) "Limiting global warming to 2°C: What do the latest mitigation studies tell us about costs, technologies and other impacts?", *Energy Strategy Reviews*, Vol. 13, pp.67-76.

25 See, for example, Gambhir, A., I. Butnar, P. H. Li, P. Smith and N. Stracham. (2019) "A review of criticisms of integrated assessment models and proposed approaches to address these, through the lens of BECCS", *Energies*, Vol. 12(9), 1747.

26 See "Representative Concentration Pathways (RCPs)", webpage on the IPCC Data Distribution Centre website (https://sedac.ciesin.columbia.edu/ddc/ar5_scenario_process/RCPs.html).

27 See Nordhaus, W. D. (2017) "Revisiting the social cost of carbon", *Proceedings of the National Academy of Sciences*, Vol. 114(7), pp.1518-1523.

Figure 5. The DICE model

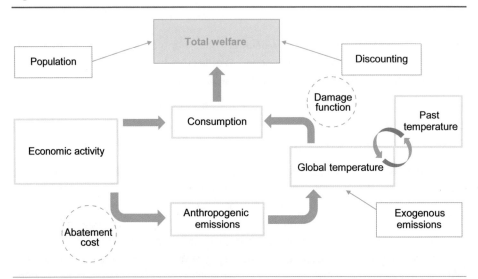

Source: Author's analysis.

IAMs may be helpful to inform strategic, sector-wide investment decisions, and are certainly useful to explore stylised implications of different risk mitigation policies on key economic sectors (the energy industry being among the most extensively studied over the years). However, they do not achieve the level of granularity required to inform asset selection, investment gradation within a sector, or tactical allocations aimed at benefiting from or hedging against climate change. Granular, bottom-up approaches can instead be tailored to particular risk exposures to (1) explicitly incorporate climate risk into valuations, and (2) refine climate risk pricing by taking into account asset characteristics. The recent push toward more transparent climate risk disclosures, as well as greater use of forward-looking risk metrics and benchmark climate scenarios, all point in the direction of such bottom-up exercises becoming prevalent in the future[28].

Among the most interesting challenges lying ahead is the improvement of companies' climate risk disclosures by using **forward-looking metrics** capturing a company's commitment to future emissions reduction, rather than its carbon footprint. The latter

---

28 See TCFD (2020).

has limited relevance for company valuations, which instead capture *future* financial prospects. Moreover, carbon footprints do not consider companies' pricing power, i.e. their ability to pass on the cost to their customers. In addition to current emissions data, companies should use forward-looking projections, such as future production curves, and disclose investments and/or strategies that companies are currently adopting to address climate risks going forward. The emergence of climate-related tail risk metrics, such as climate Value-at-Risk, is promising and supports market participants' efforts to screen for resilience to downside risks brought about by climate change.

Transparency and traceability of supply chains

Global supply chains are exposed to both physical and transition climate risks. Physical risks may impair the reliability of key nodes in supply networks and lead to their disruption. Transition risks arise from decarbonisation policies making some nodes obsolete and uneconomical to manage. Due to the many interlinking connections across supply chains, it can be challenging for investors to assess their vulnerability to climate risks and address the multiple different forms those risks take. Supply chains feature complex challenges not only in terms of mapping vulnerability to risks, but also in terms of transparency and traceability of climate risk exposures along the value chain.

Transparency refers to the disclosure of information about supply chains and sourcing to stakeholders in a way that ensures the information is communicated in an accessible and comparable manner. Traceability, on the other hand, refers to the ability to identify and track the journey of products and materials, from the beginning of the supply chain to their final distribution and application[29].

Technology is helping make progress on increasing transparency and traceability. Climate surveillance technology which relies on satellites, for example, can now track methane emissions, and asset tracking devices are increasingly allowing production and sourcing to be properly monitored[30]. Recent initiatives in climate finance also focus on the design of new instruments, such as sustainability-linked bonds (see sub-section below), which link funding and pay-outs to the achievement of sustainability goals. There is an opportunity

---

29 See United Nations Global Compact and BSR. (2014) *A Guide to Traceability: A Practical Approach to Advance Sustainability in the Global Supply Chains.*

30 See Malik, N. "Satellites put the world's biggest methane emitters on the map", *Bloomberg,* 21 October 2020.

here for blockchain technology to support the structuring of these transactions as smart contracts[31].

Sustainability-linked bonds (SLBs)

According to JP Morgan, the market for bonds linked to companies meeting specific sustainability targets could grow 20-fold in 2021 and aggregate issuance could range between US$120 billion and US$150 billion[32]. The most important feature of SLBs is that the bond's financial and/or structural characteristics can vary depending on particular Key Performance Indicators (KPIs) reaching predefined Sustainability Performance Targets (SPTs). For example, a bond could entail an increase in coupon payment triggered by failure to meet a certain carbon emissions reduction target.

There is a tight link with climate risk and broader ESG disclosures here, as best practice suggests that issuers should select KPIs that have already been included in previous annual reports (including sustainability reports or other disclosures) to allow investors to benchmark the bond's structure and subsequent performance against historical track records. According to International Capital Market Association's SLB Principles[33], a 3-year track record and third-party verification of KPIs would be desirable minimum standards. Clearly transparency, traceability, and verification are all dimensions that are bound to become increasingly important for these instruments, demonstrating organic improvement of tools needed in the context of climate risk disclosures, climate surveillance, and product design.

Insurance products

Physical risks such as floods and hurricanes are naturally related to risk transfer mechanisms such as insurance and insurance-linked securities. On the demand side, there is a clear understanding of the costs entailed by de-risking supply chain networks

---

31 See, for example, Nassiry. (2018) "The role of fintech in unlocking green finance: Policy insights for developing countries", *ADBI Working Paper*, No. 883, Asian Development Bank Institute; and Principles for Responsible Investment (PRI). (2018) *Responsible Investment and Blockchain*.

32 Source: "Sustainability-linked bond market to swell up to $150 billion: JP Morgan ESG DCM Head", *Reuters*, 22 March 2021.

33 See International Capital Market Association, *Sustainability-linked Bond Principles*, June 2020.

because of escalating insurance costs in areas more visibly exposed to the impacts of climate change. Securing longer term protection beyond the standard short-term insurance mechanisms commonly available in the marketplace seems however to be elusive: on the supply side, there is considerable aversion to engage in long-term insurance commitments, given the sizeable uncertainty surrounding climate projections. This makes the market incomplete when it comes to climate risk solutions.

A more effective contribution to climate risk transfers may be represented by the use of insurance mechanisms beyond the provision of standalone indemnities. As an example, consider agricultural production in emerging countries, which is increasingly exposed to physical risks such as drought and floods, and could therefore benefit hugely from the adoption of climate resilient production technologies[34]. In emerging markets, a large proportion of agricultural production is driven by smallholder farmers that have limited access to advanced input packages and training[35]. Access to finance is a key barrier to technology adoption, because these farmers are traditionally shunned by banks due to lack of credit history and the simple fact that for them defaulting on a loan is often a matter of survival[36]. Poor expected yields and greater frequency and severity of adverse weather events confine smallholder farmers to having low credit standing and limited resources to post as collateral: they are therefore stuck in a vicious circle preventing them from accessing the financial resources needed to adopt more sophisticated production technologies[37].

Recent innovation in insurance, including parametric weather insurance products, may offer a solution to resolve the above difficulties. Similar to derivative contracts, these instruments pay out in case specific weather conditions materialise and trigger a payment (e.g. cumulative rainfall falling below a contractually agreed threshold). Originally reliant on weather stations, these products can now leverage on satellite data and machine-learning techniques to build pay-out indices closely matching the exposure of policyholders at any location[38]. Recent large pilots in East Africa demonstrate that such

---

34 See, for example, McKinsey & Company, *Agriculture and Climate Change: Reducing Emissions through Improved Farming Practices*, 2020 (referred to as the report "McKinsey (2020b)").

35 See Duflo, E., M. Kremer and J. Robinson. (2008) "How high are rates of return to fertilizer? Evidence from field experiments in Kenya", *American Economic Review*, Vol. 98(2), pp.482-488.

36 See Dercon, S. and L. Christiaensen. (2011) "Consumption risk, technology adoption and poverty traps: Evidence from Ethiopia", *Journal of Development Economics*, Vol. 96(2), pp.159-173.

37 See, for example, Biffis, E., E. Chavez, A. Louaas and P. Picard. (2021) "Parametric insurance and technology adoption in developing countries", to be published in the *Geneva Risk and Insurance Review* (referred to as the paper "Biffis et al. (2021)").

38 See, for example, Biffis, E. and E. Chavez. (2017) "Satellite data and machine learning for weather risk management and food security", *Risk Analysis*, Vol. 37(8), pp.1508-1521.

products can deliver much more than standalone insurance coverage and can actually be used to mitigate credit rationing, promote financial inclusion, and incentivising climate resilient technology adoption. A recent study[39] focusing on Tanzania has documented that input loans embedding a parametric insurance component can de-risk agricultural bank portfolios by being recognised by loan underwriters as being a credit enhancement device, and hence circumvent credit rationing. Importantly, as insurance premiums capture the climate resilience delivered by an input package, they represent a powerful channel to convey to smallholder farmers the economic value of climate resilient production technologies.

Conclusion

This chapter has provided an overview of some of the main challenges faced by market participants when dealing with climatic risks. Some recent empirical evidence points in the direction of growing awareness of climate changes among investors having an impact on valuations and asset prices. In an environment characterised by rising regulatory intervention and increasing consumer pressure, these effects are expected to become more pronounced. Areas of climate finance that are currently receiving considerable attention and, in our view, will witness significant development in the next few years include:

- Building of granular datasets on climate risk exposures (e.g. asset locations) and climate impact (e.g. GHG emissions footprinting);

- Remote sensing and blockchain technology for GHG emissions assessment and monitoring;

- Development of climate scenarios to assess the resilience of financial institutions to climatic risks;

- Design and implementation of net-zero strategies increasingly focused on carbon reduction instead of emissions avoidance or carbon offsetting.

Remark: The author is grateful to the Ping An DERC (Digital Economic Research Centre) for giving permission to use material contained in their reports to support some of the findings discussed in this chapter.

---

39 Biffis et al. (2021). See also: Shee, A. and C. G. Turvey. (2012) "Collateral-free lending with risk-contingent credit for agricultural development: Indemnifying loans against pulse crop price risk in India", *Agricultural Economics*, Vol. 43(5), pp.561-574; Karlan, D., R. Osei, I. Osei-Akoto and C. Udry. (2014) "Agricultural decisions after relaxing credit and risk constraints", *The Quarterly Journal of Economics*, Vol. 129(2), pp.597-652.

第11章

氣候風險與金融創新

Enrico BIFFIS
倫敦帝國學院商學院
Brevan Howard 金融分析中心
發展金融部副總監

摘要

在本章中，我們概述了市場參與者在應對氣候風險時面臨的一些主要挑戰，同時也提供了一些最近為應對這些挑戰而開發的解決方案的例子。

這些挑戰包括氣候風險披露的規劃、量化、比較和評估，以足夠高的深度來監測和緩解氣候風險，從而獲取估值和監管上的效益。

在披露方面，我們參考了來自自然語言處理的最新證據，該證據表明，只有少數公司詳盡地披露了氣候風險所帶來的財務影響。

接下來，我們討論了氣候風險及其披露可以影響估值的程度，進而提供一些有關不同行業（如房地產和能源）的實證案例。

本章接着考慮了一些有代表性的氣候金融領域，這些領域中最近的創新尤其有前景。當中包括氣候風險分析和氣候監測方面的發展，以及在估值、資產定價和供應鏈風險管理方面的應用，還有證券和產品設計方面的創新，包括可持續發展掛鈎債券、參數保險和捆綁式金融解決方案方面的應用。

氣候風險及其披露

氣候變化帶來的風險有兩種[1]：因全球氣溫上升及與之相關的天氣模式變化和海平面上升所帶來的「**自然風險**」；在向低碳經濟轉型的過程中，因政策干預、消費者需求變化和商業環境拓寬所帶來的「**轉型風險**」。這些風險橫跨不同的行業和價值鏈。例如，糧食生產者從世界各地受嚴重乾旱影響較大、發生頻率較高的地區採購農產品時，供應上可能會遭遇更大的波動；物流公司可能會發現，暴雨和洪水頻繁擾亂重要的交通樞紐；房地產企業集團可能會發現，重要資產同時受海平面上升、高溫壓力和野外火災的威脅；能源公司可能會發現，排放限制所帶來的資產報廢義務使其大部分生產設備變為負擔。這樣的例子不勝枚舉。

企業正承受着來自投資者和監管機構與日俱增的壓力，它們被要求規劃、量化和披露所面臨的氣候風險。氣候風險披露只是更廣泛意義上的「環境、社會和治理」（Environment、Social、Governance，簡稱 ESG）指標的其中一部分，在過去幾年間備受關注。儘管如此，目前還沒有一套統一的規則，用以根據企業的「綠色認證」對企業進行排名，也沒有統一的框架來比較企業的供應鏈所面臨的氣候威脅和機遇。

氣候披露計劃（Climate Disclosure Project）、全球報告倡議組織（Global Reporting Initiative），以及最近成立的氣候相關財務信息披露工作組（Task Force on Climate-Related Financial Disclosures，簡稱 TCFD）均是這個背景下實行的重要舉措。近來各國加緊環境立法成為了加速發展和採用自願氣候披露機制的一大關鍵因素[2]。例如，歐盟關於可持續性相關披露的法規於 2021 年開始實施，擴大了對財務顧問將可持續性風險納入評估的要求。

市場近期有望推出一套統一的標準和方法，該標準和方法支持情景分析和細微氣候風險敞口自下而上的評估（見下文「創新」一節）[3]。儘管第三方評級與核查機制尚處於起步階段，仍待進一步完善[4]，但公司的自願披露是投資者的重要信息渠道之一。實證表明，氣候風險披露的廣度和深度因公司和司法權區的不同而存在很大差異。平安數字經濟研究中心的一

1　參閱例子：《氣候風險及應對：自然危害和社會經濟影響》（*Climate Risk and Response: Physical Hazards and Socioeconomic Impacts*）。麥肯錫公司，2020年。（報告簡稱為〈麥肯錫（2020a）〉。）

2　參閱例子：Y. J. Zhang 與 J. Y. Liu（2020年）〈碳資訊披露研究綜述〉（"Overview of research on carbon information disclosure"），載於《工程管理前沿》（*Frontiers in Engineering Management*）第7(1)卷，47-52頁；B. Walker 與 D. Salt（2006年）《恢復力思維：在不斷變化的世界中維持生態系統和人類》（*Resilience Thinking: Sustaining Ecosystems and People in a Changing World*），島嶼出版社：華盛頓特區；A. Kolk（2005年）〈三位一體的跨國公司的環境報告：趨同還是趨異？〉（"Environmental reporting by multinationals from the triad: convergence or divergence?"），載於《管理國際評論》（*Management International Review*）第45卷，145-166頁。

3　例如，根據《中國的ESG投資》這一報告，平安數字經濟研究中心《ESG報告系列》，2020年（報告簡稱為〈平安數字經濟研究中心（2020a）〉），僅在中證300指數的300家中國公司，共遵循了9套不同的指導方針。

4　參閱 F. Berg、J. F. Koelbel 與 R. Rigobon（2019年）〈綜合混亂：ESG評級的差異〉（"Aggregate confusion: The divergence of ESG ratings"），《麻省理工學院斯隆商學院工作論文》（MIT Sloan School Working Paper），編號5822-19，2020年5月17日。（報告簡稱為〈Berg等（2019）〉。）

份報告 [5] 顯示，在四大主要股票指數（滬深 300、標普 500、歐洲斯托克 50 和日經 225）中，日本公司在其報告中對氣候風險的介紹，不論從公司數量還是市值來看，均處於領先水平（見圖 1）—— 在公司報告中討論氣候風險的公司，日經 225 中有 52%（佔總市值的 68%）；標普 500 中有 33%（佔總市值的 53%）；歐洲斯托克 50 中有 40%（佔總市值的 44%）；而在滬深 300 中，將氣候風險納入其可持續性報告的公司僅佔 3%（佔總市值的 13%）。

圖 1：在 2020 年公司報告中討論氣候風險的公司的佔比

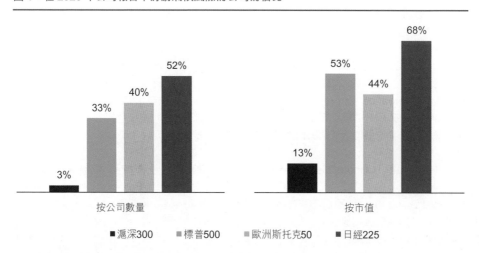

資料來源：〈我們對氣候信息披露的立場以及我們為甚麼需要披露 —— 公司可持續性報告的文本分析〉，平安數字經濟研究中心《ESG 報告系列》，2020 年（報告簡稱為〈平安數字經濟研究中心（2020b）〉）。

以 TCFD 框架作為參考基準，平安數字經濟研究中心（2020a）報告中展示的文本分析研究顯示，在提供氣候風險披露的公司中，超過 90% 的公司報告了與**碳排放**和**能源使用**相關的指標（見圖 2）。但對**水資源利用**和**土地利用**的報告卻非常缺乏。雖然對碳排放的披露程度很高，但問題出在細節上。如果在對公司營運中的碳排放作恆常披露時，亦將**間接排放**包括在內，就困難得多。這些間接排放的源頭來自於公司自身營運範圍之外（例如來自供應鏈）。這類排放通常被稱為「第三類」排放。在複雜的價值鏈中，披露間接排放需要詳細了解上下游運輸和分銷的碳足跡，以及已售產品和已購商品與服務的使用情況。這顯然在未來會成為吸引市場參與者進一步密切關注的一個領域。

5　資料來源：平安數字經濟研究中心（2020a）。

圖 2：氣候相關指標按行業的披露率

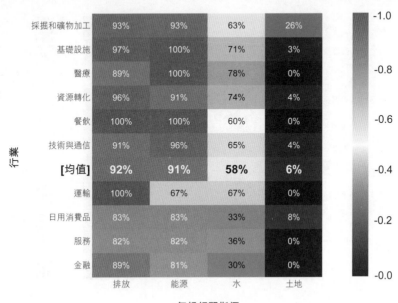

資料來源：平安數字經濟研究中心（2020b）。

從投資者的角度看，氣候風險對財務的影響顯然至關重要（見下文「估值」一節）。一些報告框架，如 TCFD 的報告框架[6]，對每個行業應披露的具體影響維度提供了明確的指導。遺憾的是，平安數字經濟研究中心（2020b）報告中進行的自然語言處理分析顯示，影響的重要維度仍沒有得到披露（見圖 3）。例如，很少有公司披露氣候風險對「資本和融資」的影響；還有，相對於「綠色」公司，「棕色」公司的披露相當程度被怠慢。與之有鮮明對比的是，樣本中卻有幾家公司都廣被認為受到重大轉型風險的影響：這些風險包括因限制排放和對陷入困境並轉變為負債的資產進行資金配給所帶來的資產報廢義務。另一方面，未被披露的氣候風險維度勢必會導致戰略性偏差，而可能影響真實報告的內容。這還更廣泛地涉及到「漂綠」的問題，各方近期都試圖通過在透明度、第三方驗證和標準化等多方面的努力來解決這個問題。

6　TCFD《氣候相關財務信息披露工作組的建議》，2017年6月（報告簡稱為〈TCFD（2017a）〉；TCFD《技術補充：在披露與氣候相關的風險和機遇中使用情景分析》（*Technical Supplement: The Use of Scenario Analysis in Disclosure of Climate-Related Risks and Opportunities*），2017年6月（報告簡稱為〈TCFD（2017b）〉）。

圖 3：財務指標按行業的披露率

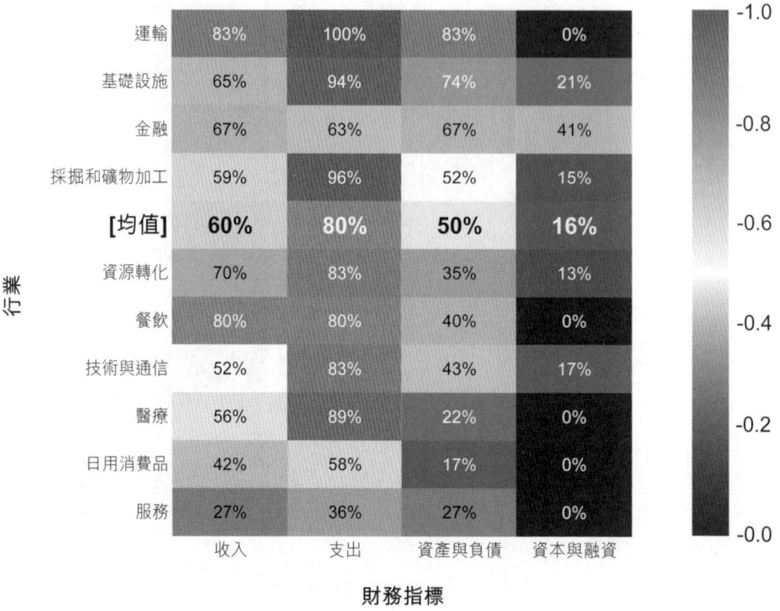

行業	收入	支出	資產與負債	資本與融資
運輸	83%	100%	83%	0%
基礎設施	65%	94%	74%	21%
金融	67%	63%	67%	41%
採掘和礦物加工	59%	96%	52%	15%
[均值]	**60%**	**80%**	**50%**	**16%**
資源轉化	70%	83%	35%	13%
餐飲	80%	80%	40%	0%
技術與通信	52%	83%	43%	17%
醫療	56%	89%	22%	0%
日用消費品	42%	58%	17%	0%
服務	27%	36%	27%	0%

財務指標

資料來源：平安數字經濟研究中心（2020b）。

估值

氣候報告框架的發展以及為提高透明度和可比性所作出的相關努力證明，氣候風險敞口越來越受到投資者的關注。一個顯而易見的問題是，公司估值是否考慮了氣候風險，如果是，在多大程度上考慮了氣候風險。關於這個問題的實證相當混雜。一方面，有證據表明，一些房地產市場已經開始就海平面上升的威脅對估值打折扣[7]，天氣衍生產品的價格會反映超出了氣象站所記錄短期天氣變化信息的氣候預測[8]。在轉型風險方面，一些研究顯示，相

7　參閱 A. Bernstein、M. T. Gustafson 與 R. Lewis（2019年）〈地平線上的災難：海平面上升的價格效應〉（"Disaster on the horizon: The price effect of sea level rise"），載於《金融經濟學雜誌》（*Journal of Financial Economics*）第134（2）卷，253-272頁。

8　參閱 W. Schlenker 與 C. A. Taylor（2019年）〈市場對氣候變化的預期〉（"Market expectations about climate change"），國民經濟調查局（National Bureau of Economic Research）的文章，編號w25554。

較於低排放企業，高排放企業的股票交易價格較低，這也證明了的確存在碳風險溢價[9]。另一方面，一些研究發現，從農業生產到房地產，許多行業和資產類別都存在錯誤定價的情況[10]。錯誤定價可能是普遍現象而非例外，原因包括：

- 相互抗衡的自然風險（如乾旱與洪水）和風險的異質性（如地理位置或產品特徵的差異）使得複雜價值鏈的脆弱性讓人捉摸不透。

- 氣候預測具有相當大的不確定性，這影響了我們對自然和轉型風險的理解，這也使得評估它們對企業現金流的影響具有高度猜測性。

- 在問題的對策方面，要想實現經濟繁榮的同時減緩氣候變化，如何權衡取捨是很複雜的，需要大量的協調，並與綠色創新的成功密不可分。

- 即使投資者可以就氣候變化對企業未來現金流的影響作出正確預期，但特定公司 / 行業對投資者的吸引力可能成為價格的重要驅動因素（例如與 ESG 投資相關的資本流動）。

面對未有結論的實證，人們可能會懷疑資產定價「理論」是否能提供一些幫助，但即使在這方面，觀點也不盡相同。一些市場參與者認為，氣候風險指標主要吸引有綠色偏好的投資者。與有關「罪惡股票」（如涉及煙草和賭博的股票）[11] 的文獻一致，這意味着出於環保考慮的投資者會因為投資主體的業務沒對其屬意的投資機會有所束縛，而在其投資中不盡佔優勢，讓該等主體有所得益。相反，有些市場參與者傾向於在適當的情況下，承認氣候風險指標對標杆公司基本面的信息價值（例如對現金流量的影響）及其總風險敞口[12]。事實上，氣候變化是系統性風險的主要來源之一，應按照標準資產定價理論進行定價。這兩種觀點是可以調和的：前一種觀點適用於均衡狀態，而後一種觀點強調向新均衡狀態的轉型，即政策、監管和市場參與者的氣候意識的改變可能導致各種資產的大規模重新定價。監管壓力測試採用了後一種觀點，目的是讓金融機構在其資本建模過程中，內化自然風險和轉型風險的影響[13]。

9　參閱 P. Bolton 與 M. Kacperczyk（2020年）〈全球的碳溢價〉（"Carbon premium around the world"），載於 SSRN。

10　參閱例子：H. Hong、F. W. Li 與 J. Xu（2019年）〈氣候風險和市場效率〉（"Climate risks and market efficiency"），載於《計量經濟學雜誌》（*Journal of Econometrics*）第208(1)卷，265-281頁；R. Jiang 與 C. Weng（2019年）〈氣候變化風險和農業相關股票〉（"Climate change risk and agriculture-related stocks"），可在SSRN上查閱，2019年12月15日；Y. Ding、C. Sun 與 J. Xu（2020年）〈氣候變化和市場可預見性：土壤濕度衛星資料證據〉（"Climate changes and market predictability: Evidence from satellite readings of soil moisture"），載於 SSRN（3637698），2020年1月1日。

11　參閱例子：E. F. Fama 與 K. R. French（2007年）〈分歧、品味和資產價格〉（"Disagreement, tastes and asset prices"），載於《金融經濟學雜誌》（*Journal of Financial Economics*）第83(3)卷，667-689頁；H. Hong 與 M. Kacperczyk（2009年）〈罪惡的代價：社會規範對市場的影響〉（"The price of sin: The effects of social norms on markets"），載於《金融經濟學雜誌》（*Journal of Financial Economics*）第93(1)卷，15-36頁。

12　參閱例子：D. Benedetti、E. Biffis、F. Chatzimichalakis、L. L. Fedele 與 I. Simm（2019年）〈氣候變化投資風險：向低碳經濟轉型前的最優投資組合構建〉（"Climate change investment risk: Optimal portfolio construction ahead of the transition to a lower-carbon economy"），載於《運籌學研究年報》（*Annals of Operations Research*）第299期，847-871頁。

13　參閱例子：英格蘭銀行（2021年）《2021年兩年期調查提綱參與者指南：氣候變化帶來的金融風險》，英國倫敦英格蘭銀行。（報告簡稱為〈英格蘭銀行(2021)〉。）

要理解氣候風險敞口和財務業績之間的聯繫是相當複雜的，因為存在幾個相互抵觸的價值驅動因素[14]，以及上文討論的自我報告披露的缺點。更廣泛的 ESG 評級問題也受到分數差異和排名不一致的困擾[15]。使用基於人工智能的指標可以揭示其中的一些關係。最近的研究表明，在控制碳排放和其他標準變數的情況下，更好地披露財務影響指標和更高的股票估值以及更低的資本成本之間存在正相關關係[16]。

儘管在過去幾年間，關於氣候風險和 ESG 評級的討論主要集中在股權領域，但債務市場同樣非常重要，也有一些證據支持了類似的發現。例如，在研究美國的銀行貸款時，一項研究[17]發現，盡社會責任公司的銀行貸款比其他公司的少支付 7 到 18 個基點息率；無擔保貸款對社會責任問題最為敏感。也有越來越多的證據表明，債務投資者的氣候意識與日俱增，一些商業貸款機構已經開始將貸款利率與 ESG 的表現掛鉤[18]。

為了說明氣候風險（及其披露）為何（以及如何）影響股權和債務，我們一起來看看圖 4。圖 4（a）展示了持有公司資產看漲期權的股權持有人所面臨的標準凸性收益曲線（深藍線），以及實質賣出公司資產看跌期權的債券持有人所面臨的標準凹性收益曲線（紅線）。在簡單的「兩日」單週期模型中，一家公司在 0 時點增加了數額為 D 的債務。當公司的現金流在該期間變現後，公司在 1 時點的資產（用 X 表示）決定了股東和債券持有人的收益。如果公司的資產低於債務的面值，股權持有人將受到有限責任的保護，而債券持有人將收回剩餘財產。市場參與者將通過理性預測這些結果，在 0 時點對股權和債務進行定價[19]。圖 4（b）展示了公司資產得以實現價值 X 的兩種可能性的概率分佈。這兩種分佈反映了不同程度的氣候風險：在所描繪的特定示例中，「一如往常」的分佈（黑色曲線）具有更高的違約率，這將使得債務價值降低；「氣候去風險化」的分佈（淺藍色曲線）通過解決自然／轉型

---

14 參閱例子：B. Cornell 與 A. Damodaran（2020年）〈評價ESG：做得好還是聽起來好？〉，載於 SSRN（3557432），2020年3月20日。

15 參閱例子：Berg 等（2019年）。

16 資料來源：平安數字經濟研究中心〈氣候資訊披露和財務業績：人工智能驅動指標、漂綠檢測和公司特徵〉，《ESG報告系列》第4期，2020年12月（報告簡稱為〈平安數字經濟研究中心(2020c)〉）。特別是，符合TCFD要求的大型公司往往估值較高，而從事氣候披露的中小型公司仍可能提供可觀的升值機會。

17 A. Goss 與 G. S. Roberts（2011年）〈企業社會責任對銀行貸款成本的影響〉（"The impact of corporate social responsibility on the cost of bank loans"），載於《銀行業與金融雜誌》（*Journal of Banking & Finance*）第35(7)卷，1794-1810頁。

18 參閱例子：S. C. Bae、K. Chang 與 H. C. Yi（2018年）〈企業社會責任、信用等級和私人債務合同：銀團貸款市場的新證據〉（"Corporate social responsibility, credit rating, and private debt contracting: new evidence from syndicated loan market"），載於《量化金融與會計評論》（*Review of Quantitative Finance and Accounting*）第50卷，261-299頁；S. Gatti 與 A. Florio（2018年）〈綠色債券市場的發行利差決定因素：第二方評審和綠色債券原則的作用〉（"Issue spread determinants in the green bond market: The role of second party reviews and of the Green Bond Principles"），載於《金融和可持續性研究手冊》（*Research Handbook of Finance and Sustainability*），Edward Elgar出版社；F. Barth、B. Hübel 與 H. Scholz（2019年）〈ESG和企業信用利差〉（"ESG and corporate credit spreads"），載於 SSRN（3179468），2021年3月30日。

19 公司進行風險管理是為了向投資者發出信號，表明此類問題已得到控制，並在必要時得到緩解。實際上，股權持有人的凸性收益所引發的冒險激勵，可能會使資產替代等代理問題變得尤為尖銳。適當的風險披露和風險管理會更緊密地協調債券持有人和股權持有人的定價看法，來緩解這些摩擦。

風險，從而使得債務價值提升，並且可能利用氣候變化機會，增加股權持有人的收益漲幅。因此，適當的披露和與市場參與者的接洽可能會大幅降低融資成本，提高公司估值[20]。

圖 4（b）佐證了就氣候風險披露所作的尾部風險措施的關注度在日益增強。這方面的實例包括使用氣候壓力測試和計算氣候風險值，試圖量化在不同全球溫度情景下，對公司前景以現值計算的影響[21]。將這種影響納入股權和債券的定價考量顯然很吸引長期投資者的興趣[22]，除此之外，監管機構也在研究氣候風險對於系統性風險的影響[23]。

圖 4：股權和債務投資的收益表

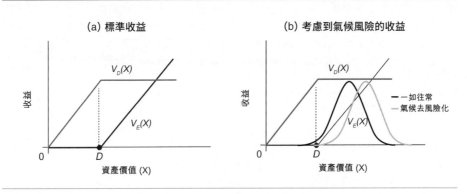

(a) 標準收益　　　　　**(b) 考慮到氣候風險的收益**

$V_D(X)$　$V_E(X)$　收益　資產價值 (X)　一如往常　氣候去風險化

註：在上圖中，y 軸代表不同利益相關者（E 代表股東，D 代表債權人）的收益，y 軸是公司資產的最終價值 X 的函數。
　　圖 4b 提供了在「一如往常」和「氣候去風險化」兩種策略下 X 軸可能性的分佈。

資料來源：平安數字經濟研究中心（2020b）。

創新

圍繞氣候風險的金融創新為分析工具和產品的創新提供了巨大機遇。我們在此討論氣候風險分析、供應鏈風險監測、保險和投資要素等領域。

20　關於進一步的討論和一些實證結果，請見平安數字經濟研究中心（2020c）。
21　參閱TCFD(2017b)和TCFD《前瞻性金融部門指標諮詢》（*Forward-Looking Financial Sector Metrics Consultation*），2020年10月（報告簡稱為〈TCFD(2020)〉。）
22　參閱例子：Gründl H.、M. Dong與J. Gal（2016）〈保險公司長期投資組合投資策略的演變〉（"The evolution of insurer portfolio investment strategies for long-term investing"），載於《經合組織雜誌：金融市場動向》（*OECD Journal: Financial Market Trends*）第2016(2)卷，1-55頁。
23　參閱英格蘭銀行(2021)。

氣候風險分析

大部分文獻側重於自上而下的方法，去理解不同技術和生活方式情景下氣候變化的經濟影響。綜合評估模型（Integrated Assessment Model，簡稱 IAM）是氣候風險建模中最受歡迎的工具之一。這些模型通過對經濟和人口增長的假設，以及溫室氣體排放的其他驅動因素，來就全球能源系統和其他溫室氣體排放行業的潛在演變建構模型。這些模型涉及將「一如往常」情景與其他推動技術和生活方式改變的路徑進行比較，這些路徑旨在遏制排放並限制長期溫度上升達到特定目標。這些模型是有力工具，能向決策者提供風險緩解措施的成本效益信息[24]。從複雜的成熟 IAM 中抽取出一套簡化板模型，並通過引入排放與經濟增長之間的簡化關係，專注於減排的成本效益分析，同時試圖將氣候變化的影響和降低氣溫上升的好處轉換成幣值[25]。這些模型的產出通常出現在政府間氣候變化專門委員會（Intergovernmental Panel on Climate Change，簡稱 IPCC）的報告中[26]。圖 5 概述了知名的「動態綜合氣候經濟」（Dynamic Integrated Climate-Economy，簡稱 DICE）模型[27]。

IAM 可能既有助於為全行業的戰略性投資決策提供信息，當然也有助於探索不同風險緩解政策對關鍵經濟行業的程式化影響（能源行業是近年來在這方面研究最廣泛的行業之一）。然而，這些模型並沒有達到所需的細微性程度，來為資產選擇、行業內投資分級或旨在從氣候變化中獲益或對沖氣候變化的分配策略提供信息。相反，可以針對特定的風險敞口定制細化的、自下而上的方法，用以：（1）明確將氣候風險納入評估；（2）考慮資產特徵，細化氣候風險定價。近期為推動更透明的氣候風險披露的舉措，以及更多地採用前瞻性風險指標和基準氣候情景，這些都表明這種自下而上的做法將在未來變得更常見[28]。

---

24 參閱例子：O. Dessens、G. Anandarajah 與 A. Gambhir（2016年）〈將全球暖化限制在2°C以內：關於成本、技術和其他影響，最新的緩解研究告訴了我們甚麼？〉（"Limiting global warming to 2°C: What do the latest mitigation studies tell us about costs, technologies and other impacts?"），載於《能源戰略評論》（*Energy Strategy Reviews*）第13卷，67-76頁。

25 參閱例子：A. Gambhir、I. Butnar、P. H. Li、P. Smith 與 N. Stracham（2019年）〈通過BECCS的視角，回顧對綜合評估模型的批評和解決這些問題的建議方法〉（"A review of criticisms of integrated assessment models and proposed approaches to address these, through the lens of BECCS"），載於《能源》（*Energies*）第12卷（9），1747頁。

26 參閱載於政府間氣候變化專門委員會資料分佈中心網頁上的〈典型濃度路徑〉（"Representative Concentration Pathways (RCPs)"）網頁（https://sedac.ciesin.columbia.edu/ddc/ar5_scenario_process/RCPs.html）。

27 參閱 W. D. Nordhaus（2017年）〈重新審視碳的社會成本〉（"Revisiting the social cost of carbon"），載於《美國國家科學院院刊》（*Proceedings of the National Academy of Sciences*）第114（7）卷，1518-1523頁。

28 參閱TCFD（2020）。

圖 5：動態綜合氣候經濟（DICE）模型

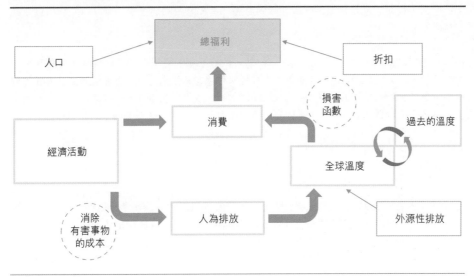

資料來源：作者的分析。

未來最有趣的挑戰之一是通過利用**前瞻性指標**，來改進公司的氣候風險披露，其體現的是企業對未來減排的承諾，而非其碳足跡。碳足跡與公司估值的相關性有限，因為公司估值反映的是**未來**的財務前景。此外，碳足跡並沒有考慮到公司的定價能力，即它們將成本轉嫁給客戶的能力。除了當前的排放數據之外，公司還應採用前瞻性預測，如未來的生產曲線，並披露公司當前為應對未來氣候風險而採取的投資及／或戰略。未來很有希望會有與氣候相關的尾部風險指標（如氣候風險值），可以支援市場參與者在氣候變化帶來的跌價風險下選擇應對措施。

供應鏈透明度和可追溯性

全球供應鏈同時面臨自然和轉型氣候風險。自然風險可能會損害供應網絡中關鍵節點的可靠性，並導致其中斷。脫碳政策導致一些節點過時且在管理上不經濟，從而產生轉型風險。由於供應鏈之間交互連接，投資者在評估自身對氣候風險的脆弱性，以及應對這些多種不同形式的風險時可能面臨挑戰。供應鏈面臨着複雜的挑戰，不僅體現在風險脆弱性方面，還體現在價值鏈上氣候風險敞口的透明度和可追溯性。

透明度是指向利益相關者披露供應鏈和採購信息，確保信息得以傳播、可獲取及可比較。另一方面，可追溯性是指從供應鏈開端到最終分銷和應用的過程中，可以識別和跟蹤產品和材料的能力 [29]。

技術正在幫助提高透明度和可追溯性。例如，依靠衛星的氣候監測技術現在可以用來追蹤甲烷排放，資產跟蹤設備也愈發能對生產和採購作適當的監測 [30]。最近在氣候融資方面的舉措還側重於設計新的工具，如可持續發展掛鈎債券（見以下分節），將融資和支出與實現可持續發展目標聯繫起來。在此，還有機會使用區塊鏈技術將這些交易構造成智慧型合約 [31]。

可持續發展掛鈎債券（SLB）

據摩根大通稱，2021 年，與實現特定可持續發展目標掛鈎的公司債券市場有望增長至 20 倍，總發行量可能在 1,200 億美元至 1,500 億美元之間 [32]。SLB 最重要的特徵是，該債券的財務及／或結構特徵可能會有變化，具體取決於達到預先設定多個可持續發展表現目標（Sustainability Performance Target，簡稱 SPT）的特定關鍵績效指標（Key Performance Indicator，簡稱 KPI）。例如，債券可能會因未能達到某個碳減排目標而導致票息率上升。

氣候風險和更廣泛的 ESG 披露之間存在一個更緊密的聯繫，最佳實務做法建議發行人應選擇已包含在以往年度報告（包括可持續性報告或其他披露）中的 KPI，以便讓投資者根據歷史記錄對債券結構和後續表現與基準作比較。根據國際資本市場協會的《可持續發展掛鈎債券原則》[33]，三年的跟蹤記錄和 KPI 的第三方驗證將是合適的最低標準。顯然，對這些工具而言，透明度、可追溯性和驗證都將變得越來越重要，它們展示了在氣候風險披露、氣候監測和產品設計背景下對各種工具所需的有機改進。

---

29 參閱聯合國全球公約和BSR（2014年）《可追溯性指南：推進全球供應鏈可持續性的實用方法》（*A Guide to Traceability: A Practical Approach to Advance Sustainability in the Global Supply Chains*）。

30 參閱Malik N.〈衛星將世界上最大的甲烷排放者繪製在地圖上〉（"Satellites put the world's biggest methane emitters on the map"），載於《彭博》，2020年10月21日。

31 參閱例子：Nassiry（2018年）〈金融科技在解鎖綠色金融中的作用：對發展中國家的政策見解〉（"The role of fintech in unlocking green finance: Policy insights for developing countries"），亞洲開發銀行學院《亞洲開發銀行研究所工作論文》編號883；責任投資原則（Principles for Responsible Investment）（2018年）《責任投資和區塊鏈》（*Responsible Investment and Blockchain*）。

32 資料來源：〈可持續發展掛鈎債券市場將膨脹至1,500億美元：摩根大通ESG DCM主管〉（"Sustainability-linked bond market to swell up to $150 billion: JP Morgan ESG DCM Head"），載於《路透社》，2021年3月22日。

33 參閱國際資本市場協會《可持續發展掛鈎債券原則》（*Sustainability-linked Bond Principles*），2020年6月。

保險產品

洪水和颶風等自然風險必然與風險轉移機制相關，例如保險和保險掛鈎證券。在需求方面，人們清楚地認識到，降低供應鏈網絡風險的成本可能很高，因為在更易受到氣候變化影響的地區，保險成本會上升。然而，在市場上常見的標準短期保險機制之外，尋求更長期的保護似乎難以實現：在供應方面，鑒於氣候預測有相當大的不確定性，保險機構非常不願意提供長期保險承諾。所以在氣候風險解決方案方面，市場是相當不完整的。

使用保險機制可能是對氣候風險轉移更有效的貢獻，而不僅是提供獨立賠償。例如，以新興國家的農業生產為例，這些國家越來越容易受到乾旱和洪水等自然風險的影響，因此可以從採用適應氣候變化的生產技術中獲得巨大益處[34]。在新興市場，小農戶佔農業生產的很大部分，他們獲得先進的一攬子投入和培訓的機會有限[35]。獲得資金與否是能否採用技術的一個關鍵，由於這些農民缺乏信用記錄，所以銀行往往會避開他們，而且對於農民來說，拖欠貸款往往事關生存[36]。預期產量低以及更頻繁、更嚴重的惡劣天氣事件將小農戶的信用狀況限制在較低的水平，也使其無法獲得足夠的資源作為抵押。因此，他們陷入了無法從金融系統中獲得貸款以資助採用更複雜的生產科技的惡性循環[37]。

最近保險領域的創新，包括參數化設計的天氣保險產品，可以為解決上述困難提供一套解決方案。與衍生工具合約類似，這些工具在特定天氣條件出現並觸發付款條件時（例如累計降雨量低於合同約定的閾值）會作出支付。這些產品最初依賴於氣象站，但現在可以利用衛星數據和機器學習技術，建立與任何地點的投保人的風險敞口密切匹配的賠付指數[38]。最近在東非進行的大規模試點表明，這類產品可以提供比獨立保險更多的保障，且實際上還可以用來緩解信用分配、促進普惠金融，以及激勵採用氣候適應型技術。最近一項重點

---

34 參閱例子：麥肯錫諮詢公司《農業與氣候變化：通過改進耕作方式減少排放》（*Agriculture and Climate Change: Reducing Emissions through Improved Farming Practices*），2020年（報告簡稱為〈麥肯錫(2020b)〉）。

35 參閱 E. Duflo、M. Kremer 與 J. Robinson（2008年）〈肥料的回報率有多高？來自肯亞實地試驗的證據〉（"How high are rates of return to fertilizer? Evidence from field experiments in Kenya"），載於《美國經濟評論》（*American Economic Review*）第98(2)卷，482-488頁。

36 參閱 S. Dercon 與 L. Christiaensen（2011年）〈消費風險、技術採用和貧困陷阱：來自埃塞俄比亞的證據〉（"Consumption risk, technology adoption and poverty traps: Evidence from Ethiopia"），載於《發展經濟學雜誌》（*Journal of Development Economics*）第92(2)卷，159-173頁。

37 參閱例子：E. Biffis、E. Chavez、A. Louaas 與 P. Picard（2021年）〈發展中國家的參數化保險和技術採用〉（"Parametric insurance and technology adoption in developing countries"），將刊登在《日內瓦風險與保險評論》（*Geneva Risk and Insurance Review*）。（報告簡稱為〈Biffis等(2021)〉。）

38 參閱例子：E. Biffis 與 E. Chavez（2017年）〈天氣風險管理和糧食安全的衛星數據和機器學習〉（"Satellite data and machine learning for weather risk management and food security"），載於《風險分析》（*Risk Analysis*）第37(8)卷，1508-1521頁。

關注坦桑尼亞的研究[39]表明，嵌入參數化保險成份的投入貸款，可以降低農業銀行投資組合的風險，因為貸款承銷商認為這是一種信用增強手段，可以規避信用分配。重要的是，由於保險費反映了一攬子投入所帶來的氣候抗禦力，它們是向小農戶傳達氣候抗禦生產技術的經濟價值的一個有力渠道。

結論

本章概述了市場參與者在應對氣候風險時面臨的一些主要挑戰。最近的一些實證表明，投資者越來越意識到氣候變化對估值和資產價格的影響。在一個監管干預力和消費者壓力都在增加的環境中，這些影響預計會變得更加明顯。目前備受關注的、亦是我們認為未來幾年將會出現重大發展的氣候融資領域包括：

- 建立關於氣候風險敞口（例如資產位置）和氣候影響（例如溫室氣體排放足跡）的精細數據庫；

- 用於溫室氣體排放評估和監測的遙感和區塊鏈技術；

- 開發氣候情景以評估金融機構對氣候風險的抵禦能力；

- 淨零戰略的設計和實施越來越注重碳減排，而不是避免排放或碳抵銷。

註1：作者感謝平安數字經濟研究中心允許使用他們報告中包含的材料，來支持本章中討論的一些發現。

註2：本文原稿是英文，另以中文譯本出版。如本文的中文本的字義或詞義與英文本有所出入，概以英文本為準。

39 Biffis等(2021)。另見：A. Shee 與 C. G. Turvey (2012年)〈農業發展中存在意外信用風險的無抵押貸款：補償印度豆類作物價格風險貸款〉("Collateral-free lending with risk-contingent credit for agricultural development: Indemnifying loans against pulse crop price risk in India")，載於《農業經濟學》(*Agricultural Economics*) 第43(5)卷，561-574頁；D. Karlan、R. Osei、I. Osei-Akoto 與 C. Udry (2014年)〈放寬信用和風險約束後的農業決策〉("Agricultural decisions after relaxing credit and risk constraints")，載於《經濟學季刊》(*The Quarterly Journal of Economics*) 第129(2)卷，597-652頁。

Chapter 12

Green and sustainable finance in private equity investment: Practical experience in Mainland China

Frankie FANG
Managing Partner, Starquest Capital

Summary

ESG stands for environmental, social and governance. It is an investment philosophy and business strategy that emphasises environment, society and governance factors more than just financial performance. Taking ESG factors into account can establish a sustainable financial market in China.

Many Western financial institutions have incorporated ESG factors into their research and investment decision-making systems far ahead of their Chinese peers. Despite low penetration and only initial adoption, as the awareness of ESG rises, the Chinese private equity (PE) industry is gradually embracing the idea and has initiated local practices.

Fund of Funds (FoFs) in the PE industry has a unique amplification effect in promoting responsible investing. For its asset diversification, long-term investment horizons, and binding terms, FoFs managers are ideally positioned to incorporate ESG considerations into their top-level strategy and extend the impact to the general partners' underlying portfolio companies. This chapter presents our thoughts on ESG investment practices of FoFs, including a quantitative evaluation system and case studies.

Looking ahead, as a result of the joint efforts from all stakeholders to actively promote responsible investing, we can confidently expect greater sustainability in the PE market and more responsible "new economy" enterprises in China.

Current development of responsible investment in Mainland China

The concepts of environment, society and governance (ESG) have been developed in western capital markets for many years, accumulating mature experience in institutional mechanisms, market services and investment practices. ESG investment practices have also become an important part of the investment process of private equity (PE) funds. Nowadays, many financial institutions around the world have incorporated ESG factors into their own research and investment decision-making systems. In recent years, the asset scale of responsible investment has been increasing rapidly around the world.

Compared to the mature ESG investments in the western markets, the responsible investment practices and ESG concepts in Mainland China started later and are still at the stage of strengthening awareness and exploring ways to improve the socially responsible investment system.

The first ESG investment in Mainland China was in 2002 when Tsing Capital established the first ESG-related fund, the China Environmental Fund, in the Mainland. This fund has a strong financial background, including the Asian Development Bank, Government funds of the Netherlands, British Petroleum, Hong Kong LESS and other renowned international investment institutions. In 2006, the Shenzhen Stock Exchange (SZSE) released the *Guidance on Social Responsibility for Listed Companies* acting as the first ESG signal sent by a stock exchange. In 2008, AEGON-INDUSTRIAL Fund Management Co., Ltd., as a public fund company, first introduced the concept of socially responsible investment and launched the first fund product on the theme of social responsibility, the Aegon-Industrial Society Responsibility Securities Investment Fund. The assets under management of relevant types of responsible investment funds in the Mainland financial market has increased significantly since 2010. A range of corresponding policies have also been promulgated, for example, in 2008, the Shanghai Stock Exchange (SSE) issued the *Notice on Strengthening Social Responsibilities of Listed Companies* and the *Issuance of the SSE Guidance on Environmental Information Disclosure of Listed Companies*, requiring listed companies to actively perform their social responsibilities while focusing on their economic interests. In addition, the Asset Management Association of China (AMAC) has also played its leading role. Since 2016, AMAC has held several domestic and international forums and seminars and conducted ESG research to promote the concept and practice of ESG. In November 2018, AMAC released the *Research Report on the ESG Evaluation System for Listed Companies in China* and the *Guidance for*

Green Investors (Trial Implementation), serving as practical guidelines for China's ESG investment markets to further promote the development of ESG in Mainland China.

As of March 2021, 3,844 institutions have signed the United Nations-supported Principles for Responsible Investments (PRI)[1], 56 of which are from China, including China Huarong, E Fund, Penghua Fund, Southern Fund, Bosera Fund, China Life and Ping An. Of these 56 institutions, 30 joined between 2019 and 2020. From the view of the growing number of UNPRI signatories in 2019, the fastest growth comes from China, showing that China has been strengthening its awareness of responsible investment in recent years.

Necessity for ESG investment in private equity

Overview of ESG investment practices of PE/VC institutions in China

The awareness of the Chinese primary market on ESG investment is generally weak. Thanks to the attention of regulatory authorities to "green finance", the call by the public on the "responsibility of capital", and the related institutional establishment in the secondary market, among the general partners (GPs) of PE fund management institutions, 50% heard of ESG but did not pay particular attention to it for the moment; a minority, such as venture capital (VC) fund management institutions, have in-depth knowledge of ESG; and 29% have never heard of ESG investment or even do not understand its basic meaning[2].

The disparity of awareness of ESG among PE funds is mainly reflected in the currency. ESG principles are of relatively high significance in US dollar (USD) funds and dual-currency funds as they are strongly influenced by international capital. These types of funds have the fund management partners directly responsible for ESG-related matters, and there have been several successful ESG investment practice cases. RMB funds, on the other hand, are observed to have a weak awareness of ESG and serious insufficient attention to ESG. Some RMB funds have the awareness of ESG but only at the fundraising stage without investment practice, while most RMB funds lack the awareness of or adequate emphasis on ESG and also have no establishment of ESG strategies and ESG systems.

---

1   Source: The *PRI* website.
2   Source: Starquest ESG Due Diligence Survey, 2020.

Looking at the practice at different stages of investment, PE funds at the middle and later investment stages would pay more attention to ESG factors. There are two reasons for this: (1) PE funds at these stages are mainly invested in enterprises with relatively strong profitability, good cash flow, rapid growth and even being mature; these enterprises usually have a large market share and a large user base, and would have spare capacity to assume social responsibility; (2) PE funds at these stages are closer to the exit window, so they are more sensitive to regulatory requirements and investor preferences in the secondary market and have realised that ESG investment is in desperate need, which are specifically reflected in the gradual introduction of disclosure standards for the Social Responsibility Report of listed companies, the ESG rating of A-shares after their inclusion in MSCI indices, etc. In comparison, angel funds and VC funds are relatively short of awareness of and attention to ESG. Nevertheless, some angel funds and VC funds have made certain progress in taking ESG as a risk control factor in early-stage project screening and post-investment management. For example, they may avoid investing in projects that may cause environmental pollution or resource waste, and may consider the moral misconduct of founders with prudence.

The short of knowledge of the industry on ESG is also reflected in industry communication and the compliance with regulations. Compared with public funds and investment funds in the secondary market, Mainland PE funds have inadequate participation in ESG training and ESG industry communication, and few of them have joined international ESG organisations. The GPs of Mainland PE fund management institutions also fail to observe industry rules and international standards in an effective way. When making ESG investment, only a few fund management institutions abide by industry self-regulatory standards, such as the A-share secondary market evaluation indicators/systems, and the international standards, such as the eight ESG performance standards established by the International Finance Corporation (IFC).

Significance and value of ESG for PE/VC investment

The most significant implication of ESG investment is to promote enterprises to conduct ESG-friendly practices through the power of capital, and to drive them to protect the ecological environment, perform social responsibility, and improve corporate governance. ESG investment has the following effects on enterprise behaviours.

In general, investors can influence enterprise behaviours in two ways: (1) for an investor who is a director of the company, it can initiate a protest at a board meeting; and (2) for an investor as an ordinary investor, it can protest by deregistering from the shareholder register. Indeed, the practice of incorporating ESG factors into corporate decision-making has been adopted in the last century, and corporate directors are increasingly putting their focus on corporate strategies and behaviours in respect of social responsibility, so called Corporate Social Responsibility (CSR). According to previous studies, since the 1990s, corporate boards have tended to require their companies to incorporate the factors of economic, environmental, and social sustainability into corporate governance and reflect these factors in management reports. Academic studies[3] have confirmed that CSR-focused companies would take environment, social sustainability, and corporate governance as key focuses of their competitive strategies to maximise corporate value; and these companies often have competitive advantages in aspects such as return on assets and systemic risks.

In addition, some scholars[4] found that social responsibility requirements initiated by long-term investors have a greater impact on enterprise behaviours. If long-term investors have a positive impact on the managers of the invested enterprise, they can help the enterprise improve its corporate governance capabilities. Specifically, long-term investors can have an impact on enterprise behaviours through shareholder proposals and changes in the board of directors and managers. In addition, as long-term investors tend to diversify their investments (such as in terms of industry, region, development stage, etc.), their impacts are related to the degree of risk control of the enterprise.

If, according to the studies, ESG investment stimulates companies to preserve the ecological environment, fulfill social responsibility and improve corporate governance, then how well are the investments performing? The relationship between ESG performance and corporate financial performance (CFP) has been a hot topic for academic research. Since the 1970s, scholars and investment institutions in the West have published numerous academic empirical studies, literature reviews, and business reports on the relationship between ESG and CFP. Gunnar Friede, Timo Busch, and Alexander Bassen have found that roughly 90% of the studies found a non-negative ESG-CPF relationship by analysing more than 2,200 individual academic studies published during 1990 to 2015[5]. The literature they reviewed have a wide scope of coverage, including portfolio research,

---

3   Albuquerque, R., A. Durnev. and Y. Koskinen, "Corporate social responsibility and firm risk: Theory and empirical evidence", 20 November 2011, available at SSRN.

4   Bebchuk, L. A. and L. A. Stole. (1993) "Do short-term objectives lead to under- or over-investment in long-term projects?", The Journal of Finance, Vol. 48, Issue 2, pp.719-729.

5   Friede, G., T. Busch and A. Bassen. (2015) "ESG and financial performance: Aggregated evidence from more than 2,000 empirical studies", Journal of Sustainable Finance & Investment, Vol. 5, No. 4, pp.210-233.

non-portfolio research, different regions and countries at different stages of development such as emerging markets, and various financial products (corporate bonds, green infrastructure, corporate equity, etc.).

FoFs as a useful tool for promoting ESG investment

Fund of Funds (FoFs) plays a pivotal role in global asset allocations. According to a research by Preqin and China Venture Institute[6], FoFs has become the second largest investor, following pension funds, in the private equity market in terms of subscription amount. According to Pitchbook data, as at the end of June 2019, FoFs worldwide had about US$360 billion of capital under management, of which, about US$295 billion was invested in projects, and US$65 billion are available for investing.

FoFs is taken as an effective tool for ESG practice for its following key characteristics.

FoFs featured by long-term investment meeting the sustainable investment principle of ESG

The ESG concept emphasises that investors are supposed to fully consider the performance of the invested company in environmental protection, social contribution, and corporate governance in making their investment decisions, implying a natural long-term investment cycle. The characteristics of ESG investment also imply the difficulty for it to be widely promoted and implemented, and so it must match with an investment method that possesses a similar investment cycle and has the same emphasis on long-term sustainability.

Active investors of PE investment in the Mainland include FoFs (including government guidance funds), pension funds, insurance companies and asset management institutions. These investors raise their funds from different sources, have different strategic focuses, and expect different investment outcomes. Among them, FoFs have the longest

---

6   *Research Report on China Market-oriented VC/PE Fund of Funds (2019)*, published on the website of Chinaventure Institute, October 2019.

investment cycle, usually up to 3-5 years, while the investment cycle of asset management companies and fund companies is just 1-3 years with high performance pressure in the short term. For insurance companies and pension funds, due to their relatively high debt pressure and the weakness of their internal team in professional investment, it is difficult for them to adopt ESG investment strategy with a relatively long investment cycle. Therefore, FoF is a more appropriate investment method to match the characteristics of ESG investment.

FoFs featured by diversified allocation covering all ESG elements and effectively controlling risks

In respect of asset allocation, FoFs exhibit diversified allocation strategies, bearing the characteristics of cross-region, multi-industry, cross-stage, cross-year and multi-strategy (including growth capital, venture capital in mergers and acquisitions (M&A), non-performing assets investment, mezzanine investments, etc.). In mature PE markets, large investment institutions often make diversified allocation at the fund level, and then strengthen their allocation in certain key fields by grasping the opportunities of follow-up investments, or reduce over-allocation in certain funds through secondary market transactions. Through a variety of investment methods and portfolios, the investment of the FoFs may cover most industries, regions and development stages, and fully balance asset allocation to avoid excessive concentrated allocation.

Over the past 10 and more years, the leading FoFs such as LGT have successfully extended ESG to hundreds of sub-funds. However, the ESG investment concept of FoFs is still very weak in the Mainland. It is therefore imminent to raise the overall ESG awareness in the industry and give them guiding strategies.

Figure 1. Diversified allocation of FoFs

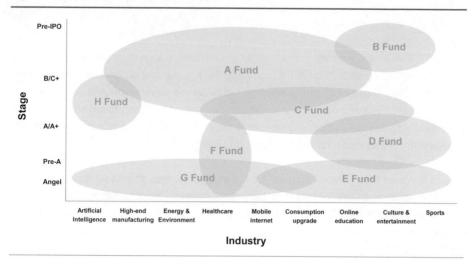

Note: "Stage" in the chart refers to the financing stage of enterprises in the PE market, including the angel round (i.e. the seed period for angel investment) and the following Pre-A round, A/A+ round, Pre-IPO round (i.e. before initial public offering), etc.

Source: Starquest Capital.

Market status and impact of FoFs effectively promoting the development of ESG investment

In respect of market impact, due to the long-term investment cycle of FoFs, once FoFs implements the relevant investment principles of ESG, it will have an impact on the invested funds and underlying projects for at least 10 years or more. In addition, fund raising will be conducted every 2-3 years to supplement with new funds, expecting existing investors to keep increasing their holdings. Therefore, by guiding, supervising the invested funds and projects and putting relevant terms in place at the level of FoFs, ESG concept can be effectively incorporated into the invested funds and invested enterprises.

Such amplification effect of FoFs plays the role as radar. Through the FoFs team's in-depth due diligence on the industries, markets, sub-funds and underlying projects, FoFs can timely detect the information of all aspects of the markets like a radar, acting as a platform for information collection and resource integration.

Terms of agreement of FoFs driving self-regulation of ESG investment

In the PE investment market, in addition to government supervision and self-regulation, the FoFs works as the third force for promoting the healthy and sustainable development of the industry. Different from government policy-based supervision and restrictions, in ESG practice, FoFs not only enact legally binding terms but also exercise supervision with relatively flexible principles, so that it may reasonably and effectively drive the development of invested funds and projects on ESG practice.

The inclusion of ESG terms in private fund agreements, though without any established global standard practices for that, has become a common practice for mainstream FoFs and PE investors in the US and Europe, and the trend has been on the rise. Conditional on the signing of an agreement by both parties, a sub-fund can exercise subjective initiative in advocating and fulfilling ESG investment, with enhanced proactivity in practice.

ESG investment strategies of FoFs

Strategies and policies

The incorporation of ESG by an FoF into its investments requires the FoF manager to reach a high degree of strategic consensus, and even to incorporate ESG into the top-level design of the fund. Specifically, the manager is supposed to abide by the following six principles:

- **Investment practice:** incorporating ESG concepts into specific investment practices, including project analysis, investment decision-making;

- **Subjective initiative:** becoming an active enabler, exercising the subjective initiative and integrating ESG concepts into investment practices;

- **Information disclosure:** requiring investment institutions to fully disclose ESG information;

- **Industry promotion:** promoting the investment industry to understand, be familiar with, and finally put into practice the PRI principles;

- **Industry exchange:** establishing cooperation and communication with pioneers in the industry to improve the efficiency of implementing the PRI principles; and

- **Regular reporting:** reporting the progress of implementation of PRI principles on a regular basis in accordance with relevant international standards.

ESG quantitative assessment system of FoFs

The ESG quantitative assessment indicators of FoFs shall be constructed from four aspects: general assessment of the institution, environment, society and corporate governance, as shown in Table 1. Different from direct investment, FoFs invest in sub-funds and their GPs. FOFs are required to consider the characteristics of the business processes of the PE investment industry prior to constructing its ESG assessment frameworks. To this end, in addition to the three conventional elements of "environment", "society" and "corporate governance", the additional element of "general assessment of the institution" of GP will be adopted.

After the FoFs builds an appropriate key indicator matrix, a variety of ways may be adopted to collect data, assign values and design weightings to the indicators, and arrive at the final assessment results. Information collection and statistics compilation are the prerequisites and basis for assessment. The common methods of information collection include interviews, ESG questionnaires, public information inquiries, and provision of supporting evidence. Indicators such as government administrative penalties, corporate public opinion information, rules violations, and defaulters may be inquired through public channels by taking advantage of the professional assessment results of the regulatory authorities. Indicators such as ESG awareness, ESG committee and execution of ESG terms are connected with the autonomous and detailed disclosure made by a sub-fund, which requires the FoFs to embed in the ESG elements at various stages for information collection.

Table 1. Foundation framework for ESG assessment indicators of FoFs

	Assessment content	Assessment indicators
General assessment of the institution	ESG awareness	The institution's following aspects in relation to ESG: strategic positioning, policy formulation, committees mechanism, advisory mechanism, terms signing, industry exchange, etc.
	Investment process	The institution's ESG investment strategies, investment practices, due diligence designs, risk reporting mechanism, etc.
	Post-investment management	The institution's following aspects in relation to invested enterprises: continuous ESG supervision and guidance, assessment mechanism, exit management, etc.
	Information disclosure	The institution's following mechanisms of reporting to the limited partners: regular ESG reporting mechanism, negative information reporting mechanism, etc.
Environment	Sub-funds	Industries and regions in which the sub-fund intends to invest
	Invested enterprises	Environmental policies, risk exposure coefficient, energy consumption indicators and carbon emissions, etc. of the invested enterprise
Society	Sub-funds	Investment returns, enterprise credibility, industry competition, protection of employees' rights and interest, etc. of a sub-fund
	Invested enterprises	Return on equity, employee policies, supply-chain relationship, public security, etc. of the invested enterprise
Corporate governance	Sub-funds	Composition of the investment and decision-making committee, voting mechanism, employee mobility, etc. of a sub-fund
	Invested enterprises	Macro strategies, level of cash returns, rules violations of the invested enterprise

Source: Starquest Capital.

Cases of PE ESG practice in China[7]

Early ESG investment practice of investment institutions in the Mainland — Company A

Company profile

Company A invests in multiple industries covering finance, industrial enterprises, media content, consumer services, retail, automobile and real estate, education and medical care. Its past investment projects included ByteDance, Meituan Dianping (3690.HK), Ke Holding (BEKE.N), Xin Chao Media, Pagoda and Li Auto.

ESG investment process

Company A has established a corresponding ESG execution system for its ESG investment to encourage employees to apply ESG in investment practice. In the investment process, Company A classifies projects' internal risks in respect of environmental and social needs according to international standards such as the eight ESG performance standards and the Environmental and Social Management toolkit of the IFC.

Strategic objectives: Company A conducts due diligence in respect of the target entity's financial, legal, tax, business and integrity areas, with the focus on its compliance with environmental, social, and governance requirements, so as to determine whether an entity has ESG risks. This will provide views and recommendations for making the subsequent investment decision.

Due diligence: At the initial stage of preliminary due diligence, Company A eliminates negative industries as those listed in the exclusion list of the IFC to avoid engaging in any "high-risk" (Category A as defined by the IFC) transactions. Upon approval of the proposed transaction, the Investment Committee/Credit Committee will conduct formal due diligence.

Post-investment management: After the initial investment, Company A will continuously monitor and provide annual reports according to the general investment standards. For

---

7   The two cases described in this section are real cases and the information disclosed is public information.

low-risk investments, Company A continuously monitors through periodic reviews and ongoing contact with customers, and requiring environmental and social action plans, etc. For high-risk investments, Company A maintains a core document containing all environmental, social, and ethical action plans and their corresponding compliance procedures in implementation and updates such document on a yearly basis.

ESG training: Company A provides training on ESG knowledge to its employees through holding training sessions and emails containing learning content.

Resources used in ESG due diligence: Company A communicates with the limited partners (LPs) of PE institutions on a regular basis. It will consider incorporating ESG-related content in the agenda of the annual investors' meeting, provide relevant ESG reports according to LPs' needs, and answer questions raised by LPs. For specific ESG risks and opportunities, it will conduct online exchanges and communications.

ESG practice cases

Company A places emphasis on the investment opportunities in the industrial internet field, and favours the empowerment of emerging technologies in traditional industries. Taking one of its invested projects, Company C, as an example, the company has developed two business modules of B2B finished product trading platform and upstream intelligent cloud factory to solve the pain points of the market by analysing circulation as a starting point and tracing back to the production of gray fabric. Company C takes mandate measures to the production capacity of the upstream textile mills, enabling higher rate of running machines for high-quality production capacities while phasing out machines with inferior quality but excess capacity. While connecting the looms through the Internet of Things (IoT), it monitors the failure data of the machines to achieve "cloud operation and maintenance", that is, helping the textile mills to maintain equipment in time at lower cost through establishing operation and maintenance centres by region, thereby obtaining positive social benefits through improving the efficiency of the industry.

During the COVID-19 pandemic in 2020, Company A donated 3 million yuan to the Chinese Red Cross Foundation, which was earmarked for a relief fund for medical workers. It also called on individuals and enterprises to actively donate to the fund for love. After the 2020 Spring Festival, the post-investment service team of Company A launched a series of courses of "Mutual Assistance against COVID-19". Experts from various fields were invited to share at the courses their opinions online on corporate finance, remote collaborative office, financial cash management and control, and local anti-epidemic policies to offer help in different aspects.

ESG investment practice of Starquest Capital's invested enterprise — Company B

Company profile

Company B is a fast-growing self-operated B2B Internet enterprise in the pharmaceutical circulation industry. It is dedicated to streamlining China's pharmaceutical circulation links. Company B provides one-stop online pharmaceutical wholesale services for downstream retail terminals such as individually-owned pharmacies, small chain pharmacies and private clinics mainly through its self-developed online platform, the close cooperation with upstream pharmaceutical enterprises, the self-built warehousing and logistics capabilities, as well as the integrated supply chain. It also provides SaaS software services to pharmacies to help them better complete customer and inventory management and greatly improve operational efficiency, so as to better serve the society and communities.

ESG practice

The enterprises participating in the pharmaceutical circulation market in Mainland China have long been characterised by "large in quantity, small in size, scattered in geographical distribution, chaotic in management, and poor in quality". The long circulation chain of pharmaceuticals and the chaotic circulation order have resulted in affiliated businesses, money laundering through invoices, fictitious transactions, rebate-driven marketing, commercial bribery, and the like.

The chaotic circulation in Mainland China has not only resulted in the unreasonably high prices of pharmaceuticals, but also led to the deterioration of the business environment. In this regard, the government has introduced the "two-invoice system" and other policies to regulate the commercial behaviour in the pharmaceutical sector. Company B mainly serves the large number of small and medium-sized pharmacies in Mainland China by cooperating directly with upstream pharmaceutical companies to streamline the redundant pharmaceutical circulation links, thereby providing a transparent pricing system for pharmacies and the society. The business development of Company B is of great significance to the standardisation and development of the pharmaceutical industry in Mainland China. Its businesses contribute to more standardised commercial operations and drug pricing system, thus making the pharmaceuticals more affordable to common people.

As one of the largest local pharmacy suppliers in Hubei Province, Company B donated needed epidemic prevention materials to Wuhan Optical Valley and Wuhan aid teams in the early stage of the COVID-19 epidemic to alleviate the shortage of medical supplies at that time. After the lockdown of Wuhan, Company B was among the first batch of reserve enterprises for emergency materials procurement in Hubei Province, and the only qualified Internet platform. During the epidemic, it provided assistance to the Epidemic Prevention and Control Headquarters in the unified procurement, distribution and settlement of medical supplies, while distributed masks, drugs and other strategic materials to all parts of Hubei, thus contributing its due efforts to the prevention and control of the epidemic.

After the epidemic subsided, Company B has increased its investment in smart pharmacies and online diagnosis and treatment. In September 2020, it launched a new healthcare platform, which has remote telemedicine service terminals set up for pharmacies. Internet technology and audio-video decoding are used to enable online prescriptions by doctors, remote prescriptions review by pharmacists, online health consultation, chronic disease management, etc. This helps solve the problems of selling prescription medicines by pharmacies. The platform also provides an enterprise resource planning and management system for pharmacies to realise real-time synchronisation with prescriptions, thus making pharmacy members' medication usage safer, as well as increasing the patients' stickiness to pharmacies and the repurchase rate.

Support from all parties in the industry

Regulatory support

AMAC is committed to effectively promoting responsible investment in China's capital market, and has undertaken various activities. Since the second half of 2016, AMAC has worked closely with international organisations such as UNPRI and the Asian Corporate Governance Association, and proactively guided the industry in exploring and practising responsible investments by holding forums, compiling topical articles, carrying out empirical research, and organising small seminars and lectures. AMAC and the Financial Research Institute of the Development Research Centre of the State Council jointly carried out a study on the topic of "ESG assessment system for Chinese listed companies". After more than a year of fundamental analysis, industry discussions and research, AMAC released the *Research Report on the ESG Assessment System for Chinese Listed Companies* in November 2018, presenting the ESG performance of investment targets from the perspective of investors. Later in November 2019, it released the second phase of research results, including the *Quality Assessment Report on the ESG Information Disclosure of Listed Companies* and the *Research Report on the ESG Assessment System for Listed Companies*.

Following on the above research, AMAC disclosed at a forum in July 2021 that it will continue to systematically promote the ESG work[8]. Firstly, it will promote the evaluation of ESG information disclosure quality of listed companies and promoted the enhancement of the information disclosure quality and corporate governance level of the invested enterprises. Secondly, it will explore and develop ESG indices to serve as benchmarks for the industry, and actively guide and regulate comprehensive ESG practices covering ESG evaluation, ESG investment strategies and ESG investment instruments.

Academic support

Major academic research institutes in the field of ESG in Mainland China include the International Institute of Green Finance (IIGF) of the Central University of Finance and Economics (CUFE) and the Green Finance Committee of the China Society for Finance and Banking (GFC). Among them, the IIGF has a wealth of research achievements in ESG data and ESG indices.

In September 2019, the IIGF released the CUFE IIGF ESG Database, an independently developed online ESG database in the Mainland[9]. At the same time, the IIGF released a number of stock indices with ESG as the core investment concept. These include the "CSI 300 Green Leading Stock Index", "CUFE-CNI Shenzhen-Hong Kong Stock Connect Green Select Index", "CSI Zhongcai Shanghai and Shenzhen 100 ESG Leading Index" and "Beautiful China ESG 100 Index", etc.

In addition, the GFC has carried out extensive and in-depth research on ESG investments, green bonds, green finance, environmental information disclosure of listed companies, etc., yielding a series of research results.

Support from exchanges

The stock exchanges in Mainland China have undertaken various ESG practices. The SZSE took the lead in releasing guidelines on social responsibility of listed companies

---

8   Source: Media reports on *Shanghai Securities News Asset Management Summit 2021* (《2021 年上海證券報資產管理高峰論壇》).

9   Source: "IIGF released online ESG database" (〈中財大綠金院發佈線上 ESG 資料庫〉), *Sina Finance*, 18 September 2019.

in September 2006, initially establishing a framework for ESG information disclosure. Between 2009 and 2010, the SZSE issued successively guidelines for regulating the operation of its three boards, in which relevant regulations have been absorbed and enhanced in two separate chapters of corporate governance and social responsibility. In 2015, the guidelines were further revised, issuing successively memoranda on information disclosure for periodic reports, mandatorily requiring listed companies included in the SZSE 100 Index to disclose social responsibility reports. In 2016, the SZSE initiated the pilot programme of green corporate bonds and launched such products as asset-backed securities (ABS) and public-private partnership (PPP). In 2017, the SZSE launched the "CUFE-CNI Green Bond Total Return Index" to promote the interconnection of green products and services in the Mainland capital market.

For the SSE, since its issuance of the *Guidance for Environmental Information Disclosure of Listed Companies* in 2008, it has continued to improve the information disclosure of environment and social responsibility of listed companies in recent years. By 2019, there were more than 600 companies on the SSE Main Board disclosing targeted poverty alleviation information and actively disclosing information of environmental protection and pollution discharge[10]. Meanwhile, the SSE has imposed mandatory disclosure requirements on the fulfilment of social responsibility by companies listed on the SSE Science and Technology Innovation Board (STAR Market), and put great emphasis on the disclosure of environmental information in the review of the issuance and listing of stocks on the STAR Market. In addition, the SSE has listed a number of green corporate bonds, ABS, and has released more than 50 green and sustainable development related indices with China Securities Index Co., Ltd. (CSI). It has also participated in green finance related work of international organisations, such as the World Federation of Exchanges, the United Nations Sustainable Stock Exchanges Initiative and the Asian Financial Cooperation Association.

The SSE and the SZSE have held ESG training sessions for listed companies successively. In April 2018, the MSCI ESG disclosure and rating training was successfully held by the SSE which mainly introduced the MSCI ESG index to A-share listed companies. In December 2019, the second session of the "MSCI ESG Training for A-share Companies" was successfully held by the SZSE. MSCI, UNPRI and other experts in relevant fields introduced and discussed topics such as global ESG investment trends, ESG data disclosure, legislation and disclosure trends on climate change, and sustainable development in China. In June 2020, under the guidance of the Investor Protection Bureau of the China Securities

---

10 Source: "SSE: Continue to jointly walk along the green path" (〈上交所：將繼續攜手市場各方同走綠色發展之路〉), *Sina Finance*, 5 June 2020.

Regulatory Commission (CSRC), the SSE and Lujiazui International City jointly launched the "Towards Better – Virtual ESG Investing Forum" with virtual livestream, introducing the latest status and legal framework of ESG investment, demonstrating the integration by the Mainland institutional investors of ESG into their practices, including investment strategic objectives, research and analysis, portfolio management, risk control and due diligence, and guiding investment institutions to implement the sustainable development concept through responsible investment, so as to form a supporting external environment for the high-quality development of listed companies.

Outlook of ESG development in the Mainland PE Market

With the strong advocacy by the regulatory authorities in China, the continued guidance by AMAC, and the continued propaganda of by UNPRI, MSCI and other international institutions/organisations, an increasing number of Chinese investment institutions turn their focus onto ESG investment. After the outbreak of the COVID-19 epidemic in 2020, the penetration of ESG investment in the Mainland capital market further accelerated. More and more investors, investment institutions and enterprises take the initiative to assume social responsibility. We believe that more PE institutions will implement ESG investment strategies in the future, and the advantages of ESG investment projects will gradually be revealed. It is an irresistible trend of the times for PE investment in the Mainland to be ESG-focused, sustainable and long-term. These are mainly reflected in the following aspects:

Stronger demand for ESG among the public and investors

In recent years, the public has paid more attention to the ESG practices of enterprises, such as environmental protection in the production process, healthy and greening of consumer goods, legal labour and corporate integrity. After a series of incidents such as the case of Chang Sheng Biotechnology[11], investors have also started to keep an eye on the ESG performance of enterprises, to avoid black swan incidents.

---

11 Changsheng vaccine incident: The Chinese vaccine company Changsheng Biotechnology Co., Ltd. produced 252,600 doses of these unqualified DPT vaccines in 2018. By the end of 2018, the company received a mandatory delisting notification from the SZSE.

Regulatory authorities' and the market's further promotion of ESG information disclosure by investment institutions and enterprises

In view of the promotion of quality assessment of the ESG information disclosure by the CSRC, SSE, SZSE and AMAC in 2019, and the ESG rating of A-share companies by MSCI and other rating agencies, we can see that the regulatory authorities and market forces will continue to promote ESG information disclosure. The gradual transition trend of ESG information disclosure from being "voluntary" to "compulsory", and of disclosing entities from listed companies to unlisted companies, will continue further.

ESG strategy becoming an important PE investment strategy

With continuous attention received from the regulatory authorities and the market advocacy by LPs of PE institutions, more and more PE fund managers are taking ESG as an important investment strategy. Since 2018, many private fund managers have practised in the field of ESG, including entering into limited partnership agreements related to ESG and abiding by UNPRI, IFC and other ESG standards. It is expected that the penetration of ESG investments will be further enhanced in 2021.

More prominent advantages of ESG projects

Since ESG projects have a certain effect of "demining", volatility and risk-adjusted returns are generally better than non-ESG projects. In addition, during the COVID-19 epidemic, enterprises that have good corporate governance and focus on ensuring people's livelihood have been fully recognised, and "ESG friendly industries" such as medical care and new energy have developed despite the economic downturn, further demonstrating the advantages of ESG projects.

We believe that sustainable investment innovations driven by diversity and ESG concepts will serve as an important way for investment institutions to protect capital from risks. All sectors should take actions and practices to continuously promote ESG responsible investment and the sustainable development of the PE market in China.

Remark: This paper has been produced in the Chinese language, published with a separate English language translation. If there is any conflict in this paper between the meaning of English words or terms in the English language version and Chinese words in the Chinese language version, the meaning of the Chinese words shall prevail.

第12章

私募股權投資中的綠色及可持續金融：中國內地實踐經驗

方遠
星界資本　創始管理合夥人

摘要

ESG 指 Environmental（環境）、Social（社會）和 Governance（治理），是一種綜合考量環境、社會、治理等因素，而非單一財務績效的投資理念和企業評價標準，充分考慮 ESG 因素能夠幫助中國逐步建設一個更為綠色、健康、共享和可持續發展的金融市場。

西方眾多金融機構都已將 ESG 因素納入到自身的研究及投資決策系統中。相較而言，中國的責任投資實踐以及 ESG 理念發展較晚。但隨着 ESG 意識不斷提升，中國私募股權市場也將進一步擁抱責任投資理念並開啟本地實踐。

在 ESG 投資的整體推進過程中，私募股權母基金作為具有資本放大效應的資產管理形式，與推動 ESG 理念和實踐的需求天然契合。通過母基金的長期性、多元化配置、行業地位和條款約束，將 ESG 納入基金的頂層設計中，形成 ESG 量化評估指標，並通過被投資子基金將 ESG 理念擴張至底層企業。本章提供了一些對於母基金 ESG 投資實踐的階段性設想，包括具備母基金特色的量化評估系統和實踐案例，供讀者們參考指正。

展望未來，在中國新經濟的浪潮中，產業各方對 ESG 的重視程度將會不斷增強，我們對私募股權市場的可持續發展充滿信心，也將催生更多負責任的中國「新經濟」企業。

責任投資在中國內地的發展現狀

環境（Environment）、社會（Society）、管治（Governance）（三者簡稱 ESG）理念在西方資本市場已經發展多年，在體制機制、市場服務、投資實踐已有成熟的經驗，ESG 投資實踐也已經成為私募股權投資基金在投資流程中重要的一部分。當前，全球範圍內眾多金融機構都已將 ESG 因素納入到自身的研究及投資決策系統中。近幾年責任投資在全球各個地區內的資產規模呈現高速增長。

相較成熟的西方 ESG 投資現狀，中國內地責任投資的實踐以及 ESG 理念發展比較晚，尚處於加強意識、探索健全社會責任投資系統的階段。

內地最早出現的 ESG 投資是在 2002 年，當時的青雲創投設立了內地首隻 ESG 相關聯的基金 —— 中國環保基金。該基金擁有強大實力的資金背景，包括亞洲開發銀行、荷蘭政府基金、英國石油、香港 LESS 公司等著名國際投資機構。深圳證券交易所（簡稱「深交所」）在 2006 年發佈了《上市公司社會責任指引》，這是證券交易市場首次發出的 ESG 信號。2008 年，興業全球基金管理有限公司是內地第一家引入社會責任投資理念的公募基金公司，並發佈內地首隻社會責任主題的基金產品 —— 興全社會責任證券投資基金。在 2010 年後，內地金融市場上相關類型的責任投資基金管理規模開始有了顯著增長。相應的政策也陸續出台，例如上海證券交易所（簡稱「上交所」）於 2008 年發佈了《關於加強上市公司社會責任承擔工作暨發佈〈上海證券交易所上市公司環境信息披露指引〉的通知》，要求上市公司在注重經濟利益時，也積極履行企業社會責任。此外，中國證券投資基金業協會（簡稱「中基協」）也逐漸發揮了其引導性作用。2016 年以來，中基協多次舉辦國內外論壇和研討會，開展 ESG 研究，大力推行 ESG 理念與實踐。2018 年 11 月，中基協發佈了《中國上市公司 ESG 評價系統研究報告》和《綠色投資者指引（試行）》，作為中國 ESG 投資市場的實踐指引，進一步推動 ESG 在中國內地的發展。

截至 2021 年 3 月，已有 3,844 家機構成為了聯合國支持的《責任投資原則》（United Nations-supported Principles for Responsible Investment，簡稱 PRI）簽署方 [1]，中國機構共 56 家，包括中國華融、易方達基金、鵬華基金、南方基金、博時基金、中國人壽、中國平安等。這 56 家機構中，有 30 家是在 2019 年至 2020 年新加入的，從 2019 年 UNPRI 的簽署機構數目增長來看，中國已成為增速最快的地區，可見中國對責任投資的意識近年來在逐步加強。

1　資料來源：《PRI》網站。

私募股權 ESG 投資的必要性

中國 PE/VC 機構的 ESG 投資實踐概況

中國一級市場 ESG 投資意識總體淡薄。受惠於監管層對於「綠色金融」的關注、社會對「資本責任性」的呼籲及二級市場的制度建設，在私募股權投資（Private Equity，簡稱 PE）基金管理機構普通合夥人（General Partner，簡稱 GP）當中，有 50% 曾聽説過 ESG，但是暫未特別關注；少數 —— 包括創業投資（Venture Capital，簡稱 VC）基金 —— 深入了解過 ESG；而 29% 則完全沒有聽説過 ESG 投資，甚至不了解其基本含義[2]。

私募股權基金之間的 ESG 認知懸殊主要體現在幣種上。美元基金及雙幣種基金受國際資本影響，相對重視 ESG 原則，由基金管理合夥人直接負責 ESG 相關事項，甚至已有多個成功的 ESG 投資實踐案例。人民幣基金 ESG 認知相對薄弱，對 ESG 重視程度嚴重不足。部分人民幣基金雖有 ESG 認知，但僅停留在募資層面，缺少投資實踐，而大部分人民幣基金不僅缺乏 ESG 認知，重視程度也不足，在 ESG 戰略制定、ESG 制度建設等多個方面均為空白。

從投資階段看，中後期的 PE 基金更加注重 ESG 因素，原因有二：第一，中後期的 PE 基金主要投向盈利能力較強、現金流狀況良好、高速成長甚至已經成熟的企業，而這些企業往往擁有着較高的市場份額、龐大的用戶羣體，有餘力兼顧社會責任甚至必須承擔社會責任；第二，中後期基金離退出窗口更近，對二級市場的監管需求及投資者偏好更加敏鋭，已意識到 ESG 投資迫在眉睫，具體而言包括上市公司《社會責任報告》披露標準逐步出台、A 股納入 MSCI 指數後的 ESG 評級等。相對而言，天使投資基金、VC 基金則在 ESG 認知及重視程度上有所欠缺。不過，部分天使投資基金及 VC 基金以 ESG 作為風險控制因素，在早期的項目篩選及投後管理中取得一定的進展，如避免投資存在環境污染或資源浪費的項目、謹慎對待創始人品德不端等。

行業 ESG 認知不足還體現在行業交流、規範認定上：相較於公募基金及二級市場的投資基金，PE 基金在內地的 ESG 培訓、ESG 行業交流上參與度不足，加入國際 ESG 組織的基金更是鳳毛麟角。內地 PE 基金管理機構的 GP 也未能有效參照行業規範及國際標準，僅個別基金管理人參照 A 股二級市場評價指標／體系等行業自律標準及國際金融公司（International Finance Corporation，簡稱 IFC）的八個 ESG 表現標準等國際標準展開 ESG 投資。

2　資料來源：星界ESG盡職調查問卷，2020年。

ESG 對於 PE/VC 投資的意義和價值

ESG 投資最重要的意義在於，通過資本的力量推動企業展開 ESG 友好型實踐，促使企業保護生態環境、履行社會責任、改進公司治理。ESG 投資對企業行為的作用可體現在如下幾方面。

投資者通常可以通過兩種方式影響企業行為：持有董事席位的投資者，可以在董事會上發起抗議；一般投資者，可以退出股東名冊來進行抗議。實際上，在公司決策過程中納入 ESG 相關因素的行為在上世紀已經出現，公司董事也越來越關注公司在社會責任方面的策略和行為，即 Corporate Social Responsibility（簡稱 CSR）。歷史研究表明，從上世紀 90 年代起，公司董事會已產生一種趨勢，即要求公司將經濟、環境和社會可持續性等因素加入公司治理的範疇中，並在管理報告中體現。有學術研究 [3] 證實，重視 CSR 的企業將環境、社會可持續性和公司治理作為競爭策略的關注點之一，以令公司價值最大化，而這些企業往往在資產回報、系統性風險等方面都佔據優勢。

此外有學者研究 [4] 發現，由長期投資者倡導下的社會責任要求，對企業行為有更大的影響。當長期投資者對被投資企業的管理者產生正面影響時，可幫助企業提高公司的治理能力。具體而言，長期投資者可以通過股東建議書、董事會和經營者變更等方式達到影響企業行為的作用。此外，由於長期投資者更傾向於投資的多元化（如在投資行業、地域、階段等），其影響與企業控制風險程度相關。

研究表明，ESG 投資能促使企業保護生態環境、履行社會責任、改進公司治理，那麼 ESG 投資的績效如何？ESG 表現與公司財務回報（corporate financial performance，簡稱 CFP）的關係，一直是學術研究的熱門領域，自 20 世紀 70 年代以來，西方大量學者及投資機構發佈了大量 ESG 與 CFP 關係的學術實證研究、文獻綜述、商業報告。Gunnar Friede、Timo Busch 和 Alexander Bassen 通過分析自 1990 年至 2015 年發表的 2,200 餘份學術文章，發現 90% 的研究發現 ESG 評價機制與公司財務回報存在着顯著的非負相關關係 [5]。Gunnar 等查閱的文獻涵蓋了投資組合研究、非投資組合研究、不同區域、不同發展程度國家例如新興市場、不同金融產品（公司債、綠色基建、公司股權等），覆蓋範圍極其廣泛。

3　R. Albuquerque、A. Durnev 與 Y. Koskinen〈Corporate social responsibility and firm risk: Theory and empirical evidence〉，載於 SSRN，2011年11月20日。

4　L. A. Bebchuk 與 L. A.Stole（1993年）〈Do short-term objectives lead to under- or over-investment in long-term projects?〉，載於《The Journal of Finance》，第48期第2卷，719-729頁。

5　G. Friede、T. Busch 與 A. Bassen（2015年）〈ESG and financial performance: Aggregated evidence from more than 2000 empirical studies〉，載於《Journal of Sustainable Finance & Investment》，第5期第4卷，210-233頁。

母基金是推進 ESG 投資的利器

母基金在全球資產配置中擔任着舉足輕重的作用。根據 **Preqin** 與投中研究院的研究[6] 表明，按照認繳金額的規模大小，母基金已經成為私募股權市場的第二大投資者，僅次於養老基金。根據 **Pitchbook** 數據，截至 2019 年 6 月底，全球母基金管理資本量約 3,600 億美元，其中在管項目合計約 2,950 億美元，可投資本量約 650 億美元。

母基金有幾個主要特徵，讓其成為了 ESG 實踐的利器，概述如下。

母基金的長期性投資特徵契合 ESG 可持續投資的要求

ESG 理念強調投資者在作出決策過程中充分考慮被投資企業在環境保護、社會貢獻和公司治理的表現，具備天然的長周期性。同時，ESG 的投資特徵也意味着其推廣和實施的難度系數較高，必須與具備類似投資周期、同樣重視長期可持續發展的投資方式相配合。

在內地私募股權投資領域中，比較活躍的投資機構包括母基金（包括政府引導基金）、養老基金、保險公司、資產管理機構等。它們資金來源不一，投資策略各有側重點，預期目標也不同。其中，母基金是這當中投資期限最長的，通常投資期可達 3-5 年；相比而言，資產管理公司和基金公司的投資期僅 1-3 年，短期內業績壓力大。而對於保險公司和養老金，由於其負債壓力相對較大，內部的團隊投資專業性也比較弱，很難採取投資周期較長的 ESG 投資策略。因而，母基金是更貼近 ESG 投資特徵的投資方式。

母基金的多元化配置全覆蓋 ESG 要素，有效控制風險

母基金在資產配置上，有跨地域、跨行業、跨階段、跨年份、跨策略（包括成長資本、併購風險投資、不良資產投資、夾層投資）等特徵，呈現多元化的配置戰略。在成熟的私募市場中，大型投資機構通常會在基金層面進行分散性配置，然後通過把握項目跟投機會加強在某幾個重點領域的佈局，或通過二級市場的交易來減持在某些基金上的過度配置。通過多樣的投資方式和投資組合，母基金的投資輻射可覆蓋大部分行業、地域和發展階段，並充分平衡資產配置，避免過多的集中性配置。

國際上如 LGT 等領先母基金，在過去十餘年成功地將 ESG 推廣到數百隻子基金中。然而，當前內地母基金的 ESG 投資理念還十分薄弱，亟需提高整體意識並給出指導策略。

---

6 《中國市場化VC/PE母基金研究報告(2019)》，載於投中研究院的網站，2019年10月。

圖 1：母基金的分散型資產配置

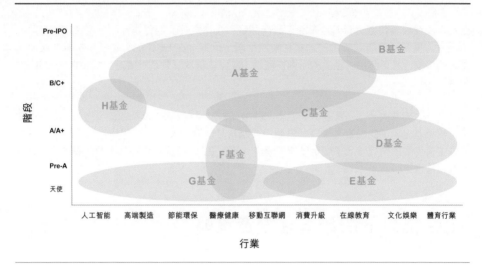

註：圖中的「階段」指私募股權市場中企業的融資階段，包括天使輪（即天使投資的種子期）與之後的 Pre-A 輪、
　　A/A+ 輪、Pre-IPO 輪（即首次公開招股前）等。

資料來源：星界資本。

母基金的地位和市場效應有效推進 ESG 投資的發展

從影響力度來看，由於母基金長期投資的特徵，一旦母基金履行 ESG 投資的相關原則，它對被投基金及底層項目的影響時間至少在 10 年及以上。而且被投基金往往會每隔 2-3 年募集新一期基金，渴望舊的投資者持續加碼。因此，通過母基金層面來對被投基金和項目進行 ESG 相關的引導、監督和條款落地，可以相對有效地將 ESG 理念深入被投基金及被投企業當中。

母基金的放大效應自然使它也擁有雷達效應。通過母基金團隊對行業、市場、子基金和底層項目的深度盡職調查，母基金可以像雷達一般，及時探測到市場各個維度的資訊，成為了一個天然信息聚焦和資源整合的大平台。

母基金的協議條款驅動 ESG 投資的自律調節

在私募股權投資領域，母基金是除了政府監督和自律之外促進行業健康、可持續性發展的第三股力量。與政府政策性的監督和限制不同，母基金在 ESG 的實踐既規定具有法律約束力的條款，又實施相對靈活的原則性監督，合理並有效驅動被投資基金和項目的 ESG 實踐發展。

雖然在全球範圍內，在私募基金的協議文件中尚未形成對 ESG 條款的標準做法，但對於歐美主流母基金及 PE 投資者來說，已屬於較為常見的實踐，而且該趨勢還在不斷擴大。在雙方簽署協議的前提下，子基金能夠在倡導和履行 ESG 投資上發揮其主觀能動性，提高實踐的積極性。

ESG 視角下的母基金投資策略

戰略及政策

母基金將 ESG 納入投資體系中，要求母基金管理人在戰略上形成高度的共識，甚至將 ESG 納入基金的頂層設計中。具體地，應遵循以下六項原則：

- **投資實踐**：將 ESG 理念納入具體的投資實踐中，包括項目分析、投資決策等；
- **主觀能動**：成為積極的推動者，發揮主觀能動性，將 ESG 理念整合至投資實踐中；
- **信息披露**：要求投資機構應當進行充分的 ESG 信息披露；
- **行業推動**：促進投資行業理解、熟悉、最終實踐 PRI 原則；
- **行業交流**：與行業先行者建立合作與溝通，提高實踐 PRI 原則的效率；
- **定期匯報**：按相關的國際準則，定期匯報 PRI 原則實施的進展。

母基金 ESG 量化評估體系

母基金的 ESG 量化評估指標，應從機構總評、環境、社會、公司治理四方面進行底層框架的構建，如表 1 所示。與直接投資不同，母基金的投資對象是子基金及其管理人（GP），母基金在構建 ESG 評估框架時，應考慮私募股權投資行業的業務流程特點。為此，除考慮環境、社會、公司治理三大常規要素外，新增對 GP 的「機構總評」要素。

表 1：母基金 ESG 評估指標底層框架

	評價內容	評價指標
機構總評	ESG 認知	機構對 ESG 的戰略定位、政策制定、委員會機制、顧問機制、條款簽署、行業交流等
	投資流程	機構的 ESG 投資策略、投資實踐、盡職調查設計、風險報告機制等
	投後管理	機構對被投企業的 ESG 持續督導、評估機制、退出管理等
	信息披露	機構向有限合夥人提供的常規 ESG 匯報機制、負面信息匯報機制等
環境	子基金	子基金擬投資的行業、地域等
	被投企業	被投企業的環境政策、風險暴露系數、能耗指標、碳排放量等
社會	子基金	子基金投資回報水平、企業信用、同業競爭情況、員工權益保障等
	被投企業	被投企業的淨資產收益率、員工政策、供應鏈關係、公眾安全保障等
公司治理	子基金	子基金投決會組成、投票機制、員工流動性等
	被投企業	被投企業的宏觀戰略、現金回報水平、公司違規等

資料來源：星界資本。

母基金在構建適當的關鍵指標矩陣後，可以採取多種方式採集、賦值、設計權重並得出最終評價結果。信息採集及統計是展開評估的前提與基礎，常見的採集方法有訪談、ESG 問卷、公開信息查詢、證明材料提供等。政府行政處罰、公司輿論信息、違規情況、失信被執行人等指標可以在公開渠道查詢，借助監管機構專業的評估結果。ESG 認知、ESG 委員會、ESG 條款簽署等指標，離不開子基金自發、詳細的披露，要求母基金在多階段嵌入 ESG 板塊，展開信息收集。

中國私募股權 ESG 實踐案例 [7]

內地早期投資機構的 ESG 投資實踐 —— 公司 A

公司概述

公司 A 投資領域涵蓋金融、產業企業、媒體內容、消費服務、零售、車與房、教育醫療等大類行業。過往投資項目包括字節跳動、美團點評（3690.HK）、貝殼找房（BEKE.N）、新潮傳媒、百果園、車和家等。

ESG 投資流程

公司 A 內部針對 ESG 投資，制定了相應的 ESG 執行制度，鼓勵員工在投資實踐中踐行 ESG。在投資過程中，公司 A 採用 IFC 的八個 ESG 表現標準、IFC 的環境與社會管理（Environmental and Social Management）工具包等國際標準，從環境、社會需求等角度，對項目進行內部風險分類。

戰略目標：公司 A 將重點放在目標實體遵守環境、社會和治理要求，進行其財務、法律、稅務、商業、誠信等方面的盡職調查，以判斷公司是否存在 ESG 風險，並為之後的投資決策提供相關意見和建議。

盡職調查：在初步盡職調查的初始階段，公司 A 將剔除負面行業，如 IFC 的排除名單，不從事任何「高風險」（相當於 IFC 界定的 A 類）交易。擬議的交易獲得批准後，投資委員會／信貸委員會進行正式的盡職調查。

投後管理：在初始投資後，公司 A 會持續監測並以一般投資標準提供年度報告。關於低風險投資，公司 A 不斷監測，包括定期審查、不斷與客戶接觸以及定期收集環境和社會行動計劃等。對於風險較高的投資，公司 A 會保存一份包括所有環境、社會和道德行動計劃及其執行合規程序的中心文件，並每年更新。

ESG 培訓：公司 A 通過舉辦培訓會議以及學習郵件的形式，對員工進行 ESG 知識培訓。

ESG 盡職調查中運用的資源：公司 A 會定期與 PE 機構的有限合夥人（Limited Partner，簡稱 LP）交流，考慮將 ESG 相關內容包含在年度投資者會議議程之中，根據 LP 需求提供相關的 ESG 報告，針對 LP 提出的相關問題予以回答，特定 ESG 風險機遇會以線上溝通的形式進行交流。

7　有關本節中兩個案例為實體個案，而當中的披露信息均屬可公開信息。

ESG 方面的實踐

公司 A 重點關注產業互聯網領域的投資機會，看好新興技術對傳統產業的賦能。以所投資項目公司 C 為例，公司 C 從流通切入往上游延伸到坯布生產，發展出 B2B 成品部交易平台和上游智能雲工廠兩大業務模塊來解決市場痛點。公司 C 對上游紡織廠的產能進行託管改造，讓優質產能的開機率更高，同時使劣質過剩產能逐步淘汰；在通過物聯網連接各個織布機的同時，對機器的故障數據進行監控，以實現「雲運維」，按區域搭建運維中心，幫助織布廠以更低成本更及時地維修設備，通過對產業效率的提升來體現正面的社會效益。

在 2020 年的新冠疫情中，公司 A 向中國紅十字基金會捐贈 300 萬人民幣，定向用於某醫務工作者人道救助基金。同時號召人員，無論個人或企業，在能力範圍內積極地向該基金捐款，共獻愛心。在 2020 年春節過後，公司 C 投後服務團隊策劃推出了碼腦「守望相助戰新冠」系列課程，邀請各領域專家就企業融資、遠程協同辦公、財務現金管控、地方抗疫政策等主題進行線上分享，從不同角度為社會提供幫助。

星界資本被投企業 ESG 投資實踐 —— 公司 B

公司概述

公司 B 是一家快速成長中的自營式互聯網 B2B 醫藥流通企業，致力於壓縮中國藥品流通環節。公司主要通過其自主開發的線上平台，以及與上游製藥企業保持密切合作，自建倉儲物流能力，整合全網供應鏈，為下游的個體藥店、小連鎖藥店和私立診所等零售終端提供一站式線上藥品的批發業務。公司也向藥房提供 SaaS 軟件服務，幫助藥房更完善地完成客戶及庫存管理，並大幅提升運營效率，從而更有效率地為社會和社區服務。

ESG 方面的實踐

中國內地醫藥流通市場參與的企業長期存在着「多小散亂差」的特點，藥品流通鏈條長、流通秩序混亂，這也導致了掛靠經營、過票洗錢、買空賣空、帶金銷售、醫藥商業賄賂等行為時有發生。

內地流通行業的亂象不僅造成了百姓承擔的藥品價格虛高，也導致了社會經商環境的惡化。為此，政府出台了「兩票制」等一系列政策，規範醫藥環節的商業行為。公司 B 重點服務於內地大量的中小藥房，在上游直接對接藥廠，壓縮並整合冗長的醫藥流通環節，為藥房和社會提供透明的價格系統。公司 B 的業務發展對於內地醫藥行業的規範和發展有着重要的意義，有助於為社會帶來更規範的商業運作以及藥品價格系統，進而為百姓帶來更多價格更便宜的藥品。

作為湖北當地最大的藥房供應商之一，公司 B 在新冠疫情初期向武漢光谷、援漢團隊捐贈緊缺防疫物資，緩解醫療物資短缺的局面。武漢封城後，公司 B 是首批湖北應急物資採購儲備企業，也是唯一一家入選的互聯網平台，在疫情期間幫助防控指揮部統一採購、配送和結算，同時將口罩、藥物等戰略物資配送到湖北各地，為疫情防控作出貢獻。

疫情緩和後，公司 B 也加大在智能藥店、在線診療等方面的投入，2020 年 9 月推出一個新型醫療健康平台，利用互聯網技術、音頻視頻解碼為藥店設置遠程醫療服務終端，提供醫生在線開方、藥師遠程審方、在線健康諮詢、慢病管理等服務，解決藥店處方藥銷售問題；提供店內企業資源規劃管理系統實現處方實時同步，同時保障藥店會員用藥更安全，增加患者和藥店的黏性與複購率。

產業各方支持

監管支持

中基協致力於在中國的資本市場中有效推進責任投資，並已開展了多項活動。自 2016 年下半年以來，中基協與 UNPRI、亞洲公司治理協會等國際組織密切合作，並通過舉辦論壇、編譯專題文章、開展實證研究、組織小型交流會和培訓講座等舉措，積極引導行業開展責任投資的探索實踐。中基協與國務院發展研究中心金融研究所合作開展了《中國上市公司 ESG 評價體系》課題研究，經過一年多的基礎分析、行業座談和調研，於 2018 年 11 月發佈了《中國上市公司 ESG 評價體系研究報告》，從投資者的角度出發理解投資標的的 ESG 表現；後於 2019 年 11 月又發佈了二期研究成果，包括《上市公司 ESG 信息披露質量評價報告》和《上市公司 ESG 評價體系研究報告》。

在以上成果的基礎上，中基協代表在 2021 月 7 月一個論壇的講話中表示，將繼續系統性推進 ESG 工作[8]，其一是推動上市公司 ESG 信息披露質量評價，促進被投企業提高信息披露質量和公司治理水平，其二是探索開發 ESG 指數，為行業提供比較基準，積極引導、規範從 ESG 評價到 ESG 投資戰略再到 ESG 投資工具的完整實踐。

8　資料來源：有關《2021年上海證券報資產管理高峰論壇》的新聞報導。

學術支持

內地 ESG 領域的主要學術研究機構包括中央財經大學綠色國際金融研究院（簡稱「綠金院」）和中國金融學會綠色金融專業委員會（簡稱「綠金委」）。其中，綠金院在 ESG 數據和 ESG 指數方面有着豐富的研究成果。

2019 年 9 月，綠金院發佈了獨立研發的線上 ESG 數據庫 —— 中財綠金院 ESG 數據庫 [9]。同時，綠金院發佈了多個以 ESG 為核心投資理念的股票指數，包括「滬深 300 綠色領先指數」、「中財 - 國證深港通綠色優選指數」、「中證 - 中財滬深 100 ESG 領先指數」、「美好中國 ESG 100 指數」等。

另外，綠金委在 ESG 投資、綠色債券、綠色金融、上市公司環境信息披露等方面持續開展了廣泛深入的研究，形成了多項研究成果。

交易所支持

中國內地各交易所在 ESG 領域已有諸多實踐。深交所於 2006 年 9 月率先發佈了上市公司社會責任指引，初步建立 ESG 信息披露的架構。2009 年至 2010 年間，深交所三個板塊先後發佈了規範運作指引文件，其中公司治理、社會責任兩個獨立章節吸納、完善了相關規定。2015 年進一步修訂指引，先後發佈了定期報告信息披露的備忘錄，對納入深證 100 指數的上市公司強制要求披露社會責任報告等。2016 年，深交所啟動綠色公司債券試點，並推出綠色資產支持證券（asset-backed securities，簡稱 ABS）、綠色公私合作夥伴關係（public-private partnership，簡稱 PPP）等產品。2017 年，深交所推出「中財 - 國證綠色債券指數」，推動內地資本市場綠色產品服務互聯互通。

上交所於 2008 年發佈《上市公司環境信息披露指引》，近年來不斷完善上市公司環境及社會責任信息披露相關工作，截至 2019 年，滬市主板中已有超過 600 家公司披露精準扶貧信息及主動披露環保排污相關信息 [10]。同時，上交所對科創板上市公司履行社會責任情況提出了強制披露要求，並在科創板股票發行上市審核過程中高度重視環境信息披露。此外，上交所上市了多隻綠色公司債、ABS，並與中證指數有限公司發佈了超過 50 隻綠色及可持續發展相關指數，並持續參與世界交易所聯合會、聯合國可持續交易所倡議、亞洲金融合作協會等國際組織的綠色金融相關工作。

9　資料來源：〈中財大綠金院發布線上ESG數據庫〉，載於《新浪財經》，2019年9月18日。
10　資料來源：〈上交所：將繼續攜手市場各方同走綠色發展之路〉，載於《新浪財經》，2020年6月5日。

上交所與深交所先後舉辦了上市公司的 ESG 培訓活動。2018 年 4 月,MSCI ESG 披露和評級培訓在上交所成功舉辦,主要為 A 股上市公司介紹 MSCI ESG 指數方面的內容。2019 年 12 月,第二屆 MSCI A 股上市公司 ESG 培訓在深交所成功舉辦,MSCI、UNPRI 組織等相關領域專家圍繞全球 ESG 投資趨勢、ESG 數據披露、氣候變化法規和披露趨勢、中國可持續發展等議題進行講解、研討。2020 年 6 月,在中國證券監督管理委員會(簡稱「中國證監會」)投資者保護局指導下,上交所聯合陸家嘴金融城啟動了「走向美好 ── ESG 投資雲講壇」系列活動,以「雲上直播」的形式介紹 ESG 投資最新狀況和法律框架,展示內地機構投資者將 ESG 融入投資戰略目標、研究分析、組合管理、風險控制、盡責管理等方面的實踐,引導投資機構踐行可持續發展理念開展責任投資,營造上市公司高質量發展的外部生態。

展望中國內地私募股權市場的 ESG 發展

隨着中國監管機構的大力倡導,中基協的持續引導以及 UNPRI、MSCI 等國際機構 / 組織的持續宣傳,越來越多中國投資機構開始關注 ESG 投資。2020 年新冠疫情爆發後,進一步加速了 ESG 投資在內地資本市場的滲透,越來越多投資者、投資機構及企業主動承擔社會責任。我們認為未來將有更多私募股權投資機構陸續踐行 ESG 投資策略,ESG 類投資項目的優勢也會逐漸顯現,內地私募股權投資的 ESG 化、可持續化、長期化是不可阻擋的時代潮流,主要表現在以下幾方面:

公眾及投資者對 ESG 需求更加強烈

近年來公眾愈發關注企業 ESG 的踐行,如生產過程中的環境保護、消費品的健康化綠色化、合法勞工、公司廉潔等。經過長生生物 [11] 等系列事件後,投資者也逐步關注企業的 ESG 表現,避免黑天鵝事件。

監管者及市場組織進一步推動投資機構、企業 ESG 的信息披露

根據 2019 年中國證監會、上交所與深交所、中基協等所推動的 ESG 信息披露質量評價,以及 MSCI 等評級機構對 A 股公司展開 ESG 評級等事件看,監管機構及各方市場力量持續推動 ESG 信息披露。ESG 信息披露從「自願」向「強制」緩慢過渡,主體從上市公司到非上市公司的趨勢將進一步延續。

11　長生生物疫苗事件:2018年,長生生物疫苗生產了252,600支不合格人用狂犬病疫苗。在2018年末,公司收到了深交所的退市要求。

ESG 策略成為重要的私募股權投資策略

隨着監管機構的持續關注與私募股權機構 LP 的市場倡導等，越來越多私募基金管理人將 ESG 設為重要的投資策略。2018 年以來，不少私募基金管理人在 ESG 領域有所實踐，包括簽署 ESG 相關的有限合夥協議（Limited Partnership Agreement）、遵守 UNPRI、IFC 等 ESG 準則。預計 2021 年，ESG 投資的滲透率將進一步提升。

ESG 類項目優勢愈加凸顯

由於 ESG 類項目具有一定的「排雷」作用，波動性及風險調整後收益普遍優於非 ESG 項目。此外，新冠疫情期間，公司治理良好、注重民生保障的企業也得到充分認可，醫療、新能源等「ESG 友好行業」也逆勢發展，進一步驗證 ESG 類項目的優越性。

我們相信多元化及 ESG 理念驅動下的可持續投資創新，將是投資機構保護資本避免風險的重要途徑，各界應以自身行動與實踐，持續推動中國的 ESG 責任投資及私募股權市場可持續發展。

Chapter 13

Financial technology applications for green and sustainable investments

Jason TU
Co-founder and Chief Executive Officer
MioTech

Summary

With the rise of both policy and social awareness on sustainability, green and sustainable investments are fast-tracking towards being mainstream investment philosophies. Unlike traditional investing, the implementation of these philosophies has challenged investors, issuers and regulators for years because of a lack of both data and technical support.

On the technology side, the rise of artificial intelligence has brought many changes to the financial markets, from digitisation to automation and access to information. New technologies such as Natural Language Processing, Knowledge Graph, and Data Governance platforms have significantly boosted investors' and issuers' productivity.

The new technologies and the trend of green and sustainable investments are set to join forces to bring investing to the next level.

Technical challenges for investors, issuers and regulators

Green and sustainable investments are mostly measured by the concept of Environmental, Social, and Governance (ESG). Compared with financial statements, trading prices and volumes, ESG data is more scattered, unstructured, often unaudited and hard to interpret from the investor's perspective. To issuers, ESG data-gathering and compliance with global or regional standards are complex processes. Regulators also need to keep track of the markets from an ESG perspective. These needs pose challenges that can be solved by technology, and have created enormous room for financial technology (fintech) applications.

Investors' perspective

After decades of market development, today's financial, compliance, and regulatory environments are highly complex. Investment opportunities have increased significantly, together with unprecedented level of risks. Data and software products can help investors scout for new investment opportunities and avoid hidden risks.

New investment strategies

Growth, profitability and cash generation are key criteria for making investment decisions. Therefore, financial statements have been the single most important source of information since modern accounting rules were established. Benjamin Graham's 1949 book, *The Intelligent Investor*, has educated generations of investors on such concepts.

However, as the world becomes increasingly digitised, investors have turned to other sources of information, in a bid to identify hidden gems in the market. Amid this trend, green and sustainable investing has evolved from a niche philosophy to a core investment strategy. This is due not just to market demand, but also to technologies that make more ESG data available to investors.

Many ESG-focused investment strategies are factor-based. Similar to conventional methods, investors test combinations of ESG data points against the history of financial instrument prices to find correlations or causal effects. For example, some stock selection strategies simply rely on an ESG rating, a score calculated from a variety of data points.

Some other trading strategies have focused more on specific aspects of issuers' ESG performance. For example, a number of investment researchers have found employee satisfaction to be a strong indicator of stock price resilience during economic downturns[1].

Some other sustainable investment strategies are framework-based, but also rely on data. Carbon transition assessment, for example, is a tool that has gained popularity with many investors. It aims to assess a company's long-term readiness to transition into a low-carbon economy, assuming a hefty carbon tax or competitive disadvantage if the company fails to do so. The analysis is usually based on multiple dimensions of data, including the company's current carbon emissions, its technology readiness, and macroeconomic conditions.

These investment strategies all require unconventional — often scattered and unstructured — datasets generated by advanced technologies such as image recognition and Natural Language Processing (NLP).

Risk, compliance and regulation

In finance, return is always accompanied by risk. In green and sustainable investing, risks can arise from a lack of understanding of the investment or non-compliance with complicated regulatory requirements.

The increasingly digitised world poses challenges for investors to understand hidden risks in data. Unlike traditional financial statements-based analysis, an executive's misconduct, product quality issues, or a negative piece of news on environmental violations can all bring substantial risks to an investment. It is important for investors to receive early warnings on these hidden vulnerabilities. One of the ways to do that is to examine historical data. For example, data has shown that in the mining industry, large-scale safety accidents and environmental pollution incidents can usually be predicted by uncovering less severe historical events that are traceable through government penalty records. Investors need timely information on such incidents, which are crucial data points in the case of green and sustainable investments.

The fast-changing global regulatory landscape also poses compliance challenges for investors. For example, the *European Union (EU) Taxonomy on Sustainable Finance,*

---

1   See, for example, Shan, C. and D. Y. Tang, "The value of employee satisfaction in disastrous times: Evidence from COVID-19", 10 July 2020, available at SSRN; Chen, C., Y. Xia and B. Zhang, "The price of integrity", 2 February 2021, available at SSRN.

though being implemented only in the EU, would be enforceable on Asia-Pacific companies that operate or raise funds in the EU as well as Asian financial market participants who sell investment products or provide financial services in the EU. In respect of the regulatory differences, the *EU Taxonomy* strictly bans coal-related business from obtaining green financing, while China previously included clean coal usage as an industry eligible for green bond issuance. Though the Green Bonds Endorsed Project Catalogue (2021 Edition)[2] excluded clean coal usage to align with the EU, global differences in regulatory policies and definitions are still prevalent, and navigating through complex policies is a challenge for many investors. Data and software systems can dramatically reduce the compliance and regulatory burden for green and sustainable investors.

Issuers' perspective

Technology, industrialisation and globalisation have helped companies to grow exponentially large. Multinationals often depend on global supply chains and, as a result, companies are faced with increasingly complex and diverse demands from stakeholders, business structures, and regulatory environments. Reporting and data management software are extremely helpful for issuers to meet green and sustainable investors' requirements.

Managing complex business structures and stakeholders

The key difference found in socially responsible investments, which include green and sustainable investments, is the shift of focus to stakeholder management, under which companies engage with their stakeholders and identify, understand and manage their needs and expectations. The broad definition of stakeholders is not only a management challenge, but also a practical data and technology challenge. This means a company's goal is no longer to simply maximise shareholders' equity, but rather to maximise their stakeholders' benefits that could include, for example, employee welfare, supply chain management, and customer wellbeing.

---

2   The Green Bonds Endorsed Project Catalogue (2021 Edition) was issued jointly by the People's Bank of China, the National Development and Reform Commission and the China Securities Regulatory Commission (CSRC) on 2 April 2021.

In green and sustainable investing, issuers usually find it difficult to cope with internal reporting and data management challenges within their own shareholding structures. Implementing an effective business reporting mechanism throughout subsidiaries and invested companies is already a challenging work, but it only becomes more of a burden when the focus is on green efforts and sustainability. To many of the issuers, simply compiling the energy consumption among all its subsidiaries is a substantial endeavour.

Externally, managing suppliers and customers is also no easy task. Modern day supply chains and customers are usually widely distributed across different regions. Gaining insights into their operational and compliance data often requires a robust reporting and tracking mechanism. Technology can significantly reduce communication and management cost, once the processes are automated.

Meeting internal and external data management and reporting needs usually requires a combination of both hardware and software technology. Internet of Things (IoT) devices, for example, are highly useful tools with which to gather energy and emissions data, on top of which software plays an important role in control, data management, analytics, and optimisation. Organisational management software provides internal data input, survey and reporting mechanisms that allow companies to manage their stakeholders.

Compliance reporting and regulatory standards

Compliance and regulatory reporting as well as data management can be as challenging as stakeholder management. Besides the internal and external data gathering discussed previously, issuers often find it difficult to navigate complex regulatory reporting requirements and traditionally, consultants fill those gaps. More automated reporting software is being used by companies to convert the same operational dataset into different reporting standards, and provide benchmarking to industry peers. Some stock exchanges have provided tools on their websites to help issuers assess their sustainability performance, while many multinational companies have adopted more complex regulatory reporting software systems to address their sustainability-related compliance and reporting needs.

Issuers' robust sustainability data management, reporting, and rigorous compliance processes can boost investors' confidence on their investments and propel healthy market growth. These needs can be better served with data, hardware and software technologies.

Cost-effectiveness considerations

Sustainability compliance reporting and stakeholder management can consume large amounts of financial and human resources. Digitisation and automation of the work can save resources and at the same time reduce error.

The cost-benefit considerations need to take into account both the complexity of business operations and the regulatory environment. There has been a quick adoption of sustainability software among large conglomerates with a large number of subsidiaries as well as suppliers and also among multinational enterprises that need to deal with different sustainability compliance standards.

An off-the-shelf Software as a Service (SaaS) product may cost anywhere between one to a dozen headcounts. A fully customised solution may cost even more. However, the price of non-compliance and poor management could be immeasurable.

Roles of data, technology, and methodology in different applications

Fintech applications for green and sustainable investment are designed to solve the challenges discussed in the previous section, and usually involve the following functionalities:

- Search and browsing for sustainability-related information at project, corporate, industry or macroeconomic level;
- Tracking and alert on investments, subsidiaries, supply chains, customers, or sustainability-related projects;
- Internal data management; and
- External compliance and regulatory reporting.

Before we delve into the pure technologies, it is important to know that most green and sustainable investment applications usually involve several key components, including analytical frameworks (such as methodologies), supporting data, and the technologies that generate the data and build the software.

Data

Data are the building blocks of all applications. From the perspective of sources, we usually classify data into four categories:

- Disclosed data;

- Alternative data from third-party sources;

- Media and social media; and

- Other datasets.

Disclosed data

Useful disclosed datasets in green and sustainable investments come from a variety of sources. For publicly listed stocks and stock-related investments, such as mutual funds and exchange-traded funds, a wealth of information can be found in the prospectuses, annual reports, as well as corporate social responsibility (CSR) reports, or equivalent sustainability reports in some jurisdictions. Fixed-income investments can be evaluated at either the issuer level or the project level, by looking into either issuer-level official reports or bond-level prospectuses and annual reports.

Despite the differences among investment products, the data points used for green and sustainable investing are similar across the board. Besides the common data points such as direct and indirect emissions — known as Scope 1, 2, and 3 emissions under the *Greenhouse Gas Protocol* — that are outlined in many global reporting standards, investors also look into other data points, such as green revenue, to examine the nature of the business. As discussed in the previous section, variations in regulatory requirements can also result in data differences across different jurisdictions.

The quality of disclosed data is usually tied to the rigour of the issuers' reporting, and how well these datasets can be extracted from their reports. The former is better supported by robust data management and reporting software that we have discussed in the previous sections. The latter usually involves optical character recognition or similar tools, as well as NLP, especially when the reports are in document or picture formats. There has also been a larger push among multiple exchanges across the globe to promote the eXtensible Business Reporting Language (XBRL) reporting framework, the open international standard for digital business reporting.

Alternative data

Disclosed data has its limitations. Although reporting standards are becoming more comprehensive and stringent globally, they cannot cover every aspect of the issuers' sustainability performance.

Alternative data, gathered from third-party sources not linked to the issuers, provide an alternative view compared to the issuers' own subjective statements, and thus would have pivotal importance in assessing an investment's true greenness.

The sources of alternative data can be very diverse. The ones that have gained popularity with sustainable investors are mostly from government, regulatory, industry, and non-government organisation websites. The format of the data is also vastly different. A penalty record from the government may be published as a document, graphic or spreadsheet file. An industry report may be published as online text. Other data may sit in interactive charts and tables.

Because of such a scattered and unstructured nature, alternative data is hard to gather, cleanse, and standardise without the help of technology. Data gathering may take form of application programming interfaces, Really Simple Syndication (RSS) feeds, web-crawling, or a direct connection to databases. Data cleansing usually involves a much more complicated technical process that can include Optical Character Recognition (OCR), NLP, dedupe, data merge, testing, as well as extraction, transformation, and load procedures. The standardisation process usually combines both statistical work and methodology mapping so that different numbers can be aligned to the same metrics.

Media and social media

Despite its alternative nature, the unofficial and high frequency nature of media and social media data distinguishes itself from other categories.

Annual or quarterly disclosure would not be able to provide investors with timely information. Especially in green and sustainable investing, investors value ex-ante indicators a lot more than ex-post analyses. Media and social media data compensate for the low frequency of disclosed data. In the meantime, since media and social media cover a broad range of topics, it is important to be able to decipher the media language, for example by labelling the topics and the entities involved.

The core of the technology here is the real-time data feed and NLP — especially in terms of named entity recognition and topic modelling. The combination of the two requires a very robust technical infrastructure upon which machine learning can be processed almost instantly.

Other datasets

There are other types of data that have gained popularity in the past decade. Satellite imagery helps investors and issuers monitor the regions in which they are interested. Using different spectrums of radio waves, satellites can not only identify real objects on the ground, but also under water, below ground and in the air.

However, like every dataset, satellite imagery has its own shortcomings. The currently available satellite products are far from the ultra-high-resolution surveillance camera concept as might be believed by many investors. Not only is it limited by its frequency of coverage and the limit of resolution, it is constantly prone to cloud and other weather disruptions. However, satellite imagery is ideal for macroeconomic analysis in green and sustainable investing, especially for surveying lands and tracking pollution. Successful satellite research has been conducted to study palm oil plantations, vegetation coverage, natural disasters, and greenhouse gas emissions.

If we put all different categories of data onto a credibility spectrum, disclosed data would be the most credible because it is tied to regulatory reporting and scrutiny, while media and social media would take the opposite end. Alternative data would stand in the middle. On the contrary, if we put these categories onto a frequency spectrum, the positions would reverse as media and social media account for the most frequent, and disclosed data occupy the other end. It is important to equip green and sustainable investors with a variety of datasets that spans the spectrum of different standards, since each of the datasets is helpful in its own way.

Methodology

Despite the prevalence of ESG ratings, indices, or other benchmarks, the ways data are analysed or used for insight into green and sustainable investments — in other words, the methodologies — vary across different financial institutions, corporate issuers, and jurisdictions.

Investor differences

Most large investors have their own evaluation systems for green and sustainable investments. Though powered by the same data, their views can be materially different.

A prominent example of debate in the industry is the treatment of alcohol-related businesses. While alcohol may be perceived as the cause of poor health and social instability — which run contrary to the United Nations Sustainable Development Goals — by some investors, others have argued in favour of the social and cultural contexts of alcohol use.

Another notable example is the focus on absolute exclusion versus graduated withdrawals. While some investors have excluded brown energy — conventional fossil fuels, such as oil or coal — from their portfolios, others have retained them, emphasising the speed of their transition to green energy. Some others have developed more sophisticated frameworks to assess the carbon transition cost.

In a multifaceted world, a unified consensus on how good is good and how bad is bad is a challenge. However, the diverse methodologies of different investors underscore the fast-developing trends around sustainable investing.

Differences in regulatory or global standards

Differences in standards are another form of methodological discrepancies that can lead to variations in data interpretation.

Disclosure on greenhouse gas emissions in Hong Kong is a very good example. While the ESG disclosure rules of the Stock Exchange of Hong Kong (SEHK) do not mandate that issuers disclose their emissions by type of greenhouse gases, the exchange has provided disclosure tools to help companies assess their emissions of each type. As a result, a large number of issuers in Hong Kong were found to have disclosed their emissions data with detailed breakdowns, such as carbon dioxide (CO_2), methane, nitrous oxide, perfluorocarbons, and hydrofluorocarbons[3].

In many other jurisdictions, issuers adopting different standards — including the most comprehensive *Global Reporting Initiative* standard — would usually only disclose the mass in tonnes of carbon dioxide equivalent (tCO2e) as a total number, or at most specify what are included in the calculation.

---

3   Source: Analysis by Mioying Financial Technology (HK) Limited (MioTech).

These different methodologies give investors more information to assess the detailed carbon profiles as well as the operating models of many listed companies.

Technology

When financial technology is applied to green and sustainable investments, it is important to know the differences among data, methodology and technology, in order to pinpoint the problems and needs. While technology can solve lots of pain points for investors such as data accuracy, data management and reporting, methodology relies more on industry and regulatory consensus, as well as the maturity of the market. We will discuss the details of different technologies in the next section.

Existing and emerging technologies in green and sustainable Investments

Several technologies have been brought up in previous sections, alongside their applications. Their technical details are worth the attention from investors, in order to understand the technology's capabilities and limitations.

NLP

Making sense of the text is a common use case in analysing disclosed, alternative, or media datasets. In green and sustainable investing, it is especially important to be able to figure out what happened to which company. In technical terms, such a process involves topic modelling, and figuring out whom it happened to involves named entity recognition. By analysing large amounts of text, NLP algorithms are able to identify the patterns and similarities in wording, rhetoric, as well as sentence structures. Current state of machine intelligence can even auto-generate abstracts for research or academic papers.

In the context of green and sustainable investing, being able to quickly summarise large chunks of text is extremely helpful. In the case of annual reports, NLP technology can be used to extract texts, tables as well as accounting items, and further identify any revenue items aligned with United Nations Sustainable Development Goals (UNSDGs). In corporate social responsibility reports, the algorithms can extract both quantitative numbers — for example related to emissions, energy consumption, water, and waste disposal — and qualitative statements such as commitments and descriptions of sustainable efforts. The same capabilities apply to alternative and media data. In legal documents, for example, NLP technology can be used to automatically assign a legal case type such as contract or labour dispute. Each media article is assigned one or multiple topic labels, such as environmental violations, immediately after it is fetched into the NLP engine.

Besides the topics, identifying people is vitally important. Entity recognition is even more challenging in Chinese, where there are no capitalised letters or middle names. After recognising the entity names, machine intelligence also needs to align the names to the existing identifiers in its own database, and further to know the subjects and objects. This is called entity alignment. As an example, at MioTech, besides being able to accurately identify entity names in both English and Chinese, an advanced feature engineering method similar to search page rank is adopted to solve the entity alignment challenge.

Machine learning requires large amounts of training data, as does NLP. A robust NLP architecture ensures high precision and recall with a relatively small training dataset. This is especially important in green and sustainable investing, because this newly established field has relatively less historical data and having finance professionals label training data is a costly work. As an example, MioTech's NLP architecture incorporates a three-layer approach: the base layer is a generalised layer based on Google's Bidirectional Encoder Representations from Transformers, known as BERT; the middle layer is a financial language layer; the top layer is the topic layer, which attempts to reach high precision and recall based on a relatively low minimum of tagged training data inputs.

Knowledge graph

Being able to identify hidden gems and risks in the market means that investors can see through the non-transparent links among entities and verify information. In previous sections, we have illustrated the importance of shareholding and supply chain information. All this relationship information can be recorded in a graphical database instead of a traditional relational database for more efficient traversal and calculations. Environmental penalties, for example, occur much more often at a subsidiary level than at a holding company level. The same applies to other controversial data points that are mostly composed of alternative data. Therefore, using a knowledge graph to unveil hidden linkages is an important feature for tracking and giving alert to investors and issuers.

Knowledge graphs also play an important role in merging and verification of new data. GraphDB-based artificial intelligence technologies, such as clustering and community studies, can determine if a new piece of data conforms to the existing knowledge. To put it in simple words, if an existing relationship between companies A and B is recorded in the knowledge graph, an additional piece of news stating a new event happened between A and B is thus more credible. This is an important technique in verifying alternative and media data.

Knowledge graphs have economies of scale — the larger the existing knowledge graph is, the better it can verify additional pieces of data and grow even larger. A rich and vivid knowledge graph can possess billions of nodes and edges, and experience growth continuously.

Data governance

Finance has very little tolerance for errors. As a financial database grows and different types of data are being processed, a single misstep can cause a cascade of misinformation. To ensure the overall validity, every piece of data in green and sustainable investing must be traceable through its entire development process.

For example, at MioTech, engineers are allowed to work on the upstream and downstream of the same piece of data simultaneously without the priority in task scheduling. This ensures that each piece of data can be traced to its original source and can independently be tested at any time. Fintech applications usually involve hundreds and thousands of data pipelines. Effective management of the data lineage and the development process requires a robust data governance platform.

Sustainability fintech applications in China

Despite the rapid growth of China's financial market, it is still lagging behind on data transparency and technology infrastructure. In green and sustainable finance, Hong Kong and the Mainland markets each has its own fintech strengths and weaknesses.

According to MioTech's statistical analysis of listed companies' data for the financial year 2019, 26% of the A-share issuers listed in the Mainland (1,030 out of 3,950) released their CSR reports, compared to 95.8% (2,418 out of 2,525) of those listed in Hong Kong. Only 168 A-share issuers, representing a mere 4.3%, disclosed their greenhouse gas emissions, compared to an overwhelmingly 77.2% disclosure rate for Hong Kong listed companies. A similar degree of contrast occurred for energy consumption data, on which A-share issuers' disclosure rate was 6%, compared to 92.8% for Hong Kong listed issuers.

However, the numbers above do not mean Hong Kong listed companies have an overwhelming data advantage. They lag behind in supplier, customer, and subsidiary disclosures. A-share listed companies are required to disclose the details of the top five suppliers and customers, while those listed in Hong Kong usually choose to disclose just the largest supplier or customer and the top five combined amount, as required by the Listing Rules. Similarly, A-share listed companies are required to disclose all their subsidiaries, but the Hong Kong listed ones are only required to disclose subsidiaries that materially contribute to the group company.[4]

Because of the detailed disclosure of subsidiaries and supply chains, A-share companies usually have abundant alternative data tracing through different stakeholders. Hong Kong companies lag behind because of their opaque disclosure of related companies. On the other hand, both the holding companies and the related companies of Hong Kong listed entities tend to be distributed across different jurisdictions, making it even more difficult to collect alternative data, for example, from government or regulatory websites.

Besides reporting, data management problems also contribute to the lack of data transparency. Companies in the Mainland and Hong Kong are still late adopters of enterprise software despite the rapid technology development in the consumer area. ESG reporting, monitoring, and energy efficiency tools are still rare in the market. Data collection and management are still manual in many organisations.

Today's financial market relies heavily on technology. The fast-rising trend of green and sustainable investment will nurture a new wave of fintech to empower investors and issuers in China.

---

4   Source: Appendix 16 ("Disclosure of Financial Information") to SEHK's *Main Board Listing Rules,* available on the website of Hong Kong Exchanges and Clearing Limited, viewed on 7 May 2021; *Standards Concerning the Contents and Formats of Information Disclosure by Companies Offering Securities to the Public No. 2 — Contents and Formats of Annual Reports* (《公開發行證券的公司信息披露內容與格式準則第 2 號──年度報告的內容與格式》), available on the CSRC's website, viewed on 7 May 2021.

第13章

綠色及可持續投資的
金融科技應用

涂鑒彧
妙盈科技　創始人兼行政總裁

摘要

隨着政策制定與社會各界對可持續發展的意識愈來愈高，綠色及可持續投資急速發展，且逐漸成為主流投資理念。與傳統投資不同，有關理念的實施多年來均為投資者、發行人及監管機構帶來挑戰，原因在於數據及技術兩方面的支援仍存在不足。

技術方面，人工智能的崛起為金融市場帶來不少改變，涉及方面包括數碼化、自動化及資料存取。自然語言處理、知識圖譜及數據治理平台等新科技大大提升了投資者與發行人的生產力。

新科技結合綠色及可持續投資的趨勢，勢將投資活動提升到另一層次。

投資者、發行人及監管機構在技術上面對的挑戰

綠色及可持續投資主要是環境、社會及管治（Environment, Social, Governance，簡稱 ESG）的概念實踐。相較於財務報表、交易價格及交易量，ESG 數據較為分散、非結構化，且通常未經審核，難以從投資者的角度詮釋。對發行人而言，ESG 數據的收集以及遵守全球或地區標準是相當繁複的過程。監管機構亦須從 ESG 的角度留意市場發展。這些需要所帶來的挑戰均可由科技解決，為金融科技的應用提供了龐大的空間。

投資者角度

經過數十年的市場發展，現時的金融、合規及監管環境已變得非常複雜。投資機會大幅增加，但風險之高也前所未見。數據及軟件產品可協助投資者探索新的投資機會，同時避開潛藏的風險。

新投資策略

增長、盈利能力及現金流是投資決策的主要考慮因素。因此，自現代會計準則面世以來，財務報表一直是唯一最重要的資料來源。本杰明・格雷厄姆（Benjamin Graham）於 1949 年的著作《聰明的投資者》（*The Intelligent Investor*）向一代又一代的投資者灌輸的，便是這些概念。

然而，由於全球趨向數碼化，投資者開始轉向其他信息來源，務求在市場尋寶。在此趨勢下，綠色及可持續投資已由小眾概念演變成核心投資策略。這不僅歸因於市場需求，亦是由於新技術讓投資者可取得更多 ESG 數據。

不少以 ESG 為重點的投資策略均以因子為基礎。與傳統方式類似，投資者會對照金融產品過往價格回測不同的 ESG 數據點組合，以找出相關性或因果效應。例如，有部分選股策略僅依賴 ESG 評級（根據不同的數據點計算得出的分數）；另一些交易策略則更着重發行人 ESG 表現的特定範疇，例如不少投資研究員發現，在經濟下滑期間，員工滿意度是股價韌力的重大指標[1]。

另一些可持續投資策略則以框架為基礎，但同時亦依賴數據。舉例而言，碳轉型評估就是一種很受投資者歡迎的工具，其目標在於評估公司長遠而言過渡至低碳經濟的準備程度，

1　參閱以下例子：C. Shan 與 D. Y. Tang〈艱難時代下員工滿意度的價值：新冠肺炎一疫所見〉（"The value of employee satisfaction in disastrous times: Evidence from COVID-19"），載於 SSRN，2020年7月10日；C. Chen、Y. Xia 與 B. Zhang〈廉正的代價〉（"The price of integrity"），載於SSRN，2021年2月2日。

假設的是若該公司未能成功過渡，便可能要面對沉重的碳稅或競爭力不足的問題。有關分析通常以不同層面的數據為基礎，包括公司現時的碳排放、技術成熟度及宏觀經濟條件。

這些投資策略均需要由先進技術如圖像識別及自然語言處理（Natural Language Processing，簡稱 NLP）等所產生的非傳統（通常是分散和非結構性的）數據集所支持。

風險、合規及監管

在金融學中，回報往往伴隨風險。在進行綠色及可持續投資時，若對投資缺乏了解或不遵守複雜的監管規定，便可能產生風險。

隨着全球環境趨向數碼化，投資者須了解數據當中潛藏的風險。與基於財務報表進行的傳統分析不同，高層管理人員的不當行為、產品質素問題或有關違反環保意識的不利消息，均可能會對投資帶來重大風險。因此，投資者有必要盡早注意這類潛在風險，而其中一個方法就是檢查歷史數據。以礦業為例，相關數據顯示，大型的安全意外及環境污染事件通常都可以透過政府罰款紀錄，追溯過往一些沒那麼嚴重的事件而預測得到。此類事件的資料對綠色及可持續投資而言都是關鍵數據，投資者須及時取得。

急速發展的全球監管環境亦為投資者帶來合規方面的挑戰。例如，《歐盟可持續金融分類標準》（European Union (EU) Taxonomy on Sustainable Finance）儘管現時僅於歐盟實施，但其對於在歐盟經營業務或集資的亞太區公司，又或於歐盟銷售投資產品或提供金融服務的亞洲金融市場參與者而言，都同樣有執行力。在監管上的差異方面，《歐盟可持續金融分類方案》嚴格禁止與煤炭有關的業務取得綠色資金；而在中國，使用潔淨煤的行業則以往是被列為合資格發行綠色債券的行業。儘管《綠色債券支持項目目錄（2021 年版）》[2] 已經撤除使用潔淨煤的項目，與歐盟的標準一致，但全球監管政策及定義仍存在各種差異，要一一翻查這許多的複雜政策，對不少投資者來說極不容易。數據及軟件系統可大幅減低綠色及可持續投資者面對的合規及監管負擔。

發行人角度

在科技、工業化及全球化的推動下，不少公司增長成規模極大的企業。跨國公司通常都依賴全球供應鏈，來自利益相關方、業務結構及監管環境各方面的要求越來越複雜及多元化。匯報及數據管理軟件會對發行人達到綠色及可持續投資者的要求非常有幫助。

2　《綠色債券支持項目目錄(２０２１年版)》由中國人民銀行、中國國家發展和改革委員會與中國證券監督管理委員會(簡稱「中國證監會」)於2021年4月2日聯合發佈。

管理複雜的業務結構及利益相關方

社會責任投資（包括綠色及可持續投資）中可以見到的最主要差異，就是焦點轉移至利益相關方管理 —— 公司會與其利益相關方溝通互動，識別、了解並管理利益相關方的需求及期望。利益相關方的定義廣泛，不僅造成管理方面的困難，同時亦為數據及技術的應用帶來挑戰。這表示公司的目標不再只是將股東權益最大化，而是要盡量提升利益相關方的權益，包括員工福利、供應鏈管理及客戶優惠等。

在綠色及可持續投資方面，發行人在其本身股權結構下，通常難以應對內部匯報及數據管理上的挑戰。要在附屬公司及其所投資的公司內部實行有效的業務匯報機制本身已不容易，如果還要聚焦在綠色工作及可持續發展上，整個機制的運作負擔就更大。對不少發行人而言，光是編備所有附屬公司的能源消耗資料便已是一項龐大的工程。

對外方面，管理供應商和客戶亦不輕鬆。現今的供應鏈及客戶通常廣泛分佈於不同地區，要了解其營運及合規資料，往往需要穩健的匯報及追蹤機制。科技可大大減低溝通及管理成本 —— 只要有關程序自動化即可。

要滿足內部及外部的數據管理及匯報需求，往往需要結合硬件及軟件技術。舉例而言，物聯網（Internet of Things，簡稱 IoT）裝置是非常有用的工具，可收集有關能源及排放的數據，而在此之上的軟件則可在監控、數據管理、分析及優化等工作上發揮重要作用。用於機構管理的軟件會提供內部數據輸入、調查及匯報機制，協助公司處理利益相關方管理的工作。

合規匯報及監管標準

合規及監管匯報以及數據管理跟利益相關方管理一樣困難。除上文提到的內部及外部數據收集外，發行人亦經常感到難以通覽各種複雜的監管匯報規定，所以傳統上這項工作會交由顧問公司負責。現今越來越多公司開始採用自動化匯報軟件，將同一組營運數據集轉換成不同的匯報標準，並提供同業基準資料以作對比。部分證券交易所亦於其網站提供了相關工具以協助發行人評估其可持續表現，同時不少跨國公司均採用了較複雜的監管匯報軟件系統，以解決與可持續發展有關的合規及匯報需求。

發行人在可持續數據管理、匯報及嚴格遵守合規程序等方面做得穩妥，可大大提高投資者的投資信心、促進健康的市場發展。通過數據、硬件及軟件技術，可進一步滿足有關需求。

成本效益方面的考量

可持續發展方面的合規匯報及利益相關方管理，可以花費大量財務和人力資源。若將有關程序數碼化及自動化，便可節省資源，同時減少出錯。

在考慮成本效益時，亦須考慮業務運作的複雜性及監管環境。不少擁有許多附屬公司和供應商的大型企業集團，以及須符合不同可持續合規標準的跨國企業，正紛紛採用可持續發展軟件。

現成的「軟件即服務」(SaaS) 產品所需要的管理人手由一個到數十個不等。若完全度身訂造解決方案，則可能花費更多成本，但不合規和管理不良的代價卻無法估量。

數據、技術及方法論在不同應用層面的角色

綠色及可持續投資的金融科技應用程式是專為解決上一節所述的困難而設，當中通常涉及以下功能：

- 在項目、公司、行業或宏觀經濟層面搜尋並瀏覽可持續發展的相關資料；
- 追蹤及提示有關投資、附屬公司、供應鏈、客戶或可持續發展相關項目的消息；
- 內部數據管理；及
- 外部合規及監管匯報。

在進入純技術的探討前，我們必須了解到大部分綠色及可持續投資應用程式通常涉及數項主要元素，包括分析框架（例如方法論）、數據以及生成數據並建立軟件的技術。

數據

數據是構成所有應用程式的元素。就來源而言，我們通常會將數據分成四類：

- 披露數據；
- 第三方來源的另類數據；
- 傳媒及社交媒體；及
- 其他數據集。

披露數據

有關綠色及可持續投資的有用披露數據集可來自不同的地方。就公開上市股份或股份相關投資產品（例如互惠基金及交易所買賣基金）而言，從招股章程、年報及企業社會責任報告

（或部分司法權區所要求的可持續發展報告）便可取得大量相關資料。固定收益投資可按發行人層面或項目層面評估，方法是查看發行人的官方報告或債券的招股章程及年報。

儘管投資產品各有不同，但用於綠色及可持續投資的數據點均大同小異。除不少全球匯報標準均有概述的常見數據點（例如《溫室氣體協議》（Greenhouse Gas Protocol）中稱為範圍 1、2 及 3 排放的直接及間接排放物）外，投資者亦會參考其他數據點（例如綠色收入）來檢查有關業務性質。如上一節所述，合規規定的差異亦可能會造成不同司法權區的數據各有不同。

披露數據的質素通常與發行人的匯報是否嚴謹，以及有關數據集是否可輕易由其報告取出有關。前者可在上一節所述的穩健數據管理及匯報軟件的幫助下達成，後者則通常會利用到圖像識別（或類似工具）以及 NLP，尤其在報告是以文件或圖片形式呈現的情況下。全球多家交易所亦大力推動採用可擴展商業報告語言（XBRL）的匯報框架（用於數碼商業匯報的公開國際標準）。

另類數據

披露數據有其限制。儘管全球匯報標準越來越全面及嚴格，卻未能涵蓋發行人可持續表現的每一個範疇。

來自與發行人沒有關聯的第三方來源的其他數據，便可提供對照發行人本身主觀陳述的另類觀點，因此就評估某項投資是否真正綠色而言至關重要。

另類數據的來源可以很廣泛。可持續投資者較常用的大多是政府、監管機構、行業及非政府組織的網站。數據的形式亦差異甚大。政府罰款紀錄可以是載於文件、圖表或試算表中，行業報告可以是以網上文本形式發佈，還有其他數據可能是載於互動的圖表中。

由於另類數據如此分散及欠缺結構，因此若沒有科技的幫助，便難以收集、清洗及標準化。數據收集可通過應用程式介面、簡易資訊聚合（Really Simple Syndication，簡稱 RSS）饋送、網絡爬蟲或直接連接數據庫等形式進行。數據清洗通常涉及更複雜的技術程序，當中可包括光學字元辨識（Optical Character Recognition，簡稱 OCR）、NLP、數據去重複、數據合併、測試，以及提取、轉換與載入程序。標準化程序通常會結合統計工作和方法映射，讓不同數據符合相同指標。

傳媒及社交媒體

傳媒及社交媒體的數據儘管性質也較另類，但其非官方再加上高頻的屬性，相對於其他類型的數據即顯得自成一類。

年度或季度披露無法為投資者提供及時的資料。尤其是就綠色及可持續投資而言，投資者對事前指標的重視遠高於事後分析。傳媒及社交媒體數據可彌補披露數據頻率偏低的問題。同時，由於傳媒及社交媒體涵蓋一系列不同種類的主題，能夠辨識媒體語言（例如通過標籤主題及所涉及的實體）便至關重要。

有關技術的核心是即時數據饋送及 NLP（尤其是實體辨識及主題模型）。結合這兩項技術需要非常穩健的技術基礎設施，讓機器學習可近乎即時進行。

其他數據集

過去十年亦有其他類型的數據興起。衛星影像可幫助投資者及發行人關注其感興趣的地區。利用不同頻譜的無線電波，衛星可識別陸地上以至水底、地底及空中的實物。

然而，與所有數據集一樣，衛星影像亦有其本身的缺點。現有的衛星產品並非超高像素的監視攝影機，仍遠遠不符投資者的期望。衛星影像不僅受限於覆蓋頻率和偏低的解像度，還容易受雲層及其他天氣影響。不過，衛星影像非常適用於綠色及可持續投資的宏觀經濟分析，尤其是用於測量土地及追蹤污染情況。在棕櫚油種植、植被覆蓋、自然災害及溫室氣體排放的研究中，衛星研究都成功發揮其作用。

若比較不同類別數據的可信度，披露數據因與監管及審查掛鈎，因此是最可信的，相反，傳媒及社交媒體的可信度最低，而另類數據則居中。另一方面，若比較不同類別數據的頻率，上述排位便會倒轉過來 —— 傳媒及社交媒體的頻率最高，披露數據則最低。每一類數據集都有其可幫助投資者的長處，因此綠色及可持續投資者需要有不同類型及標準的數據集以協助其投資。

方法論

儘管 ESG 評級、指數或其他基準在市場上均十分普遍，但不同金融機構、公司發行人及司法權區將數據用於分析或了解綠色及可持續投資的方法（即方法論）各有不同。

投資者差異

大部分大型投資者均有其本身用於評估綠色及可持續投資的系統。儘管使用同樣的數據，他們的觀點亦可能有很大的差異。

業內一項重大爭議，就是如何對待與酒精類有關的業務。有部分投資者認為酒精可危害健康及破壞社會穩定（而這與聯合國可持續發展目標有衝突），但亦有其他投資者從社會及文化的角度支持飲酒。

另一項值得一提的爭議，就是：到底該是「徹底排除」還是「逐步排除」？部分投資者的投資組合裏已剔除棕色能源（指傳統化石燃料，例如石油和煤），但亦有些投資者保留有關能源的投資，説其所強調的是過渡至綠色能源的速度。還有一些投資者建立了精密的框架，用以評估碳過渡成本。

在包羅萬象的環境下，要就如何定義「好」和「壞」達到共識相當困難。不過，正因為不同投資者使用的方法各異，可持續投資的發展才會如此迅速。

監管或全球標準的差異

方法論的差異亦體現在標準方面的差異，而這可能會造成不同的數據闡釋。

香港有關溫室氣體排放的披露是個很好的例子，儘管香港聯合交易所（簡稱「聯交所」）的 ESG 披露規則並未規定發行人須披露不同類型溫室氣體的排放，但聯交所亦提供了披露工具，協助公司評估各類溫室氣體的排放。因此，香港若干數量的發行人已分門別類地詳細披露了其排放數據，例如二氧化碳（CO_2）、甲烷、一氧化二氮、全氟碳化合物及氫氟碳化合物 [3]。

在很多其他的司法權區，採納不同標準〔包括最全面的《全球報告倡議組織》（Global Reporting Initiative）的標準〕的發行人通常只會披露二氧化碳當量的總噸數（tCO2e），最多也只會列明其計算中包含了哪些溫室氣體。

上述不同的方法論可為投資者提供更多資料，讓其評估許多上市公司的詳細碳排狀況及營運模式。

技術

在綠色及可持續投資應用金融科技，必須了解數據、方法論及技術之間的差異，以準確針對問題及需要。一方面，科技可為投資者解決很多痛點（例如數據準確度、數據管理及匯報），另一方面，方法論更依賴行業及監管方面的共識，以及市場的成熟程度。關於不同技術的詳情在下一節作討論。

3　資料來源：Mioying Financial Technology (HK) Limited（妙盈科技）的分析。

綠色及可持續投資的現有及新興技術

我們在上幾節提到了數項技術及其應用。要了解有關技術的能力及限制，投資者值得注意當中的技術細節。

NLP

不論是分析披露數據、另類數據，還是媒體數據，通常都涉及解構文字的意思。就綠色及可持續投資而言，從文字中了解公司情況的能力尤為重要。從技術角度來看，這過程涉及建構主題模型，而要識別有關對象，則涉及實體識別。通過分析大量文字，**NLP** 演算法可識別出文字、修辭及句子結構的模式和相似之處。現時的機器智能更可自動生成研究或學術論文的摘要。

對綠色及可持續投資而言，能從大量文字裏快速得出總結概要的幫助甚大。以年報為例，**NLP** 技術可用於摘取文字、表格及會計項目，並進一步識別任何符合《聯合國可持續發展目標》的收入項目。從企業社會責任報告中，有關演算法可同時摘取定量數據（例如有關排放、能源消耗、用水及廢物處理的數據）及定性陳述（例如有關可持續發展工作的承諾及陳述）。有關功能亦適用於另類及媒體數據。以法律文件為例，使用 **NLP** 技術可將文件自動編配其所屬法律個案類型（例如合約或勞資糾紛）。每篇媒體文章在輸入 **NLP** 引擎後，立即會被打上一個或多個主題標籤（例如環保違規）。

除主題外，識別人物亦非常重要。由於中文沒有大寫字母和中間名，從中文中識別實體會更難。辨識實體名稱後，機器智能亦須將有關名稱與其數據庫中的既有身份標識配對，並進一步分辨主體及對象。有關程序稱為「實體匹配」。以妙盈科技的技術為例，除可準確辨識實體的中英文名稱外，更採用了類似搜尋網頁排名的先進特徵工程方法，以解決實體匹配方面的困難。

NLP 與其他機器學習一樣，都需要大量訓練數據。強大的 **NLP** 架構應能確保高精確率及召回率，而需要的訓練數據集的規模又相對較小。這就綠色及可持續投資而言尤其重要，因為這是全新的領域，歷史數據相對較少，而採用金融專家標籤訓練數據的成本又高昂。以妙盈科技的技術為例，**NLP** 架構採用三個層次的構思 —— 底層是通用層，建基於 **Google** 的基於變換器的雙向編碼器表示技術（Bidirectional Encoder Representations from Transformers，簡稱 BERT）；中層是金融語言層；而頂層則是主題層，旨在根據有限的已標記訓練數據集達到高精確率及召回率。

知識圖譜

若想找出市場潛藏的機遇和風險，投資者需要能看穿實體之間各種不透明的聯繫，再加以驗證。在以上幾節中，我們展示了持股及供應鏈資料的重要性。所有這些關聯性資料均可記錄於圖數據庫（而非傳統的關聯式數據庫）中，以提升搜索及計算效率。舉例而言，環保罰款在附屬公司層面出現的頻率比起在控股公司層面出現的較高。這在其他主要屬於另類數據的具爭議性數據點亦見如是。因此，利用知識圖譜找出潛藏關聯是一項重要功能，有助追蹤並向投資者及發行人發出警示。

知識圖譜在合併和驗證新數據方面亦發揮重大的作用。以圖數據庫（GraphDB）為基礎的人工智能技術（例如聚類及社羣研究）可釐定個別新數據是否與現有知識吻合。簡而言之，若 A 公司及 B 公司的現有關聯性被記錄於知識圖譜中，顯示 A 公司與 B 公司之間有新事件發生的消息便更為可信。這是驗證另類及媒體數據的一項重要技術。

知識圖譜具有規模經濟的特徵 —— 現有知識圖譜越大，便越容易驗證新數據，並可進一步增大。豐富而不斷更新的金融知識圖譜會有數以十億計的節點和連線，其數量會持續增長。

數據治理

金融領域的容錯率極低。隨着金融數據庫不斷增長並處理不同類型的數據，只要走錯一步亦可導致資料出現極大量的錯誤。為確保整體的有效性，綠色及可持續投資的每項數據均必須可在其整個發展過程中被持續追蹤。

以妙盈科技的做法為例，工程師可同時處理同一項數據的上游及下游程序，毋須排定先後次序。這可確保每一項數據均可追溯至其源頭，並可隨時作獨立測試。金融科技應用程式通常涉及成千上萬的數據來源，要有效管理數據處理歷程及發展過程，必須有穩健的數據治理平台。

中國的可持續金融科技應用

儘管中國金融市場的發展相當迅速，但其在數據透明度及科技基礎設施方面仍較為落後。就綠色及可持續金融而言，香港與內地市場的金融科技各有其強弱項。

根據妙盈科技就上市公司 2019 財政年度的統計數據，於內地上市的 A 股發行人當中，26%（3,950 家中的 1,030 家）發佈了企業社會責任報告，而香港上市發行人的數字是 95.8%（2,525 家中的 2,418 家）。只有 168 家 A 股發行人（僅 4.3%）披露了其溫室氣體排放，而香港上市公司的有關披露率卻高達 77.2%。能源消耗數據方面亦同樣有相當大的差異：A 股發行人的披露率為 6%，香港上市發行人則達 92.8%。

然而，上述數字並不代表香港上市公司在數據方面有壓倒性的優勢。香港上市公司在供應商、客戶及附屬公司的披露方面較為落後。A 股上市公司須披露最大的五家供應商及客戶細節，而香港上市公司則通常選擇只按上市規則的要求，披露最大的供應商或客戶，以及首五大的合計數字；同樣地，A 股上市公司須披露旗下所有附屬公司，但香港上市公司只須披露對集團公司有重大貢獻的附屬公司[4]。

由於 A 股公司有詳細披露附屬公司及供應鏈，他們通常亦有充足的另類數據，可通過不同利益相關方作追蹤。香港公司在有關聯的公司方面的披露並不透明，因此較為落後。另一方面，香港上市公司的控股公司及關聯公司大多遍佈不同司法權區，收集另類數據（例如從政府或監管機構網站收集有關數據）便更為艱難。

除匯報方面外，數據管理問題亦是數據缺乏透明度的原因之一。儘管內地與香港在消費領域的科技發展迅速，但兩地的公司在採用企業軟件方面仍較為遲緩。市場上的 ESG 披露、監控及能源效益工具仍不多，不少機構仍以人手進行數據收集及管理。

現今的金融市場非常倚重科技。綠色及可持續投資急速發展的趨勢將醞釀出金融科技新浪潮，為中國的投資者及發行人提供強大的助力。

註：本文原稿是英文，另以中文譯本出版。如本文的中文本的字義或詞義與英文本有所出入，概以英文本為準。

4　資料來源：聯交所《主板上市規則》附錄十六（「財務資料的披露」），載於香港交易及結算所有限公司的網站，於2021年5月7日閱覽；《公開發行證券的公司信息披露內容與格式準則第 2 號 —— 年度報告的內容與格式》，載於中國證監會的網站，於2021年5月7日閱覽。

3

The role of exchanges in green and sustainable finance

交易所在綠色及可持續金融中的角色

Chapter 14

On policy and regulation for the development of green and sustainable finance

Cary Steven KROSINSKY
Lecturer, Yale and Brown University
Co-founder, Sustainable Finance Institute

Summary

China has emerged as a global leader on green finance policy creativity over the last five years, much to its credit, and this leadership has the potential to catalyse necessary action on climate change across Asia where transitions will be particularly challenging to achieve, and these transitions are poised to create significant financial opportunity across the world.

There will be significant learnings to be taken from evolving policy implementations that will continue to emerge in countries such as China, as will be necessary to achieve ambitious carbon peaking by 2030 targets as well as carbon neutrality by 2060 goals.

Accordingly, in this chapter, we will describe five aspects regarding the importance of policy in enabling green and sustainable transitions more generally, those being:

1. Why policy is a key enabler;

2. Specific existing policies which can enable successful transitions to occur;

3. Challenges which remain;

4. Reporting and disclosure requirements which can further assist; and

5. Implications of the policy and regulatory landscape for stock exchanges in supporting green and sustainable finance.

Introduction

A successful green and sustainable transition in China is essential for helping solve climate change on a global basis, and policy will be a key driver of the changes that must occur in order for the long envisioned ecological civilisation to become fully realised. The very good news is that China, which has the second largest pool of wealth capital in the world[1], has emerged as an important global leader on green finance policy creativity over the last five years, much to its credit, and its leadership on policy has the potential to catalyse necessary action across Asia where transitions will be more challenging to achieve. China's recent pledges to achieve carbon peaking by 2030, and carbon neutrality by 2060, as well as related ambitions on finance only continue to accelerate as of this writing and are increasingly well received, creating significant opportunities for strategic investors across the world.

It is important to note that successful green and sustainable transitions only occur when there is economic vibrancy; hence we see China's green transition alongside better financial outcomes for investors as an essential and necessary enabler of this climate change resolution dynamic. The rest of the world in effect must partner with China so that the rest of Asia can learn from China's transition success, and with Asia representing something like half of the world's economy, nothing is arguably more important to achieve in the battle to solve climate change.

Why policy is a key enabler

It would be nice to think that policy was not necessary. That a global financial system, empowered by the best features of free market capitalism could bring in all necessary considerations to ensure the ongoing health of the global economy in perpetuity on its own, but that is not how markets actually function in practice.

The dichotomy of market behaviour is perhaps best illustrated by the Nobel Prize for Economics having been awarded in 2013[2] to Eugene Fama for his efficient market

---

1   Source: Credit Suisse Research Institute, *Global Wealth Databook 2019*.
2   See "Prize in Economic Sciences 2013", press release of the Royal Swedish Academy of Sciences on the website of the Nobel Prize, 14 October 2013.

hypothesis work, which argues that everything eventually gets priced in, and at the same time to Yale's Robert Shiller for his work on Animal Spirits[3], calling specifically for active government policymaking to ensure that expectations of the behaviour of people circumventing systems to be fully reflected in decision making. The combination of Fama and Shiller being awarded the Nobel Prize really tells the story here, especially when it comes to necessary transitions from business as usual. People will seize opportunities when and where they can, that's just human nature.

Therefore, policy is necessary to allow markets to function properly, baking in necessary climate change transitions, whereas a purely free market approach inevitably contains different actors with differing goals, interests and priorities.

Market actors such as public companies across all sectors, as well as within all global financial institutions, are filled with employees who fully care about the well-being of environmental conditions being caused by pollution, for example, and of the health of their societies more generally. Yet adequate checks and balances remain largely not in place to ensure that the worst of global climate change will occur, and the ongoing effects of pollution are quite likely to continue to affect lives, and other concerns remain among issues such as global levels of biodiversity, the health of oceans and more, making necessary policy mandatory for achieving societal outcomes such as the United Nations Sustainable Development Goals (SDGs) as have been well documented are needed to be achieved by 2030 and for the optimising of financial outcomes more generally going forward for financial systems themselves.

The final report of the United Nations Environment Programme (UNEP) Inquiry into the Design of a Sustainable Financial System[4] in which we had a role in 2015-16 in fact identified three specific categories of gaps in the financial system on such matters concerning societal outcomes, those three being (1) a gap on effectiveness, (2) an efficiency gap, and (3) a gap on resilience as well. Efficiency is about the outsized contemporary nature of the financial services sector which helps cause something of an ongoing overall disconnect from the real economy, which only represents half of global financial system value as of today[5]. Resilience is about the ability to stress test the financial system or any part thereof regarding green and sustainable considerations, but the biggest issue of all is arguably effectiveness.

3   Akerlof, G. A. and R. J. Shiller. (2010) *Animal Spirits: How Human Psychology Drives the Economy, and Why It Matters for Global Capitalism*, Princeton University Press.
4   See "Final UNEP Inquiry Report reviews prospects for global sustainable financial system", *NEWS* webpage on the *IISD SDG Knowledge Hub* website, 24 April 2018.
5   See Cary Krosinsky. (2015) "The value of everything", *UNEP Inquiry Working Paper*, December 2015.

Effectiveness is the degree to which green and sustainable considerations are baked into the financial system today and the gap here remains sizeable for example as was recently outlined by the Organisation for Economic Co-operation and Development (OECD) at US$2.5 trillion per year[6].

Box 1 gives an illustration of China's green finance policy approach[7]. China's ability to drive top-down policy has become a clear and distinct global competitiveness advantage over countries such as the United States (US), Australia and other nations across Europe, where policies such as feed-in tariffs on renewable energy or establishing a price on carbon can get fully set up by one government only to get overturned by a subsequent regime. This sort of "yoyo effect" leads to less confidence by investors and corporations seeking to ensure that their strategies and investments will not fail financially, and also puts a damper on commitments to innovation and research and development, which has faded in recent years in the US for example, giving fully dedicated countries such as China a distinct advantage going forward. Chinese companies have clear signals on carbon neutrality alongside other policies and incentives mentioned in this chapter, encouraging them to innovate and diversify, making this all strategic and materially relevant for investors to fully consider going forward. Just imagine what would be possible if the US and China do fully cooperate on climate change going forward; this would become an unstoppable force for solving climate change as opposed to what we have now, some progress mixed in with hesitation and doubt, and again such cooperation would position the financial market to benefit from such confidence and cooperation.

US President Biden in his speech to a Joint Session of Congress on 28 April 2021 recognised the challenge to democracies in achieving consensus on what is necessary which only then can translate to consistency in policy[8]. Once consistency in wanting to achieve desired outcomes is achieved, there will also be a need for monitoring and evolving policies, including what can be achieved on global policy through ongoing global collaborations and negotiations, again the advantage here is to countries and their organisations that are best positioned to help achieve alignment of purpose. Dialogues between the US and China, two of the largest economies and capital markets in the world, to collaborate to solve climate change together are helpful.

Solving climate change should not be a debate, in fact it must not be.

---

6   Source: Jean-Philippe de Schrevel, "How blended finance can plug the SDG financing gap", published on the *OECD Development Matters* website, 22 January 2020.

7   Quoted from Dr. Ma Jun's introduction to the book by Cary Krosinsky, *Modern China, Financial Cooperation for Solving Sustainability Challenges*, Palgrave Macmillan, 2020.

8   Source: "Remarks by President Biden in address to a joint session of Congress", published on the *Briefing Room* webpage of the White House website, 28 April 2021.

Box 1. Five steps for China's progress on green finance policy

First, China started its green finance agenda by building a political consensus, not merely holding the technical debate. China backed green finance with a political push from the very top. The highest decision-making bodies in China, including the Central Committee of the Chinese Communist Party and the State Council, endorsed a 14-action roadmap for developing the green finance system as early as 2015. The political backing by China's president and premier carried enormous weight in setting policies, mobilising resources and facilitating inter-departmental consensus on green finance.

Second, China's approach to designing the green financial system has been top-down and not purely market-led. The successful development of green finance requires essential ingredients including green taxonomies and definition of green activities, environmental disclosures by corporations and financial institutions, rules and standards for green finance products, and incentives to corporations and financial institutions. The effective development of these arrangements, in developing countries like China, requires strong actions from government bodies and regulators which has the convening power.

Third, China emphasised coordination among key ministries, division of labour and an implementation timetable. China recognised at the policy-designing stage that green finance was not merely the responsibility of the central bank or a financial regulator, rather it requires policy support and resources from many other agencies and regulators, including fiscal support, environmental regulations, and industrial policies. That is why seven ministries jointly developed the green finance guidelines in 2016.

Fourth, China defined roles of industrial bodies such as national and local Green Finance Committees. In 2015, the People's Bank of China (PBOC) launched the Green Finance Committee (GFC) of China Society for

Finance and Banking. The GFC, with 240 financial institutions, environment-related companies and research bodies as members, quickly became the main disseminator of green finance knowledge, the organiser of green finance product innovations, a key source of policy recommendations, and the coordinator for capacity-building and international collaboration. At the local level, about 20 regional GFCs play similar roles promoting green finance market development.

Fifth, China encourages regional innovations in green finance. Since China's economy has vast regional differences, it is imperative to encourage local players to innovate in their approaches. In June 2017, the State Council approved pilot programmes on green finance reform and innovation in five provinces and eight cities. In the last two years, many valuable experiences and innovations were identified. The PBOC organises annual meetings of these pilot cities, summarises the best practices and promotes them throughout the country.

Specific existing green finance policies which enable successful transitions to occur

Categories where China has either emerged as a leader or is known to be actively considering taking further steps includes those on green bond issuance and related incentives, establishing bank incentives or penalties on minimum green finance percentage activity, as well as on pollution pricing mechanisms, mandatory recycling, electric vehicle incentives, mandatory corporate disclosure and standards including as relates to emerging global green taxonomies.

As mentioned, green and sustainable finance policy is something that will continue to evolve for purpose, therefore by the time you read this chapter additional policies may well have been introduced already or will be under consideration given the urgency of solving climate change alongside government goals on carbon neutrality. Nevertheless, the following are some examples of what effective policy has started to look like.

Green finance minimum percentage requirements for banks, green bond and green credit incentives

One of a number of policy moves is appearing in China now, arguably for the first time anywhere in the world. The *Green Finance Performance Evaluation Scheme for Banks (Draft for Comments)*[9] clearly stated that all banks will subject to qualitative and quantitative standards for achieving minimum percentages of green finance, in China's case 25%. Banks, corporations and other financial institutions around the world are beginning to commit to the concept of "Net Zero" (carbon emissions) by 2050 or otherwise participating in new coalitions on Net Zero such as the Race to Zero, Net Zero Asset Managers or similar, but there is not always a specific roadmap or short-term goals that can help achieve progress. Morgan Stanley was the first major bank to sign up for the Partnership for Carbon Accounting Financials (PCAF)[10], now representing over US$38 trillion of assets, as was previously championed by Dutch banks such as ASN, who now also champion what they call Climate Positive by 2030[11], and which is great to see. Aligning financial institutions to their past, present and future issuance is a key enabler of what businesses which are public, private and state-owned will do going forward, including what gets financed as concerns the "Belt and Road" Initiative. Companies that position themselves accordingly will experience lower costs of capital and will have partner institutions eager to drive their own transitions, an opportunity for investors to focus on such companies that are listed on Chinese exchanges. Green bond incentives have also been fully considered and are an important area to watch in China. Specific coupon rates can be tweaked based on analysis of specific intended issuance to either discourage lending to "brown" projects or encourage green projects by making them more financially desirable. More recently, green credit incentives have been applied to Chinese automobile manufacturers to help hasten the development of green vehicles or they must pay rivals according to a tradeable green car credit scheme[12].

As known, no other country in the world has minimum green finance penalties and incentives applied to its financial institutions, or have green credit incentives applied to other significant sectors, or have specific efforts to encourage these institutions to support green projects and startups. Such also includes providing lower rates to banks from the PBOC as well as green credits awarded to banks which can over-achieve on their green

---

9   《關於印發〈銀行業存款類金融機構綠色金融業績評價方案〉的通知（徵求意見稿）》, issued by the PBOC, 21 July 2020.
10 See PCAF's website (https://carbonaccountingfinancials.com/).
11 Source: ASN Bank's website.
12 Source: "China's green car credit scheme turns up heat on carbon-emitters", *Reuters*, 18 April 2021.

financing goals. Further creativity in this regard can be expected as China from a top-down perspective, specifically as it approaches 2025-2030, seeks to achieve its clearly stated goal of carbon peaking and is expected to plan in advance for how to achieve this. Recently, central bank governor Yi Gang spoke to the expectations and incentives the government is planning to make of China's financial institutions as regards green finance requirements[13]. Western financial institutions do not have these same incentives, but can China's leadership and vision inspire these institutions to follow suit in their own countries and the rest of the world? Here specifically is just one case where Chinese leadership could be so important for helping solve climate change and why global investors should encourage and participate in this transition as well, so that it can be fully effective.

Carbon and pollution pricing

The notion of a price on carbon emissions is a longstanding concept, though one that has struggled to become fully implemented and take specific effect. The concept is clear, that through the establishment of an adequate price on carbon dioxide and perhaps other greenhouse gas (GHG) emissions, a clear disincentive to pollute creates an incentive to accelerate lower carbon strategies and considerations instead for financial reasons. The challenge however is that a price on carbon needs to be globally implemented or another major region of the world may just continue to pollute instead, gaining business where it would be more economic short term to avoid such prices on carbon. Hence, China's initial efforts to create carbon emissions trading schemes had slowed down, understandably to be sure especially the last few years as economic conditions changed including during the recent coronavirus pandemic. Here in 2021, China's efforts to re-establish carbon emissions trading and a corresponding price on carbon have been rekindled. On 5 January 2021, the Ministry of Ecology and Environment disclosed the *Measures for the Administration of Carbon Emissions Trading (Trial Implementation)*[14]. The measures came into effective on 1 February 2021 and the national emissions trading scheme in the Mainland made debut on 16 July 2021. But full adoption should not be expected until the world can come to an agreement on carbon pricing for the reasons mentioned above.

It was great to see former US Secretary of State John Kerry mentioned in April 2021 in Shanghai that the Biden administration believes an effective global price on carbon will be

---

13 Source: "China to require financial institutions to move towards green finance — central bank gov", *Reuters*, 20 April 2021.

14 《碳排放權交易管理辦法（試行）》, issued by the Ministry of Ecology and Environment, 31 December 2020.

necessary to achieve[15]. But one challenge for achieving a price on carbon is the US itself. While many US cities and states favour action on climate change, no jurisdiction has established a carbon pricing mechanism.

If we do get to an agreed global price on carbon, what could be specifically useful would be gradual, predictable carbon price increases over a period of something like 5-10 years to incentivise entrepreneurs, corporates and investors and increase carbon market liquidity while also giving existing organisations and investors time to adjust.

Also, nationwide data infrastructure for modelling, gathering, reporting, monitoring and tracking carbon emissions would be important to achieve, without which it would be challenging to know what was being priced on, what would be enforced and how. Building a carbon credit score system for corporates and startups could also help, which would allow such a score to be used in line with the company's (or project's, government's, and other entities') overall credit scores as the basis of funding.

It is somewhat useful perhaps to look at case studies of carbon pricing and how effective or not such approaches have been. British Columbia in Canada has implemented a carbon price, but not necessarily at levels which change behaviour, so one challenge is how to establish a carbon price which can stand up over time. Providing money back to people is one key mechanism for ensuring success in jurisdictions where governments can be voted out of office, but even then fairly liberal states such as Washington in the US have failed to have carbon legislation passed by voters. Canada has established a national carbon price target, but its elections are affected by this, and Canada's present minority government may well have been weakened by a lack of understanding that Canada's plans for carbon pricing would not negatively affect consumers. Australia implemented a carbon tax and its government was voted out, and climate-denial governments have held power since. In France, the *Gilet Jaunes* movement triggered by the increase in tax on gas (including the proposed carbon tax) led to protests in the streets of Paris. For these sorts of reasons, politicians in the West hesitate to fully and immediately impose carbon pricing, and this all remains an obstacle to expecting China to just establish its own carbon pricing mechanisms, even though European ETS (Emissions Trading System) markets are now fully robust as one example to look for and watch closely.

---

15 Source: "Briefing with Special Presidential Envoy for Climate John Kerry", *Remarks* webpage on the website of the U.S. Department of State, 8 April 2021.

Regardless of struggles to establish carbon pricing mechanisms, pollution pricing and related policies have been in place for some time, allowing for increasingly successful transitions to occur. China has increasingly been setting more stringent pollution level goals for its Mainland cities, for example, and air pollution remains a significant environmental challenge for China to overcome making transitioning away from fossil fuel power generation an imperative in order not to have such restrictions be at ongoing odds with goals on the country's overall economic growth. Air pollution levels have been declining due to increasing regulation of the country's power generation sector. Such efforts have not received as much publicity as carbon-specific efforts, yet improvements in this sector serve as a useful example of implemented policy which has brought about direct, tangible outcomes.

Box 2 outlines a case study on China's success with pollution pricing mechanisms[16], providing a useful example of how policy over time has enabled successful transitions.

---

16 Source: Papapanou, E. (2020) "China as a leader in green finance", in the book by Cary Krosinsky, *Modern China, Financial Cooperation for Solving Sustainability Challenges*, Palgrave Macmillan.

Box 2. China and pollution pricing mechanisms

Over the past decade and a half, the Chinese power sector has steadily increased emissions limits and regulations. The first important standard was implemented in 2003, with the government requiring that scrubbers be put in sulphur dioxide (SO_2) factories. Notable progress began to surface in 2006 with the announcement of the national 11th Five-Year Plan, where hard targets were put in place for SO_2 levels. In 2007, the State Council passed a law known as the "Reduction of the Three Ways"[17]. This law profoundly altered regulators' capacity to monitor SO_2 pollution, working both to suppress tampering with SO_2 data collection at the political level, as well as to install appropriate monitoring equipment to enable frequent statistical inspections[18]. In 2013, China released the "Action Plan on the Prevention and Control of Air Pollution"[19]. This plan is regarded as perhaps the country's most influential environmental policy in recent years, helping China attain significant improvements in air quality by setting PM2.5 targets for key regions. PM2.5 refers to atmospheric particulate matter with a diameter of less than 2.5 micrometers, harmful to human health in high levels. In order to attain these ambitious targets, a nationwide cap on coal use, divided among provinces, was imposed. The plan also banned new coal-burning capacities and speeded up the use of filters and scrubbers. These measures were considered harsh, yet effective, distinguishing the plan from others with its imposition of an outright ban on polluting activities as opposed to a provision of incentives to clean up production.

Though new targets to decrease emissions are frequently released, proper enforcement is also required to ensure that such standards are truly being met consistently. Key to this enforcement is the Continuous Emissions

---

17 *Notice of the State Council on Approving and Forwarding the Implementation Plan and Measures for the Statistical Monitoring and Evaluation on Energy Saving and Emissions Reduction* (《國務院批轉節能減排統計監測及考核實施方案和辦法的通知》), 17 November 2007.

18 Source: Thomas Stoerk. "Effectiveness and cost of air pollution control in China", Grantham Research Institute on Climate Change and the Environment of the London School of Economics and Political Science, Working Paper No. 273, November 2018.

19 Source: "China: Action Plan on the Prevention and Control of Air Pollution (2013)" (〈中國：大氣污染防治行動計劃 (2013)〉), published on the website of the Air Quality Life Index (AQLI).

Monitoring System (CEMS) spot checking, which keep factories accountable to adhering by these standards. Recent improvements in both technology and policy have made these checks a much more effective procedure, as inspections prior to these improvements were easy to evade: factories were generally aware of roughly when inspectors were coming, and if a factory had just undergone inspection, it was likely that they would not have to entertain another visit for a while (given that these assessments were known to be time consuming and costly). As such, the introduction of CEMS with telemetry — which initiated 24/7 monitoring — and proved to be an extremely effective tool in increasing the accountability of factories.

However, it is important to note that the development and installation of such technology alone is not enough — *proper pollution pricing* has also played a crucial role in Chinese air pollution mitigation efforts. When the CEMS was first put in use, the fines for violations were too low, and local governments remained under pressure from local industries to turn a blind eye to violators. However, as fines were eventually raised to levels which proved to be prohibitive, the sector began to witness meaningful reductions in air pollution.

The effectiveness of these pollution pricing mechanisms rests in the way in which the country's power sector operates. In China, the grid operator must pay the power plant two separate prices: a base price and a pollution subsidy price. Since all prices in the power market are controlled, the prices the grid receives are unrelated to its payments. Given this, the system is essentially self-reinforcing: by hooking the grid up to CEMS, any time the power plant stops running its pollution abating equipment, the grid can stop paying the power plant the subsidy. The power plant therefore has an incentive to obtain the abatement subsidy (by continuously running pollution abating equipment), and the grid has an incentive to continuously monitor the plant (as to not pay extra money in subsidies to power plants failing to adhere to the standards in place)[20].

---

20 Source: Ma, J., C. Krosinsky, D. Seligsohn and X. Wang. "When finance goes green: A Chinese solution to environmental changes", Watson Events webcast, Watson Institute for International and Public Affairs, Brown University, accessed on 19 April 2018.

Disclosure and transparency

Mandatory disclosure on topics of interest to investors that participate in green and sustainable finance will only increasingly be important, particularly on carbon emissions disclosure. Western corporations continue to innovate successfully on their own reporting across dimensions of capital including natural, employees, communities where they operate and financial capital as well and how these all intersect. It is also important to consider scopes of reporting and how this connects to concepts of carbon peaking and carbon neutrality. One clear path to carbon neutrality will be achieving an understanding of the carbon footprint of all businesses to see if they are in line with protocols. The GHG Protocol[21] has done a fantastic job outlining what are Scope 1 (direct emissions from operation), Scope 2 (externally purchased electricity, etc.) and Scope 3 (15 categories of indirect emissions, including upstream and downstream). Indirect or Scope 3 emissions are often the majority of a company's footprint, such as in the automobile manufacturing sector where use of cars and trucks make up 90% of the footprint of companies such as Ford or two thirds of consumer goods companies such as Unilever (see their sustainability reports). Scope 3 emissions also include investments. For example, the loan books of financial institutions on a global basis have not been transparent, but if they were, a simple brown/green loan ratio would be very useful to understand from a carbon neutrality perspective, and as loan books take a long time to change, understanding well in advance that such disclosure is coming would help ensure changes occurred that can ensure carbon neutrality. Financial institutions when considering the carbon emissions of their investments have a footprint that is very different than if they only consider their office buildings, travel and computers. Investors appreciate when companies are fully transparent, especially mature companies with long history of trading on exchanges. Especially as China looks to encourage the lessening of the effects of day-trading volatility, it will be useful for companies to fully report regularly on their green and sustainability performance in a way that satisfies due diligence requirements. This will allow for investor confidence to increase and encourage long-term buy-and-hold investors to come in with confidence, creating a useful pool of investors willing to stick out any inevitable market ups and downs, something which has long benefited western markets.

Stock exchanges such as those in Brazil and South Africa have created separate categories of listing for companies which have done a particularly good job on sustainability reporting but it is hard to see how this has benefited those countries' economies with a bit

---

21 See the *Greenhouse Gas Protocol* website (https://ghgprotocol.org/).

of time having passed. Rather, the opportunity is to require mandatory corporate reporting on green and sustainability dimensions which has been rumoured and would be another global leading achievement for any major stock exchange which takes this sort of step. Climate risk reporting is expected from the Securities and Exchange Commission (SEC) in the US and from the EU, but this is also likely to be insufficient as there are many other cross cutting issues, especially the opportunities for innovation and transition which are only likely to accelerate.

Mandatory information disclosure would be an advantage to the jurisdictions and exchanges who fully take on this opportunity going forward, especially as the climate transition will need to rapidly accelerate in the years to come. Exchanges who do not take these steps may well end up being less competitive in the not-too-distant future.

We do not want to be prescriptive on this, but one company as a potential model to consider is a company in France (referred to as Company A below). France requires its listed companies to fully report on its sustainability and financial dimensions in what is called a reference document. Accordingly, Company A detailed out all of its strategies, initiatives and financial results across its many luxury goods brands. It also reports on its Scope 3 emissions and natural capital to a detailed degree that few other public companies have ever achieved, and it has also made its methodology fully open via what is known as the Natural Capital Protocol, and has also created investment funds for nature-based solutions. Company A is partly closely held by a family, much as the Chinese government understandably plays a strategic role as an owner of significance in public companies headquartered in China. It has also worked with development banks to consider and improve the bearing of its suppliers such as those in Mongolia who make the raw materials for their goods, a parallel in China being how the country has worked hard and achieved poverty alleviation through specific, successful interventions.

Other important categories of policy

China has also helped lead the way on a variety of other policy categories which have enabled its competitiveness as a country allowing for its listed companies to become increasingly entrusted by investors. These include electric vehicle incentives, such as giving drivers the ability to drive every day in major cities in China if they have a green licence plate, incentivising buying of electric vehicles, something you do not see at all in the West. Major cities such as Shenzhen long ago converted to electric bus fleets, and such moves also provide guaranteed revenue to manufacturers. This also incentivises global manufacturers to switch gears, given companies such as General Motors sell a significant percentage of its products in regions with increasingly stringent requirements such as China, and also California. Whole of sector policy approaches to Chinese cities and major technologies have also been put forward by the likes of the World Economic Forum[22], which if implemented could well become quite effective. No other global country is as positioned to be effective in this regard as China with few obstacles to putting in such long range transformation plans in place which could benefit its competitiveness and its economy. Other large Western firms such as Boston Consulting Group (BCG) have made clear what China needs to achieve to successfully reach its carbon goals as a country across sectors which would result in significant economic advantages including increases to gross domestic product and not a financial burden as might otherwise be assumed[23]. Goldman Sachs in its January 2021 Carbonomics Briefing further estimated such systemic transformations that meet carbon neutrality goals would create 40 million net new jobs, further aiding local employment and well-being. While it might not seem as significant, mandatory recycling in cities such as Shanghai and Beijing has also become an important part of the overall landscape, creating early pathways to circularity, which will increasingly also need to have businesses to consider reusing rare earths and other metals in the creation of electric vehicles, cell phones and more. Societies which best modernise in this fashion further increase their competitiveness for attracting talent, ensuring further benefit for investors.

Training, culture development, assistance and advisory services

With China making admirable steps on green and sustainable finance policy, often demonstrating global leadership, another step that will be required is ensuring its financial institutions are also fully fit for purpose in these modern times. Business schools and universities in the West continue to this day to largely not focus on green and sustainable finance, other than niche offerings. There are few leading academic programmes preparing financial professionals for what is required in a world where green and sustainable finance needs to become fully embedded in daily practice. China's business schools were largely modelled off of Western examples, and so there is an opportunity here as well for China to show leadership and educate its own professionals on green and

---

22 See World Economic Forum White Paper, *Major Green Technologies and Implementation Mechanisms in Chinese Cities*, September 2020.

23 Source: "How China can achieve carbon neutrality by 2060", published on BCG's website, 14 December 2020.

sustainable finance but also the next generation of financial professionals and this could also become useful model for other Asian and global professionals as well. Corporations also would benefit from having senior executives, board members and decision makers fully versed and making decisions based on where this is all headed. Stock exchanges can help provide such training, as well as provide present day competitive intelligence and strategic assistance to its listed companies to help best position its listed issuers.

Challenges that remain

1. There remains a lack of professionals at investors and corporations trained to meet the explosive demand for sustainability reporting, business reorientation, and investor communications. The China Securities Regulatory Commission in early 2021 mandated public companies in China, for example, established modernised investor relations functions[24]. Stock exchanges can help ensure that such professionalism is established alongside providing related services to its listed companies and such companies could also be required to demonstrate their capacities as an important component of ongoing listing requirements. Government can also create policies to encourage investments in education in this regard as human capital is the foundation of a sustainable financial system.

2. There is also a lack of adequate green disclosure by corporations. Investors and lenders have a hard time evaluating the physical and transitional risks associated with their investments as well as whether they are investing in reliable opportunities. Policy can help address this including setting standards that take local realities into consideration, allowing for transitions to evolve from voluntary to mandatory disclosure in an expedited manner over a number of years at most as investor demands are only likely to accelerate.

3. When looking to require companies to disclose on its green and sustainable performance, it will also be important to recognise the weakness in many so-called ESG (environment, social, governance) ratings which in addition do not take local considerations into account, also do not adequately consider important intangible factors such as human or employee capital, community well-being, culture, the benefit of political support and related policy infrastructure — which would figure to advantage Chinese companies, something Western companies do not enjoy (i.e. knowing

---

24 Source: "China mulls strengthening regulations on investor-relations management", *Xinhua*, 5 February 2021.

what policies are to be put in place on climate), something ESG frameworks do not consider properly in our view.

4. A lack of sufficient data is often cited as one of the biggest challenges for investors. Governments are the only entities that can carry out large scale, meticulous data gathering and monitoring efforts. Building a trusted, verifiable and detailed data infrastructure for modelling, gathering, reporting and tracking GHG emissions and other key sustainability indicators would go a long way towards building trust and no country has taken this step, so it is an opportunity category and a likely issue of future competitiveness as well for the benefit of that country's financial system. Without sufficient sustainability data, corporations themselves also often do not have a clear view of their standing on sustainability or carbon neutrality transition curves. The more complete and accurate the data is the better decisions investors can make with confidence as countries such as China progress towards their carbon-specific goals.

5. There is also a lack of something like a Net Zero Credit Score (NZCS) system for corporates, governments and institutions to consider aligning with. Such an NZCS could incentivise all actors much as existing corporate credit rating systems do.

Conclusion — Implications for stock exchanges

Financial institutions such as stock exchanges stand to contribute and benefit from the global imperative to solve climate change, led by countries like China, creating significant opportunities for investors. With a large pool of wealth capital in China, it should not be any wonder that regardless of political rhetoric coming from the West, every financial institution of significance is full speed ahead in China, trying to position themselves to capitalise on what many have long anticipated would be the Asian Century, with China at its heart driving necessary environmental change. Listing requirements and transparency becomes an important driver for ensuring investor confidence. Transparency and reporting on strategy which can be used with confidence by investors, along with related taxonomies and regulation, helps ensure the necessary flow of capital to enable the green and sustainable transition. This will drive the societal success one hopes to see in this field of sustainable finance.

Remark: With great thanks to Dr. Ma Jun, Huang Zhong, Chloe Wang, Eleni Papapanou and Justin Kew for their thoughts and related contributions.

第14章

推動綠色及可持續金融發展的
政策與法規

Cary Steven KROSINSKY
耶魯大學 及 布朗大學 講師
Sustainable Finance Institute　聯合創始人

摘要

在過去的五年裏，中國已經成為全球綠色金融政策創新領域中名副其實的領導者。而這種領導力也將有助推動整個亞洲必不可少的氣候行動。的確，在亞洲實現氣候轉型非常具有挑戰性，但這種轉型將會為全世界創造重要的投資機會。

我們可以從中國等國家正在如火如荼地實踐和發展的綠色及可持續金融政策中學到很多有用的經驗。這些經驗也必將對實現 2030 年碳達峰、2060 年碳中和的目標提供寶貴的經驗。

我們在本章中將從五個方面闡述政策在促進綠色及可持續轉型方面的重要性，即：

1. 政策是推動轉型的關鍵因素；
2. 現行的特定綠色金融政策助力成功轉型；
3. 轉型過程中的挑戰；
4. 助力轉型的匯報和信息披露機制；
5. 證券交易所的政策與監管措施在支持綠色及可持續金融方面的作用。

前言

中國成功的綠色及可持續發展轉型對於幫助解決全球氣候變化問題至關重要，而政策將是推動變革的關鍵驅動力之一。事實上，也只有持續推動這樣的變革，才能真正實現人類長期倡導的生態文明。好消息是，中國擁有世界第二大資本池[1]。過去五年裏，中國已經成為值得稱道的全球綠色金融政策創新者和重要領導者。而這種領導力也將有助於推動整個亞洲必不可少但極具挑戰性的氣候行動。中國最近承諾到 2030 年實現碳達峰、2060 年實現碳中和；中國在金融領域也同樣雄心勃勃 —— 截至本文撰寫之時，中國仍在加大力度推動更多的偉大目標和行動，在全球廣受認可，也為全球戰略投資者創造了重要的投資機遇。

我們認為，綠色及可持續轉型的成功實現，必須依賴於充滿活力的經濟基礎；因此，我們認為中國的綠色轉型能否為投資者提供投資回報，是解決氣候變化問題的一個重要且必要的條件。實際上，只有與中國合作，亞洲和世界其他地區才能真正從中國的成功轉型中獲得有益的經驗。亞洲佔世界經濟的一半左右，可以說在全球氣候變化的戰鬥中，沒有比這個地區更重要的戰場了。

政策是推動轉型的關鍵因素

當然，如果認為政策不是必須的話，那事情就簡單多了 —— 例如，理想的自由市場模型，能綜合各種因素並實現自我調節，從而保持資本市場的健康發展。但我們知道事實並非如此。

2013 年的諾貝爾經濟學獎被同時授予尤金·法瑪（Eugene Fama）[2] 以表彰他的「有效市場假說」，以及耶魯大學的羅伯特·席勒（Robert Shiller）以表彰他的「動物精神」理論[3]。法瑪認為價格本身最終會反映出所有影響它的因素；而席勒則呼籲政府積極制定政策，以確保各項決策可充分計及預期中人們用以規避規則的行為。法瑪和席勒被授予諾貝爾獎，說明了尋找機會和漏洞是人類的天性，特別是當市場從舊常態過渡到新常態的過程中，人類的這種天性特徵表現得更加明顯。

1　資料來源：Credit Suisse Research Institute，《Global Wealth Databook 2019》。
2　參閱〈Prize in Economic Sciences 2013〉，Royal Swedish Academy of Sciences 於其《諾貝爾獎》網站上的新聞稿，2013年10月14日。
3　參閱 G. A. Akerlof 與 R. J. Shiller（2010年）《Animal Spirits: How Human Psychology Drives the Economy, and Why It Matters for Global Capitalism》，Princeton University Press出版。

自由市場機制不可避免地存在諸多擁有不同目標、利益和訴求的參與者。因此，在應付氣候變化須作轉型的背景下，政策監管是使市場仍然得以正常運作的必要一環。

包括上市企業和金融機構在內的廣大市場參與者和它們的員工都越來越關心污染等環境問題，以及社會健康等更廣泛的議題。然而，我們目前仍然沒有有效的手段來避免人類歷史上最嚴重的氣候災難的發生，我們仍然無法完全降低和消除污染對生活的影響，我們仍然無法解決生物多樣性問題並確保海洋生態健康等等。因此，為了到 2030 年基本實現聯合國可持續發展目標、優化金融和市場體系，合理制定並強制執行相關的監管政策是十分有必要的。

2015 年至 2016 年期間，我們在參與編寫聯合國環境規劃署（United Nations Environment Programme，簡稱 UNEP）的《可持續金融體系設計調查報告》[4] 中，實際上已經明確了金融體系中關於社會效用等問題的三大差距：(1) 效能差距；(2) 效率差距；(3) 抗逆力差距。金融系統的效率問題，在於金融服務行業的規模之大長期與實體經濟整體脫節 —— 目前實體經濟僅佔全球金融系統所反映的價值的一半 [5]；金融系統的抗逆力是指對金融系統或其中的一部分進行涉及綠色及可持續發展考慮的壓力測試後的抗逆能力，涉及金融系統的穩定性；而最大的問題其實是效能差距。

效能是指金融系統的綠色及可持續程度。目前這方面的差距巨大，例如經濟合作與發展組織（Organisation for Economic Co-operation and Development，簡稱 OECD）認為，這方面的缺口每年至少為 2.5 萬億美元 [6]。

專欄 1 概述了中國制定綠色金融政策的步驟和方法 [7]。

中國自上而下推動政策的能力已成為其明顯的全球競爭優勢之一。在美國、澳洲和其他歐洲國家，諸如可再生能源上網電價或建立碳定價的政策，可能在一屆政府制定出來以後，立即又被下一屆政府推翻。這種「搖擺效應」會削弱投資者和企業的信心，同時也阻礙了對創新和研發的投入 —— 近年來美國的創新和研發優勢已經減弱，使中國等致力於創新的國家在未來具有明顯優勢。中國企業在碳中和方面獲得政府非常明確的信號，同時還有本章提到的其他政策和激勵措施的支持，鼓勵他們在這個領域進行大膽創新和多面發展。這就不得不使投資者充分考慮這一切的戰略價值和投資意義。試想一下，如果美國和中國在氣

4　參閱〈Final UNEP Inquiry Report reviews prospects for global sustainable financial system〉，載於《IISD SDG Knowledge Hub》網站上的《新聞》（*NEWS*）網頁，2018年4月24日。

5　參閱 Cary Krosinsky (2015年)〈The value of everything〉，UNEP 查考性工作報告，2015年12月。

6　資料來源：Jean-Philippe de Schrevel〈How blended finance can plug the SDG financing gap〉，載於《OECD Development Matters》網站，2020年1月22日。

7　摘自：Cary Krosinsky《Modern China, Financial Cooperation for Solving Sustainability Challenges》一書中馬駿博士的介紹編，Palgrave Macmillan出版，2020年。

專欄 1：中國制定綠色金融政策的五個步驟

首先，通過建立政治共識來啟動綠色金融議程，而不僅僅是停留在技術辯論階段。 中國通過最高層的政治推動來支持綠色金融。中國的最高決策機構，包括中共中央和國務院，早在 2015 年就批准了發展綠色金融體系的 14 項行動路線圖。中國國家主席和總理的政治支持在制定政策、調動資源和促進部門間對綠色金融的協調方面具有巨大的影響力。

第二，中國設計綠色金融體系的方法是自上而下的，而不是純粹由市場主導。 綠色金融的成功發展需要包括綠色分類標準和綠色活動的定義、企業和金融機構的環境資訊披露、綠色金融產品的規則和標準，以及對企業和金融機構的激勵。在像中國這樣的發展中國家，此類安排的有效推展需要政府和監管機構採取強而有力的措施，以發揮它們強大的執行能力。

第三，中國強調關鍵部門之間的協調、分工和實施時間表。 中國在政策設計階段就認識到，綠色金融不僅是央行或金融監管部門的責任，而且還需要其他許多機構和監管部門的政策和資源支持，包括財政支持、環境法規和產業政策等。七部委為此還在 2016 年聯合制定了《綠色金融指南》。

第四，中國強調發揮國家和地方綠色金融委員會等組織的作用。 2015 年，中國人民銀行推動成立了中國金融學會綠色金融專業委員會。由 240 家金融機構、環境相關企業和研究機構組成的綠色金融專業委員會迅速成為綠色金融知識的主要傳播者、綠色金融產品創新的組織者、政策建議的主要來源，以及能力建設和國際合作的協調者。在地方層面上，大約有 20 個區域性的金融專業委員會在促進綠色金融市場發展方面發揮着類似的作用。

第五，中國鼓勵綠色金融的區域性創新。 由於中國的經濟具有巨大的地區性差異，因此必須鼓勵地方在各自的方法上進行創新。2017 年 6 月，國務院批准了五省八市的綠色金融改革與創新試點方案，在過去的幾年中見證了許多有價值的經驗和創新。中國人民銀行組織這些試點城市的年度會議，總結最佳實踐方法，在全國範圍內推廣。

候變化方面進行全面合作，會有甚麼樣的願景？那將成為解決氣候變化一股不可阻擋的力量，而且也將使金融市場從這股信心和合作中受益。而現狀是：這方面的進展卻充滿了猶豫和懷疑。

美國總統拜登在 2021 年 4 月 28 日的國會聯席會議的講話中承認，民主國家在達成必要的共識方面面臨挑戰，而只有達成共識才能轉化為政策上的一致性[8]。即使達成了政策上的共識，也還需要監測政策的效果，並持續改善政策，這包括通過合作和談判在全球政策上逐步取得一致。同樣，政策與目標一致的國家和組織具有明顯的優勢。美國和中國這兩個世界上最大的經濟體和資本市場之間的對話合作，必將有助解決氣候變化問題。

解決氣候變化問題不應該是一場辯論。因為這場辯論本就不該存在。

綠色金融政策助力成功轉型

中國在包括綠色債券發行和相關激勵措施、銀行綠色金融激勵措施、綠色金融業務佔比要求、污染定價機制、強制回收、電動汽車補貼，以及強制性企業資訊披露和各項標準（包括綠色金融分類標準）等多方面都是全球領先者或積極推進者。

如前所述，綠色及可持續金融政策將會繼續演變，因此當你閱讀本章時，鑒於解決氣候變化和政府碳中和目標的緊迫性，決策者可能已經在考慮，甚至出台了更多的相關政策。下面我們列舉一些有效的綠色金融政策的案例。

對銀行的綠色金融業務的比例要求、綠色債券和綠色信貸激勵措施

中國推出了一系列有關綠色及可持續金融的政策舉措，有一項可能在其他任何地區都沒有見過。這項是《銀行業金融機構綠色金融評價方案》[9]，當中明確指出，所有銀行都要遵守綠色金融的質量和數量標準，並實現綠色金融業務達 25% 的最低佔比。全球的銀行、企業和其他金融機構都紛紛承諾到 2050 年實現「淨零」（碳排放），或以其他方式加入各種「碳中和」組織或倡議 —— 如「爭分奪秒」（Race to Zero）、「淨零資產管理者聯盟」（Net Zero

---

8　資料來源：〈Remarks by President Biden in address to a joint session of Congress〉，載於白宮網站上的《簡報室》（*Briefing Room*）網頁，2021年4月28日。

9　《關於印發〈銀行業存款類金融機構綠色金融業績評價方案〉的通知（徵求意見稿）》，中國人民銀行發佈，2020年7月21日。

612

Asset Managers）等，但並非每家金融機構、企業或組織有具體的路線圖和明確的短期目標。樂見的是：摩根士丹利是率先簽署「碳會計金融合作夥伴關係」（Partnership for Carbon Accounting Financials，簡稱 PCAF）[10] 的全球主要銀行，PCAF 簽署方現控制着 38 萬億美元資產；荷蘭的銀行如 ASN，也在積極倡導所謂的「2030 年氣候積極性」（Climate Positive by 2030）[11]。使金融機構過去、現在和將來發行的金融產品逐步與企業實現可持續轉型的目標相一致，是金融機構自身實現轉型的關鍵。「一帶一路」的成功與否，也與項目的綠色投融資活動有密切關係。與此目標相符的企業可以獲得較低的融資成本，並擁有一批渴望推動其自身轉型的金融機構的支持。投資者可以密切關注在中國交易所上市的此類公司。中國的綠色債券是需要關注的另一個重要領域。債券的利率可以根據對具體發行項目的分析進行調整，即通過財務誘因來鼓勵綠色項目的發展，或減少對「棕色」項目的貸款。最近，綠色信貸激勵措施還被應用到中國的汽車貸款領域，幫助加速新能源汽車產業的發展 [12]。

中國人民銀行採取的激勵措施包括向滿足綠色金融要求的銀行提供更低的利率，向能夠超額完成綠色金融指標的銀行提供獎勵等。據知，世界上沒有任何一個國家通過政策對其金融機構的綠色金融目標或綠色信貸比例設置過獎懲制度，也沒有通過監管政策來鼓勵這些機構支持綠色項目和綠色創新企業。從自上而下的角度來看，特別是在接近 2025 年至 2030 年時，相信中國會逐步加強實現碳達峰目標的力度，甚至會計劃如何提前實現這一目標。因此我們可以期待這方面的政策會出現更多的創新。最近，央行行長易綱也談到了政府計劃對中國的金融機構在綠色金融方面的願景和激勵 [13]。而西方的金融監管機構則並沒有此類激勵措施。問題是中國能否啟發其他國家進行仿效？

綠色金融激勵政策只是展現中國解決氣候變化問題的案例之一，全球投資者也應該鼓勵並積極參與這種轉變。只有這樣我們才能整體實現轉變。

碳定價與污染定價

碳排放價格（碳定價）的概念由來已久，但始終無法得到全面的實施並產生預期的效果。

碳定價的概念很明確：通過對二氧化碳等溫室氣體的排放制定一個適當的價格，足以限制排放所產生的污染，從而通過財務誘因來加速低碳轉型。然而這一概念面臨的挑戰是，碳定價需要在全球範圍內實施。如果某一個地區能繼續產生碳排放而無需為此付費，那麼這

10　參閱 PCAF 的網站（https://carbonaccountingfinancials.com/）。

11　資料來源：ASN 銀行的網站。

12　資料來源：〈China's green car credit scheme turns up heat on carbon-emitters〉，載於《路透社》，2021 年 4 月 18 日。

13　資料來源：〈China to require financial institutions to move towards green finance — central bank gov〉，載於《路透社》，2021 年 4 月 20 日。

個地區就會因成本較低而獲得更多業務優勢。因此，中國最初創建碳排放交易的計劃在過去幾年已經有所放緩，特別有見過去幾年裏全球經濟狀況的變化（包括新冠疫情的出現）。

進入 2021 年，中國重新建立排放權交易市場和相應的碳定價的意願已被重新點燃。2021 年 1 月 5 日，生態環境部披露了《碳排放權交易管理辦法（試行）》[14]。該辦法於 2021 年 2 月 1 日生效，並在 2021 年 7 月 16 日於內地正式啟動了全國性的碳交易市場。但由於前面提到的各種原因，在各國就碳定價達成共識之前，我們不應期待全球會普遍採用碳市場的機制。

很高興看到美國前國務卿約翰·克里（John Kerry）在 2021 年 4 月訪問上海時提到，拜登政府支持建設一個有效的全球碳價格的必要性[15]，但實現碳定價的挑戰之一恰恰是美國自身。雖然許多美國城市和州份都贊成對氣候變化採取行動，但沒有一個相應的司法權區真正設立了碳定價機制。

如果我們真的達成了一致的全球碳定價，那麼在 5-10 年內逐步的、可預測的碳價增長會對碳金融市場的發展十分有益，因為如此可將激勵企業和投資者的加入，增加碳市場的流動性，也給各方足夠的時間來調整。

同時，全國範圍內的數據基礎設施對於有關碳排放的數據建模、收集、報告，以及監測和跟蹤也同樣重要。如果沒有這些數據，那麼要知道甚麼該定價及如何定價等都將是挑戰。為企業與初創建立一個碳信用評分系統，使之與企業（或項目、政府和其他實體）的信用評級於融資時作一併考慮，亦會有所幫助。

通過碳定價的案例研究或許會給我們一些啟示。加拿大不列顛哥倫比亞省（British Columbia）已經實施了碳定價，但還沒有達到可以改變行為的程度。挑戰之一是如何建立一個長期穩定的碳交易市場。在政府可以通過換屆選舉投票被趕下台的體制下，財政理應取之於民用之於民。但即使如此，美國華盛頓等自由派當權的州份也未能讓選民通過碳市場立法。加拿大已經有設立全國性碳市場的目標，而選舉也受到了這個目標的影響：由少數派組成的執政聯盟不了解碳定價的計劃是不會對消費者產生負面影響，因此加拿大政府的碳市場執行力很可能會打折扣。澳洲實施了碳稅，但推動碳稅的政府卻被投票趕下了台。此後否認氣候變化的一派則持續掌權。在法國，也因增加汽油稅（含碳稅）等原因引發的「黃背心」運動至今未能徹底平息。正是由於這些原因，西方的政治家們對全面和立即實施碳定價猶豫不決。因此雖然歐洲的排放權交易機制（Emissions Trading System，簡稱 ETS）現在已經比較健全，但各國不太成功的實踐也為中國建立自己的碳市場機制形成了一定的障礙。

---

14 《碳排放權交易管理辦法（試行）》，生態環境部發佈，2020 年 12 月 31 日。
15 資料來源：〈Briefing with Special Presidential Envoy for Climate — John Kerry〉，載於美國國務院的網站上的《備註》（Remarks）網頁，2021 年 4 月 8 日。

專欄 2：中國的污染定價機制

在過去 15 年裏，中國的電力行業不斷提高排放限制和規定。2003 年實施的第一個重要標準是要求強制安裝二氧化硫洗滌裝置。2006 年，隨着國家「十一五規劃」的公佈，污染控制工作開始取得顯著進展，二氧化硫排放的硬性指標也隨之出台。2007 年，國務院發佈新法規 [16]，徹底改變了監管機構監測二氧化硫污染的能力，規定了對二氧化硫數據不得篡改，同時要求安裝監測設備，以便頻密進行統計核查 [17]。2013 年，中國發佈了可能是近年來中國最具影響力的環境政策 ──《大氣污染防治行動計劃》[18]，這項計劃通過為關鍵地區設定 PM2.5（指直徑小於 2.5 微米的大氣顆粒物，超過一定濃度對人體健康有害）目標，幫助顯著改善空氣質量。為了實現這些雄心勃勃的目標，中國在全國範圍內對煤炭的使用設定了上限，並具體落實到各個省份。該計劃還包括對新的燃煤機組增加了限制條件，促進過濾和洗滌裝置的使用等內容。這些措施嚴厲但有效 ── 與其他計劃不同，該計劃可以直接禁止污染活動，而非提供獎勵來增加淨化裝置。

雖然經常發佈新的減排目標，但目標也需要執法推行才能確保達到目標並持之以恆。執法的關鍵是通過連續排放監測系統（Continuous Emissions Monitoring System，簡稱 CEMS）進行抽查，迫使排放污染物的工廠能切實遵守這些標準。最近在技術和政策方面的改進使這些檢查變得更加有效。此前工廠很容易逃脱檢查，因為它們一般都知道檢查員大概甚麼時候到來：如果一家工廠剛剛接受了檢查，很可能在一段時間內不會再有人來檢查（耗時又耗錢）。而引入具有遠端功能的 CEMS，則可以每天 24 小時不間斷地對工廠進行連續監測，非常有效地作出問責。

然而需要注意的是，僅僅開發和安裝這種技術是不夠的 ── 適當的**污染定價**也在中國的空氣污染緩解工作中發揮了重要作用。在 CEMS 剛投入使用時，對違法行為的罰款太低，地方政府仍然受到當地經濟和產業發展的壓力，對違法者睜一隻眼閉一隻眼。然而，隨着罰款額最終提高到令人望而卻步的水平，才開始見到空氣污染正在改善。

16　《國務院批轉節能減排統計監測及考核實施方案和辦法的通知》，2007年11月17日。

17　資料來源：Thomas Stoerk〈Effectiveness and cost of air pollution control in China〉，Grantham Research Institute on Climate Change and the Environment of the London School of Economics and Political Science，工作報告第273號，2018年11月。

18　資料來源：〈中國：大氣污染防治行動計劃(2013)〉，載於Air Quality Life Index(AQLI)網站。

這些污染定價機制之所以有效，關鍵在於中國電力行業的運作方式。在中國，電網營運商必須向發電廠支付兩個獨立的價格：一個基本價格和一個污染補貼價格。由於電力市場的價格嚴格受控，因此上網電價與它的成本無直接關聯。鑒於此，該系統基本上是自我強化的：通過將電網與 CEMS 掛鈎，任何時候發電廠停止運行其污染消除設備，電網就可以停止向發電廠支付補貼。因此，電廠有動力獲得減排補貼（通過持續運行污染減排設備），而電網有動力持續監測電廠（停止向未能遵守規定的電廠支付額外的補貼）[19]。

雖然碳定價機制面臨各種各樣的問題，但污染定價和相關政策機制已經存在了一段時間，這就使得轉型逐漸變得有可能成功。例如，中國一直在為內地各城市制定更嚴格的污染控制目標，而空氣污染是中國需要克服的一個重大環境挑戰，這就促使將基於化石燃料的電力系統轉型成為了當務之急，以避免與國家整體的經濟增長目標發生衝突。由於對發電企業的監管不斷加強，中國的空氣污染水平也因此得以持續下降。這些努力並沒有像控制碳排放那樣得到廣泛宣傳，但這個例子説明政府主導的相關政策帶來了直接、切實的成效。

專欄 2 概述了中國在污染定價機制方面的成功案例[20]。它説明了政策是如何假以時日幫助實現成功轉型。

信息披露與透明度

就碳排放等綠色及可持續金融市場投資者感興趣的內容進行強制披露顯得越來越重要。西方企業不斷地在其報告中創新地加入各項資本的匯報，包括自然資本、員工、經營所在地的社區狀況和財務資本等信息，以及這些要素之間的關聯性，而企業也同樣要考慮其報告的內容如何與碳達峰和碳中和相聯繫。實現碳中和的一個明確途徑是了解各個行業的企業所有的碳足跡，看它們是否符合要求。《溫室氣體核算體系》（Greenhouse Gas Protocol）[21] 已經做了很好的工作，概述了甚麼是《範圍 1》（營運中的直接排放）、《範圍 2》（外部購買的電力等）和《範圍 3》（15 類間接排放，包括產業鏈上、下游的排放）。間接

---

19 資料來源：J. Ma、C. Krosinsky、D. Seligsohn 與 X. Wang〈When finance goes green: A Chinese solution to environmental changes〉,《Watson Events》網播，Watson Institute for International and Public Affairs，Brown University，於 2018年4 月19日閲覽。

20 資料來源: E. Papapanou（2020 年）〈China as a leader in green finance〉，載於 Cary Krosinsky《Modern China Financial Cooperation for Solving Sustainability Challenges》書中的文章，Palgrave Macmillan出版。

21 參閲：《Greenhouse Gas Protocol》網站（https://ghgprotocol.org/）。

（或《範圍 3》）的排放通常佔一家公司最大部分的碳足跡 —— 例如在汽車製造業中，汽車和卡車的使用佔福特等公司碳足跡的 90%，而就聯合利華等消費品公司而言，《範圍 3》排放佔其整體碳足跡的三分之二（見該等公司的《可持續發展報告》）。《範圍 3》的排放還包括投資相關業務所產生的排放。例如，金融機構在全球範圍內的貸款賬目並不透明，但如果它們賬目透明，其所顯示的棕色 / 綠色貸款比例，從碳中和的角度來看將會非常有用。由於貸款組合一般需要很長的時間才會轉型，因此通過信息披露，將有助我們提前了解碳中和的目標何時能實現。若金融機構考慮其投資組合所產生的碳排放，比起只考慮其自身在辦公樓、差旅，和電腦使用等所產生的碳排放，會有完全不同的效果。投資者欣賞完全透明的公司，尤其是在交易所有着長期交易歷史的成熟企業。這對中國而言尤為重要，因其希望減少市場上「即日鮮」買賣引致的波動：公司若以滿足盡職調查要求的方式定期全面報告其綠色和可持續發展的表現，將對此有所幫助。這將使投資者信心增加，鼓勵採取長期「買入並持有」策略的投資者滿懷信心地入場，建立起一個有利的投資者羣體，願意忍受不可避免的市場起伏，這是長期以來一直有利於西方市場的投資行為。

巴西和南非的證券交易所已經為那些在可持續發展報告方面做得特別好的公司設立了單獨的上市類別，但現已過了一段時間，我們仍很難看到這對上述國家的經濟帶來甚麼好處。相反，現在的機會是要求企業在綠色及可持續發展方面進行強制披露。這方面的傳聞存在已久，對於任何採取此類措施的證券交易所來說，都將是一個引領全球的成就。美國證券交易委員會（Securities and Exchange Commission）和歐盟都可能會要求上市公司提供氣候風險報告，但這可能還是不夠的，因為還會有許多其他的交叉議題會出現，特別是逐漸加速的創新和轉型的機會。

對於充分把握這一機會的地區和交易所來說，強制信息披露將是一個優勢，特別是因為在未來幾年氣候轉型將會顯著加快。不採取這些措施的交易所很可能在不久的將來失去競爭力。

我們不想在這方面做任何預設，但有一家公司的做法值得我們參考，那就是法國的一家公司（以下稱「A 公司」）。法國要求上市公司在一名為「參考文件」中全面報告其可持續發展和財務方面的情況，A 公司在這方面詳細介紹了該公司的所有發展戰略、舉措及其眾多奢侈品品牌的相關財務表現。A 公司同時也報告了《範圍 3》的排放和自然資本，詳細程度可以說是其他上市公司所沒有的。它還通過《自然資本議定書》（Natural Capital Protocol）將其方法論完全公開，並且還為基於自然的解決方案設立了專門的投資基金。A 公司有一部分股份是由一個家族所持有，就像中國政府是很多上市公司的戰略股東一樣。A 公司還與多家開發銀行合作，例如為蒙古的原料供應商改善生產能力；而中國與之類似，努力地通過具體的、成功的干預措施來實現精準扶貧。

其他重要的政策類別

中國在其他一些政策領域也起到了帶頭作用，使其國家競爭力得以迅速提升，也使其上市公司越來越受到投資者的信任。這些政策包括新能源汽車激勵措施 —— 例如，如果司機擁有綠色車牌，就可以於主要城市不限日子行駛，以鼓勵用家購買電動車 —— 這種措施在西方是完全看不到的。深圳等主要城市早已更換使用全電動的公共交通車輛，這種舉措也為相關製造商提供了收入保障。鑒於通用汽車等公司有相當比例的產品在中國和加州等要求日益嚴格的地區進行銷售，這也同樣激勵並幫助了全球其他汽車製造商的轉型。世界經濟論壇等機構也提出了針對中國城市和主要技術的政策建議[22]，這些政策一旦實施，很可能會相當有效。全球沒有任何一個國家像中國這樣，在實施長期的轉型計劃方面幾乎沒有障礙，而這些計劃的施行對於其競爭力的提升和經濟的發展顯然是十分有利的。波士頓諮詢公司（Boston Consulting Group，簡稱 BCG）明確指出，中國為實現跨行業的碳目標所採取的措施將會帶來巨大的經濟優勢（例如國內生產總值的增長），而不是像通常認為的那樣帶來財政負擔[23]。高盛在其 2021 年 1 月的《碳經濟學簡報》（Carbonomics Briefing）中進一步估計，這種滿足碳中和目標的系統性轉變將會創造 4,000 萬個新增淨額的就業機會，從而促進當地就業和福利的改善。上海和北京等城市實施的強制垃圾回收，雖然看起來沒有那麼重要，也已成為整體解決方案的重要組成部分，創造了循環發展模式的早期路徑。此模式將迫使越來越多的企業在生產電動汽車、手機等產品時需要考慮回收使用電子垃圾裏的稀土和其他金屬。以這種方式實現社會發展，會進一步提高其吸引人才的競爭力，確保投資者也受益。

培訓、文化發展、援助和諮詢服務

隨着中國在綠色及可持續金融政策方面邁出令人欽佩的步伐，並展現出全球領導力，另一個需要採取的步驟是確保其金融機構也完全適合這個時代的需要。西方的商學院和大學至今仍不是非常重視綠色及可持續金融，只是提供了有限的小眾課程產品。只有少部分領先的學術課程可以培養專業金融人士，為綠色及可持續金融扎根於日常實踐中作準備。中國的商學院在很大程度上是以西方為藍本的，因此，中國在這方面也有機會表現出領導力，對專業人員進行綠色及可持續金融的培訓，同時也開始對下一代的金融人才進行基礎教育。這也可以反過來對亞洲和其他地區的專業人員提供模範。企業也將受益於高級管理人員、董事會成員和決策者對於可持續金融的充分了解，並根據這一領域的發展方向作出正確決策。證券交易所可以幫助提供這種培訓，並為其上市公司提供最新情報和戰略支援，幫助發行人尋找最佳定位。

22　參閱世界經濟論壇白皮書《Major Green Technologies and Implementation Mechanisms in Chinese Cities》，2020年9月。
23　資料來源：〈How China can achieve carbon neutrality by 2060〉，載於BCG的網站，2020年12月14日。

存在的挑戰

1.　投資者和企業仍然缺少受過培訓的專業人員，以滿足對可持續發展報告、業務調整和投資者溝通等方面的爆炸式需求。例如，中國證券監督管理委員會在 2021 年初要求中國的上市公司建立現代化的投資者關係機制 [24]。證券交易所在提供相關服務的同時可以幫助上市公司建立這種專業團隊，而且還可以明確要求上市公司具備這方面的能力，作為維持上市企業身份的一個持續性要求。人才是可持續金融體系的基礎，因此政府也可以制定政策，鼓勵在這方面的教育和培訓投入。

2.　上市公司缺乏足夠的綠色信息披露。投資者和貸款人很難評估與他們投資相關的物理風險和過渡性風險，以及與之相關的投資安全性信息。而政策可以幫助部分解決這個問題，比如在制定標準時考慮到當地實際情況，容許在若干年內從自願性披露快速發展到強制性的可持續相關信息披露，以滿足投資者日益增強的需要。

3.　在要求公司披露其綠色及可持續表現時，我們也應認識到，許多所謂的 ESG（即 Environment — 環境、Social — 社會和 Governance — 治理）評級是有弱點的。這些評級除了沒有考慮到本地因素外，也沒有充分考慮對業務有實質性影響的無形要素，如人力或員工資本、社區福祉、文化、政治支持和政策基礎設施等。這些都是中國公司的有利因素，也是西方公司所不具備的（即知道要針對氣候制定哪些政策）。我們認為目前西方主流的 ESG 框架並沒有充分考慮無形要素。

4.　投資者的最大挑戰之一常常是缺乏足夠的數據。唯一能夠進行大規模、細緻的數據收集和監測工作的是當地政府。為建模、收集、報告和跟蹤溫室氣體排放及其他關鍵的可持續發展指標建立一個可信賴、可查核和詳細的數據基礎設施，需要一段時間才能得到投資者的信任。目前還沒有一個國家採取這個行動，所以這也可能是體現未來國家金融體系競爭力的一個機會。如果沒有足夠的可持續發展數據，企業也就往往對自身在可持續發展或碳中和過渡路徑上的位置沒有清晰的認識。數據越完整、越準確，投資者就越能在中國等國家向其特定的碳目標邁進的過程中更加自信地作出投資決定。

5.　目前還缺乏類似「碳中和信用評分」（Net Zero Credit Score）這樣的系統，供企業、政府和投資機構參考。這樣的系統可以像現有的企業信用評級系統一樣，對各參與方都可起到激勵作用。

24　資料來源：〈China mulls strengthening regulations on investor-relations management〉，載於《新華網》，2021年2月5日。

結語 —— 對證券交易所的意義

證券交易所等金融機構須為解決氣候變化這全球的迫切問題作出貢獻,而亦會從中受益。由中國這樣的國家牽頭,可以為投資者創造大量機會。由於中國有大量的資金,不管西方國家的政治言論如何,每一個重要的金融機構都在中國全速推進,試圖在許多人早已預料會到來的「亞洲世紀」當中確立自己的位置來獲益,因為這「亞洲世紀」正是以中國為核心推動着必要的變革。上市要求和透明度成為確保投資者信心的重要元素。企業戰略的透明度和匯報機制有助提高投資者的信心,配以相關的分類標準和法規,可以促使資本的有序流動來實現綠色及可持續轉型,這最終也將促使每個人都樂見可持續金融能達致的社會層面上的成功轉型。

附言:感謝馬駿博士、黃忠、汪雨晴、Eleni Papapanou 和 Justin Kew 為本文作出的貢獻。

註:本文原稿是英文,另以中文譯本出版。如本文的中文本的字義或詞義與英文本有所出入,概以英文本為準。

Chapter 15

Returns and sustainability: ESG equity indices for global, regional and home markets

Chief China Economist's Office
Hong Kong Exchanges and Clearing Limited

Summary

"ESG" stands for "Environment", "Social" and "Governance". ESG investment refers to financial investment taking into consideration these three performance areas to support sustainable long-term economic and business developments. The transition into a greener and more sustainable economy would involve tens of trillion dollars and such ESG investments might be considered to be based on ethical standards rather than financial standards. There may therefore be concerns about a dilemma in pursuing financial returns and sustainable development. As a matter of fact, ESG investment has experienced strong growth, in particular ESG equity investment which has been supported by the development of ESG equity indices. ESG equity indices are performance benchmarks and have been widely used as the underlying assets of passive investment tools like exchange traded funds. Related risk management tools like index futures are also introduced.

ESG indices are usually constructed from parent indices with the incorporation of ESG investment styles. The risk-return performances of these indices may be different from those of their parent indices with traditional investment strategies. Would ESG indices offer investment opportunities as good as, if not better than, traditional indices?

An empirical study found that the investment return and return volatility, i.e. the risk-return performance, of ESG indices in many cases were found to be similar to that of their parent indices for different investment horizons and under different market conditions. Some ESG indices, mainly regional ESG indices, had shown better return and/or lower volatility than their parent indices at times. In other words, in many cases, ESG indices tended to have similar, if not better, risk-return performances than their parent indices.

The empirical findings imply that individual ESG indices may have their own specific characteristics contributing to their outperformance relative to their parent indices, which would not be common across the whole spectrum of ESG indices. As constituents of ESG indices are companies regarded to have better ESG performance, the potential outperformance of ESG indices relative to their parent indices may owe to the better corporate financial performance and/or the higher investor valuation of constituents with better ESG performance, or investors' preferences for specific ESG investment strategies. ESG indices of different ESG investment strategies in different markets would therefore offer alternative investment choices with potentially better returns to global investors.

By and large, supported by empirical findings, ESG investment does not necessarily sacrifice financial returns, and may even enjoy better returns, while pursuing ethical investment.

ESG investment: A dilemma in pursuing financial returns and sustainable development?

"ESG" stands for "Environment", "Social" and "Governance". ESG investment refers to financial investment taking into consideration these three performance areas to support sustainable long-term economic and business development.

ESG investment has been on the rise since United Nations (UN) member countries reached a consensus on the 2030 Agenda for Sustainable Development in 2015 and signed the Paris Agreement (within the United Nations Framework Convention on Climate Change (UNFCCC)) to address global climate change. It was estimated that the transition into a greener and more sustainable economy would require about US$80 trillion to US$90 trillion of infrastructure investments during 2015 to 2030[1]. ESG investment tends to be considered as a kind of ethical investment in a moral sense, which may be contradictory to the principle of the financial world in search of high investment returns. Is it really a dilemma in pursuing financial returns and sustainable development at the same time?

As a matter of fact, there are increasing market initiatives and participation that have supported the rapid growth of ESG investment in recent years. An increasing number of asset owners, investment managers and market intermediaries became the signatories of UN-Supported Principles for Responsible Investments (PRI) to demonstrate their commitments to integrate ESG factors into their investment policies. The PRI was launched in 2006 to promote responsible investment and the number of signatories rose from 1,013 institutions in 2014 to 3,509 institutions in 2020[2]. In terms of scale, the total assets under management (AUM) of global sustainable investments rose from US$18.3 trillion in 2014 to US$35.3 trillion in 2020. Europe and the US dominated the market in 2020 while the Asia-Pacific region has the highest 6-year growth rate in asset size (17.9 times). (See Figure 1.)

---

1   Source: "Delivering on sustainable infrastructure for better development and better climate", published on Brookings Institution's website, December 2016.
2   Source: "Signatory directory", webpage on the *PRI* website, viewed on 28 July 2021.

Figure 1. Total assets of global sustainable investments by region (2014 – 2020)

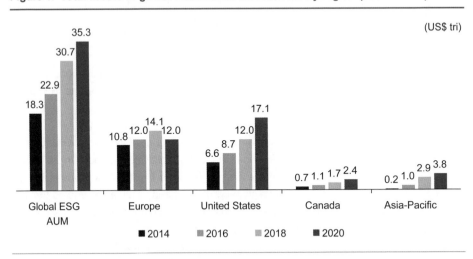

Source: "Global sustainable investment review", 2016, 2018 and 2020 issues, published on the website of Global Sustainable Investment Alliance.

The asset allocation of ESG investment are mostly in equities and bonds, which accounted for 51% and 36% respectively of total global sustainable investment assets as of end-2018[3]. The rest of 13% were allocated to other asset classes covering real estate/property, private equity/venture capital, hedge funds, cash/deposits, commodities and infrastructure.

The dominance of equities in ESG investments has been supported by the development of ESG equity indices. The first ESG index is MSCI KLD 400 Social Index launched in 1990, covering 400 stocks listed in the US[4]. To date, there are more than 1,000 ESG indices to meet investors' growing appetite for ESG investment[5]. ESG equity indices are used as benchmarks for ESG investment and as the underlying assets of passive ESG investment tools such as exchange traded funds (ETFs). The number of ESG ETFs globally rose from 46 in 2010 to 497 in 2020 and their total AUM rose from US$22 billion

---

3   Source: "Global sustainable investment review", 2018 issue, published on the website of Global Sustainable Investment Alliance.
4   It was previously called the Domini 400 Social Index. Source: "Fact sheet of MSCI KLD 400 Social Index (USD)", published on the website of MSCI, 30 June 2020.
5   Source: "An evolution in ESG indexing", published on Blackrock's iShares website, viewed on 1 September 2020.

in 2010 to US$187 billion in 2020 (see Figure 2). Another source reported that over 90% of ESG ETFs were equity ETFs as of end-June 2020 and these were dominated by those tracking ESG equity indices on blue-chip equities[6]. Besides, the rapid growth of ESG equity investment has increased the demand for ESG risk management tools. The first ESG equity index futures was launched for the benchmark equity index in Sweden in October 2018[7]. An increasing number of ESG equity index futures on blue-chip equity indices were subsequently launched. The total trading volumes of these futures rose from 1.45 million contracts in 2019 to 2.61 million contracts in 2020[8].

Figure 2. The number and AUM of ESG ETFs in the world (2010 – 2020)

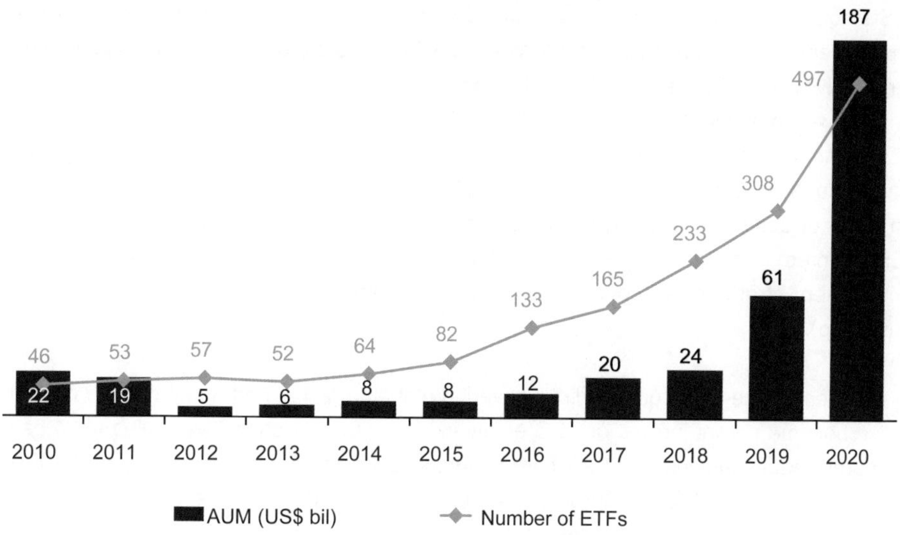

Source: "ETFGI reports assets invested in ESG (Environmental, Social, and Governance) ETFs and ETPs listed globally reach a new milestone of US$187 billion at end of 2020", published on ETFGI's website, 22 January 2021.

6   Source: "Passive sustainable funds: The global landscape 2020", published on Morningstar's website, 4 September 2020.
7   This was OMXS30 ESG Responsible Index (OMXS30ESG) futures. See "Nasdaq Launches ESG futures in the Nordics", news release on NASDAQ's website, 15 October 2018.
8   Source: Calculated based on daily trading volume of individual index futures from Bloomberg. The list of ESG equity index futures was consolidated from the information in news reports and Bloomberg as of 12 April 2021, and is not exhaustive.

ESG equity indices, particular blue-chip equity indices, are starting point for ESG investment. Compared to traditional benchmark indices, ESG equity indices adopt different investment strategies. Therefore, the risk-return patterns of these indices may be different from those of traditional investment strategies. An empirical study was conducted to examine if, and how, the risk-return patterns of ESG equity indices are different from those of the corresponding traditional indices.

The study on ESG equity index performance

ESG equity indices are usually constructed from parent equity indices to align with ESG investment styles. The investment styles of ESG indices are generally divided into "avoid" and "advance". For "avoid" style, the exposures to controversial sectors/companies that have significant negative impact on ESG performance are excluded (in line with sustainable investment strategies of negative screening or norms-based screening). For "advance" style, capital will be allocated to exposures to specific business activities/sectors in hope of achieving desired ESG outcomes (ESG achievement can be measured by ESG scores) and expected positive ESG impacts of investments (in line with sustainable investment strategies of positive screening, sustainability themed investing or impact investing).

A number of blue-chip equity indices covering global, regional and home country markets have become parent indices of ESG equity indices. Table 1 shows examples of 24 pairs of parent equity indices and their corresponding ESG equity indices. Some of the ESG indices have related futures products traded on exchanges. These ESG-parent index pairs are the subjects of the current study.

Table 1. List of selected ESG equity indices and their parent indices

Parent equity indices	ESG equity indices	ESG index short name (used in this chapter)
Global		
MSCI World Index	MSCI World ESG Leaders Index*	MSCI World L
	MSCI World ESG Screened Index*	MSCI World S
FTSE Developed Index	FTSE Developed ESG Low Carbon Emission Select Index	FTSE Dvp
S&P Global LargeMidCap Index	S&P Global LargeMidCap ESG Index	S&P Global
Regional		
MSCI EM Index	MSCI EM ESG Leaders Index*	MSCI EM L
	MSCI EM ESG Screened Index*	MSCI EM S
FTSE Emerging Index	FTSE Emerging ESG Low Carbon Emission Select Index	FTSE EM
S&P Emerging LargeMidCap Index	S&P Emerging LargeMidCap ESG Index	S&P EM
MSCI Europe Index	MSCI Europe ESG Leaders Index*	MSCI Eur L
	MSCI Europe ESG Screened Index	MSCI Eur S
Stoxx Europe 600 Index	Stoxx Europe 600 ESG-X Index*	Stoxx Eur 600
Stoxx Europe Select Dividend 30 Index	Stoxx Europe ESG Leaders Select 30 Index*	Stoxx Eur S
MSCI EAFE Index	MSCI EAFE ESG Leaders Index*	MSCI EAFE L
	MSCI EAFE ESG Screened Index*	MSCI EAFE S
Home country		
MSCI USA	MSCI USA ESG Leaders Index*	MSCI USA L
	MSCI USA ESG Screened Index*	MSCI USA S
Stoxx USA 500 Index	Stoxx USA 500 ESG-X Index*	Stoxx USA 500
S&P 500	S&P 500 ESG Index*	S&P 500 ESG
FTSE 100 Index	FTSE UK 100 ESG Select Index	FTSE UK 100
MSCI Japan Index	MSCI Japan ESG Leaders Index	MSCI Jpn L
	MSCI Japan ESG Screened Index*	MSCI Jpn S
CSI 300 Index	CSI 300 ESG Index	CSI 300
Hang Seng Index (HSI)	HSI ESG Index	HSI ESG
Hang Seng China Enterprises Index (HSCEI)	HSCEI ESG Index	HSCEI ESG

* ESG equity indices with index futures available for trading on exchange(s).

Source: Bloomberg.

These parent indices can be classified into the following categories:

- **Global market indices** — These are dominated by large-and-mid-cap companies listed on developed markets.

- **Regional market indices** — These include indices on emerging markets, Europe, Australasia, and the Far East (EAFE).

- **Home country market indices** — These include indices tracking the market performance of major financial centres, including the US, the UK, Japan, the Mainland and Hong Kong.

Risk-return performance of ESG equity indices versus their parent indices

Do ESG equity investments outperform traditional equity investments? An analogue is: do ESG equity indices outperform their respective parent equity indices? To answer this question, the return performance of ESG indices and parent indices listed in Table 1 (except CSI ESG 300 Index[9]) are compared. The study period covers 10 years spanning from 1 July 2010 to 30 June 2020. Due to different launch dates of the ESG indices, the actual study period for analysis varies across index pairs — only 12 out of 23 index pairs got observations throughout the entire 10 years' period.

The measures used for comparison are the daily returns and the standard deviation (SD) of daily returns (a measure of return volatility) of the indices. Statistical tests were conducted to test for the significance of differences in the returns and SDs of the ESG indices and their parent indices:

1. **_t_-test for difference in daily returns:** The daily returns were calculated for all available observations for each of the 23 ESG indices and their parent indices. _t_-test

---

9   As the study aims to examine the risk-return performance of ESG indices in a reasonably long investment horizon, indices included in the study shall have data of at least five years. The CSI ESG 300 Index, launched on 30 April 2020, is not included because it has data back to 30 June 2017 only. (See "Announcement on the launch of five indices including CSI ESG benchmark indices"〈關於發佈滬深 300 ESG 基準指數等五條指數的公告〉, published on the website of China Securities Index Company Limited, 8 April 2020).

was conducted to see if the daily returns of the ESG indices were higher than those of their parent indices.

2. **F-test for difference in volatility of daily returns:**   The SD of daily returns were calculated for each of the 23 ESG indices and their parent indices, for all ESG/ parent indices in each of the three index categories of "global", "regional" and "home country", and for all ESG/parent indices under study. F-tests were conducted to see if the SDs of the ESG indices were larger than those of their parent indices.

The above t-test and F-test were conducted to examine the risk and return performances of ESG indices relative to their parent indices for the entire study period, for different investment horizons, and under different market conditions. The analysis results of each of these are presented in the following sub-sections[10].

Index performance over the entire study period

Daily return

To perform t-test, the average of the daily returns of each of the ESG indices and their parent indices during the entire study period[11] were computed. Independent sample t-test was then performed on the difference in the average daily returns for (1) each ESG-parent index pair; (2) all ESG indices against all parent indices in each of the three index categories; and (3) all ESG indices against all parent indices under study. Figure 3 presents the average daily returns of the indices and the test results.

---

10 For detailed tabulations of the quantitative analysis results, please refer to appendices in the HKEX research paper, "Performance of ESG equity indices versus traditional equity indices", published on HKEX's website, 26 November 2020.

11 Noting that the study period with data of each ESG-parent index pair available for the analysis may be different.

Figure 3. Average daily returns of ESG indices and their parent indices

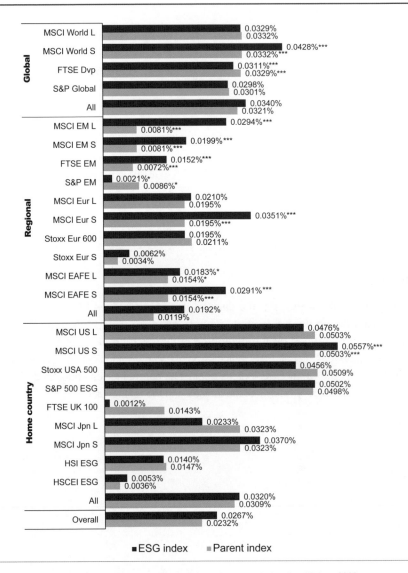

Note: Each ESG-parent index pair may have different length of study period ending 30 June 2020.

    *** Statistically significant difference at 0.1% level.

   ** Statistically significant difference at 1% level.

  * Statistically significant difference at 5% level.

Source: Computed from daily closings of indices obtained from Bloomberg.

The average daily returns of ESG indices were higher than those of their parent indices for 13 out of the 23 index pairs under study; of these, statistical significance in the difference were found for eight pairs (one global, six regional and one home country). Alongside, two index pairs (one global and one regional) were found to have the ESG index having a lower average daily return than its parent index, with statistically significant difference.

However, test for difference in the **average daily returns** of the ESG-parent index pairs may not be able to reflect the true return performance of an ESG index relative to its parent index on a daily basis, i.e. their relative return performance under the market conditions on the same day. To examine this, paired *t*-test was performed on the difference in returns on the same day for (1) each ESG-parent index pair; (2) all index pairs in each of the three index categories; and (3) all index pairs under study. Figure 4 presents the averages of these daily return differences and the test results.

Figure 4. Average of daily return differences between ESG indices and their parent indices

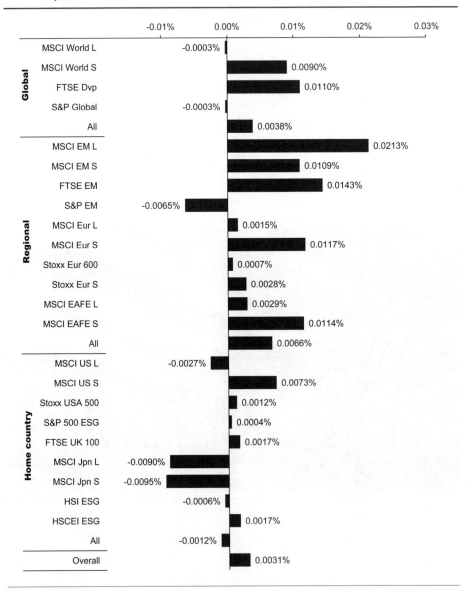

Note: Each ESG-parent index pair may have different length of study period ending 30 June 2020. None of the daily return differences was found to be statistically significant.

Source: Computed from daily closings of indices obtained from Bloomberg.

It was found that the differences between the returns of the ESG indices and their corresponding parent indices on the same day, whether for each index pair or for all ESG indices against all parent indices in each of the index categories or for all ESG indices against all parent indices under study, were not statistically significant.

Volatility of daily returns

To perform F-test on the volatility of daily returns, the SD of daily returns during the entire study period were computed (1) for each of the ESG indices and their parent indices[12]; (2) separately for all ESG indices and for all parent indices in each of the three index categories; and (3) separately for all ESG indices and for all parent indices under study. F-test was then performed to see if there was statistically significant difference between the SD of ESG and parent indices. Figure 5 presents the difference in the average of the SDs of daily returns of indices and the test results.

The overall SDs of daily returns of all ESG indices was lower than that of all parent indices during the entire study period and the difference (-0.0214%) was statistically significant. In respect of index category, the SDs of ESG index returns in each category were lower than those of the parent index returns in each of the three categories, albeit only the difference in SD for the regional category was found to be statistically significant. In respect of individual index pairs, the SDs of ESG indices were lower than those of their parent indices, with statistical significance, for 6 out of 23 index pairs (1 global index pair, 3 regional index pairs and 2 home country index pairs), but higher for 2 index pairs (2 regional index pairs), with statistical significance.

The above findings indicate that in many cases ESG indices tended to have similar, if not better, risk-return performances — higher return and/or lower risk (SDs of daily returns), compared to their parent indices.

---

12 Noting that the study period with data of each ESG-parent index pair available for the analysis may be different.

Figure 5. **Differences between the SDs of daily returns of ESG indices and their parent indices**

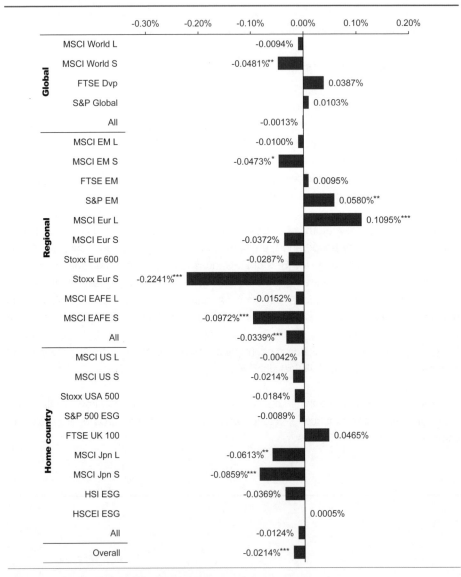

Note: Each ESG-parent index pair may have different length of study period ending 30 June 2020.
    *** Statistically significant difference at 0.1% level.
    ** Statistically significant difference at 1% level.
    * Statistically significant difference at 5% level.

Source: Computed from daily closings of indices obtained from Bloomberg.

Index performance over investment horizons up to 5 years

The risk-return performance of ESG indices compared to that of their parent indices may vary over different investment horizons. As all ESG indices under study have at least 5 years of available data, the risk-return performance for different investment horizons up to 5 years were analysed for the entire sample. The period returns[13] and SDs of daily returns of the indices were computed for the investment horizons of 3 months, 6 months, 1 year, 3 years and 5 years from the base date of 30 June 2015. The differences in the two measures of return and risk between ESG indices and their parent indices were examined by applying t-test and F-test respectively as in the sub-section above.

Period returns

More than half of the ESG indices outperformed their parent indices in terms of period returns for the different short- and medium-term investment horizons under study (3-month, 6-month, 1-year, 3-year and 5-year holding periods). However, when looking into the performance of individual indices in each index category, more than half of the home country ESG indices (5 out of 9) underperformed their parent indices in 6-month and 3-year holding periods. Nevertheless, it was found that the differences between the period returns of the ESG indices and their corresponding parent indices for all holding periods, whether across all index pairs in each of the index categories or across all index pairs under study, were not statistically significant[14].

Volatility of daily returns

More than half of the ESG indices were less volatile (had a lower SD of daily returns) than their parent indices for different short- and medium-term investment horizons under study (3-month, 6-month, 1-year and 5-year but not 3-year holding periods). In respect of each index category, more than half of the regional ESG indices had lower volatilities for all investment horizons and more than half of the global and home country ESG indices had lower volatilities for short-term investment horizons of 3 months, 6 months and 1 year. Nevertheless, the differences between the volatilities of the ESG indices and their corresponding parent indices for all holding periods, whether for each index pair or for

---

13 "Period return" is defined as the percentage change of the index closing at the end of the period of a given investment horizon relative to the index closing on the base date.

14 A limitation of t-test applied onto period returns is the small number of index pairs in the sample, which may contribute to a high standard error of the test. This limitation also applies to t-test results presented in the sub-sections below.

all ESG indices against all parent indices in each of the index categories or for all ESG indices against all parent indices under study, were not statistically significant except one regional index pair at 5-year holding period[15].

Figures 6 to 8 present the risk-return pattern of ESG indices versus their parent indices for the respective index categories of global, regional and home country for 1-year, 3-year and 5-year holding periods. As an investment doctrine, one would expect a higher return for a higher risk level. An ESG index is considered having a better risk-return performance vis-à-vis its parent index if it has a higher return at the same risk level or a lower risk at the same return level or a higher return and lower risk at the same time.

About half of the ESG indices under study, particularly regional index pairs, had better risk-return performance than their parent indices for 1-year and 5-year holding periods. In contrast, only a few ESG indices (less than three) had worse risk-return performance than their parent indices for each of the 1-year, 3-year and 5-year holding periods.[16]

---

15 This was Stoxx Europe ESG Leaders Select 30 index, which had a lower return volatility than its parent index (1.14% vs 1.29%), with statistical significance.

16 It has to be noted that such observations of better/worse performances of the ESG indices relative to their parent indices are not supported by statistical tests for significant difference, which have been conducted separately for period returns and SD of daily returns with results presented above. The same applies to the observations from scatterplots in the sub-section below.

Figure 6. Scatterplot risk-return profiles of ESG indices and parent indices
      —— **Global indices (base date: 30 Jun 2015)**

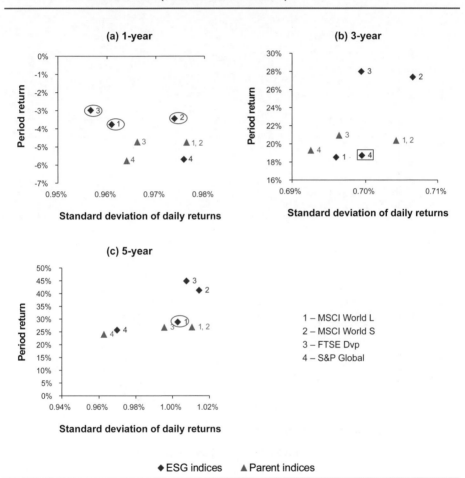

Note: An ESG index symbol in circle represents the ESG index appeared to have a better risk-return performance
than its parent index (higher return and/or lower risk) and an ESG index symbol in rectangle represents the
ESG index appeared to have a worse risk-return performance than its parent index (lower return and/or
higher risk). ESG index symbols not in circle or rectangle appeared to follow the normal high-risk-high-return
relationship with their parent indices (including those with return and risk very close to their parent indices).

Source: Calculation based on daily index closings from Bloomberg.

Figure 7. Scatterplot risk-return profiles of ESG indices and parent indices
—— Regional indices (base date: 30 Jun 2015)

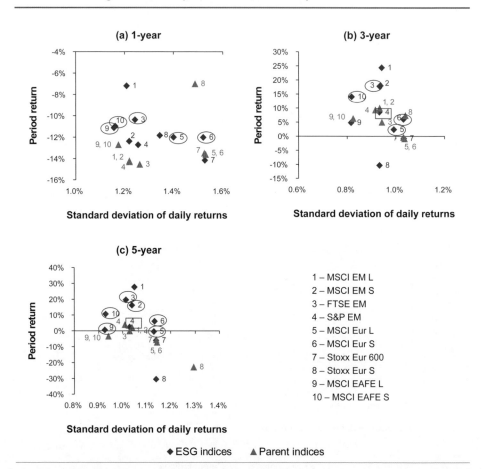

(a) 1-year

(b) 3-year

(c) 5-year

1 – MSCI EM L
2 – MSCI EM S
3 – FTSE EM
4 – S&P EM
5 – MSCI Eur L
6 – MSCI Eur S
7 – Stoxx Eur 600
8 – Stoxx Eur S
9 – MSCI EAFE L
10 – MSCI EAFE S

◆ ESG indices   ▲ Parent indices

Note: An ESG index symbol in circle represents the ESG index appeared to have a better risk-return performance than its parent index (higher return and/or lower risk) and an ESG index symbol in rectangle represents the ESG index appeared to have a worse risk-return performance than its parent index (lower return and/or higher risk). ESG index symbols not in circle or rectangle appeared to follow the normal high-risk-high-return relationship with their parent indices (including those with return and risk very close to their parent indices).

Source: Calculation based on daily index closings from Bloomberg.

**Figure 8. Scatterplot risk-return profiles of ESG indices and parent indices
——— Home country indices (base date: 30 Jun 2015)**

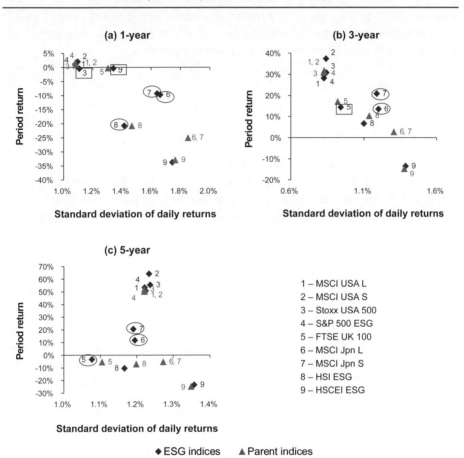

Note: An ESG index symbol in circle represents the ESG index appeared to have a better risk-return performance
than its parent index (higher return and/or lower risk) and an ESG index symbol in rectangle represents the
ESG index appeared to have a worse risk-return performance than its parent index (lower return and/or
higher risk). ESG index symbols not in circle or rectangle appeared to follow the normal high-risk-high-return
relationship with their parent indices (including those with return and risk very close to their parent indices).

Source: Calculation based on daily index closings from Bloomberg.

The above findings indicate that in many cases ESG indices tended to have similar, if not better, risk-return performances for different investment horizons up to 5 years — higher return and/or lower risk (SDs of daily returns), compared to their parent indices. Certain regional and home country ESG indices[17] were found to consistently outperform their parent indices (though not necessarily with statistical significance).

Index performance over investment horizons up to 10 years

Analyses on index performance over different investment horizons up to 10 years, were performed on 12 index pairs with data available throughout the 10-year period (2 global index pairs, 5 regional index pairs and 5 home country index pairs). The period returns and SDs of daily returns of the indices were computed for the investment horizons of 3 months, 6 month, 1 year, 3 years, 5 years, 7 years and 10 years from the base date of 30 June 2010. Similar analyses and statistical tests were performed as in the previous section.

Period returns

About half of the ESG indices outperformed their parent indices in terms of period returns for a number of short-, medium- and long-term investment horizons under study (3-month, 3-year and 10-year holding periods), but less than a half did so for other investment horizons (6-month, 1-year, 5-year and 7-year holding periods). In respect of index category, two global ESG indices underperformed their parent indices for all holding periods while about a half of the regional and home country ESG indices outperformed their parent indices for all holding periods. Nevertheless, it was found that the differences between the period returns of the ESG indices and their corresponding parent indices across all index pairs under study for all holding periods were not statistically significant.

Volatility of daily returns

More than half of the ESG indices were less volatile than their parent indices for different short-, medium- and long-term investment horizons under study (except for 3-month holding period). In respect of index category, all home country ESG indices had lower

---

17 These include FTSE Emerging ESG Low Carbon Emission Select Index, MSCI Europe ESG Leaders Index, MSCI Europe ESG Screened Index, MSCI EAFE ESG Screened Index, MSCI Japan ESG Leaders Index and MSCI Japan ESG Screened Index.

volatilities than their parent indices for medium-term investment horizons (3-year, 5-year and 7-year holding periods). Nevertheless, it was found that the differences between the volatilities of the ESG indices and parent indices in each index category and those between all ESG indices and all parent indices under study for all holding periods were not statistically significant. For individual index pairs, only three regional index pairs were found to have statistically significant difference in volatilities (two for 6-month, 1-year, 3-year, 5-year, 7-year and 10-year holding periods; one for 5-year and 7-year holding periods).

Figures 9 to 11 present the scatterplots of the risk-return patterns of ESG indices and their parent indices for 1-year, 5-year and 10-year holding periods. The risk-return performance of many ESG indices appeared to be similar to that of their parent indices for short-, medium- and long-term investment horizons. Less than half of ESG indices were better but even less were worse (others follow the normal high-risk-high-return pattern).

**Figure 9. Scatterplot risk-return profiles of ESG indices and parent indices
—— Global indices (base date: 30 Jun 2010)**

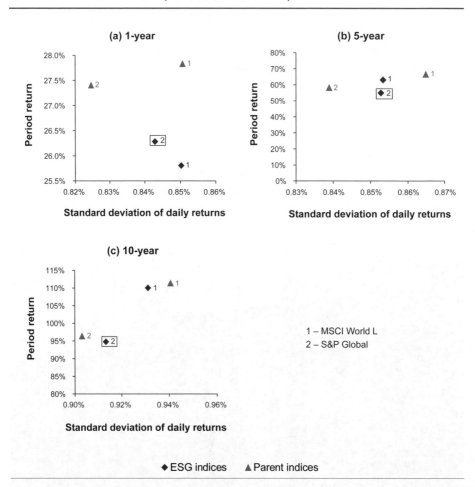

Note: An ESG index symbol in circle represents the ESG index appeared to have a better risk-return performance
than its parent index (higher return and/or lower risk) and an ESG index symbol in rectangle represents the
ESG index appeared to have a worse risk-return performance than its parent index (lower return and/or
higher risk). ESG index symbols not in circle or rectangle appeared to follow the normal high-risk-high-return
relationship with their parent indices (including those with return and risk very close to their parent indices).

Source: Calculation based on daily index closings from Bloomberg.

**Figure 10. Scatterplot risk-return profiles of ESG indices and parent indices
─── Regional indices (base date: 30 Jun 2010)**

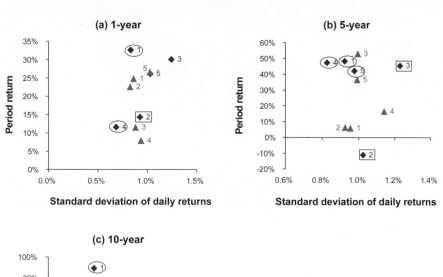

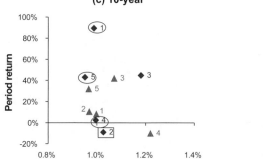

1 – MSCI EM L
2 – S&P EM
3 – MSCI Eur L
4 – MSCI Eur S
5 – MSCI EAFE L

◆ ESG indices   ▲ Parent indices

Note: An ESG index symbol in circle represents the ESG index appeared to have a better risk-return performance than its parent index (higher return and/or lower risk) and an ESG index symbol in rectangle represents the ESG index appeared to have a worse risk-return performance than its parent index (lower return and/or higher risk). ESG index symbols not in circle or rectangle appeared to follow the normal high-risk-high-return relationship with their parent indices (including those with return and risk very close to their parent indices).

Source: Calculation based on daily index closings from Bloomberg.

Figure 11. Scatterplot risk-return profiles of ESG indices and parent indices
—— Home country indices (base date: 30 Jun 2010)

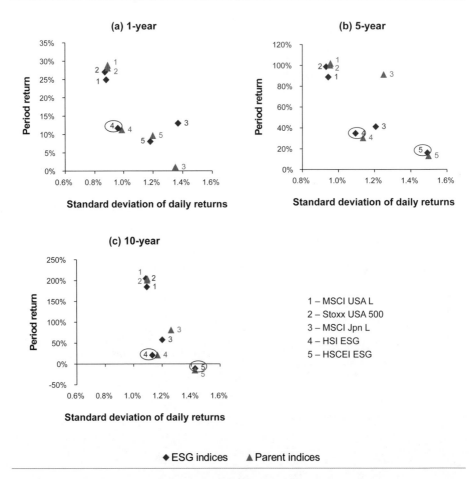

(a) 1-year

(b) 5-year

(c) 10-year

1 – MSCI USA L
2 – Stoxx USA 500
3 – MSCI Jpn L
4 – HSI ESG
5 – HSCEI ESG

◆ ESG indices ▲ Parent indices

Note: An ESG index symbol in circle represents the ESG index appeared to have a better risk-return performance than its parent index (higher return and/or lower risk) and an ESG index symbol in rectangle represents the ESG index appeared to have a worse risk-return performance than its parent index (lower return and/or higher risk). ESG index symbols not in circle or rectangle appeared to follow the normal high-risk-high-return relationship with their parent indices (including those with return and risk very close to their parent indices).

Source: Calculation based on daily index closings from Bloomberg.

The above findings indicate that in many cases ESG indices tended to have similar, if not better, risk-return performances for different investment horizons up to 10 years, compared to their parent indices. Nevertheless, certain regional and home country ESG indices[18] were found to consistently outperform their parent indices (though not necessarily with statistical significance).

Index performance in selected bull and bear markets

To examine the risk-return patterns of ESG indices versus their parent indices under different market conditions, three bull market periods and three bear market periods were identified judgementally based on the peaks and troughs of global indices between 16 October 2014 and 23 March 2020 for analysis (see Figure 12).

The three bull market periods are (period number in brackets for reference purpose):

- 16 October 2014 — 21 May 2015 (P1);

- 11 February 2016 — 26 January 2018 (P2); and

- 25 December 2018 — 12 February 2020 (P3).

The three bear market periods are:

- 21 May 2015 — 11 February 2016 (P4);

- 26 January 2018 — 25 December 2018 (P5); and

- 12 February 2020 to 23 March 2020 (P6).

The period returns and SDs of daily returns of the indices during the respective bull/bear periods were calculated. The differences in these two variables between ESG indices and their parent indices were analysed with the same statistical tests as in the above sub-sections.

---

18 These include MSCI Emerging ESG Leaders Index, Stoxx Europe ESG Leaders Select 30 Index and Hang Seng ESG Index.

Figure 12. The performance of major global equity indices (2014 – June 2020)

Note: P1 to P3 are bull market periods; P4 to P6 are bear market periods.

Source: Bloomberg.

Period returns

More than half of the ESG indices outperformed their parent indices in terms of period returns for the different bull and bear market periods and the proportion of ESG indices with outperformance was higher in the most recent bull/bear periods (18 out of 23 ESG indices in bull market period P3 and in bear market period P6). However, when looking into the performance of indices in each index category, half of the global ESG indices (2 out of 4) underperformed their parent indices in the bull market periods of P1 and P2 and more than half of the home country ESG indices (5 out of 9) underperformed their parent indices in the bull and bear market periods of P1, P4 and P5. Nevertheless, it was found that the differences between the period returns of the ESG indices and their corresponding parent indices for all the bull/bear market periods under study, whether across all index pairs in each of the index categories or across all index pairs under study, were not statistically significant.

Volatility of daily returns

More than half of the ESG indices were less volatile than their parent indices in the earlier bull market period of P1 and in all the bear market periods of P4, P5 and P6, but not for the more recent bull market periods of P2 and P3. However, when looking into the performance of indices in each index category, less than half of the global ESG indices (1 out of 4) had lower volatilities in the more recent bull market periods of P2 and P3 and the more recent bear market periods of P5 and P6; and less than half of the home country ESG indices had lower volatilities than their parent indices in the bull market periods of P1 and P2. Nevertheless, the differences between the volatilities of the ESG indices and their corresponding parent indices, whether for each index pair or for all ESG indices against all parent indices in each of the index categories or for all ESG indices against all parent indices under study, were not statistically significant for all bull/bear market periods.

Figures 13 to 15 present the scatterplots of risk-return patterns of ESG indices versus their parent indices in each bull/bear market period[19]. A number of ESG indices showed a risk-return performance dis-aligned with the high-risk-high return pattern relative to their parent indices in the bull and bear market periods — about a half of ESG indices were better than their parent indices in the bear market periods of P4 and P6 and only a few ESG indices were worse than their parent indices in the periods of P1, P2, P3 and P5.

---

19 In Figures 13 to 15, an ESG index symbol in circle represents the ESG index appeared to have a better risk-return performance than its parent index (higher return and/or lower risk) and an ESG index symbol in rectangle represents the ESG index appeared to have a worse risk-return performance than its parent index (lower return and/or higher risk). ESG index symbols not in circle or rectangle appeared to follow the normal high-risk-high-return relationship with their parent indices (including those with return and risk very close to their parent indices).

Figure 13. Scatterplot risk-return profiles of ESG indices and parent indices in bull/bear markets ⸺ Global indices

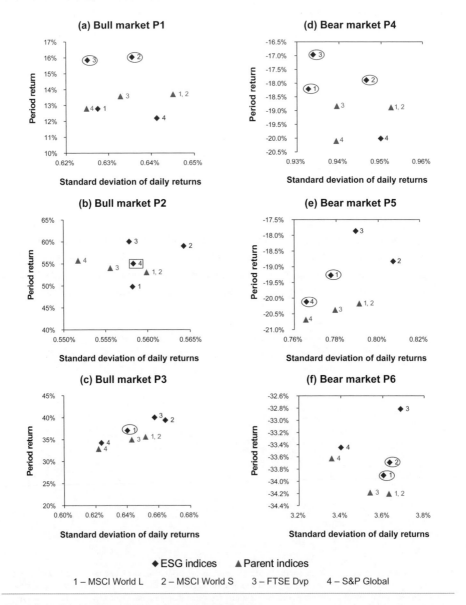

Source: Calculation based on daily index closings from Bloomberg.

Figure 14. Scatterplot risk-return profiles of ESG indices and parent indices in bull/bear markets ── Regional indices

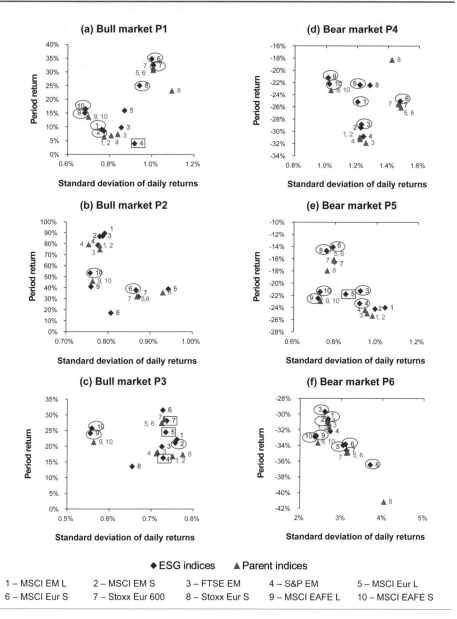

◆ ESG indices   ▲ Parent indices

1 – MSCI EM L	2 – MSCI EM S	3 – FTSE EM	4 – S&P EM	5 – MSCI Eur L
6 – MSCI Eur S	7 – Stoxx Eur 600	8 – Stoxx Eur S	9 – MSCI EAFE L	10 – MSCI EAFE S

Source: Calculation based on daily index closings from Bloomberg.

Figure 15. Scatterplot risk-return profiles of ESG indices and parent indices in bull/bear markets —— Home country indices

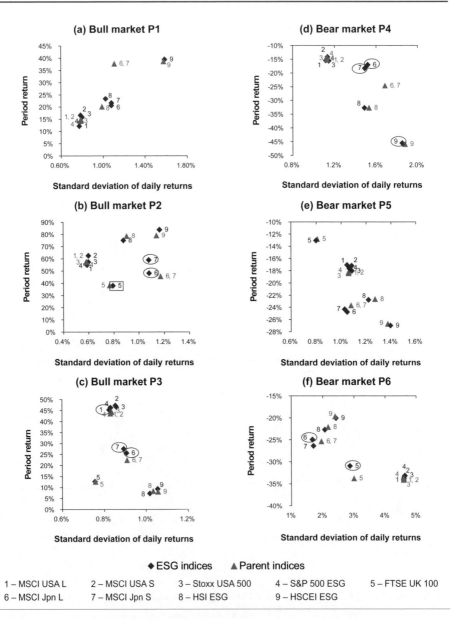

◆ ESG indices   ▲ Parent indices

1 – MSCI USA L	2 – MSCI USA S	3 – Stoxx USA 500	4 – S&P 500 ESG	5 – FTSE UK 100
6 – MSCI Jpn L	7 – MSCI Jpn S	8 – HSI ESG	9 – HSCEI ESG	

Source: Calculation based on daily index closings from Bloomberg.

The above results showed that in many cases the ESG indices under study tended to have similar, if not better, risk-return performances under different bull and bear market conditions, compared to their parent indices. One regional ESG index[20] was found to consistently outperform its parent index in the bull market and a few global and regional indices[21] did so in the bear market periods (though not necessarily with statistical significance).

Empirical findings in summary

Based on the above analysis results, the investment return and return volatility of ESG indices in many cases were found to be similar to that of their corresponding parent indices for different investment horizons and under different market conditions. Some ESG indices had shown better return and/or lower return volatility than their parent indices at times; these cases were often more in number than cases of ESG indices with worse return and/or higher return volatility than their parent indices at times[22].

A number of ESG indices, mainly regional indices, were found to outperform their parent indices in terms of risk-return pattern consistently across different investment horizons.

The empirical findings may imply that individual ESG indices may have their own specific characteristics contributing to their outperformance relative to their parent indices, which would not be common across the whole spectrum of ESG indices. These are discussed in the section below.

Factors contributing to the performance of ESG indices

There are a large number of empirical studies on the performance of ESG investment. In line with the findings of our study presented in the previous section, although there was no

---

20 This is MSCI EAFE ESG Screened Index.
21 These include MSCI World ESG Leaders index, FTSE Emerging ESG Low Carbon Emission Select Index, MSCI Europe ESG Screened Index, MSCI EAFE ESG Leaders Index and MSCI EAFE ESG Screened Index.
22 Note that the difference in performance between the ESG indices and their parent indices may or may not be statistically significant.

evidence to support the *consistent* outperformance of ESG investments across markets and study periods[23], individual ESG indices were found to outperform their parent indices at times. As constituents of ESG indices are companies recognised to be have better ESG performance, the outperformance of ESG indices could be attributable to a positive relationship between corporate financial performance and ESG ratings of the constituent companies, a higher investor valuation of companies with better ESG performance and investor preferences of different ESG investment strategies. These factors are discussed below.

Corporate financial performance

A study on the MSCI index[24] (referred to as "MSCI ESG Study") showed that the constituents of the MSCI World Index with the highest ESG ratings had better corporate financial performance during January 2007 to May 2017 through better cash flows generation and company-specific risk mitigation. The study argued that companies with better ESG ratings are usually more competitive than a comparable company in the same sector and can generate better financial returns, leading to higher business profitability and dividend payments. These companies are also better at managing company-specific risks and therefore have a lower probability of suffering from incidents that can impact their share prices. Consequently, their stock prices display lower company-specific tail risks.

The impact of ESG ratings may be different across different geographical markets. A research[25] reviewed 2,250 empirical studies on various markets between 1970 and 2014. From this review, the proportion of the number of empirical studies with findings supporting the positive relationship between corporate financial performance and ESG performance was the highest in emerging markets (65.4%) and the lowest in developed Europe (26.1%) (see Figure 16). In other words, corporate financial performance in emerging markets was likely to be better for companies with high ESG ratings. This could be a possible reason for better risk-return patterns of certain ESG indices on emerging markets. The research also found that the relationship between corporate financial performance and ESG performance was less ascertained in developed Asia, Australia and New Zealand. The research put forward a possible reason: the ESG reporting in Asia-Pacific markets was in the early stage of development during the study period of 1970 – 2014.

---

23 See Henriksson, R., J. Livnat, P. Pfeifer, M. Stumpp and G. Zeng, "ESG literature review", working paper published on the website of Quantitative Management Associates LLC (qma.com), June 2018.

24 Giese, G., L. Lee, D. Melas, Z. Nagy and L. Nishikawa. (2019) "Foundations of ESG investing: How ESG affects equity valuation, risk, and performance", *Journal of Portfolio Management*, Vol. 45, pp.69-83. The authors of the paper are all executives at MSCI, Inc.

25 Friede, G., M. Lewis, A. Bassen and T. Busch. (2015) "ESG and Financial Performance: Aggregated Evidence from More than 2000 Empirical Studies", *Journal of Sustainable Finance and Investment*, Vol. 5, pp.210-233.

Figure 16. Proportion of reviewed empirical studies finding positive and negative relationships between ESG performance and corporate financial performance

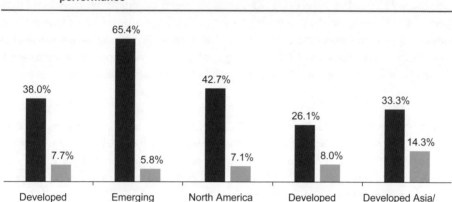

Note: The number of reviewed empirical studies was 2,250 which were conducted between 1970 and 2014.

Source: Friede, G., M. Lewis, A. Bassen and T. Busch. (2015) "ESG and Financial Performance: Aggregated Evidence from More than 2000 Empirical Studies", *Journal of Sustainable Finance and Investment,* Vol. 5, pp.210-233.

Investor valuation of ESG performance

The MSCI ESG Study found that the constituents with the highest ESG rating had a higher valuation in terms of price-to-earnings (PE) ratio and price-to-book (PB) ratio during January 2007 to May 2017. The study interpreted that the higher valuation of high ESG-rated companies can be attributable to their lower volatility of earnings and systematic risks, which could lead to a lower cost of capital and hence support the stock's valuation.

Empirical evidence showed that investments in high ESG-rated companies can generate an alpha return (additional return on top of the return on low ESG-rated companies) among companies with similar corporate financial performance. ESG performance is usually assessed by comparing companies' disclosure (within the same industry sector) in accordance with ESG reporting standards[26]. An empirical study[27] looked into the returns of 2,307 US companies during 1992 to 2002 and identified the "material" and "immaterial" sustainability issues in companies' ESG disclosure based on international ESG reporting standards. This study found that there was a significant alpha return for companies with better ESG performance in "material" issues. This study finding highlights the relationship between stock valuation and ESG reporting quality. However, there are a wide range of international standards on ESG reporting and the adoption of these standards varies significantly across markets and companies[28].

Besides, as investors value more about ESG performance, they would be more willing to pay higher prices on high ESG-rated companies than on low ESG-rated but similar companies. This behaviour would further support the valuation of high ESG-rated companies. However, investors' valuation of ESG performance was found to vary across region — a survey found that institutional investors in the US and Europe see ESG of a higher value than those in Asia, Canada and Hong Kong (see Figure 17).

---

26 In assessing the ESG rating of a company, the rater may evaluate the company's ESG performance against certain ESG reporting standards of their choice. These ESG reporting standards may be internally developed by the rater itself or with reference to those developed by international organisations such as Carbon Disclosure Project (CDP), Global Reporting Initiative (GRI), Sustainability Accounting Standards Board (SASB) or other market institutions. (See, for example, "Big four accounting firms reveal ESG reporting standards", published on the website of Business Green, 25 September 2020.)

27 Khan, M., G. Serafeim and A. Yoon. (2015) "Corporate sustainability: First evidence on materiality", *Harvard Business School Working Paper*, No. 15-073.

28 Zembrowski, P., M. Leung and K. Schacht, "ESG disclosure in Asia Pacific: A review of ESG disclosure regimes for listed companies in selected markets", published on the website of CFA Institute, 21 July 2019.

Figure 17. Proportion of institutional investors in different markets viewing environmental and social issues as "very important" (2019)

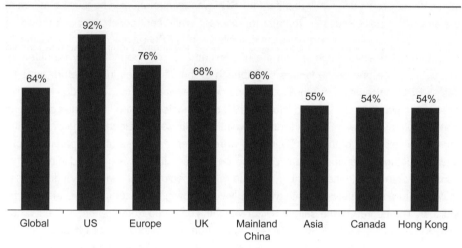

Source: "Sustainable Financing and Investing Survey 2019: Markets alert to the environment and society", published on the website of HSBC Group, 24 September 2019.

In addition to varying investor demand, there is an uncertainty about the persistency of investor demand for high ESG-rated companies. A study[29] argued that the outperformance of high ESG-rated stocks may decay or vanish over time as investors may not react positively to simple ESG information (e.g. ESG ratings) in the long run. Investors may rush to buy high ESG-rated stocks and sell low ESG-rated stocks in the short and medium term but this may reverse in the long term. In contrast, the MSCI ESG Study found that the impact of ESG ratings was lower than certain traditional factors (e.g. price momentum) but the impact could last for a longer period up to several years (compared to a few months in respect of momentum factor).

29 Hvidkjær, S., "ESG investing: A literature review", published on the website of Dansif (a forum to promote ESG investment in Denmark), September 2017.

Differences in ESG investment strategies

Investors may react differently to different ESG investment strategies because of different preferences in ESG issues[30]. To cater for different investment appetites, index providers adopt a wide range of methodologies to compile internal ESG ratings of index constituents such that the relative emphasis on the "E", "S" and "G" components may be different. These would be one of the factors contributing to the differences in risk-return patterns across ESG indices even for those on the same underlying market. Take the US market as an example. A study[31] looked into five ESG equity indices on the US market and found that the returns of these ESG indices were similar to those of their parent indices, but the short-term volatilities of these ESG indices were higher than those of their parent indices because of the differences in index construction. These differences occurred in respect of constituent stocks and their number, and the relative sector weightings. Such differences may lead to a shift of investment style (e.g. value, growth, size) compared to their parent indices. The degree of the shift in sector weights compared to the parent indices varied across ESG indices (see Figure 18) — ranging from -0.1% to 0.3% for MSCI USA ESG Leaders Index and from -3.7% to 5.8% for MSCI KLD 400 Social Index as of end-June 2020.

---

30 A survey found diverse views of consumers on climate change and consumption of tobacco and alcohol across different markets worldwide. See "Demystifying negative screens: The full implications of ESG exclusions", published on the website of Schroders, December 2017.

31 O'Brien, A., L. Liao and J. Campagna, "Responsible investing: Delivering competitive performance", published on the website of Nuveen, summer 2018.

Figure 18. Difference in sector weights for selected US ESG indices and their parent indices (June 2020)

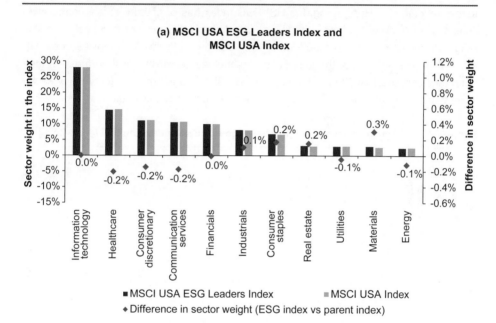

(a) MSCI USA ESG Leaders Index and MSCI USA Index

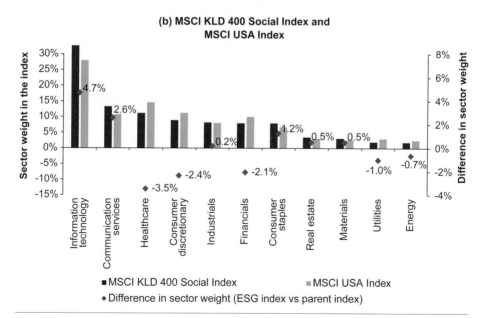

(b) MSCI KLD 400 Social Index and MSCI USA Index

Source: Fact sheets of MSCI USA ESG Leaders Index, MSCI KLD 400 Social Index, MSCI USA Index and MSCI USA IMI (June 2020).

The ESG assessment may also be different between index providers across markets. This might affect the shift of sector weights in ESG indices relative to their parent indices across markets. In Hong Kong, the HSI ESG Index has a different sector composition compared to its parent index — the Hang Seng Index (HSI). The shift of sector weights ranged from -4.6% to 6.0% (see Figure 19). Compared to the ESG indices in the US which have the weights of the information technology sector higher than those in their parent indices, the HSI ESG Index has the weight of the information technology sector lower than its parent index; vice versa is true for the sector weights of utilities.

Figure 19. Difference in sector weights between HSI ESG Index and HSI (June 2020)

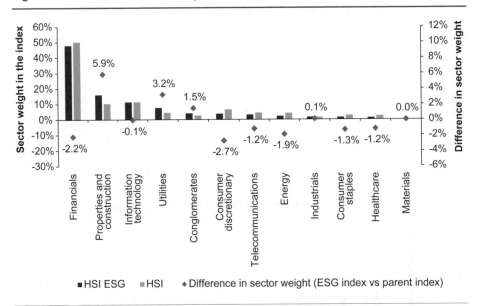

Source: Fact sheets of HSI ESG Index and HSI (June 2020).

Conclusion

ESG equity indices are performance benchmarks for ESG investments and have been widely used as the underlying assets of passive investment tools like ETFs, covering global, regional and home-country markets. Related risk management tools like ESG index futures are also introduced.

From the analysis results of 23 pairs of ESG equity indices and their parent indices covering global, regional and home country markets, the investment return and return volatility of ESG indices in many cases were found to be similar to those of their parent indices for different investment horizons and under different market conditions. Moreover, individual ESG indices were found to outperform their parent indices at times. Compared to their parent indices, the potentially better returns of ESG indices may owe to the better corporate financial performance and/or the higher investor valuation of constituents with better ESG performance, or investors' preferences for specific ESG investment strategies. ESG indices of different ESG investment strategies in different markets would therefore offer alternative investment choices with potentially better returns to global investors.

The empirical findings indicate that in many cases ESG indices tended to have similar, if not better, risk-return performances. This implies that investment through ESG indices does not necessarily sacrifice financial returns, and may even enjoy better returns, while pursuing ethical investment.

第15章

投資回報與可持續性：
全球、地區及本地市場
的ESG股票指數

香港交易所
首席中國經濟學家辦公室

摘要

「ESG」是「環境」、「社會」與「管治」的簡稱。ESG 投資是指着眼於這三方面表現而作出的金融投資,以支持長遠經濟及業務的可持續發展。向更綠色及更可持續的經濟轉型或需要數以十萬億元計的資金,而這些 ESG 投資或會循道德標準(而非財務標準)去考量,因此投資者可能會關注在追求財務回報與可持續發展之間出現的矛盾。事實上,ESG 投資增長強勁,特別在 ESG 股票指數發展的支持下,ESG 股票投資的增長勢頭尤甚。ESG 股票指數作為表現基準,已被廣泛用作交易所買賣基金等被動型投資工具的相關資產。另外,指數期貨等相關的風險管理工具亦相繼推出。

ESG 指數通常基於某隻母指數,再結合 ESG 投資風格編制而成。這些指數的風險回報表現或有別於其採用傳統投資策略的母指數。ESG 指數會否帶來媲美傳統指數(甚至更勝一籌)的投資機遇?

實證研究發現,許多時候 ESG 指數在不同長短的投資期和不同市況之下的投資回報率和回報率波幅(即風險回報表現)均與其母指數相若;而在一些情況下,有些 ESG 指數(主要是地區性的 ESG 指數)甚至比其母指數有較高的回報率及 / 或較低的波幅。換言之,許多時候 ESG 指數的風險回報表現就算不是比其母指數更勝一籌,也傾向不相伯仲。

這些實證意味着個別 ESG 指數可能是因自有的特色令其表現優於其母指數,而這些特色未必適用於所有 ESG 指數。由於 ESG 指數的成份股都是被認為是 ESG 表現良好的公司,這些指數的表現可以勝過其母指數的原因,也許是 ESG 表現較好的成份股都有較佳的企業財務表現及 / 或投資者對 ESG 表現較好的公司的評價更高,又或是投資者對特定的 ESG 投資策略有偏好。由此可見,ESG 指數在不同的市場中採用不同的 ESG 投資策略,可為全球投資者提供另類投資選擇,或可帶來更佳回報。

大致來說,從實證可見,ESG 投資在追求合乎道德投資的同時,不一定會犧牲財務回報,其回報更可能會比傳統的投資優勝。

ESG 投資：追求財務回報與可持續發展之間的矛盾？

「ESG」是「環境」、「社會」與「管治」的簡稱。ESG 投資是指着眼於這三方面表現而作出的金融投資，以支持長遠經濟及業務的可持續發展。

聯合國各成員國於 2015 年就《2030 可持續發展議程》達成共識，並簽訂《巴黎協定》（在《聯合國氣候變化框架公約》之下的協定），以期應對全球氣候變化的問題，ESG 投資自此崛起。預計 2015 年至 2030 年間向更綠色及可持續發展的經濟轉型將涉及基礎設施方面約 80 萬億至 90 萬億美元的投資 [1]。ESG 投資傾向被當成道德投資，因此可能與金融世界追求高投資回報的原則有衝突。到底同時追求財務回報和可持續發展是否真的存在矛盾？

事實上，近年市場推出多項相關舉措，以及日益增長的參與度，支持了 ESG 投資的急速發展。越來越多資產擁有人、投資管理人和市場中介機構已成為聯合國支持的《責任投資原則》的簽署成員，以證其致力將 ESG 元素融入投資政策之中。《責任投資原則》於 2006 年推出，旨在推動負責任投資。簽署成員的機構數目已由 2014 年的 1,013 家增至 2020 年的 3,509 家 [2]。全球可持續投資所涉及的資產總值亦由 2014 年的 18.3 萬億美元升至 2020 年的 35.3 萬億美元。在 2020 年，歐美主導這個市場，不過亞太區的資產規模的六年間增長率（17.9 倍）卻較其他市場為高。（見圖 1。）

1　資料來源：〈建設可持續基礎設施，以促進發展、改善氣候〉（"Delivering on sustainable infrastructure for better development and better climate"），載於Brookings Institution網站，2016年12月。

2　資料來源：〈簽署成員名冊〉（"Signatory directory"），載於《責任投資原則》網站，於2021年7月28日閱覽。

圖 1：全球可持續投資按地區劃分的資產管理規模（2014 年至 2020 年）

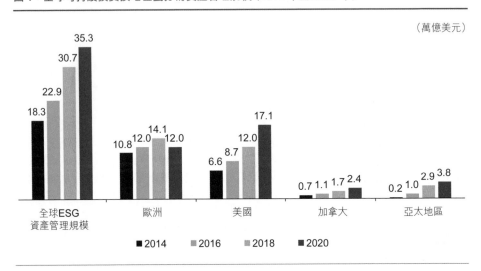

（萬億美元）

資料來源：〈全球可持續投資回顧〉（"Global sustainable investment review"），載於全球永續投資聯會的網站，2016 年、2018 年及 2020 年刊。

ESG 投資的資產配置大多集中於股本證券和債券，此兩類投資截至 2018 年年底分別佔全球可持續投資資產總額的 51% 及 36%[3]。總額其餘的 13% 所配置的其他資產類別包括房地產／物業、私募股權／創投基金、對沖基金、現金／存款、大宗商品及基建。

ESG 投資中以股票佔最大比重，主要是受到 ESG 股票指數發展的支持。首隻 ESG 指數是於 1990 年推出的 MSCI 凱特 400 社會指數，包含 400 隻美國上市的股票[4]。現時市場上可供投資者選擇的 ESG 指數已過千隻[5]。ESG 股票指數會用作 ESG 投資的基準，亦會用作交易所買賣基金（ETF）等被動型 ESG 投資工具的相關資產。全球 ESG ETF 的數量由 2010 年的 46 隻增至 2020 年的 497 隻，總資產管理規模由 2010 年的 220 億美元增至 2020 年的 1,870 億美元（見圖 2）。另一資料來源顯示，於 2020 年 6 月底，超過 90% 的 ESG ETF 均為股票 ETF，當中大部分均追蹤藍籌股的 ESG 股票指數[6]。此外，ESG 股票

3　資料來源：〈全球可持續投資回顧〉（"Global sustainable investment review"），載於全球永續投資聯會的網站，2018年刊。

4　前稱多米尼400社會指數。資料來源：〈MSCI凱特400社會指數（美元）資料表〉（"Fact sheet of MSCI KLD 400 Social Index (USD)"），載於MSCI網站，2020年6月30日。

5　資料來源：〈ESG指數的演變〉（"An evolution in ESG indexing"），載於貝萊德安碩的網站，於2020年9月1日閱覽。

6　資料來源：〈被動型可持續基金：2020年全球市況〉（"Passive sustainable funds: The global landscape 2020"），載於晨星的網站，2020年9月4日。

投資急速發展亦提高了對 ESG 風險管理工具的需求。首個 ESG 股票指數期貨在 2018 年
10 月推出，是追蹤瑞典的基準股票指數的期貨產品[7]，其後越來越多追蹤藍籌股票指數
的 ESG 股票指數期貨相繼推出。有關期貨的成交合約總數由 2019 年的 145 萬張增至
2020 年的 261 萬張[8]。

圖 2：全球 ESG ETF 的數目及資產管理規模（2010 年至 2020 年）

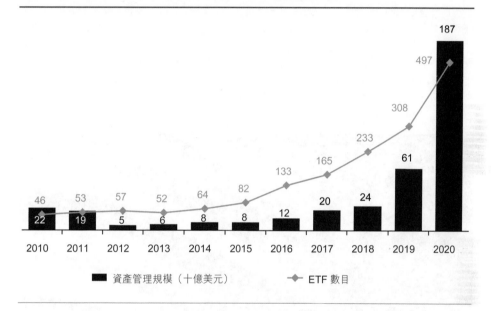

資料來源：〈ETFGI：全球上市 ESG（環境、社會及管治）ETF 及 ETP 的資產投資額於 2020 年年底達 1,870 億美
元新高〉（"ETFGI reports assets invested in ESG (Environmental, Social, and Governance) ETFs and
ETPs listed globally reach a new milestone of US$187 billion at end of 2020"），載於 ETFGI 的網站，
2021 年 1 月 22 日。

ESG 投資的起步點往往是 ESG 股票指數，尤其是藍籌股票指數。與傳統基準指數相比，
ESG 股票指數採用的投資策略並不一樣。因此，這些指數相較於傳統的投資策略可能有着
不一樣的風險回報模式。我們進行了一項實證研究，看看 ESG 股票指數的風險回報模式
是否及如何與其相應的傳統指數有所不同。

7　即OMXS30 ESG責任指數(OMXS30ESG)期貨。見〈納斯達克於北歐推出ESG期貨〉（"Nasdaq Launches ESG futures
　　in the Nordics"），載於納斯達克網站的新聞稿，2018年10月15日。

8　資料來源：按來自彭博的個別指數期貨每日交易數量計算。ESG股票指數期貨的清單是從截至2021年4月12日的新聞報
　　告和彭博整理出來，其資料未必完整。

ESG 股票指數表現的研究

ESG 股票指數通常以母股票指數為基礎，再配合 ESG 主題的投資風格。ESG 指數的投資風格一般分為「規避型」和「進取型」。前者是指剔除對 ESG 表現有重大負面影響的具爭議性行業或公司（與負面篩選或規範性篩選的可持續投資策略一致）；後者是指將資金分配至有望達到理想 ESG 成果（能以 ESG 評分計量）及投資預期對 ESG 會有正面影響的特定業務活動或行業（與正面篩選、可持續發展主題投資或影響力投資的可持續投資策略一致）。

不少全球性、地區性及本地市場的藍籌股票指數都成為 ESG 股票指數的母指數。表 1 列出 24 隻 ESG 股票指數及其對應的母股票指數。當中有部分 ESG 指數有相關期貨產品在交易所買賣。這次研究的對象便是這些 ESG 指數及其母指數。

表 1：若干 ESG 股票指數及其母指數的名單

母股票指數	ESG 股票指數	ESG 指數簡稱 （僅本章內使用）
全球指數		
MSCI 全球指數	MSCI 全球 ESG 領導指數 *	MSCI 全球 L
	MSCI 全球 ESG 篩選指數 *	MSCI 全球 S
富時已發展指數	富時已發展 ESG 低碳排放精選指數	富時已發展
標準普爾全球大中型指數	標準普爾全球大中型 ESG 指數	標準普爾全球
地區指數		
MSCI 新興市場指數	MSCI 新興市場 ESG 領導指數 *	MSCI 新興市場 L
	MSCI 新興市場 ESG 篩選指數 *	MSCI 新興市場 S
富時新興指數	富時新興 ESG 低碳排放精選指數	富時新興市場
標準普爾新興大中型指數	標準普爾新興大中型 ESG 指數	標準普爾新興市場
MSCI 歐洲指數	MSCI 歐洲 ESG 領導指數 *	MSCI 歐洲 L
	MSCI 歐洲 ESG 篩選指數	MSCI 歐洲 S
Stoxx 歐洲 600 指數	Stoxx 歐洲 600 ESG-X 指數 *	Stoxx 歐洲 600
Stoxx 歐洲精選紅利 30 指數	Stoxx 歐洲 ESG 領導精選 30 指數 *	Stoxx 歐洲 S
MSCI 歐澳遠東指數	MSCI 歐澳遠東 ESG 領導指數 *	MSCI 歐澳遠東 L
	MSCI 歐澳遠東 ESG 篩選指數 *	MSCI 歐澳遠東 S
本地指數		
MSCI 美國指數	MSCI 美國 ESG 領導指數 *	MSCI 美國 L
	MSC 美國 ESG 篩選指數 *	MSCI 美國 S
Stoxx 美國 500 指數	Stoxx 美國 500 ESG-X 指數 *	Stoxx 美國 500
標準普爾 500 指數	標準普爾 500 ESG 指數 *	標準普爾 500 ESG
富時英國 100 指數	富時英國 100 ESG 精選指數	富時英國 100
MSCI 日本指數	MSCI 日本 ESG 領導指數	MSCI 日本 L
	MSCI 日本 ESG 篩選指數 *	MSCI 日本 S
滬深 300 指數	滬深 300 ESG 指數	滬深 300
恒生指數	恒指 ESG 指數	恒指 ESG
恒生國企指數	恒生國指 ESG 指數	恒生國指 ESG

* 有指數期貨在交易所買賣的 ESG 股票指數。

資料來源：彭博。

這些母指數可分為以下類別:

- **全球市場指數** —— 在已發展市場上市的大中型公司於當中佔多數。

- **地區市場指數** —— 包括新興市場、歐洲、澳紐及遠東的指數。

- **本地市場指數** —— 追蹤美國、英國、日本、中國內地及香港等主要金融中心的市場表現的指數。

ESG 股票指數與其母指數的風險回報表現的比較

ESG 股票投資是否比傳統股票投資得到更高回報?與之對應的是:ESG 股票指數的表現是否優於其各自的母指數?為回答這些問題,我們將表 1 所列出的 ESG 指數(滬深 300 ESG 指數除外[9])與對應的母指數的回報表現作了比較。研究期為 2010 年 7 月 1 日至 2020 年 6 月 30 日的 10 年間。由於該等 ESG 指數的推出時間各異,每對指數的實際分析期長短不一 —— 23 對指數中只有 12 對的觀察數據橫跨整個十年的研究期。

這次研究比較了 ESG 指數與母指數的每日回報率及每日回報率標準差(用以衡量回報的波幅),並對這些每日回報率與每日回報率標準差的差異進行了統計檢驗,以探討這些差異是否在統計學上具有顯著性。

1. **用 *t-* 檢驗方法檢驗每日回報率的差異**:根據 23 對 ESG 指數與其母指數的所有現有數據計算其每日回報率,然後進行 *t-* 檢驗以檢定 ESG 指數的每日回報率是否高於其母指數。

2. **用 *F-* 檢驗方法檢驗每日回報率波幅的差異**:計算以下三者的每日回報率標準差,然後進行 *F-* 檢驗以檢定 ESG 指數的標準差是否大於其母指數:(1) 23 對 ESG 指數與其母指數;(2) 在全球、地區及本地三個指數類別中的所有 ESG 指數 / 母指數;及 (3) 研究中的所有 ESG 指數 / 母指數。

本文透過進行上述 *t-* 檢驗和 *F-* 檢驗,比較 ESG 指數與其母指數在整個研究期內、在不同長短投資期內和不同市況下的風險回報表現。分析結果見以下各分節[10]。

---

9   由於研究是要分析ESG指數在相當長的投資期內的風險回報表現,因此作為研究對象的指數應有至少5年的數據 。於 2020年4月30日推出的滬深300 ESG指數的數據僅追溯至2017年6月30日,因此未有涵蓋在研究範圍內。(見〈關於發佈 滬深300 ESG基準指數等五條指數的公告〉,載於中證指數有限公司網站,2020年4月8日)。
10 有關定量分析結果的詳細列表,請參閱香港交易所研究報告〈ESG股票指數與傳統股票指數的表現比較〉,載於香港交易 所網站,2020年11月26日。

在整個研究期內的指數表現

每日回報率

為進行 *t-* 檢驗，研究中計算了所有 ESG 指數與各自的母指數在整個研究期內的平均每日回報率 [11]，然後對以下三者的每日回報率的差異進行了獨立樣本 *t-* 檢驗：(1) 每對 ESG 指數與其母指數；(2) 在三個指數類別中每個類別的所有 ESG 指數與所有母指數；及 (3) 研究中的所有 ESG 指數與所有母指數。圖 3 顯示各指數的平均每日回報率及檢驗結果。

在所研究的 23 對指數中，有 13 對的 ESG 指數的平均每日回報率高於其母指數，當中 8 對（全球 1 對、地區 6 對、本地 1 對）在統計學上有顯著差異。另外，有 2 對（全球 1 對、地區 1 對）的 ESG 指數的平均每日回報率則比其母指數低，並在統計學上有顯著差異。

但是，檢驗各對 ESG 指數與其母指數的**平均每日回報率**的差異，未必能反映 ESG 指數相對於其母指數的每日真正回報表現，即兩者在同一天的市況下的相對回報表現。因此，我們對以下三者在同一天的回報率差異進行了 *t-* 檢驗：(1) 每對 ESG 指數與其母指數；(2) 在三個指數類別中的所有指數對；及 (3) 研究中的所有指數對。圖 4 顯示這些每日回報率差異的平均數及檢驗結果。

11　須注意的是，每對ESG指數與其母指數具有可供分析數據的研究期長短各有不同。

圖 3：ESG 指數與其母指數的平均每日回報率

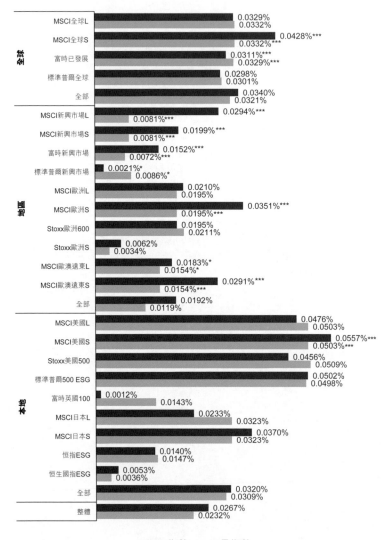

■ESG指數   ■母指數

註：每對 ESG 指數與其母指數的研究期同樣截至 2020 年 6 月 30 日，但覆蓋的時間長短或各有不同。
　　*** 差異在統計學上的顯著水平達到 0.1%。
　　** 差異在統計學上的顯著水平達到 1%。
　　* 差異在統計學上的顯著水平達到 5%。

資料來源：按取自彭博的每日指數收市點數計算。

圖 4：ESG 指數與其母指數的每日回報率差異的平均數

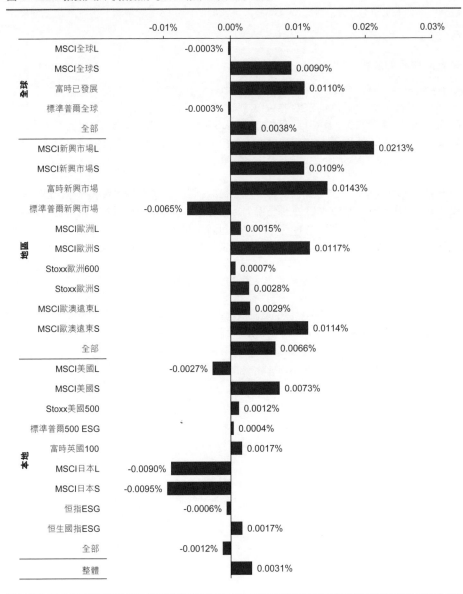

註：每對 ESG 指數與其母指數的研究期同樣截至 2020 年 6 月 30 日，但覆蓋的時間長短或各有不同。分析並無發現任何差異值在統計學上有顯著性。

資料來源：按取自彭博的每日指數收市點數計算。

結果顯示，無論是每一指數對、每個指數類別中的所有 ESG 指數相對於所有母指數，還是研究中的所有 ESG 指數相對於所有母指數，其於同日的回報率差異，在統計學上均無顯著性。

每日回報率的波幅

為了對每日回報率的波幅進行 *F-* 檢驗，研究中分別計算了以下三者在整個研究期間的每日回報率的標準差：(1) 每對 ESG 指數與其母指數 [12]；(2) 三個指數類別中每個類別的所有 ESG 指數與所有母指數；及 (3) 研究中的所有 ESG 指數與所有母指數。然後我們進行了 *F-* 檢驗，以檢定 ESG 指數與母指數的標準差在統計學上是否有顯著差異。圖 5 顯示指數在每日回報率標準差的平均值上的差異及檢驗結果。

所有 ESG 指數在整個研究期間的整體每日回報率標準差低於所有母指數的整體每日回報標準差，而其差異 (-0.0214%) 在統計學上有顯著性。就指數類別而言，在三個類別中的每一個類別，ESG 指數回報率的標準差均低於母指數的標準差，儘管只有在「地區」類別的標準差的差異在統計學上有顯著性。就個別指數對而言，在 23 對指數中有 6 對（全球 1 對、地區 3 對、本地 2 對）的 ESG 指數的標準差低於其母指數（在統計學上有顯著性），另有 2 對（地區指數）的 ESG 指數的標準差高於其母指數（並在統計學上有顯著性）。

上述結果顯示，許多時候 ESG 指數的風險回報表現就算不是比其母指數更勝一籌，也傾向不相伯仲，意即有較高回報及 / 或較低風險（每日回報率的標準差）。

---

12 須注意的是，每對ESG指數與其母指數具有可供分析數據的研究期長短各有不同。

圖 5：ESG 指數與其母指數每日回報標準差的差異

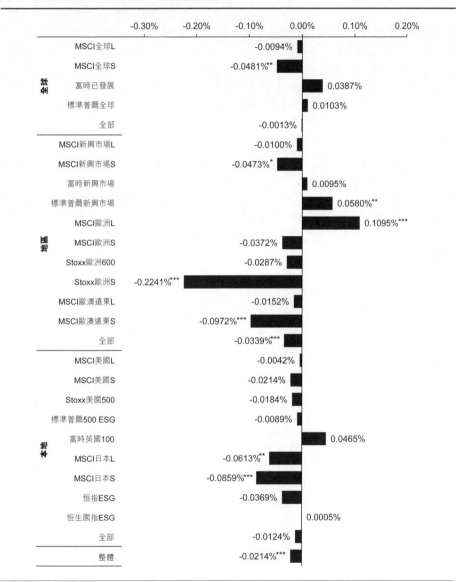

註：每對 ESG 指數與其母指數的研究期同樣截至 2020 年 6 月 30 日，但覆蓋的時間長短或各有不同。

　　*** 差異在統計學上的顯著水平達到 0.1%。

　　** 差異在統計學上的顯著水平達到 1%。

　　* 差異在統計學上的顯著水平達到 5%。

資料來源：按取自彭博的每日指數收市點數計算。

指數在 5 年或以下投資期內的表現

ESG 指數相對於其母指數的風險回報表現可能於不同長短的投資期有所不同。由於研究中的所有 ESG 指數均有至少 5 年的數據，因此本文分析了整個樣本在 5 年或以下的不同投資期的風險回報表現。研究中計算了這些指數從 2015 年 6 月 30 日基準日起在 3 個月、6 個月、1 年、3 年和 5 年的投資期的期內回報率 [13] 和每日回報率的標準差。如上一分節，研究採用了 *t-* 檢驗和 *F-* 檢驗探討 ESG 指數與其母指數在回報率和風險方面的差異。

期內回報率

超過一半的 ESG 指數在所研究的不同短期和中期投資期內（3 個月、6 個月、1 年、3 年和 5 年持有期）的期內回報率都高於其母指數。但是，當研究每個指數類別中個別指數的表現時，超過一半的本地 ESG 指數（9 隻中有 5 隻）在 6 個月和 3 年的持有期內的表現遜於其母指數。不過，研究發現，無論是每個指數類別中的所有指數對，還是研究中的所有指數對，ESG 指數與對應的母指數於所有持有期的期內回報率的差異在統計學上並無顯著性 [14]。

每日回報率的波幅

超過一半的 ESG 指數在所研究的不同短期和中期投資期內（3 個月、6 個月、1 年和 5 年持有期，但不包括 3 年持有期）的波幅比其母指數的小（即每日回報率的標準差低於其母指數）。就每個指數類別而言，超過一半的地區 ESG 指數在所有投資期內均錄得比母指數小的波幅，而全球和本地 ESG 指數中也有一半以上在 3 個月、6 個月和 1 年的較短投資期內錄得較小波幅。然而，無論是每一指數對、每個指數類別中的所有 ESG 指數相對於所有母指數，還是研究中的所有 ESG 指數相對於所有母指數，其波幅差異於所有持有期均在統計學上無顯著性（除了有 1 對地區指數於 5 年持有期內的波幅差異在統計學上具顯著性 [15]）。

圖 6 至 8 顯示了全球、地區和本地指數三類 ESG 指數與其母指數在 1 年、3 年和 5 年持有期內的風險回報情況。理論上，風險越高，投資者會期望回報也越高。若一隻 ESG 指數相對於其母指數有相同風險但較高回報，或有相同回報率但較低風險，又或有較高回報率同時有較低風險，該 ESG 指數的風險回報表現就被認為比其母指數優勝。在所研究的 ESG 指數中，約有一半（尤其是地區指數）在 1 年和 5 年的持有期比其母指數有更佳的風險回報表現。反之，只有少數 ESG 指數（少於 3 隻）在 1 年、3 年和 5 年的持有期的風險回報表現遜於其母指數。[16]

---

13 「期內回報率」是指指數於指定投資期的最終收市點數相對於基準日收市點數的百分比變化。

14 對期內回報率進行「*t-*檢驗」的其中一個限制在於樣本中的指數對並不多，或會導致檢驗標準誤差較高 。以下兩個分節中所述的「*t-*檢驗」結果也有此限制。

15 那是Stoxx 歐洲ESG 領導精選30指數，其回報率的波幅（1.14%）低於其母指數（1.29%）（在統計學上具顯著性）。

16 須注意的是，這些對照ESG 指數與其母指數表現的觀察結論，並無相關統計學上的顯著差異檢驗作支持（上文已分別就期內回報率和每日回報率標準差進行相關的檢驗並論述結果）。以下兩個分節中的散點圖的觀察結論同樣要注意這點。

圖 6：ESG 指數與母指數的風險回報散點圖 —— 全球指數（基準日：2015 年 6 月 30 日）

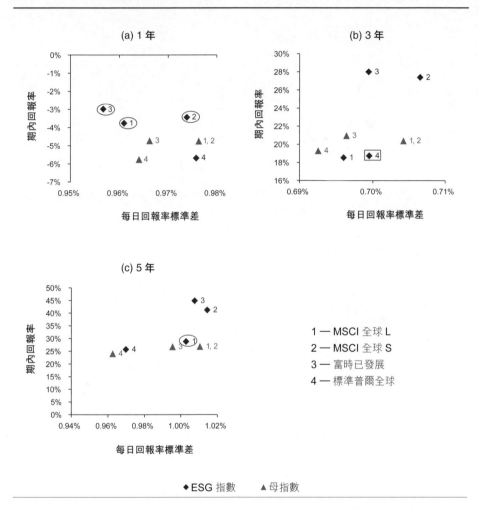

1 —— MSCI 全球 L
2 —— MSCI 全球 S
3 —— 富時已發展
4 —— 標準普爾全球

◆ESG 指數　　▲母指數

註：若 ESG 指數標誌在圓圈內，表示該 ESG 指數的風險回報表現優於其母指數（較高回報及 / 或較低風險）；若 ESG 指數標誌在長方形內，表示該 ESG 指數的風險回報表現遜於其母指數（較低回報及 / 或較高風險）。不在圓形或長方形中的 ESG 指數，則與其母指數屬於正常的「高風險 - 高回報」關係（當中包括回報及風險非常接近其母指數的指數）。

資料來源：按取自彭博的每日指數收市點數計算。

圖 7：**ESG 指數與母指數的風險回報散點圖 —— 地區指數**（基準日：**2015 年 6 月 30 日**）

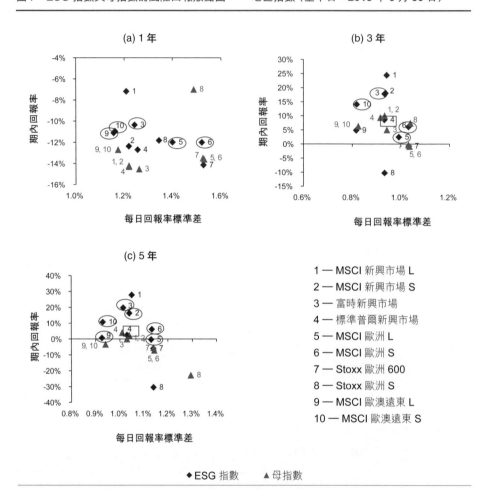

(a) 1 年

(b) 3 年

(c) 5 年

1 — MSCI 新興市場 L
2 — MSCI 新興市場 S
3 — 富時新興市場
4 — 標準普爾新興市場
5 — MSCI 歐洲 L
6 — MSCI 歐洲 S
7 — Stoxx 歐洲 600
8 — Stoxx 歐洲 S
9 — MSCI 歐澳遠東 L
10 — MSCI 歐澳遠東 S

◆ ESG 指數　▲ 母指數

註：若 ESG 指數標誌在圓圈內，表示該 ESG 指數的風險回報表現優於其母指數（較高回報及 / 或較低風險）；若 ESG
　　指數標誌在長方形內，表示該 ESG 指數的風險回報表現遜於其母指數（較低回報及 / 或較高風險）。不在圓形或
　　長方形中的 ESG 指數，則與其母指數屬於正常的「高風險 - 高回報」關係（當中包括回報及風險非常接近其母指
　　數的指數）。

資料來源：按取自彭博的每日指數收市點數計算。

圖 8：ESG 指數與母指數的風險回報散點圖 —— 本地指數（基準日：2015 年 6 月 30 日）

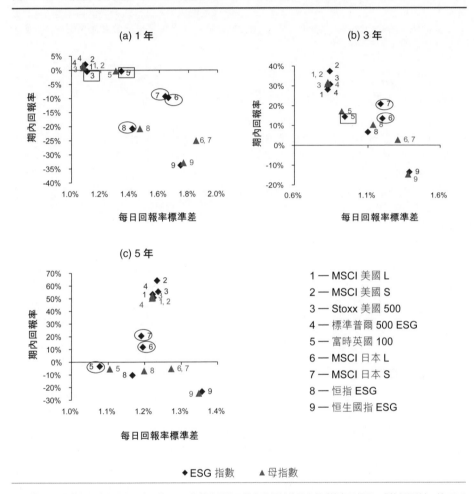

(a) 1 年

(b) 3 年

(c) 5 年

1 — MSCI 美國 L
2 — MSCI 美國 S
3 — Stoxx 美國 500
4 — 標準普爾 500 ESG
5 — 富時英國 100
6 — MSCI 日本 L
7 — MSCI 日本 S
8 — 恒指 ESG
9 — 恒生國指 ESG

◆ ESG 指數　　▲ 母指數

註：若 ESG 指數標誌在圓圈內，表示該 ESG 指數的風險回報表現優於其母指數（較高回報及 / 或較低風險）；若 ESG 指數標誌在長方形內，表示該 ESG 指數的風險回報表現遜於其母指數（較低回報及 / 或較高風險）。不在圓形或長方形中的 ESG 指數，則與其母指數屬於正常的「高風險 - 高回報」關係（當中包括回報及風險非常接近其母指數的指數）。

資料來源：按取自彭博的每日指數收市點數計算。

上述結果顯示，許多時候 ESG 指數在 5 年或以下的不同長短投資期內的風險回報表現就算不是比其母指數更勝一籌 —— 即較高回報及／或較低風險（每日回報率的標準差），也傾向不相伯仲。研究也發現一些地區和本地 ESG 指數 [17] 的表現持續地較其母指數優勝（雖然未必在統計學上有顯著性）。

指數在 10 年或以下投資期內的表現

研究分析了 12 對有 10 年數據的 ESG 指數與其母指數（全球 2 對、地區 5 對、本地 5 對）在 10 年或以下的不同長短投資期內的表現，計算了指數從 2010 年 6 月 30 日基準日起在 3 個月、6 個月、1 年、3 年、5 年、7 年和 10 年的投資期內的期內回報率和每日回報率標準差。所採用的分析和統計檢驗如上一分節所述。

期內回報率

在所研究的指數中，約有一半的 ESG 指數在若干短、中和長期的投資期（3 個月、3 年和 10 年持有期）的期內回報率高於其母指數，但在其他投資期（6 個月、1 年、5 年和 7 年持有期）則少於一半有此表現。按指數類別來說，2 隻全球 ESG 指數在所有持有期內的表現均不及其母指數，而大約一半的地區和本地 ESG 指數則在所有持有期的期內回報率均較其母指數為佳。然而，研究中的所有指數對在所有持有期內，ESG 指數與相應的母指數的期內回報率差異在統計學上並無顯著性。

每日回報率的波幅

在所研究的指數中，超過一半的 ESG 指數在不同短、中和長期的投資期內（3 個月持有期除外）的波幅比其母指數的小。就每個指數類別而言，所有本地 ESG 指數均在中期投資期內（3 年、5 年和 7 年持有期）與其母指數相比錄得較小的波幅。然而，研究發現，無論是每個指數類別中的所有 ESG 指數相對母指數，還是研究中的所有 ESG 指數相對母指數，在所有持有期內的波幅差異在統計學上均無顯著性。就個別指數對而言，只有 3 對地區指數（其中 2 對的相關持有期是 6 個月、1 年、3 年、5 年、7 年和 10 年；另一對的相關持有期是 5 年和 7 年）的波幅差異在統計學上有顯著性。

圖 9 至 11 為 ESG 指數與其母指數在 1 年、5 年和 10 年持有期內的風險回報情況的散點圖。許多 ESG 指數的風險回報在短、中和長期的投資期內似乎與其母指數不相伯仲。雖然少於一半的 ESG 指數的表現較其母指數優勝，但表現遜於其母指數的卻更少（其他的都是正常的高風險 - 高回報情況）。

---

17 包括MSCI新興市場ESG低碳排放精選指數、MSCI 歐洲ESG 領導指數、MSCI 歐洲ESG 篩選指數、MSCI 歐澳遠東 ESG 篩選指數、MSCI 日本ESG 領導指數及MSCI 日本ESG 篩選指數。

圖 9：ESG 指數與母指數的風險回報散點圖 —— 全球指數（基準日：2010 年 6 月 30 日）

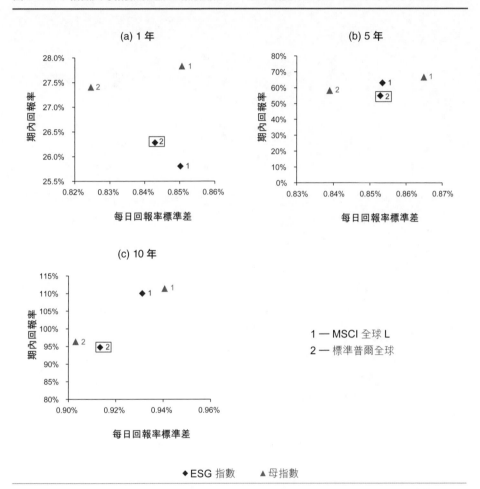

(a) 1 年

(b) 5 年

(c) 10 年

1 — MSCI 全球 L
2 — 標準普爾全球

◆ESG 指數　　▲母指數

註：若 ESG 指數標誌在圓圈內，表示該 ESG 指數的風險回報表現優於其母指數（較高回報及 / 或較低風險）；若 ESG 指數標誌在長方形內，表示該 ESG 指數的風險回報表現遜於其母指數（較低回報及 / 或較高風險）。不在圓形或長方形中的 ESG 指數，則與其母指數屬於正常的「高風險 - 高回報」關係（當中包括回報及風險非常接近其母指數的指數）。

資料來源：按取自彭博的每日指數收市點數計算。

圖 10：ESG 指數與母指數的風險回報情況散點圖 ── 地區指數（基準日：2010 年 6 月 30 日）

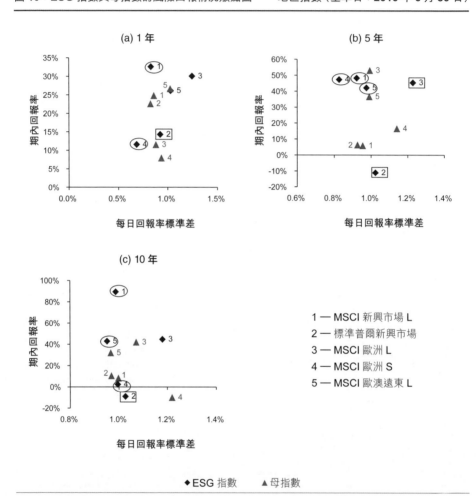

1 ── MSCI 新興市場 L
2 ── 標準普爾新興市場
3 ── MSCI 歐洲 L
4 ── MSCI 歐洲 S
5 ── MSCI 歐澳遠東 L

◆ESG 指數　▲ 母指數

註：若 ESG 指數標誌在圓圈內，表示該 ESG 指數的風險回報表現優於其母指數（較高回報及／或較低風險）；若 ESG 指數標誌在長方形內，表示該 ESG 指數的風險回報表現遜於其母指數（較低回報及／或較高風險）。不在圓形或長方形中的 ESG 指數，則與其母指數屬於正常的「高風險 - 高回報」關係（當中包括回報及風險非常接近其母指數的指數）。

資料來源：按取自彭博的每日指數收市點數計算。

圖 11：ESG 指數與母指數的風險回報散點圖 —— 本地指數（基準日：2010 年 6 月 30 日）

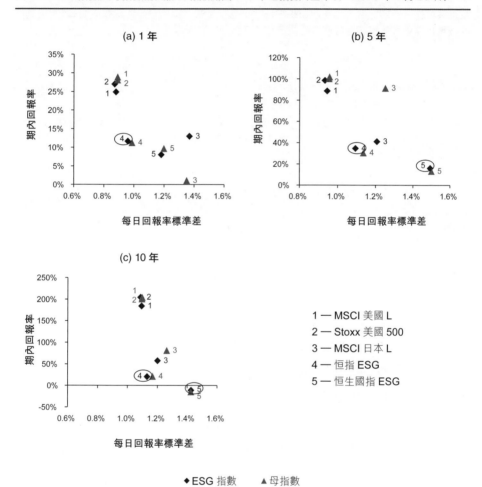

註：若 ESG 指數標誌在圓圈內，表示該 ESG 指數的風險回報表現優於其母指數（較高回報及 / 或較低風險）；若 ESG 指數標誌在長方形內，表示該 ESG 指數的風險回報表現遜於其母指數（較低回報及 / 或較高風險）。不在圓形或長方形中的 ESG 指數，則與其母指數屬於正常的「高風險 - 高回報」關係（當中包括回報及風險非常接近其母指數的指數）。

資料來源：按取自彭博的每日指數收市點數計算。

上述結果顯示，許多時候 ESG 指數在 10 年或以下的不同長短投資期內的風險回報就算不是比其母指數更勝一籌，也傾向不相伯仲。不過，研究也發現一些地區和本地 ESG 指數[18]的表現持續地較其母指數優勝（雖然未必在統計學上有顯著性）。

特定牛市和熊市的指數表現

為了研究 ESG 指數及其母指數在不同市況下的風險回報情況，本研究按主觀判斷從全球指數在 2014 年 10 月 16 日至 2020 年 3 月 23 日期間的高低起跌中辨別出三個牛市期和三個熊市期（見圖 12）。

三個牛市期是（括號內為時期編號以作辨認之用）：

- 2014 年 10 月 16 日至 2015 年 5 月 21 日（P1）；
- 2016 年 2 月 11 日至 2018 年 1 月 26 日（P2）；及
- 2018 年 12 月 25 日至 2020 年 2 月 12 日（P3）。

三個熊市期是：

- 2015 年 5 月 21 日至 2016 年 2 月 11 日（P4）；
- 2018 年 1 月 26 日至 2018 年 12 月 25 日（P5）；及
- 2020 年 2 月 12 日至 2020 年 3 月 23 日（P6）。

研究中計算了各指數在各段牛／熊市期的期內回報率和每日回報率的標準差，並使用上文相關分節所述的統計檢驗，分析 ESG 指數與其母指數在這兩方面的差異。

---

18 這些包括MSCI 新興市場ESG 領導指數、Stoxx 歐洲ESG 領導精選30指數及恒生ESG指數。

圖 12：主要全球性股票指數的表現（2014 年至 2020 年 6 月）

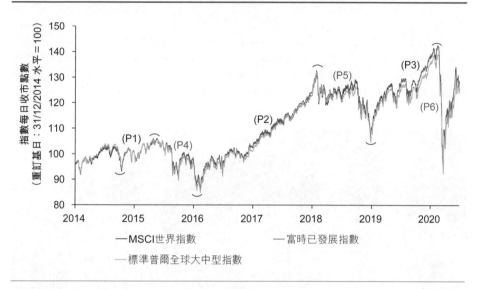

註：P1 至 P3 為牛市期；P4 至 P6 為熊市期。

資料來源：彭博。

期內回報率

超過一半的 ESG 指數在不同的牛／熊市期的期內回報率均高於其母指數，而在最近的一個牛／熊市期內，ESG 指數佔優的比例較高（在牛市期 P3 和熊市期 P6，23 隻 ESG 指數中有 18 隻回報表現較其母指數為佳）。但是，在每個指數類別中，全球 ESG 指數當中有半數（4 隻中有 2 隻）在牛市期 P1 和 P2 的表現遜於其母指數，而本地 ESG 指數中超過一半（9 隻中有 5 隻）在牛市期 P1 和熊市期 P4 和 P5 表現遜於其母指數。不過，無論是每個指數類別中的所有指數對，還是所研究的所有指數對，ESG 指數與對應的母指數在研究中的所有牛／熊市期內的期內回報差異在統計學上並無顯著性。

每日回報率的波幅

超過一半的 ESG 指數在研究期內首個牛市期 P1 及全部三個熊市期 P4、P5 和 P6 的波幅均比其母指數的小，但較近期的兩個牛市期 P2 和 P3 則不然。但是，在每個指數類別中，少於一半的全球 ESG 指數（4 隻中有 1 隻）在較近期的牛市期 P2 和 P3 和較近期的熊市期 P5 和 P6 錄得比對應的母指數小的波幅；而少於一半的本地 ESG 指數在牛市期 P1 和 P2 錄得較其母指數小的波幅。不過，無論是每一指數對、每個指數類別中的所有 ESG 指數相對於所有母指數，還是研究中的所有 ESG 指數相對於所有母指數，其波幅差異於所有牛 / 熊市期在統計學上均無顯著性。

圖 13 至 15 為 ESG 指數與其母指數在各牛 / 熊市期內的風險回報情況的散點圖[19]。若干 ESG 指數在各牛 / 熊市期內的風險回報年其母指數的有偏離「高風險 - 高回報」關係的現象 —— 約有一半的 ESG 指數在熊市期 P4 和 P6 的表現較其母指數佳，而只有少數的 ESG 指數在牛 / 熊市期 P1、 P2、 P3 和 P5 的表現較其母指數遜色。

---

19 圖13至15中，若ESG指數標誌在圓圈內，表示該ESG指數的風險回報表現優於其母指數(較高回報及/或較低風險)；若 ESG指數標誌在長方形內，表示該ESG指數的風險回報表現遜於其母指數(較低回報及/或較高風險)。不在圓形或長方形中的ESG指數，則與其母指數屬於正常的「高風險-高回報」關係(當中包括回報及風險非常接近其母指數的指數)。

圖 13：牛 / 熊市期內 ESG 指數及母指數的風險回報散點圖 —— 全球指數

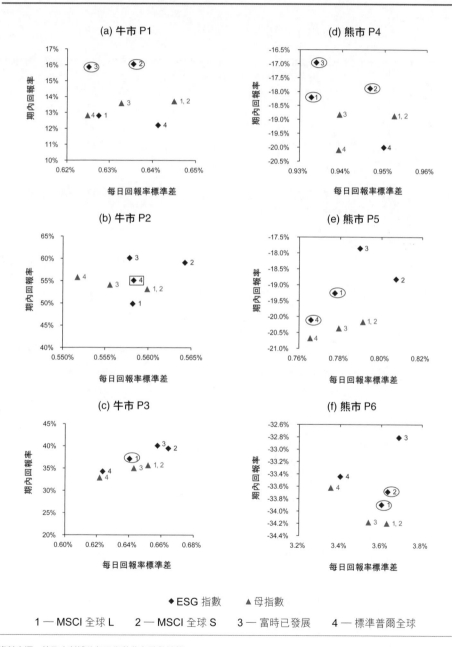

◆ ESG 指數　　▲ 母指數

1 — MSCI 全球 L　　2 — MSCI 全球 S　　3 — 富時已發展　　4 — 標準普爾全球

資料來源：按取自彭博的每日指數收市點數計算。

圖 14：牛 / 熊市期內 ESG 指數及母指數的風險回報散點圖 —— 地區指數

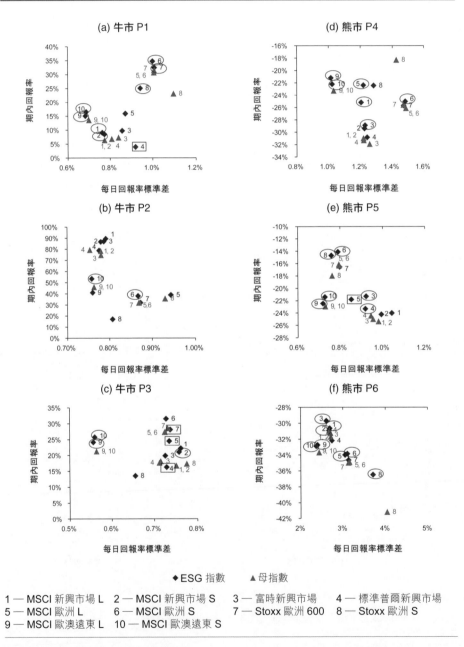

(a) 牛市 P1

(b) 牛市 P2

(c) 牛市 P3

(d) 熊市 P4

(e) 熊市 P5

(f) 熊市 P6

◆ ESG 指數　　▲ 母指數

1 — MSCI 新興市場 L　　2 — MSCI 新興市場 S　　3 — 富時新興市場　　4 — 標準普爾新興市場
5 — MSCI 歐洲 L　　　　6 — MSCI 歐洲 S　　　　7 — Stoxx 歐洲 600　　8 — Stoxx 歐洲 S
9 — MSCI 歐澳遠東 L　　10 — MSCI 歐澳遠東 S

資料來源：按取自彭博的每日指數收市點數計算。

圖 15：牛 / 熊市期內 ESG 指數及母指數的風險回報散點圖 —— 本地指數

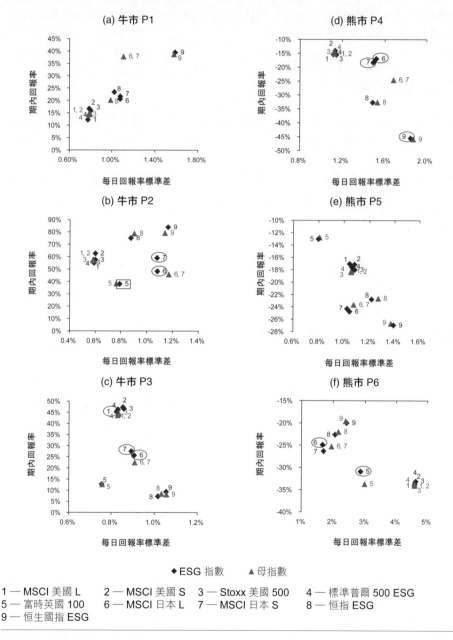

(a) 牛市 P1

(b) 牛市 P2

(c) 牛市 P3

(d) 熊市 P4

(e) 熊市 P5

(f) 熊市 P6

◆ ESG 指數　　▲ 母指數

1 — MSCI 美國 L　　2 — MSCI 美國 S　　3 — Stoxx 美國 500　　4 — 標準普爾 500 ESG
5 — 富時英國 100　　6 — MSCI 日本 L　　7 — MSCI 日本 S　　8 — 恒指 ESG
9 — 恒生國指 ESG

資料來源：按取自彭博的每日指數收市點數計算。

上述結果顯示，所研究的 ESG 指數許多時候在不同牛熊市況下的風險回報表現就算不是比其母指數更勝一籌，也傾向不相伯仲。研究也發現一隻地區 ESG 指數 [20] 在牛市期的表現持續地較其母指數優勝，也有數隻全球及地區指數 [21] 在熊市期的表現持續地較其母指數優勝（雖然在統計學上未必有顯著性）。

實證結果概要

根據以上的分析結果，許多時候 ESG 指數的投資回報率和回報率波幅在不同長短投資期和不同市況下均與對應的母指數不相伯仲。在一些情況下，有些 ESG 指數比其母指數有較高的回報率及 / 或較小的回報率波幅，這些情況通常較出現 ESG 指數比其母指數有較低回報率及 / 或較大回報率波幅的情況更多 [22]。

研究發現多隻 ESG 指數（主要是地區指數）在不同長短投資期內的風險回報都持續地優於其母指數。

這些實證或意味着個別 ESG 指數可能是因自有的特色令其表現優於其母指數，而這些特色未必適用於所有 ESG 指數。詳細討論見下文。

影響 ESG 指數表現的因素

有關 ESG 投資表現的實證研究有很多。正如我們在上一節中所展示的研究結果，雖然沒有實證證明於不同市場與研究期內的 ESG 投資的表現能**持續地**較母指數優勝 [23]，但個別 ESG 指數在一些情況下卻表現出較其母指數優勝。由於 ESG 指數的成份股都是公認為 ESG 表現良好的公司，ESG 指數有出色的表現，可能是因為這些公司的 ESG 評級與其財務業績有正向的關係，以及投資者對 ESG 表現良好的公司評價較高，以及投資者對不同的 ESG 投資策略有所偏好。下文對這些因素逐一討論。

---

20 指MSCI 歐澳遠東ESG 篩選指數。
21 指MSCI全球ESG領導指數、富時新興ESG低碳排放精選指數、MSCI 歐洲ESG 篩選指數、MSCI 歐澳遠東 ESG 領導指數和MSCI 歐澳遠東ESG 篩選指數。
22 須注意的是，ESG指數與其母指數的表現差異不一定在統計學上有顯著性。
23 見 R. Henriksson、J. Livnat、P. Pfeifer、M. Stumpp 與 G. Zeng〈ESG文獻綜述〉("ESG literature review")，載於在 Quantitative Management Associates LLC（qma.com）網站上的工作論文，2018年6月。

企業的財務業績

一項有關 MSCI 指數的研究[24]（以下稱為「MSCI ESG 研究」）顯示，MSCI 世界指數的成份股中，ESG 評級最高者於 2007 年 1 月至 2017 年 5 月的財務業績比其他成份股公司較佳，歸因於他們能產生更多的現金流，並較有效地減低公司特有的風險。該研究指出，ESG 評級較高的公司通常比行業內的同類公司更具競爭力，能賺取更理想的財務回報，且有更高的業務盈利能力和股息分配。這些公司也較擅長管理公司特有的風險，能有更大機會避免股價受到風險事件影響。因此，這些公司的股價反映其有較低的特有極端風險（tail risks）。

ESG 評級的影響在不同的地區市場或有不同。一項研究[25]檢視了 1970 年至 2014 年間有關不同市場的 2,250 項實證研究，發現這些實證研究中所得結果證明企業財務業績與 ESG 表現屬正向關係的研究數目在新興市場的研究中有較高佔比（65.4%），而在已發展的歐洲市場的佔比則最低（26.1%）（見圖 16）。換句話説，新興市場中有較高 ESG 評級的公司，其財務業績通常較佳。這或可解釋為何一些新興市場的 ESG 指數錄得較佳的風險回報。該研究也發現，在已發展的亞洲、澳洲和紐西蘭市場，企業財務業績與 ESG 表現的關係不太明確。該研究指出這可能是因為亞太市場的 ESG 匯報工作於 1970 年至 2014 年的研究期內尚在發展初期。

24　G. Giese、L. Lee、D. Melas、Z. Nagy 與 L. Nishikawa（2019年）〈ESG投資之基礎：ESG如何影響股權估值、風險和表現〉（"Foundations of ESG investing: How ESG affects equity valuation, risk, and performance"），載於《Journal of Portfolio Management》第45期，69-83 頁。此文的作者均為MSCI, Inc.的行政人員。

25　G. Friede、M. Lewis、A. Bassen 與 T. Busch（2015年）〈ESG及財務表現：超過2000份實證研究的綜合證據〉（"ESG and Financial Performance: Aggregated Evidence from More than 2000 Empirical Studies"），載於《Journal of Sustainable Finance and Investment》第五期，210-233頁。

圖 16：所檢視的實證研究中發現 ESG 表現與公司財務表現之間有正向或反向關係的數量所佔比例

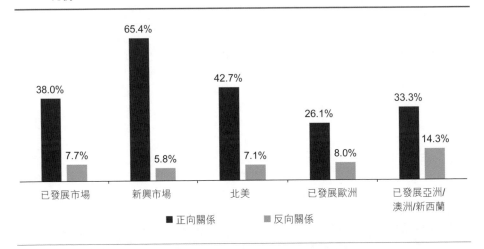

註：所檢視的實證研究數量共 2,250 份，進行研究的時間在 1970 年至 2014 年間。

資料來源：Friede, G.、M. Lewis、A. Bassen 與 T. Busch（2015 年）〈ESG 及財務表現：超過 2000 份實證研究的綜合證據〉（"ESG and Financial Performance: Aggregated Evidence from More than 2000 Empirical Studies"），載於《Journal of Sustainable Finance and Investment》第五期，210-233 頁。

投資者對 ESG 表現的重視

「MSCI ESG 研究」發現 ESG 評分最高的成份股於 2007 年 1 月至 2017 年 5 月期間有較高的估值（以市盈率和市賬率計算）。據這項研究的解釋，估值較高的原因可能是因為 ESG 評級較高的公司的盈利波動較低、系統性風險較低，連帶資金成本也可降低，對其股價支持較大。

面對財務業績相類似的公司，實證表明投資於 ESG 評級較高的公司能產生「alpha」回報（即相對於投資 ESG 評級較低公司所得的額外回報）。對公司 ESG 表現所作的評估，通常是根據 ESG 匯報準則所作的資料披露與同一行業公司作比較[26]。一項實證研究[27]分析

---

26 在評估公司的ESG評級時，評估員會根據他們選擇的ESG匯報準則來作出評估 。這些ESG匯報準則可能是評估員自行內部制定，或參考國際機構，例如《碳信息披露項目》（Carbon Disclosure Project）、《全球報告倡議組織》（Global Reporting Initiative）、《永續會計準則委員會》（Sustainability Accounting Standards Board）或其他市場機構所制定的標準。（例子可見2020年9月25日在Business Green網站上刊發的題為〈四大會計師事務所披露ESG匯報標準〉（"Big four accounting firms reveal ESG reporting standards"）的文章。）

27 M. Khan、G. Serafeim 與 A. Yoon（2015年）〈企業可持續性：辨認「重大」議題的首要證據〉（"Corporate sustainability: First evidence on materiality"），Harvard Business School的工作報告，第15-073號。

690

了 2,307 家美國公司於 1992 年至 2002 年間的回報，並根據國際 ESG 匯報標準，界定了公司所披露的 ESG 資料中屬於「重要」和「不重要」的可持續性議題。這項研究發現，在「重要」議題上 ESG 表現較佳的公司，有顯著的「alpha」回報。研究結果凸顯出股票估值與 ESG 匯報質量兩者的密切關係。但是，市場上有許多不同的國際 ESG 匯報準則，不同的市場和公司採用哪一套，也極之不同 [28]。

此外，由於投資者越來越重視 ESG 表現，在云云相類似的公司之中，他們更願意為 ESG 評級高的公司支付高一點的股價，令這些公司的估值有更大支持。不過，研究發現投資者對 ESG 表現的重視程度因地區而異 —— 一項調查發現，美國和歐洲的機構投資者較亞洲、加拿大和香港的機構投資者更重視 ESG（見圖 17）。

圖 17：不同市場中認為環境及社會議題「十分重要」的機構投資者的佔比（2019 年）

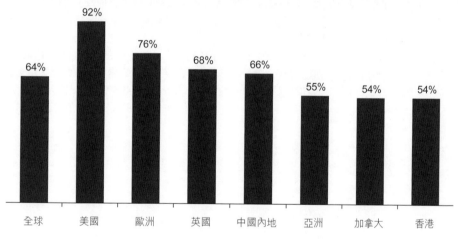

資料來源：〈2019 年可持續金融及投資研究：關注環境及社會事宜的市場〉（"Sustainable Financing and Investing Survey 2019: Markets alert to the environment and society"），載於滙豐集團的網站，2019 年 9 月 24 日。

---

28 P. Zembrowski、M. Leung 與 K. Schacht（2019年）〈亞太地區的ESG披露：特定市場的上市公司的ESG披露制度一覽〉（"ESG disclosure in Asia Pacific: A review of ESG disclosure regimes for listed companies in selected markets"），載於特許金融分析師協會網站，2019年7月21日。

投資者對 ESG 評級高的公司的需求，除了可能因地而異之外，也未必能一直持續。一項研究[29] 指出，ESG 評級較高的股票的出色表現可能會隨時間逐漸遜色或消失，因為長遠而言投資者對簡單的 ESG 信息（例如 ESG 評級）未必永遠有正面回應。投資者或會在短中期追捧高 ESG 評級的股票而出售低 ESG 評級的股票，但這情況在長期或會逆轉。另一方面，「MSCI ESG 研究」卻發現，ESG 評級的影響雖然低於某些傳統因素（例如價格動力），但其影響可能會維持較長時間，長達數年（而動力因素則只維持數月）。

ESG 投資策略的差異

投資者對不同 ESG 議題的關注程度不一，所以對不同 ESG 投資策略的反應亦可能各異[30]。為滿足不同的投資偏好，指數公司用許多方法來編制指數成份股的內部 ESG 評級，以至不同指數成份股在「環境」、「社會」及「管治」三方面各有不同比重，因此即使是涵蓋同一相關市場的 ESG 指數，也有不同的風險回報情況。以美國市場為例，一項研究[31] 分析了美國市場上的五隻 ESG 股票指數，發現這些 ESG 指數的回報與其母指數相似，短期波幅卻高於其母指數，就是因為這些指數的編制各有不同。當中的差異涉及成份股及其數量，以及相關行業的權重方面，這些差異或會導致 ESG 指數的投資風格（例如價值、增長、規模）有別於其母指數。ESG 指數與其母指數比較之下的行業權重變化，在不同的 ESG 指數當中有所不同（見圖 18）── 截至 2020 年 6 月底，MSCI 美國 ESG 領導指數的行業權重變化為 -0.1% 至 0.3% 不等，MSCI 凱特 400 社會指數的變化則為 -3.7% 至 5.8% 不等。

29 S. Hvidkjær,〈ESG投資：文獻綜述〉（"ESG investing: A literature review"），載於Dansif（旨在促進丹麥ESG投資的論壇）的網站，2017年9月。

30 一項調查發現，全球不同市場的消費者對氣候變化及煙草和酒精消費各有不同看法。見〈揭開負面篩選的神秘面紗：ESG 篩選因素的影響一覽〉（"Demystifying negative screens: The full implications of ESG exclusions"），載於 Schroders的網站，2017年12月。

31 A. O'Brien、L. Liao 與 J. Campagna〈責任投資：做出具有競爭力的業績〉（"Responsible investing: Delivering competitive performance"），載於Nuveen的網站，2018年夏。

圖 18：若干美國 ESG 指數與母指數的行業權重差異（2020 年 6 月）

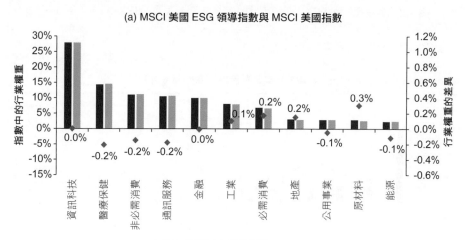

(a) MSCI 美國 ESG 領導指數與 MSCI 美國指數

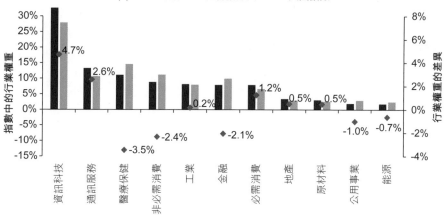

(b) MSCI 凱特 400 社會指數與 MSCI 美國指數

資料來源：MSCI 美國 ESG 領導指數、MSCI 凱特 400 社會指數、MSCI 美國指數及 MSCI 美國可投資市場指數的資料頁（2020 年 6 月）。

指數公司對不同市場的 ESG 評估或各不相同,因而可能會影響不同市場 ESG 指數相對其母指數的行業權重變化。在香港,恒指 ESG 指數與其母指數 (恒生指數) 的行業結構不同,行業權重變化為 -4.6% 至 6.0% 不等 (見圖 19)。有別於美國的 ESG 指數中資訊科技的行業權重高於其母指數,恒指 ESG 指數中資訊科技的行業權重則比其母指數為低;而公用事業的行業權重情況則剛剛相反。

圖 19:恒指 ESG 指數與恒生指數的行業權重差異 (2020 年 6 月)

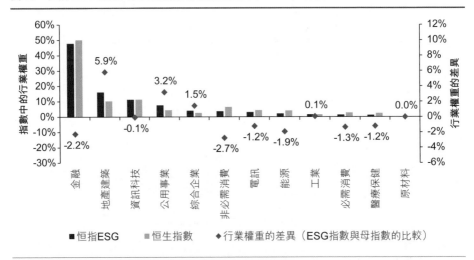

資料來源:恒指 ESG 指數及恒生指數的資料頁 (2020 年 6 月)。

總結

ESG 股票指數是衡量 ESG 投資表現的基準，亦已被廣泛用作 ETF 等被動型投資工具的相關資產，所涉及的範圍同時包括全球、地區及本地市場。另外，ESG 指數期貨等相關的風險管理工具亦相繼推出。

從本研究對 23 對覆蓋全球、地區和本地市場的 ESG 股票指數與對應的母指數的分析結果可見，許多時候 ESG 指數在不同長短的投資期和不同市況之下的回報率和回報率波幅都與其母指數相若；而在一些情況下，有些 ESG 指數的表現甚至比其母指數更勝一籌。ESG 指數的表現可以勝過其母指數的原因，也許是 ESG 表現較好的成份股都有較佳的企業財務表現及 / 或投資者對 ESG 表現較好的公司的評價更高，又或是投資者對特定 ESG 投資策略有所偏好。由此可見，ESG 指數在不同的市場中採用不同的 ESG 投資策略，可為全球投資者提供另類投資選擇，或會帶來更佳的回報。

從實證可見，許多時候 ESG 指數的風險回報表現就算不是比其母指數更勝一籌，也傾向不相伯仲。這意味着 ESG 指數方面的投資在追求合乎道德投資的同時，不一定會犧牲財務回報，其回報更可能會比傳統的投資優勝。

Chapter 16

ETFs and index funds are accelerating adoption of sustainable investing

Carolyn WEINBERG
Global Head of Product for iShares and Index Investments
BlackRock

Abdelhamid BIZID
Head of iShares Product, Platform and Markets, Asia Pacific
BlackRock

Chris DIETERICH
Editorial Director, iShares and Index Investments
BlackRock

Sunita SUBRAMONIAM
Head of Sustainable for iShares and Index Investments, Asia Pacific
BlackRock

Summary

This chapter discusses four forces that we believe will help triple assets under management in global sustainable exchange traded funds (ETFs) and index mutual funds by the end of this decade:

• Recognition that sustainability influences risk and return;

• Richer data leading to better indices;

• Investors can access sustainability at a fraction of the cost through ETFs; and

• Investors can use sustainable ETFs in a variety of ways in their portfolios.

We outline our framework for building sustainable products, then expand upon this framework by laying out a classification system for climate-oriented sustainable investment products. We conclude with client case studies in Asia Pacific that demonstrate the myriad ways in which all types of investors are using ETFs and index funds to make sustainability the new standard of investing.

Introduction

Exchange traded funds (ETFs) and index funds are expanding the market for sustainable investing and will play an integral role in facilitating one of the most consequential changes to the investment landscape in a generation.

By providing convenient, transparent, and affordable ways to access sustainable investment strategies, ETFs and index funds are helping to spread the idea that climate risk is investment risk and underscoring that sustainable characteristics of securities are consequential to returns.

Sustainable investing is a transformative trend that can help drive capital to companies best positioned to compete in a rapidly evolving economy. This point is crucial: BlackRock believes that sustainable investing starts with the proposition of better long-term, risk-adjusted returns. The coming years represent a critical period for environmental, social, and governance (ESG) issues, including climate change, and record damages from extreme weather events in 2020 have underscored to investors the importance of re-pricing climate risks[1]. Over time, we believe the search for enhanced returns will drive an enduring investor reallocation into sustainable strategies and out of traditional ones.

Sustainable strategies have been around for decades, often in niche active mutual fund vehicles, but recent years have seen a rapid acceleration in investment sentiment and demand. This tectonic shift in investor preference is due to durable investment performance, advances in data collection and analytics, and the proliferation of sustainable strategies that can fit into many investor portfolios at a low cost.

Importantly, the convenience that ETFs and index funds provide, is attracting more and more investors to sustainable assets. Globally, indexed assets under management (AUM) as a proportion of the US$1.8 trillion market for sustainable funds has quadrupled to 24% in 2020, up from 6.3% in 2014[2]. And there is still considerable room for growth. In 2020,

---

1   Source: United Nations Development Programme, "Peoples' Climate Vote", 26 January 2021. The Peoples' Climate Vote involved two "big picture" questions followed by six policy questions where the respondent could select up to three preferences per question (18 in total). The survey was distributed to people via advertising on mobile gaming networks. Some 30.7 million invitations were issued, and the survey yielded 1.4 million responses, a response rate of 4.6% across the 50 countries. Data report is based on analysis of the 1.22 million respondents who answered all three demographic questions and at least the first question on climate change.
2   Source: BlackRock analysis of data from Morningstar (as of March 2021).

BlackRock predicted that global AUM in sustainable ETFs and index mutual funds could rise to US$1.2 trillion by 2030, roughly triple the US$426 billion total as at the end of 2020[3].

Sustainable investing through indexing is becoming mainstream

Historically, accessing sustainability across asset classes was challenging due to limited product availability. Sustainable investing used to be a niche set of products, catering to values-focused (rather than performance-driven) investors. Due to the selective scope of this offering, sustainable mutual funds often came at a significantly higher expense ratio[4] than traditional products.

ETFs and index funds have expanded the availability of sustainable investment options for investors and every portfolio. Consider the growth of ETFs in particular: there are now nearly 600 sustainable ETFs globally, up from around 30 a decade ago, and a growing number of which have climate-oriented considerations[5]. The increasing number of sustainable ETFs, including climate-oriented ETFs, offers new and convenient ways for all investors to access innovative strategies.

Disruptions brought on by the global COVID-19 pandemic have only served to intensify the demand for sustainable

Sustainable terminology

Sustainable investing refers to any investment approach that combines traditional security analysis with environmental, social, and governance (ESG) insights. It is an umbrella category that captures different investment strategies.

ESG describes the data or metrics that derive insights about the environment, society, and governance, such as but not limited to climate risk, human capital management, and board structure and independence.

---

3   Source: BlackRock, "Reshaping sustainable investing", April 2020.
4   The expense ratio is a measure of the total costs associated with managing and operating the product; it typically includes the management fee and other expenses such as trustee, custody, registration fees and other operating expenses.
5   Source: BlackRock analysis of Morningstar global data (as of 31 December 2020).

investing and, globally, ETFs and index funds took in a record US$110 billion in inflows in 2020 — nearly double the prior year's mark[6]. Looking ahead, BlackRock clients recently reported plans to double their sustainable assets over the next five years, and we expect a growing share of assets to accumulate through ETFs and index funds[7].

Recognition that sustainability influences risk and return

More investors recognise that companies with favourable ESG characteristics may provide competitive performance and relatively less sustainability-related risk over the long term.

ESG insights uncover potential risks and opportunities that are not captured by traditional financial analysis. Companies that fail to manage ESG issues may be exposed to wide-ranging risks. For example, companies that produce poor quality products may face costs related to product recalls, litigation, and reduced customer loyalty. Companies exposed to increasingly frequent extreme weather events may face disruptions to their operations. What's more, companies that face sustainability-related controversies, like major data breaches, may experience reputational risk.

On the other hand, we believe companies that demonstrate positive ESG characteristics may benefit over the long term. For example, companies with strong human capital management practices may benefit from low employee turnover and high employee productivity. Companies delivering innovating solutions to improve water efficiency may benefit from the rising demand for such products, due to worsening water scarcity. Companies that manage their consumption of natural resources or reduce their waste may benefit from more efficient operations.

While modern sustainable investment indices are new, their track records reflect comparable and sometimes superior returns versus their traditional market-weighted index counterparts and higher ESG scores. For example, the MSCI USA SRI Select Reduced Fossil Fuels

---

6   Source: BlackRock analysis of Morningstar global data (as of 31 December 2020).

7   Source: *BlackRock Global Client Sustainable Investing Survey,* July – September 2020. Respondents included 425 investors in 27 countries representing an estimated US$25 trillion in AUM. Sustainable investments are defined as portfolios which have a distinct ESG objective (such as thematic or impact), apply exclusionary screens, or optimise towards ESG. It does not include ESG-integrated portfolios, company engagement or proxy voting. There is no guarantee that any forecasts made will come to pass.

Index, which selects the top 25% of companies in each sector based on ESG score and screens out companies with exposure to fossil fuels, has delivered a 17.41% return over the past five years, 1.32% more on an annualised basis than the MSCI USA Index[8].

Recent evidence suggests that sustainability may be a source of resilience. Sustainable indices are generally comprised of securities issued by companies with higher profitability and lower levels of leverage than the broader market, and Figure 1 shows certain ESG index strategies that emphasise stable businesses may potentially help investors manage market downturns. Companies with solid balance sheets may be better positioned to focus on mitigating ethical issues and introducing sustainable practices than their less-profitable peers. And conversely, companies with strong sustainable practices may need to allocate less resources on resolving controversies and litigations than their less sustainable peers.

Our view is that investors who move quickest to reallocate toward sustainability have the highest probability of financial benefit as, over time, the most sustainable assets become more valuable and the least sustainable assets become less valuable. Figure 2 illustrates the dispersion in performance between equities issued by companies with the highest and lowest ESG ratings, according to index provider MSCI — the AAA-rated companies outperformed the CCC-rated companies by 122% for the period from April 2018 to March 2021.

Figure 1. Percentage of sustainable indices that have outperformed during downturns

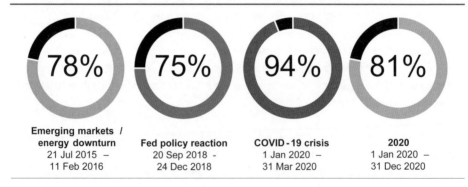

| Emerging markets / energy downturn 21 Jul 2015 – 11 Feb 2016 | Fed policy reaction 20 Sep 2018 - 24 Dec 2018 | COVID-19 crisis 1 Jan 2020 – 31 Mar 2020 | 2020 1 Jan 2020 – 31 Dec 2020 |

Note: For illustrative purposes only.

Source: BlackRock Sustainable Investing as of 31 December 2020, Morningstar as of 11 May 2020. This is a set of 32 globally representative, widely analysed sustainable indices and their non-sustainable counterparts. Indices are unmanaged and used for illustrative purposes only and are not intended to be indicative of any fund's performance. It is not possible to invest directly in an index.

---

8   Source: MSCI, as of 31 March 2021.

Figure 2. Cumulative total returns of companies with different MSCI ESG Ratings

Source: BlackRock, using underlying company ESG Rating data from MSCI ESG Research and performance data from MSCI, from 1 April 2018 to 31 March 2021. Cumulative Total Return of MSCI USA Index and company MSCI ESG Ratings within the MSCI USA Index (99.8% MSCI ESG coverage). As of 31 March 2021, there were 18 securities in the MSCI USA Index rated AAA, 96 rated AA, 131 rated A, 188 rated BBB, 123 rated BB, 54 rated B, 7 rated CCC, and 5 securities with no ESG ratings out of 622 total in the MSCI USA Index. The MSCI ESG Rating is calculated as a direct mapping of ESG Quality Scores to letter rating categories (e.g. AAA = 8.6-10). The ESG Ratings range from leader (AAA, AA), average (A, BBB, BB) to laggard (B, CCC). Index performance is for illustrative purposes only. Index performance does not reflect any management fees, transaction costs or expenses. Indices are unmanaged and one cannot invest directly in an index. Past performance does not guarantee future results and there is no guarantee that companies with higher ESG ratings will outperform companies with lower ESG ratings.

Richer data leading to better indices

The information that feeds into sustainable indices that power ETFs is improving, a trend that will help expand the market in the years ahead.

Capturing ESG insights and climate-oriented data through indices used to be challenging because information about corporate sustainability practices was scattered and hard to find. Companies are increasingly disclosing ESG metrics to help measure and communicate their efforts at managing risk and creating value through sustainability. What's more, companies are increasingly disclosing information under standardised frameworks that make information more readily comparable.

Efforts abound in creating standardisation across various sustainability reporting frameworks, and we believe there will be greater convergence in 2021. In 2020, there was a 363% increase in Sustainability Accounting Standards Board (SASB) framework disclosures and more than 1,700 organisations expressing support for the Task Force on Climate-related Financial Disclosures (TCFD)[9].

Newly equipped with standardised frameworks, companies are divulging more information about their sustainability practices and have a greater incentive to improve their corporate behaviours. This is due in part to demands from investors, governments, regulators, and the public that companies provide stakeholders with a clearer picture of how they are addressing sustainability-related business risks such as climate change. For example, the proportion of S&P 500 companies that published a sustainability or corporate responsibility report rose to 90% in 2019 from 20% in 2011[10]. Since 2013, the number of companies that disclose climate-related metrics has more than doubled — to more than 9,500[11].

Greater disclosure means more comprehensive coverage by the ESG rating firms, data aggregators, and specialised data providers. For instance, MSCI has expanded the number of ESG ratings it provides to companies by more than one-third, to 9,070, since 2018[12].

Advances in climate and data science now enable investors to better model how steadily rising temperatures affect the frequency and severity of natural catastrophes, as well as potential investment exposure and vulnerability to such hazards[13]. Big data science allows investors to review not only disclosed standardised data and third-party research, but also unstructured data, which gives rise to return-generating insights.

The range of security and portfolio metrics will look very different in a few years and it is clear that better data and disclosure is accelerating climate-oriented investing and indexing. More robust metrics will also provide investors with the ability to better frame their sustainable investing strategies by focusing on metrics that matter most to them, or which they believe can provide better outcomes.

---

9   Source: "Larry Fink's 2021 letter to CEOs", published on BlackRock's website.
10 Source: G&A Institute, *Annual S&P 500 Sustainability Reporting Analysis (2020)*, available on their website.
11 Source: Morningstar (data as of 31 December 2020).
12 Source: MSCI, April 2021
13 Source: BlackRock Investment Institute, "Getting physical: Scenario analysis for assessing climate-related risks", April 2019.

Investors can access sustainability at a fraction of the cost through ETFs

ETFs and index funds are convenient and efficient to operate, allowing fund providers to pass on cost savings to investors. The affordability of ETFs and index funds relative to other sustainable investment products will bolster demand in the years ahead.

Over the long term, there can be a steep cost in paying more than you need to in annual fund fees or to source high-quality sustainable data. A few decades ago, sustainable fund investors could either pick securities themselves (and pay for sourcing sustainable data information) or pay a high price for actively managed mutual funds, many of which had inconsistent track records.

Sustainable indices and ETFs are helping drive down the total costs of investing sustainably while broadening the variety of available exposures. Globally, in March 2020, the average actively managed sustainable equity mutual fund had a total cost of 1.15 percentage points per year on an asset-weighted basis — that was more than four times higher than the 0.28 percentage point total cost for the average sustainable equity ETF[14]. More recently, BlackRock found that the average US domiciled sustainable equity mutual fund with climate components in their investment strategies has an average net expense ratio of 1.17 percentage points per year, more than double the 0.46 percentage point for comparable ETFs[15].

As with traditional indexing, lower fees give investors a better chance of tracking or potentially beating a benchmark, when possible. Investors are transitioning money into sustainable and climate-oriented investments and we believe they will increasingly do so in the most cost-effective way possible — through sustainable ETFs and index funds.

---

14 Source: BlackRock, Bloomberg (ETFs); Morningstar (mutual funds) as of 31 March 2020.
15 Source: BlackRock analysis of Morningstar global data (as of 31 December 2020).

Investors can use sustainable ETFs in a variety of ways inside portfolios

Historically, accessing sustainability across asset classes and investment styles was a challenge, and creating an entire portfolio out of sustainable funds was nearly impossible. Today, it is easier than ever before with an expanding menu of ETF choices for investors looking to implement sustainable investing strategies. The growing number of ETFs will be a powerful force for expanding the market for sustainable investing.

Sustainability is no longer only a European trend or a niche product segment. ESG considerations can be implemented across asset classes in a variety of ways while pursuing competitive performance. In all cases, ESG ETFs provide investors large and small with the opportunity to invest sustainably across asset classes and regions.

Investors can replace traditional core exposures with sustainable building blocks or use them as unique satellite exposures to express their views on structural environmental or social trends and even seek to create a positive, measurable impact with their investments. More investors are looking to incorporate ESG in their model portfolios, since many ESG ETFs are built from the industry's most popular broad benchmarks, so investors can take a sustainable approach without fundamentally changing their asset allocations and investment strategies.

The inherent transparency that ETFs provide — transparent methodologies, frequent (often daily) transparency of holdings, transparent sustainability metrics and characteristics — makes it possible for investors to clearly articulate their objectives to stakeholders. Figure 3 presents the different ways of constructing sustainable strategies with ETFs and indexed mutual funds.

Figure 3. Five ways to align client goals with sustainable strategies

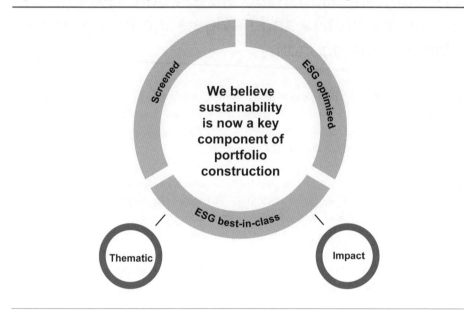

- **Screened** (often used by benchmarked institutions) — Eliminate exposure to areas such as civilian firearms and controversial weapons. These strategies tend to have low tracking error as they are usually market capitalisation weighted.

- **Optimised** (often used by asset owners in Asia) — Maximise exposure to high ESG-rated companies while closely tracking parent indices. These strategies are often used when clients / investors do not want to change their benchmarks but want to enhance their ESG scores.

- **Best-in-Class** (often used by asset managers and wealth managers in portfolios) — Access the highest-scoring ESG companies while applying extensive screens. These strategies are mostly used by high conviction clients, ready to invest in concentrated portfolios.

- **Thematic** (often used by asset managers and private banks for distribution to end investors) — Focus on a particular environmental, social or governance issue. These high-conviction strategies use a societal trend narrative (for instance, clean energy), which tends to resonate with retail and wealth investors.

- **Impact** (often used by wealth managers) — Invest for a measurable sustainable outcome alongside financial returns.

ETFs are enabling investors to address the climate imperative and navigate the transition to a low-carbon economy

BlackRock believes climate risk is investment risk, and market participants increasingly share this view. While "broad" ESG strategies have been growing and developing over the past few years, the focus on climate risk is relatively new and we believe that it is transforming the sustainable investment landscape.

Reshaping the global economy to meet the climate threat will have major financial ramifications — and not just far in the future. Investors may begin to see the effects of climate in the years ahead, and valuation trends could be magnified over the coming decades by growing investor demand for sustainable assets[16]. We do not believe that the risks and opportunities presented by climate change are yet priced into the markets. Therefore, the biggest potential benefits may accrue to the global investors, who are quickest to ready their portfolios for the new era of climate investing.

Increasingly, investors are asking us for more choices related to climate change, and in particular how to ensure that investments are aligned with commitments to a "net zero" economy — one that emits no more carbon and other greenhouse gases than are removed from the atmosphere.

A broad spectrum of investors, from asset owners to wealth managers, are turning to climate-oriented ETFs for a liquid, transparent, and efficient way to help build portfolios for the transition to a low-carbon economy.

Until recently, divestment was the predominant way to express climate-oriented objectives, for instance by excluding fossil fuels producers or reducing exposure to carbon emissions. However, the advancements in data and analytical tools

Climate terminology

Paris-alignment refers to whether business activities and portfolios are aligned with the emissions reductions trajectory necessary to meet the goal of the Paris Agreement objective of containing global warming to "well below" 2 degrees Celsius above pre-industrial era.

---

16 See BlackRock Investment Institute, "Climate change — Turning investment risk into opportunity". 21 February 2021.

have enabled more sophisticated approaches to climate investing, which can replace or complement traditional investing.

For instance, it is now possible to construct benchmarks that are closely aligned to the objectives of the Paris Agreement. The European Commission was first to define Paris-aligned Benchmarks, which index providers are using to construct Paris-aligned indices. These Paris-aligned versions of popular benchmarks are designed to reduce exposure to transition and physical climate risks and manage climate change opportunities, as well as help investors seeking to align with a decarbonation trajectory that is compatible with the Paris Agreement.

Figure 4 shows BlackRock's framework for approaching climate-focused investing with ETFs.

Figure 4. Focusing on climate using ETFs

Broad building blocks		Targeted exposure
Reduce exposure to carbon emissions or fossil fuels	Prioritise investments based on climate opportunities and risks	Target climate themes and impact outcomes

Case studies in Asia Pacific (APAC) ETF adoption

There has been a remarkable acceleration in the ways that investors are using sustainable ETFs. What follows are examples of different APAC regional investors taking different approaches to sustainability through ETFs. This shift is relatively recent and the examples below all have been implemented in the past couple of years.

- **Blending faith-based investing with global diversification**

    The investor: An insurance firm based in a Muslim-majority country in Asia wanted to provide its clients a way to help them diversify away from domestic equities while still investing in line with Shariah principles.

    Faith-based investing often entails exclusions of business activities that may be perceived to be violating certain values. Such exclusions can be codified systematically through faith-based indices that can be replicated across various markets. In this case, the insurance firm opted for Islamic ETFs as portfolio building blocks to create well diversified portfolios.

- **Combining lower volatility with ESG ratings**

The investor: A prominent insurer in Hong Kong was looking to reduce greenhouse gas emission intensity relative to a broad US equity benchmark and tilt the exposure of its portfolio to equities with lower expected volatility than the overall market.

The investor opted for an ETF whose index was optimised to minimise the expected volatility while also reducing emission intensity and exposure to fossil fuel reserves was an ideal choice for this selective investor, who provided cornerstone funding for the exposure. In addition to reducing emissions risk, the index-tracking ETF improved the ESG score for the US equity exposure.

- **Improving the sustainability credentials of discretionarily managed portfolios**

The investor: A sophisticated private bank based in Hong Kong implemented minimum ESG threshold requirements in their wealth clients' discretionarily managed portfolios and was looking for products that would enable them to improve the sustainability profile of their mandates without changing their asset allocation strategy.

Comparing products and portfolios based on metrics such as ESG score, carbon emission intensity, etc. helped them establish a baseline and define a pathway towards more sustainable portfolios. ETFs were particularly suited to their strategy, due to the transparency of the holdings and index methodologies. The bank selected a majority of best-in-class sustainable versions of popular market benchmarks to include in model portfolios for potentially better risk and return characteristics, and to help meet sustainability and climate goals. In this case, switching out of traditional equity and fixed income ETFs and into ESG equivalents helped the bank create globally diversified multi-asset portfolios of higher-rated ESG companies, while extensively screening out companies that were involved in controversial activities and / or had adverse effects on climate.

- **Reducing exposure to fossil fuels in private bank portfolios**

  The investor: An Asian private bank was looking for stringent screens around fossil fuels to replace long-term developed market equity holdings for their advisory clients. Although excluding fossil fuels was the investor's highest priority, they were also very receptive to wider ESG opportunities that could help them outperform conventional equities in the long term. Sustainable ETFs that combine screens and higher ESG ratings can serve investors as convenient equity building blocks.

  Developed market best-in-class equity ETFs as part of a strategic allocation helped the private bank prioritise higher-rated ESG companies while extensively screening out controversial activities, including fossil fuel-related ones. Additionally, the selected ETFs helped them improve carbon emission intensity in their clients' portfolios.

- **Equity opportunities in low-carbon transition readiness**

  The investor: A large asset owner in South East Asia was interested in investing in new equity ETFs that seek to overweight companies that may be better positioned to benefit from the transition to a low-carbon economy and underweight ones that may not be as well-positioned.

  ETFs can now offer investors convenient, transparent market access and a way to democratise carbon transition readiness strategies. Drivers of the low-carbon transition include physical climate risks, shifting energy mix, tighter environmental regulations, and technological innovation. Examples include a company's involvement with energy extraction and clean energy, as well as how efficiently they manage natural resources. The investor allocated to low-carbon transition readiness ETFs offering convenient, low-cost access to an innovative equity investment strategy that captures the company's exposure and management of transition risks and opportunities.

- **Bringing global net-zero opportunities to the retail segment in Thailand**

  The investor: A prominent asset manager in Thailand recognised the growing demand for sustainable thematic investing among retail investors in the country. They wanted to bring to market a simple, targeted offering that reflected opportunities that would arise from the transition to a low-carbon economy.

Investors who believe in the upside potential and who want to allocate to niche but growing areas like clean energy, electric vehicles, and green bonds may benefit from a targeted approach that is narrower in scope than a broad ESG or climate benchmark. The asset manager set up a feeder fund on the back of a pure-play ETF focusing on companies producing energy from wind, solar, and other renewable sources.

- **Building a more sustainable and diversified fixed income portfolio in Australia**

The investor: An Australian superannuation fund with strong aspirations towards sustainable and climate investing wanted to incorporate ESG across their entire portfolio, including their fixed income book. While the fund manager privileged direct investments in equities, as they considered exercising their voting rights as an integral part of active ownership, they chose to use ETFs to implement their sustainable views in fixed income and help enhance the profile of their overall portfolios.

Sustainability considerations can be implemented in a variety of fixed income markets through ESG best-in-class indices while keeping tracking error to the parent index relatively low, thereby simplifying the transition from standard to sustainable. The superannuation fund opted to switch their international fixed income allocation to a range of fixed income ESG ETFs across emerging markets debt, high yield and investment grade products.

An overview of APAC's sustainable ETF landscape

The APAC region was relatively late to sustainable investing, especially compared with Europe, but has seen significant regional momentum in the adoption of sustainable investing in recent years. A South Korean pension, a Hong Kong insurance firm, a Singapore-based robo-advisor, an asset manager in Thailand: each investor or money manager is engaged in the shift towards sustainable assets, as the previous use cases have shown.

Importantly, a select few investors in the region, typically large asset owners, have pivoted towards bespoke sustainable policy benchmarks. As early as 2016, Taiwan's Bureau of Labor Funds launched the first multi-billion US dollar mandate in Asia that combined ESG and multifactor strategies[17]. More recently, Japan's Government Pension Investment Fund (GPIF) selected broad and thematic ESG benchmarks for foreign equities in line with their objective of "improving long term returns through enhanced sustainability of individual issuers and the market as a whole"[18]. Similarly, the Hong Kong Monetary Authority (HKMA) has articulated its responsible investment policy for its Exchange Fund across public and private market investments, including adopting ESG indices as a benchmark for passive portfolios[19].

BlackRock believes that decisions made by large asset owners in the region to ratify sustainable indices will play an important role in influencing the course of investing by setting an example for other investors in their respective local markets to follow.

In the retail fund segment, and specifically in ETFs, mainland China, Australia and Japan exchanges currently dominate with a total of US$9.8 billion in assets across over 50 products[20], although the Taiwan stock exchange is not far behind, with two large local equity ETF launches in 2019 and 2020[21]. Elsewhere in APAC, the sustainable landscape is heterogeneous and very much in its infancy. Approaches differ across markets, and several local and global index providers have played a role in catering to the bespoke sustainability needs of these local markets.

Even among the largest markets, the heterogeneity of offering persists. China's net-zero ambition is echoed in the local ETF marketplace, as many new product launches and most of the asset gathering appear to be focused on climate-related thematic exposures, such as electric vehicles and clean energy. In Australia, the offering is rapidly expanding beyond domestic equities to now cover international equities, thematic ideas, and fixed income. The development of these sustainable building blocks has been fuelled by increased demand by wealth managers and financial advisors for sustainable model portfolios. In Japan, several ETFs cover a variety of niche ESG themes in local equities, aligned with some of the investments made by GPIF (focused on corporate governance or gender diversity) or with retail-focused themes (technology in particular). Since the issuance by the Securities and Futures Commission (SFC) of its first circular on green and

---

17 Source: "MSCI wins benchmark for $2.4 billion ESG and factors mandate from Taiwan's Bureau of Labor Funds", press release on MSCI's website, 19 December 2016.

18 Source: "GPIF selects two ESG-themed foreign equity indexes", published on GPIF's website, 18 December 2020.

19 See "Responsible Investment", webpage on the HKMA's website.

20 Source: BlackRock analysis of exchange traded products (ETP) data from Bloomberg, WIND, ASX, as of 31 January 2021. Excludes SOE (stated-owned enterprises) Reform ETFs in China.

21 Source: "Cathay launches Taiwan dividend ETF with ESG screening" (31 July 2020) and "Yuanta partners with FTSE Russell on Taiwan's first ESG ETF" (26 August 2019), published on the website of ETF Strategy.

ESG funds[22], the number of sustainable ETFs in Hong Kong has grown, helping investors access broad ESG and climate-themed investments, with a particular focus on China. Furthermore, the Hong Kong Exchanges and Clearing Limited (HKEX) has set up the Sustainable & Green Exchange (STAGE), a portal to provide information on sustainable, green and social investment products, from green bonds to ESG ETFs.

The future of sustainable ETFs is promising globally and in APAC

ETFs and index mutual funds are showing that sustainable investing does not need to be complex, exclusive, or expensive. In recent years, index development and democratisation of sustainable ETFs have expanded the choices for investing sustainably, and are driving new standards of quality in markets, and a longer-term orientation for companies and economies.

There is a lot of room for future growth in index investing overall and in sustainable ETFs. In 2020, BlackRock predicted that global AUM in sustainable ETFs and index funds could hit US$1.2 trillion by the end of this decade, nearly tripling the US$425 billion market where the industry left off in 2020 (see Figure 5).

BlackRock believes that there is significant potential for regional growth in APAC's sustainable ETFs. This is predicated on two factors. First, end investors in the region are just as keen to invest sustainably as their peers in the US or Europe. Through BlackRock's 2020 People & Money Survey, we asked over 8,000 individuals in Asia about their attitudes towards money, investing, and financial well-being; we discovered that people in Asia are passionate about the environmental and societal challenges faced by the world today and this trend transcended generational differences. Further, 79% of investors surveyed in Asia and 81% in Hong Kong said that they would switch to sustainable investments if all things remained equal. BlackRock believes that ETF issuers will move to address this demand gap over the medium term.

---

22 "Circular to management companies of SFC-authorised unit trusts and mutual funds — Green or ESG funds", circular on the SFC's website, 11 April 2019.

Figure 5. AUM of sustainable ETFs and index mutual funds (2016 – 2020)

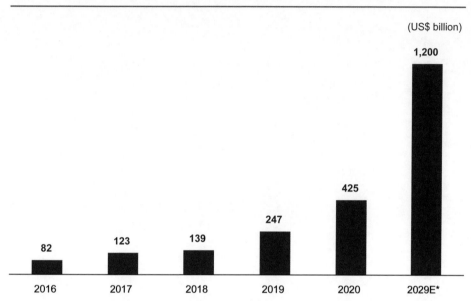

* BlackRock's estimate.

Source: BlackRock analysis of Morningstar data (as of March 2021).

The second factor relates to accessing sustainable assets in local markets. Despite the recent growth in sustainable ETFs in the region, there are several local markets where there are no or few sustainable propositions. For example, at the time of writing, there are no equity sustainable ETFs with exposure to Hong Kong, Singapore or ASEAN stocks. In other cases, the offering is not commensurate with the growth of sustainability in the underlying. For example, China is among the world's largest issuers of green and sustainable bonds, yet there are few ETFs for investors to access this segment. BlackRock believes that, with better sustainable data for the region and broader coverage of local companies, the ETF landscape will grow in local markets to fill this product gap and provide more sustainable choices for local equities and local fixed income.

The future of sustainable ETF and index mutual funds is bright globally as well as in the Asia Pacific region.

第16章

ETF及指數基金加快可持續投資的步伐

Carolyn WEINBERG
貝萊德　全球 iShares 及指數投資產品主管

Abdelhamid BIZID
貝萊德　亞太區 iShares 產品、平台及市場主管

Chris DIETERICH
貝萊德　iShares 及指數投資編輯總監

Sunita SUBRAMONIAM
貝萊德　亞太區 iShares 及指數投資可持續發展主管

摘要

本章嘗試探討我們認為有助於全球可持續交易所買賣基金（Exchange Traded Fund，簡稱 ETF）及指數互惠基金的資產管理規模在 2030 年前擴大三倍的四大動力：

- 可持續發展可影響風險及回報；

- 豐富的數據可優化指數；

- 投資者可透過 ETF 以高的成本效益涉獵可持續發展方面的投資；及

- 投資者可以在其投資組合中以多種方式使用可持續 ETF。

我們先勾畫出用以搭建可持續產品的框架，然後進一步羅列以氣候為本的可持續投資產品的分類系統。最後，我們列出一些亞太區客戶的個案，展示不同類型投資者使用 ETF 及指數基金時靈活多變的方法，使得可持續發展成為時下投資的新標準。

引言

交易所買賣基金（Exchange Traded Fund，簡稱 ETF）與指數基金正不斷擴大可持續投資方面的市場，為投資造就和推動最重要的改變，扮演着不可或缺的角色。

ETF 與指數基金為投資者實行可持續投資策略提供了便利、透明及具成本效益的途徑，有助於宣揚「氣候風險也是投資風險」的概念，也令人關注到證券的可持續特徵可以影響回報。

可持續投資是一項變革性的趨勢，可助市場資金導向有能力應變及具競爭力的公司。這一點非常關鍵：貝萊德認為可持續投資的首要前提是要提升經風險調整後的長線收益。未來數年是應對氣候變化等環境、社會及管治（Environment、Social、Governance，簡稱 ESG）問題的關鍵期，而 2020 年出現的極端天氣造成前所未有的損害，亦強調了投資者注意為氣候風險重新定價的重要性[1]。假以時日，我們相信對較佳回報的探求會驅使投資者逐步捨棄傳統策略，而轉投可持續策略的懷抱，並且是持續可見的大勢所趨。

可持續策略存在已有數十年，通常用於小眾主動型互惠基金，只是近年相關投資氣氛及需求均急速膨脹。投資者偏好有此重大轉移，可歸因於持久的投資表現往績、數據收集與分析技術進步，以及可持續投資策略越來越多，很多投資者的投資組合均可應用這些策略而所費不多。

重要的是，ETF 與指數基金提供的便利吸引了越來越多的投資者涉足可持續資產。全球以指數為基礎資產的資產管理規模在可持續基金市場（共 1.8 萬億美元）中的佔比，由 2014 年的 6.3% 增至 2020 年的 24%，升幅達三倍[2]，且仍有不少增長空間。2020 年，貝萊德曾預計，到 2030 年時，可持續 ETF 及指數互惠基金的全球資產管理規模可達 1.2 萬億美元，約為 2020 年末總數（4,260 億美元）的三倍[3]。

1　資料來源：聯合國開發計劃署（United Nations Development Programme）〈人們對於氣候的表決〉（"Peoples' Climate Vote"），2021年1月26日。〈人們對於氣候的表決〉包括兩個「大方向」問題再加另外六個政策性問題，回應人士可就每個問題（共18個）選擇最多三個答案。該項調查透過手機遊戲網絡的廣告向公眾發出，共發出了約3,070萬個邀請，獲得140萬個來自50個國家的回應，回應率為4.6%。數據報告是以回答了全部三條人口統計問題及至少第一條有關氣候變化的問題的122萬名回應人士所提供的回應作為分析基礎。

2　資料來源：貝萊德按Morningstar數據的分析（截至2021年3月）。

3　資料來源：貝萊德〈重塑可持續投資〉（"Reshaping sustainable investing"），2020年4月。

透過指數進行可持續投資漸成主流

過往由於市場上相關產品不多，要在不同資產類別實現可持續發展相當困難。可持續投資原是小眾系列產品，客戶對象是注重價值（而非表現）的投資者。由於選擇範圍甚窄，可持續互惠基金的開支比率[4] 往往遠高於傳統產品。

ETF 與指數基金為投資者及所有投資組合帶來了更多的可持續投資產品選擇。尤其是 ETF 方面的增長：現時全球有近 600 隻可持續 ETF（10 年前只有約 30 隻），注重氣候方面考量的 ETF 亦越來越多[5]。可持續 ETF（包括注重氣候的 ETF）數目不斷增加，為所有投資者接觸創新策略提供了方便的新渠道。

2020 年新冠肺炎疫情肆虐全球，所造成的破壞更深化了市場對可持續投資的需求，全球 ETF 與指數基金全年錄得創新高的 1,100 億美元現金流入，幾乎是 2019 年的兩倍[6]。展望將來，貝萊德部分客戶最近表示計劃將其可持續資產於未來五年增加一倍，我們預期透過 ETF 與指數基金累積的資產會越來越多[7]。

可持續詞彙

可持續投資是指任何結合傳統證券分析與環境、社會及管治（ESG）因素的投資方法，是一個涵蓋不同投資策略的廣泛類別。

ESG 是指可讓人洞識有關環境、社會及管治表現的數據或指標，包括但不限於氣候風險、人力資本管理，以及董事會架構和獨立性。

可持續發展可影響風險及回報

越來越多投資者認知到，有積極處理 ESG 工作的公司長遠來說可能會有更出色的表現，與可持續發展相關的風險亦相對較少。

4　開支比率是用來計算與管理及營運產品有關的總成本，一般包括管理費及其他支出，例如受託人、託管、註冊費及其他營運支出。

5　資料來源：貝萊德按Morningstar全球數據的分析（截至2020年12月31日）。

6　資料來源：貝萊德按Morningstar全球數據的分析（截至2020年12月31日）。

7　資料來源：《貝萊德全球客戶可持續投資調查》（*BlackRock Global Client Sustainable Investing Survey*），2020年7月至9月。回應人士包括來自27個國家的425名投資者（資產管理規模約為25萬億美元）。可持續投資被定義為具有獨特ESG目標（例如主題或影響力）、進行各式篩選又或向ESG方面進行優化的投資組合，但並不包括ESG整合投資組合、公司議合或委派代表投票。任何預測並沒有保證會實現。

從 ESG 角度出發可以看出傳統財務分析方法看不到的潛在風險和機遇。未能有效管理 ESG 事宜的公司可能會面對許多不同的風險。例如，產品質素低劣的公司可能須承擔有關產品回收及訴訟的成本，客戶忠誠度亦會因此減少。受到越來越頻繁的極端天氣所困擾的公司，亦可能要面對業務運作受阻的風險。此外，公司若面對與可持續發展有關的爭議（例如涉及重大數據洩密等違規情況），可能會承擔商譽風險。

另一方面，我們相信，有正面 ESG 特徵的公司可長遠得益。例如：公司注重人力資本管理，其員工流失率會較低，員工生產力較高；在水資源短缺問題日益嚴重之下，提供創新解決方案提升用水效益的公司，市場對其產品的需求或會越來越高；又例如有效管理天然資源消耗或減少廢棄物的公司，其營運效率亦或會有所提升。

儘管現時的可持續投資指數歷史仍很短，但這些指數的往績紀錄反映其回報可媲美（有時甚至勝過）傳統的市場加權指數，ESG 分數亦較後者高。例如，MSCI 美國社會責任投資精選減少化石燃料指數（MSCI USA SRI Select Reduced Fossil Fuels Index）從每個行業挑選 ESG 分數最高的 25% 的公司，並剔除使用化石燃料的公司，而該指數於過去五年的回報率達 17.41%，按年較 MSCI 美國指數高 1.32%[8]。

近期有證據顯示可持續發展或可增加投資韌性。可持續指數的成份股一般是盈利能力高於、且槓桿水平低於大市的公司，而按圖 1 所顯示，一些強調業務穩定的 ESG 指數策略或會有助投資者應付跌市。相較於盈利能力較低的公司，資產負債表較扎實的公司或會較有能力緩解道德方面的問題，亦較有能力實行有關可持續發展的做法；反過來說，相較於不太着重可持續發展的公司，嚴格實行有關可持續發展做法的公司需要在解決爭議及訴訟方面投放的資源或可以少一些。

我們的看法是，投資者越快將投資以可持續發展方向重新分配，能獲得經濟利益的機率便越大，因為隨着時間流逝，最注重可持續的資產將會變得更有價值；相反地，最不關注可持續的資產則會隨之貶值。圖 2 所示的是根據指數供應商 MSCI 的資料，就 ESG 評級最高與最低的公司所發行的股票的表現所作的對照 —— 由 2018 年 4 月至 2021 年 3 月，評級 AAA 的公司的收益較評級 CCC 的公司高 122%。

8　資料來源：MSCI，數據截至2021年3月31日。

圖 1：跌市期間跑贏大市的可持續指數佔比

78%	75%	94%	81%
新興市場/能源低迷	對聯儲局政策的反應	新冠肺炎疫情肆虐	**2020 年**
2015 年 7 月 21 日至	2018 年 9 月 20 日至	2020 年 1 月 1 日至	2020 年 1 月 1 日至
2016 年 2 月 11 日	2018 年 12 月 24 日	2020 年 3 月 31 日	2020 年 12 月 31 日

註：僅供説明。

資料來源：《貝萊德可持續投資》（截至 2020 年 12 月 31 日），Morningstar（截至 2020 年 5 月 11 日）。有關資料包括
32 隻涉及全球市場、廣受分析的可持續指數及其非可持續版本指數。有關指數未受管理且僅用作説明用
途，亦不反映任何基金的表現。投資者無法直接投資任何指數。

圖 2：不同 MSCI ESG 評級的公司的累計總回報率

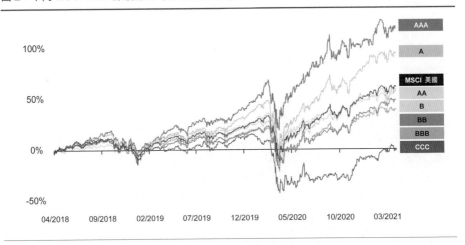

資料來源：貝萊德（採用由 MSCI ESG 研究部提供的相關公司 ESG 評級數據及由 MSCI 提供的表現數據，2018 年 4
月 1 日至 2021 年 3 月 31 日）。MSCI 美國指數的累計總回報及 MSCI 美國指數中的公司 MSCI ESG 評級
（MSCI ESG 覆蓋率達 99.8%）。於 2021 年 3 月 31 日，在 MSCI 美國指數的 622 隻證券當中，有 18 隻
為 AAA 級，96 隻為 AA 級，131 隻為 A 級，188 隻為 BBB 級，123 隻為 BB 級，54 隻為 B 級，7 隻為
CCC 級，5 隻沒有 ESG 評級。MSCI ESG 評級的計算方法為將 ESG 質素分數直接轉成字母評級類別（例
如 AAA = 8.6-10）。ESG 評級分為「領先（leader）」（AAA、AA）、「平均（average）」（A、BBB、BB）及「落
後（laggard）」（B、CCC）。指數表現僅供説明，概不反映任何管理費用、交易成本或支出。有關指數未
受管理，投資者無法直接投資任何指數。過去表現並不保證未來業績，亦不保證 ESG 評級較高的公司表
現會優於 ESG 評級較低的公司。

豐富的數據可優化指數

現在，ETF 背後涉及的可持續指數所包含的資訊質素越來越高，當有助於這方面市場的未來拓展。

在過往，透過指數獲取 ESG 方面的信息與氣候相關的數據可說相當困難，因為有關企業可持續做法的資訊較為零散，不易收集。而現在，越來越多公司披露其 ESG 指標，以協助計量並讓市場知道其在透過可持續發展來管理風險並創造價值方面所付出的努力。還有就是越來越多公司會按規範化的框架披露信息，令不同公司的資訊更容易和更方便地作比較。

此外，市場積極推動不同的可持續匯報框架之間相互協調以達到標準化、規範化，我們相信 2021 年可以見到更大程度的接軌和一體化。2020 年，根據永續會計準則委員會（Sustainability Accounting Standards Board）的框架披露的資訊增加了 363%，逾 1,700 家機構表示支持氣候相關財務信息披露工作組（Task Force on Climate-related Financial Disclosures）[9]。

多了標準化的框架，公司開始披露越來越多有關其可持續做法的資訊，改善本身企業行為的動力也越來越大。這部分歸因於投資者、政府、監管機構及公眾都要求公司更清晰地向持份者展示其如何解決與可持續發展有關的業務風險（例如氣候變化）。例如，標準普爾 500 指數公司當中，刊發了可持續或企業責任報告的公司佔比由 2011 年的 20% 增至 2019 年的 90%[10]。自 2013 年起，披露氣候相關指標的公司數目超過 9,500 家，增幅逾倍[11]。

披露水平的提升，意味着 ESG 評級機構、數據集成商和專門數據供應商的覆蓋範圍變得更全面。例如，2018 年以來，MSCI 向公司提供的 ESG 評級數目增至 9,070 項，增幅逾三分之一[12]。

氣候科學與數據科學的進步，讓投資者可更有效地用模型預測氣溫持續上升會如何影響天然災害的頻密度和嚴重程度，以及投資時須面臨或容易受其影響的相關風險[13]。透過大數據科學，投資者除可檢視已披露的標準化數據與第三方研究外，還可研究零散數據，從中得出或可為其帶來回報的啟示。

9　資料來源：〈Larry Fink給各行政總裁的信2021〉（"Larry Fink's 2021 letter to CEOs"），載於貝萊德的網站。

10　資料來源：G&A Institute《年度標準普爾500可持續匯報分析（2020年）》（*Annual S&P 500 Sustainability Reporting Analysis (2020)*），載於G&A Institute的網站。

11　資料來源：Morningstar（2020年12月31日的數據）。

12　資料來源：MSCI，2021年4月。

13　資料來源：貝萊德 Investment Institute〈實際行動：評估氣候相關風險的情境分析〉（"Getting Physical: Scenario analysis for assessing climate-related risks"），2019年4月。

可以預見，不出數年內，證券及投資組合指標的範圍便會跟現在所見的大不相同，而很清楚的是，高質素的數據及信息披露正加快市場在投資和指數上注重氣候考量的步伐。較全面的指標亦有助於投資者更有效地制定其可持續投資策略，包括集中考量對其最相關又或其認為能達到較好結果的指標。

投資者可透過 ETF 以高的成本效益涉獵可持續發展方面的投資

ETF 與指數基金的操作方便且高效，基金供應商節省成本的效益可傳導給投資者。ETF 與指數基金也較其他可持續投資產品便宜，而這一優勢料將推高其未來的市場需求。

長遠而言，支付高於所需的基金年費又或搜尋優質可持續數據所涉及的成本都可以很昂貴。數十年前，可持續基金投資者只得兩個選擇：(1) 親自挑選證券 (同時支付搜尋可持續數據資料的成本)；(2) 付出高昂費用惠顧主動管理型互惠基金 (但基金往績紀錄多不穩定)。

通過可持續指數及 ETF，現在可持續投資的總成本正漸漸降低，可投資的產品範圍也越來越大。於 2020 年 3 月，全球的主動管理型可持續股票互惠基金的總成本平均為每年 1.15 個百分點 (按資產加權基準計算)，是一般可持續股票 ETF 的平均總成本 (0.28 個百分點) 的四倍有多 [14]。再近期一點，貝萊德發現，投資組合中包含氣候成份股的一般美國註冊可持續股票互惠基金，其平均淨支出比率為每年 1.17 個百分點，為可比 ETF 的平均淨支出比率 (0.46 個百分點) 的一倍以上 [15]。

一如傳統指數產品，較低的費用使投資者有更好的機會跟蹤或甚至有可能超過基準指數的表現。投資者的資金都紛紛轉投可持續及注重氣候因素的投資，我們相信這趨勢只會更加明顯，而過程中他們會儘可能以最具成本效益的方法進行，也就是投資於可持續 ETF 與指數基金。

---

14 資料來源：貝萊德、彭博 (ETF)：Morningstar (互惠基金) (截至2020年3月31日)。
15 資料來源：貝萊德按Morningstar全球數據的分析 (截至2020年12月31日)。

投資者可以在其投資組合中以多種方式使用可持續 ETF

過往，在各種資產類別中以不同投資風格來追求可持續發展相當困難，要完全以可持續基金組成一個完整的投資組合更是近乎不可能。現時，尋求實行可持續投資策略的投資者可以選擇的 ETF 越來越多，要實現上述追求變得前所未有的容易。ETF 數目不斷增加，將為可持續投資市場的進一步拓展提供強大動力。

可持續發展的趨勢不再局限於歐洲或小眾產品市場。投資於不同的資產類別都可透過各種方法納入 ESG 考慮因素，同時追求具競爭力的表現。無論如何，透過 ESG ETF 產品，大小投資者都有機會進行跨資產類別和跨地區的可持續投資。

投資者可以把傳統的核心投資換成可持續的元素，或將可持續元素作為獨特的周邊元素，以之反映其對環境或社會的結構性趨勢的見解，甚至利用其投資帶出正面、可計量的影響。越來越多投資者擬於其標準投資組合中加入 ESG 因素，而由於不少 ESG ETF 都是取材自業內最受歡迎的廣泛基準，故投資者在採取可持續做法時，也不用徹底改變其原有的資產配置和投資策略。

ETF 產品由於先天具備透明度 —— 方法透明、持倉更新的披露頻繁（通常為每日）、可持續指標及特徵透明，這讓投資者得以向持份者清晰表達其目標。圖 3 顯示利用 ETF 與指數互惠基金制定可持續策略的各種方法。

圖 3：滿足客戶可持續策略目標的五大方案

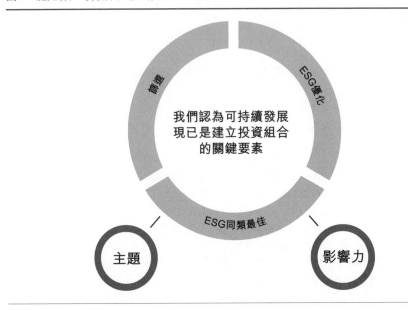

- **篩選**（基準機構常用）—— 將民用軍火和具爭議性武器等範疇剔出投資組合。這類策略通常屬市值加權性質，追蹤誤差偏低。

- **優化**（亞洲資產擁有人常用）—— 投資組合儘量增加對 ESG 評級較高的公司的投資，同時緊貼追蹤母指數，通常是在客戶 / 投資者不欲改變其基準但又想提升 ESG 評分時採用。

- **同類最佳**（資產管理人及財富管理人常用於投資組合）—— 投資 ESG 評分最高的公司，同時進行大量篩選。採用這類策略的，多是有高信念、隨時願意投資於集中型投資組合的客戶。

- **主題**（資產管理人與私人銀行分發給終端投資者時常用）—— 專注於特定的環境、社會或管治議題。這類高信念策略皆以社會趨勢作表述（例如潔淨能源），散戶和財富投資者對此通常都有共鳴。

- **影響力**（財富管理人常用）—— 投資尋求財務回報的同時也追求可計量的可持續發展成果。

ETF 有助於投資者了解和應對迫在眉睫的氣候問題，並引導他們過渡至低碳經濟

貝萊德認為氣候風險等於投資風險，市場參與者對此亦越來越認同。儘管過去數年廣泛的 ESG 策略不斷增加及發展，但着重氣候風險的也是近期才出現，我們相信可持續投資環境將會由此改寫。

重塑全球經濟以應對氣候威脅會產生重大的財務影響，而這種影響並非出現於遙不可及的未來。投資者可能於數年內已開始體驗到氣候變化帶來的影響，加上投資者對可持續資產的需求日增，未來數十年的估值趨勢可能也更加明顯[16]。我們不認為市場價格已計及氣候變化所呈現的風險和機遇的價值。因此，全球投資者中誰能最快準備妥當、調整好名下投資組合來迎接氣候投資的新時代，誰就有機會早着先機，獲利最豐。

越來越多投資者要求我們提供更多有關氣候變化的投資選擇，尤其是要求說明如何確保投資符合達到「淨零」經濟的承諾（「淨零」是指碳排放量與其他溫室氣體排放量不多於從大氣層中清除的量）。

不少投資者（包括資產擁有人以至財富管理人）紛紛轉投以氣候為本的 ETF，取其可以流動性高、透明及高效的方式協助其建立投資組合，以過渡至低碳經濟。

直至最近，撤資才成為展示以氣候為本的目標的主要方法（例如剔除化石燃料製造商或減少對碳排放的投資）。然而，數據及分析工具的進步已造就更精細的氣候投資方法，可取代傳統投資或與之相輔相成。

舉例而言，現在已可建立緊貼《巴黎協定》（Paris Agreement）各項目標的基準。歐洲委員會（European Commission）率先定義符合《巴黎協定》的基準，指數供應商都使用這些基準建立符合《巴黎協定》的指數。這些從熱門基準衍生出來、符合《巴黎協定》的基準，旨在減低轉型及實際氣候風險，並管理有關氣候變化的機遇，同時協助投資者走上與《巴黎協定》一致的脫碳軌道。

圖 4 顯示貝萊德透過 ETF 進行氣候投資的框架。

> **氣候詞彙**
>
> **符合《巴黎協定》**是指業務活動及投資組合與實現《巴黎協定》的目標所必需的減排軌跡保持一致，《巴黎協定》的目標是將全球暖化的程度控制在比工業革命前的氣溫升高「遠低於」攝氏 2 度。

16　參閱貝萊德 Investment Institute〈氣候變化 —— 將投資風險轉化為機遇〉（"Climate change — Turning investment risk into opportunity"），2021年2月21日。

圖 4：利用 ETF 進行氣候投資

主要投資資產		目標持倉
減少涉及碳排放或化石燃料的投資	投資時優先考量氣候機遇及風險	以氣候方面的主題及影響力結果為目標

亞太區 ETF 投資個案研究

投資者使用可持續 ETF 的方法有顯著的進展。下文載列亞太區不同投資者以各種方法透過 ETF 進行可持續發展投資的例子。有關轉變是較近期才出現，以下所有例子均是在過去幾年內實施。

- **結合全球多元化和信仰為本的投資**

  投資者：一家位於亞洲穆斯林國家的保險公司擬為客戶提供方案，協助其在投資組合中以不違背伊斯蘭教條加入本地股票以外的投資。

  信仰為本的投資通常會排除可能被認為違背某些價值的業務活動。這種排除法可透過以信仰為本的指數（不同市場皆可複製）——系統化。在此個案中，該保險公司選擇以伊斯蘭 ETF 作為投資組合的基本元素，再分別建立充分多元化的投資組合。

- **結合低波動性和 ESG 評級**

  投資者：香港一家著名的保險公司擬減低溫室氣體排放密度（相對於一廣泛的美國股票基準），並讓投資組合偏重預期波幅較整體市場低的股本證券。

  該投資者選擇了一個將指數優化以減少預期波幅、同時亦減低排放密度及化石燃料儲量風險的 ETF，對於這位講究的投資者而言，這是個理想的選擇，因該投資者為這項化石燃料儲量的投資提供了基石資金。除減低排放風險外，該追蹤指數的 ETF 提高了所涉美股投資的 ESG 評分。

- **提升自主管理投資組合的可持續認證**

  投資者：香港一家高端私人銀行對其財富客戶的自主管理投資組合實施最低 ESG 門檻規定，可讓其毋須改變資產配置策略而能夠提升其獲授權投資的產品組合的可持續發展水平。

根據 ESG 評分及碳排放密度等指標比較產品與投資組合後，該私人銀行訂立了基準線並設定如何建立可持續發展水平更高的投資組合。由於 ETF 的持倉和指數方法論均較透明，因此尤其適合他們的策略。該銀行最後挑選加入其標準投資組合的，大多是熱門市場基準指數的「同類最佳」可持續版本基準指數，以提升風險回報特徵，也協助其達到可持續及氣候目標。在此個案中，從傳統股票與定息 ETF 轉向與 ESG 有關的同類產品，有助於該銀行建立包括 ESG 評級較高的公司、分散全球的多元資產投資組合，同時篩出許多參與具爭議性的活動及 / 或對氣候有不良影響的公司。

- **私人銀行投資組合減少化石燃料方面的投資**

投資者：一家亞洲私人銀行擬為其顧問客戶對涉及化石燃料的投資嚴加篩選，以換掉其對發達市場方面股票的長期持倉。儘管排除化石燃料是該投資者的首要事項，但他們亦很樂意嘗試其他範圍更廣的 ESG 機遇，以助其長線跑贏傳統股本證券。所以，對投資者來說，結合篩選與較高 ESG 評級的可持續 ETF 可以是很方便的組合元素。

發達市場同類最佳股票 ETF 作為策略性配置的一部分，有助於該私人銀行優先選擇 ESG 評級較高的公司，同時大量篩出具爭議性的活動（包括與化石燃料有關的活動）。此外，所選的 ETF 有助於其改善客戶投資組合中的碳排放密度。

- **作低碳過渡準備的股票投資機遇**

投資者：一名東南亞的大型資產擁有者有意投資一些新的股票型 ETF，該等 ETF 會增持那些或較能在低碳經濟過渡中得益的公司，而減持在這方面實力較遜的公司。

ETF 現時可讓投資者以便利及透明的方式參與市場，並使碳過渡準備策略大眾化。過渡至低碳經濟的推動因素包括實際氣候風險、能源組合轉移、環境規例收緊，以及科技方面的創新等，例如公司在能源提取及潔淨能源方面的參與，以及其管理天然資源的效率。該投資者將其投資分配至低碳過渡準備型 ETF，有關 ETF 讓其輕易地、並且低成本地採用創新的股票投資策略，掌握該公司對過渡風險與機遇的投資及管理。

- **為泰國散戶帶來全球淨零機遇**

投資者：一名泰國的著名資產管理人看到泰國個人投資者對可持續主題投資的需求越來越大，希望可為市場引進能反映過渡至低碳經濟所帶來機遇的簡單、定向投資產品。

投資者若相信潔淨能源、電動車及綠色債券等小眾、但正不斷發展的範疇具有增長潛力，可能更容易在採用比泛 ESG 或氣候基準範圍較窄的定向投資法中獲益。該資產管理人最後設立了一個聯接基金，聯接至一個專項 ETF 來集中投資於透過風力、太陽能及其他可再生資源來生產能源的公司。

- 建立更加可持續及多元化的澳洲定息投資組合

  投資者：一隻對可持續及氣候投資有強烈興趣的澳洲退休基金擬在其整個投資組合（包括定息投資）中加入 ESG 元素。儘管基金經理很重視直接投資股本證券（因為他們認為行使投票表決權是積極所有權的重要一環），但還是選擇利用 ETF 在定息投資組合中實現其在可持續方面的理念，並協助提升整體投資組合的質素。

  可持續方面的考慮因素可透過 ESG 同類最佳指數於不同的定息市場執行，同時將與母指數之間的追蹤誤差維持在較低水平，使得從「標準」過渡至「可持續」的過程簡單一點。該退休基金最後選擇將其國際定息投資轉為投放於一系列的定息 ESG ETF，涉及新興市場債務、高收益及投資級產品等。

亞太區可持續 ETF 概覽

相對於其他地區（尤其是歐洲），亞太區接觸可持續投資較遲，但近年區內採用可持續投資的勢頭相當強勁。就像上文個案所述，一隻南韓養老基金、一家香港保險公司、一名新加坡機械人投資顧問、一名泰國資產管理人：每個投資者或資金管理人都先後轉投可持續資產的懷抱。

重要的是，區內有少數投資者（一般為大型資產擁有者）轉向了度身訂造的可持續政策基準。早於 2016 年，台灣勞動基金運用局已發出亞洲首項結合 ESG 與多重因素策略的數十億美元委託經營[17]。較近期一點，日本年金積立金管理運用獨立行政法人（Government Pension Investment Fund，簡稱 GPIF）就海外股本證券挑選了廣泛及主題性的 ESG 基準，符合其「透過提升個別發行人以至整體市場的可持續發展水平來提升長期回報」的目標[18]。無獨有偶，香港金融管理局（簡稱「香港金管局」）就其外匯基金在公開及私人市場的投資發佈其負責任投資政策，包括採納 ESG 指數作為被動式投資組合的投資基準[19]。

貝萊德認為，該地區大型資產所有者對可持續指數的認可，將為當地市場的其他投資者樹立榜樣，在影響、推動可持續投資的進程中發揮重要作用。

---

17 資料來源：〈MSCI獲台灣勞動基金運用局發出24億元ESG及因素委託經營基準〉（"MSCI wins benchmark for \$2.4 billion ESG and factors mandate from Taiwan's Bureau of Labor Funds"），MSCI網站上的新聞稿，2016年12月19日。

18 資料來源：〈GPIF挑選了兩隻以ESG為主題的海外股票指數〉（"GPIF selects two ESG-themed foreign equity indexes"），載於GPIF 的網站，2020年12月18日。

19 參閱香港金管局網站上的《負責任投資》網頁。

零售基金（尤其是 ETF）方面，現時是中國內地、澳洲和日本等交易所主導，涉及 50 多隻產品合共 98 億美元的資產 [20]，但臺灣證券交易所亦距離不遠 —— 2019 年和 2020 年推出兩隻大型本地 ETF[21]。亞太區其他地方的可持續市場發展則較為混雜，且仍在發展初期。不同市場的投資方法各有不同，而數家本地和全球指數供應商已着手回應這些本土市場的需要，為它們度身訂造可持續發展的相關服務。

就算是在最大型的市場，產品的參差度仍然存在。中國的本土 ETF 市場均配合國家的淨零排放目標，不少新推出的產品及匯聚的大部分資產均趨向注重氣候主題（例如電動車和潔淨能源）。澳洲方面，投資產品急速拓展，不僅有本地股本證券，現時更涵蓋國際股本證券、主題性概念及定息產品。財富管理人及財務顧問對可持續標準投資組合的需求日益增加，推動了這類在投資組合中的可持續元素的發展。在日本，數隻 ETF 涵蓋了各種本地股票中的小眾 ESG 主題，與 GPIF 所進行的部分投資（着重企業管治或性別多元化）或以零售為重心的主題（尤其是科技）的投資一致。在香港，證券及期貨事務監察委員會（簡稱「香港證監會」）就綠色及 ESG 基金刊發首份通函後 [22]，香港的可持續 ETF 數目有所增加，有助於投資者進行廣泛的 ESG 及氣候主題投資（尤其是以中國為重心）。此外，香港交易及結算所有限公司（簡稱「香港交易所」）設立了可持續及綠色交易所（Sustainable & Green Exchange，稱為 STAGE）—— 一個提供有關可持續、綠色及社會責任投資產品（包括綠色債券以至 ESG ETF 等）資訊的平台。

可持續 ETF 在亞太區以至全球的前景樂觀

ETF 與指數互惠基金告訴我們，可持續投資不一定複雜、獨有或昂貴。近年的指數發展加上可持續 ETF 的普及化，可持續投資的選擇增多，市場也出現新的質量標準，推動公司和經濟體擁有更具遠見的發展目標。

指數投資整體和可持續 ETF 的未來仍有許多增長空間。於 2020 年，貝萊德預計全球可持續 ETF 與指數基金的資產管理規模可於未來十年內達到 1.2 萬億美元，幾乎是 2020 年數字（4,250 億美元）的三倍（見圖 5）。

20　資料來源：貝萊德按取自彭博、WIND、ASX的交易所買賣產品數據（於2021年1月31日）的分析。數據不包括中國的國有企業改革ETF。

21　資料來源：〈國泰推出採用ESG篩選的台灣股息ETF〉（"Cathay launches Taiwan dividend ETF with ESG screening"）（2020年7月31日）和〈元大與富時羅素合作推出台灣首隻ESG ETF〉（"Yuanta partners with FTSE Russell on Taiwan's first ESG ETF"）（2019年8月26日），載於ETF Strategy的網站。

22　〈致證監會認可單位信託及互惠基金的管理公司的通函 —— 環境、社會及管治基金〉，香港證監會網站上的通函，2019年4月11日。

圖 5：可持續 ETF 與指數互惠基金的資產管理規模（2016 年至 2020 年）

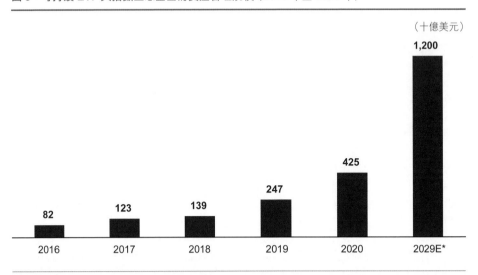

（十億美元）

* 貝萊德的估計。

資料來源：貝萊德按 Morningstar 數據的分析（截至 2021 年 3 月）。

貝萊德相信亞太區的可持續 ETF 有極大的地區增長潛力。有關預測是基於兩項因素作出：第一，區內的終端投資者對可持續投資的熱衷不遜於歐美投資者。在貝萊德的 2020 年人口及金錢調查（People & Money Survey）中，我們訪問了亞洲區逾 8,000 名個人受訪者對金錢、投資及財務狀況的態度；我們發現亞洲人對於現時全球面對的環境及社會挑戰非常在意，而該趨勢不受年代差距影響。此外，在受訪的亞洲及香港投資者當中，分別有 79% 及 81% 表示若一切對等，他們都會轉向可持續投資。貝萊德認為在不久將來，ETF 發行人會着手填補這需求上的缺口。

第二項因素關乎本土市場有否投資可持續資產的渠道。儘管區內可持續 ETF 近期有所增長，但還有幾個本土市場完全沒有（或只有極少）與可持續發展相關的投資渠道。例如截至執筆之時，沒有任何投資於香港、新加坡或東南亞國家聯盟的股票可持續 ETF；或有關投資產品並不符合所涉及相關資產的可持續水平。例如，中國是全球最大的綠色及可持續債券發行人之一，但僅有少數可供投資者選擇的可持續 ETF。貝萊德相信，只要區內可持續數據質素提升、更多本地公司獲涵蓋，各個 ETF 市場均可進一步增長，來填補當中的產品缺口，為不同市場的當地股本證券及定息產品提供更多可持續方面的選擇。

亞太區以至全球的可持續 ETF 與指數互惠基金的前景均一片光明。

註：本文原稿是英文，另以中文譯本出版。如本文的中文本的字義或詞義與英文本有所出入，概以英文本為準。

Chapter 17

Fixed income markets:
The rapid global development
of sustainable bonds

Chaoni HUANG
Head of Sustainable Capital Markets
Global Markets Asia Pacific
BNP Paribas S.A.

Summary

Green, social and sustainability financing is growing rapidly, with implications for investors and companies globally. This chapter seeks to discuss key developments in the sustainable bonds market. The paper covers the definitions and landmark developments for each of the main sub-categories of the sustainable bond market, namely, green bonds, social bonds, sustainability bonds, transition bonds, and sustainability-linked bonds. Special attention is given to developments in the Asia Pacific region, and specifically in China, which already accounts for a lion's share of the global green bond market.

The paper argues that further regulatory harmonisation and developments in China will provide a substantial boost to the sustainable bonds market beyond green bonds. This trend will be accompanied by further action by multilateral development banks and other supranational organisations, also in light of the impact of the COVID-19 pandemic in triggering the need for innovative sources of financing to address challenges that are inherently part of the green, social and sustainability agenda.

Overview of the sustainable bond market

There is broad consensus among global multilateral institutions such as the United Nations, the World Bank and a majority of nation states around the world on the need for urgent action that will drive the transition towards a more sustainable and ultimately carbon-neutral development model. The massive funding needs associated with this task are a historic challenge, and opportunity, for international and local capital markets.

Bond and loan markets are responding to this challenge with the rapid development of Green, Social and Sustainability (GSS) financing products, which are part of the broader growth of financing and investment that aligns with Environmental, Social and Governance (ESG) principles. This chapter will focus on the fixed income component of sustainable financing, or what we can broadly refer to as sustainable bonds. This category covers a variety of instruments, ranging from the now well-established green bonds, to newer formats such as social bonds, sustainability bonds, transition bonds and sustainability-linked bonds (SLBs).

In this chapter, sustainable bonds and SLBs will refer to those which the World Bank defines as instruments that can deliver outcomes to support the Sustainable Development Goals (SDGs)[1] agenda set by the United Nations in 2015 and adopted by all 195 member states. A more precise discussion on the definitions is found in the next section of this chapter.

Over the past decade and a half, the development of the sustainable bond market has followed a pattern found in other areas of financial innovation. Multilateral Development Banks (MDBs) were the catalyst, first making the transition from policy goals, such as climate finance and the SDGs, to commercially viable issuance structures that could be widely adopted by market participants. MDBs have driven innovation in a number of areas: the World Bank issued the first blockchain bond in 2018 and, with some prescience, the first pandemic bond in 2017[2].

---

1   See United Nations' website (https://sdgs.un.org/goals) on the 17 SDGs.

2   Source: "World Bank launches world-first blockchain bond", *Reuters*, 23 August 2018; "World Bank launches first-ever pandemic bonds to support $500 million pandemic emergency financing facility", press release on World Bank's website, 28 June 2017.

MDBs were followed quickly by issuers from the banking and broader financial institutions segment, who were in turn followed by multinationals and other corporations.

The first green bond, which can be credited with launching climate finance in the capital markets, was issued in 2007 by the European Investment Bank. This was labelled as a "Climate Awareness Bond" and its proceeds were directed towards financing renewable energy and energy efficiency projects[3]. The first step for bonds linked to the SDGs came with a World Bank issuance in March 2017 under the "SDGs Everyone" initiative it announced in January of the same year[4]. Mexico became the first sovereign issuer in September 2020 with a US$890 million SDG offering[5].

In the green bond market, Asian sovereigns were among the pioneers, with the Republic of Indonesia being the first sovereign from the region to issue in the format with a US$1.25 billion five-year Sukuk in March 2018[6]. The Hong Kong Special Administrative Region has also been among the trailblazers: in February 2018, Hong Kong became one of the few sovereign issuers to establish a green bond programme, with a ceiling of HK$100 billion, or nearly US$13 billion[7]. In his 2021-22 Budget speech, Financial Secretary Paul Chan proposed doubling that ceiling to allow for further issuance of HK$175.5 billion (US$22.6 billion) over the next five years[8].

Figure 1 offers an overview of sustainable finance categories, in accordance with the International Capital Market Association (ICMA).

---

3   Source: International Finance Corporation, "Mobilizing private climate finance — Green bonds and beyond", *EMCompass*, Note 25, December 2016.
4   Source: "World Bank issues first UN sustainable development bond", *Reuters*, 9 March 2017.
5   Source: United Nations Development Programme (UNDP), "Historic $890 million Sustainable Development Goals Bond issued by Mexico", 14 September 2020.
6   Source: UNDP, "Indonesia's green sukuk", 8 October 2018.
7   Source: Government of the Hong Kong Special Administrative Region of the People's Republic of China, "Government Green Bond Programme", 15 November 2018.
8   Source: "Speech by the Financial Secretary, the Hon Paul MP Chan moving the Second Reading of the Appropriation Bill 2021", 24 February 2021.

Figure 1. ICMA's categories of sustainable finance

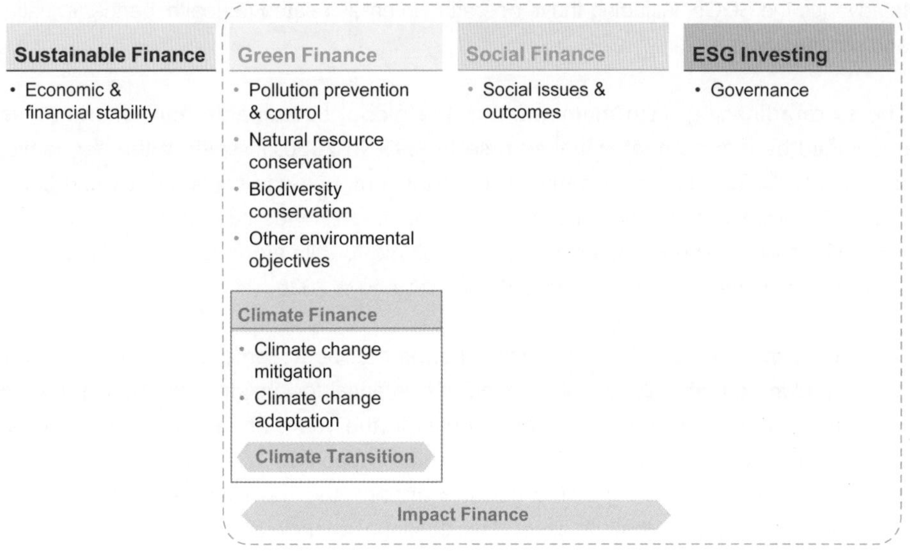

Source: ICMA, "Green, Social and Sustainablility Bonds: A High-Level Mapping to the Sustainable Development Goals", June 2020.

Sustainable bond markets are now on the cusp of the final transition from a niche segment to one with broad appeal across the institutional and retail investor bases. Today, sustainable bonds cover a wide range of thematic uses of proceeds, from climate to any of the 17 SDGs, which include gender equality, poverty elimination, good health and well-being and sustainable cities and communities.

Globally, retail investors have demonstrated their support for the sustainable finance agenda with an estimated US$715 billion of accumulated investments, according to a recent survey, with the most targeted sectors for capital allocations being energy and financial services, excluding microfinance[9]. In Asia, SDG-linked bonds have been made specifically available to retail investors since December 2018, when the World Bank

---

9   Source: "Global impact investment market going strong despite pandemic – GIIN", published on the website of Pensions & Investments, 11 June 2020.

launched SDG index-linked bonds in Hong Kong and Singapore[10]. These bonds offered returns linked to an equity index tracking the performance of companies that are deemed to advance the SDGs, including those operating in areas related to health, gender equality and climate.

The extraordinary growth momentum in the global sustainable bond market was underlined by the fact that issuance rose by 29% in 2020, in spite of the pandemic, reaching US$732.1 billion. Nearly a fifth of this amount was social bonds and close to US$70 billion was sustainability bonds, while green bonds surged to a new high of US$305.3 billion. The cumulative issuance volume for climate finance alone is around US$1 trillion between its inception in 2007 and the end of 2020[11].

The global growth trend for sustainable bonds has been remarkable, but historical numbers alone do not fully reveal the market's potential for growth, especially given the role that Asia and China in particular can play in the years ahead. Alongside further enhancements to the architecture and frameworks supporting sustainable bond markets, their application to Asia's growing need to finance the transition towards net-zero emissions should ensure that the asset class continues to grow and flourish.

Indeed, China is already a powerful catalyst for the growth of sustainable bonds. Total green bond issuance from the country in 2020 was US$37.6 billion, down from the record volume of US$55.58 billion in 2019[12], mainly due to COVID-19 disruption. In 2020, China was the fourth largest country for green bond issuance globally, following the US, Germany and France[13].

Chinese issuance that only adhered to domestic green bond standards was US$15.33 billion, or 41% of the total volume[14]. A more detailed discussion on the various regulators involved in regulating China's market follows in subsequent sections, but for now it is worth noting that domestic green bonds issued under the framework established by the National Development and Reform Commission (NDRC) had until early 2021 primarily differed from those following international standards in that they allowed issuers to allocate up to 50% of

---

10 Source: "World Bank introduces sustainable development goals index-linked bonds for retail investors in Hong Kong and Singapore", press release on World Bank's website, 17 December 2018.

11 Source: "Social bonds propel ESG issuance to record $732 billion in 2020", *Bloomberg*, 11 January 2021.

12 Source: "China's next energy transition plan set to boost green bond issuance in 2021", published on the *S&P Global – Market Intelligence* website, 28 February 2021.

13 Source: Ditto.

14 Source: Ditto.

proceeds to repay loans or invest in general working capital. However, the People's Bank of China (PBOC), NDRC and China Securities Regulatory Commission jointly released an updated green bond framework — the *Green Bonds Endorsed Project Catalogue (2021 Edition)* — in April 2021 (referred to as the "Green Bond Catalogue" hereinafter). The Catalogue excludes any fossil fuel projects from the eligible uses of proceeds and was considered to be a step forward in the convergence of Chinese and global green bond standards.[15]

However, China's environmental policy ambitions are set to further accelerate the development of its sustainable bond market. President XI Jinping announced in September 2020 during a United Nations General Assembly meeting that the country is committed to achieving carbon neutrality by 2060. That announcement is set to have profound and far-reaching impacts on the entire Chinese economy, driving changes that will require vast investment. Hong Kong, as a two-way bridge between Mainland China and the global capital markets, can also play an important role with its own sustainability initiatives, including its 2050 net-zero emissions target, pioneering sovereign green bond programme and the launch of Sustainable and Green Exchange (STAGE), a platform for the listing and cataloguing of data relating to sustainable bond issuance done through the Stock Exchange of Hong Kong.

This commitment from China — as the world's second-largest economy[16], biggest source of carbon emissions and one of its leading sustainable bond issuers, will require capital from around the world. And this globalisation of China's sustainable bond market should support the continued harmonisation of global standards for this asset class, which remain fragmented.

Definitions of sustainable bond categories

Before proceeding to a further discussion of the development of the sustainable bond markets, some additional details may be helpful in clarifying the differences between the various categories of such bonds. As mentioned above, this paper refers to developments

---

15 Source: *China Green Bond Market 2019 Report*, Climate Bonds Initiative and CCDC, supported by HSBC; "Earth Summit 2021: China excludes fossil fuel projects from green bonds, taking a step towards global standards on the path to 2060", published on the *South China Morning Post* website, 22 April 2021; "Notice on Issuing the Green Bond Endorsed Projects Catalogue (2021 edition)," unofficial translation published on the Climate Bonds Initiative website.

16 Source: World Bank, *Gross Domestic Product 2019*.

covering **green bonds, social bonds, sustainability bonds, transition bonds, and SLBs**. Each of these categories has been the subject of a variety of global consultations and working groups with the aim of standardising as much as possible the guidance for private and public sector issuers seeking to link their social and environmental agendas with their financing objectives.

While the matter of definitions may seem academic, we concur with the ICMA position, outlined in a May 2020 paper, that a tendency towards the interchangeable use of terms such as "climate", "green" and "sustainable" may dilute the urgency of making progress in the achievement of specific policy targets, whether climate mitigation or sustainable growth policy goals, as outlined in the Paris Agreement or in the United Nations Sustainable Development Goals[17].

As the Asian Development Bank noted in a 2020 paper, there remain differences of opinion about what actually constitutes a green bond. Domestic definitions are often looser than international ones, and there are diverging views on the specific eligibility of investment in clean coal and the maximum allowable use of proceeds for repaying debt and for general corporate purposes[18].

Starting with green bonds, the Green Bond Principles (GBP) issued by ICMA in June 2018 and updated in June 2021 defined them as "any type of bond instrument where the proceeds will be exclusively applied to finance or re-finance, in part or in full, new and/or eligible green projects, and which are aligned with the four core components of the GBP," namely use of proceeds, process for project evaluation and selection, management of proceeds and reporting[19].

Next, social bonds finance projects that directly aim to address or mitigate a specific social issue and/or seek to achieve positive social outcomes, especially but not exclusively for a target population[20].

---

17 Source: ICMA, *Sustainable Finance: High-level Definitions*, May 2020.
18 Source: Hao Zhang, "Regulating green bonds in the People's Republic of China: Definitional divergence and implications for policy making", Asian Development Bank Institute (ADBI) Working Paper Series, No. 1072, January 2020.
19 Source: ICMA, *Green Bond Principles: Voluntary Process Guidelines for Issuing Green Bonds*, June 2018.
20 Source: ICMA, *Green, Social and Sustainablility Bonds: A High-Level Mapping to the Sustainable Development Goals*, June 2020.

Sustainability bonds, also according to the 2018 ICMA definition, are "bonds where the proceeds will be exclusively applied to finance or re-finance a combination of both green and social projects. Sustainability Bonds are aligned with the four core components of both the GBP and Social Bond Principles (SBP) with the former being especially relevant to underlying green projects and the latter to underlying social projects"[21].

In June 2020, ICMA offered a definition of SLBs. These are any type of bond instrument for which the financial and/or structural characteristics can vary depending on whether the issuer achieves sustainability or ESG objectives. For instruments in this category, issuers are committing explicitly to future improvements in sustainability outcomes within a timeline. SLBs are a forward-looking and performance-based instrument, whose objectives are measured through Key Performance Indicators (KPIs) and assessed against Sustainability Performance Targets (SPTs).[22]

The more loosely defined label is that of transition bonds, for which ICMA provided a handbook instead of a formal principles paper, given that the goals of such bonds may fall either partially or entirely under the purview of any of the categories of green bonds, social bonds and sustainability bonds as defined above[23]. The main target of the transition bond handbook are carbon-intensive companies without a substantial pipeline of sustainable projects. These companies are critical to the broader adoption of sustainable financing given that around 100 companies globally are responsible for 70% of greenhouse gas emissions. Transition bonds can help these companies build pathways towards the Paris Agreement target by progressively decarbonising their business models. Without the participation of such large emitters — who cannot issue green bonds because of their restrictions to use of proceeds — the Paris Agreement target set in 2015 to limit global warming to a two degrees Celsius increase compared to pre-industrial levels would remain out of reach[24].

Furthermore, ICMA has mapped the four key categories above to the 17 SDGs set by the UN in order to further guide issuers in their choice of the appropriate category[25].

---

21 Source: ICMA, *Sustainability Bond Guidelines*, June 2018.
22 Source: ICMA, *Sustainability-Linked Bond Principles: Voluntary Process Guidelines*, June 2020.
23 Souce: ICMA, *Climate Transition Finance Handbook: Related questions*, 9 December 2020.
24 Source: "Climate Transition Finance Handbook bridges the sustainable finance gap for carbon-intensive issuers", published on the website of White & Case, 17 December 2020.
25 See ICMA, *Green, Social and Sustainablility Bonds: A High-Level Mapping to the Sustainable Development Goals*, June 2020.

Investor demand

The meteoric growth of sustainable investing is reflected by *Bloomberg Intelligence's* forecast that ESG assets under management will reach US$53 trillion by 2025, up from a 2018 total of US$30.6 trillion and accounting for more than a third of all projected assets under management[26].

In its October 2020 Global Financial Stability Report, the International Monetary Fund (IMF) noted the resilience of green financing even in the face of the global pandemic[27]. Flows into sustainable and environmental equity funds suffered a slowdown in the first quarter of 2020 but the multi-year trend of inflows remained positive, in particular for fixed income funds, while small declines were observed in the other asset classes (see Figure 2).

Figure 2. Sustainable and environmental fund flows as a share of fund size — moving average (2003Q1 – 2020Q1)

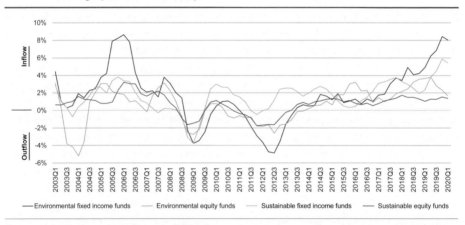

Source: *IMF Global Financial Stability Report 2020.*

---

26 Source: "ESG assets may hit $53 trillion by 2025, a third of global AUM", published on the *Bloomberg Intelligence* website, 23 February 2021.

27 Source: *Global Financial Stability Report: Bridge to Recovery*, published on the IMF's website, October 2020.

Meanwhile, ESG exchange traded funds are set to be a key driver of that growth, with as much as US$1 trillion of expected inflows over the next five years[28].

Despite the COVID-19 pandemic, investor demand remains strong across sustainable asset classes, especially bonds. As shown in Table 1, over-subscription ratios for US dollar (USD) sustainable bond sales by Asia-Pacific (APAC) issuers hit a record of 6.35 times for the first half of 2020, up 29% compared with the same period a year earlier.

Table 1. Over-subscription ratios of APAC sustainable bonds in USD (2019 – 2020)

Period		Over-subscription ratio (times)
2019 H1		4.94
2019 H2		4.26
2020 H1		6.35
2020 H2		6.03
2019 – 2020	**All**	**5.33**
	Investment grade	**4.96**

Source: BNP Paribas, Bloomberg.

While the green bond segment has continued to attract strong demand, there are reasons to believe that other types of sustainable bonds will also grow in popularity. Social bonds, for example, were until recently a niche product but have surged in issuance volume as a result of the COVID-19 pandemic, which has put factors such as equality and social justice on the policy agenda alongside climate change.

Out of the US$400 billion of sustainable debt issuance in 2019, social bonds totalled just US$20 billion, according to the Climate Bonds Initiative (CBI)[29]. But there was a clear shift in 2020, though, with issuers like the International Finance Corporation (IFC) embracing social bond issuance as a tool to finance their response to the corona virus. The African Development Bank also launched a US$3 billion "Fight COVID-19" social bond in March

---

28 Source: "ESG assets may hit $53 trillion by 2025, a third of global AUM", published on the *Bloomberg Intelligence* website, 23 February 2021.
29 Source: "A pandemic-driven surge in social bond issuance shows the sustainable debt market is evolving", published on the website of S&P Global Ratings, 22 June 2020.

2020^{30}. According to the Institute of International Finance (IIF), this was the world's largest US dollar-denominated social bond transaction to date. In April 2020, Guatemala became the first sovereign issuer of a social bond aimed at financing COVID-19 response efforts. The bond's proceeds were allocated to health infrastructure improvements and food security, as well as support for preventative health and medical practices.

Issuance of SLBs also gathered momentum in 2020, receiving an important boost in September of that year when the European Central Bank (ECB) announced that it would accept SLBs as collateral and start buying them under its asset purchase programmes[31].

Role of exchanges

The range of market participants contributing to the development of the sustainable bond market continues to broaden. Securities exchanges are an important example of this dynamic.

For example, US-based Nasdaq launched a Sustainable Bond Network at the end of 2019. As at the end of February 2021, this covers some 4,800 bonds from 350 issuers out of a total global sustainable bond universe of around 7,000 bonds[32]. The network is not a listing venue for such bonds, but instead aims to collect as much information as possible from issuers on sustainable bonds' use of proceeds, impact, frameworks and certifications, thereby offering investors a comprehensive picture that can help them select which instruments to add to their portfolios.

There are also important initiatives underway in Asia. In December 2020, Hong Kong Exchanges and Clearing Limited (HKEX) launched STAGE, Asia's first multi-asset sustainable investment product platform, covering primarily bonds and exchange traded products.

---

30 Source: "African Development Bank launches record breaking $3 billion 'Fight COVID-19' Social Bond", press release on the website of the African Development Bank, 27 March 2020.
31 Source: "ECB to accept sustainability-linked bonds as collateral", press release on ECB's website, 22 September 2020.
32 Source: "Bringing transparency to the sustainable bond market", published on the website of Environmental Finance, 22 February 2021.

STAGE acts as an online repository for sustainable finance instruments, launching with 29 such products in December 2020[33]. HKEX said that, while there is more than US$30 trillion invested in sustainable assets, less than one per cent of that investment comes from Asia[34]. Through the STAGE platform, US$28.7bn billion of sustainability, green, social or transition bonds had been listed on the exchange as of 31 December 2020, HKEX added[35]. As at the end of February 2021, STAGE data showed that instruments from 21 issuers in five currencies — Euro, US Dollar, Hong Kong Dollar, Renminbi, and Macau's Pataca — had been listed on the venue.

Overall, the availability of platforms such as STAGE in Asia will facilitate the growth of the sustainable bond market in the region by bringing together issuers and investors as well as making more data available.

Outlook for sustainable bonds in Asia

A comprehensive overview of the development of sustainable bonds in each Asian jurisdiction would exceed the scope of this chapter, but it is crucial to note the important function of the region in general, and China in particular, in the development of this market.

China

China's key role in the sustainable bond market is widely acknowledged. Its green bond market has grown from less than US$1 billion of issuance at the end of 2014 to US$164.9 billion in 2020 up to the end of November, according to Fitch Ratings[36]. Hong Kong is making its own contribution to China's outsized role in sustainable bonds, including through its January 2020 US$2.5 billion green bond offering, followed by another transaction of the same size a year later[37]. But while there has been issuance under non-

---

33 Source: "HKEX launches stage, its sustainable and green exchange", news release on HKEX's website, 1 December 2020.

34 Source: Ditto.

35 Source: *STAGE* webpage on HKEX's website, viewed on 19 April 2021.

36 Source: "China Corporates Snapshot — December 2020: China's green bond market to stay robust amid policy support", special report published on the website of Fitch Ratings, 23 December 2020.

37 Source: "HKSAR Government's green bonds offering", press release on the website of the Hong Kong Monetary Authority, 27 January 2021.

green sustainable bond labels, such as in the categories of so-called blue bonds and COVID-19 bonds by Chinese state- and privately-owned banks, these segments have yet to find real foothold.

Sustainable bond issuance from China has remained largely domestic: over 80% of its outstanding green bonds were issued in the onshore market, according to Fitch[38]. But demand from global investors for Chinese bonds has been growing, with the foreign share of ownership rising to around 10% for Chinese government bonds as at the end of 2020[39]. This has been driven by sustained efforts by Mainland and Hong Kong regulators and exchanges opening up investment channels such as the Bond Connect link with Hong Kong and the China Interbank Bond Market Direct scheme.

Historic differences in practice between the Chinese sustainable bond market and its international counterpart have caused concern for some international investors. However, China's new Green Bonds Endorsed Project Catalogue is seen to have narrowed this gap. As well as ending support for carbon-intensive projects involving the use of fossil fuels, it adopts more scientific and precise definitions of green projects, unifies different regulatory authorities' criteria for defining green projects for the first time and achieves alignment in its Level-II and Level-III Categories with the world's mainstream taxonomy of green assets, according to Moody's Analytics[40].

Nonetheless, NDRC guidelines still allow for half of a transaction's proceeds to be used for general corporate purposes, which remains a sticking point for ESG-oriented international investors and contrasts with the approach taken by the CBI and ICMA, which require all proceeds to be used for sustainable projects. A continued drive towards greater convergence should help to increase global demand for Chinese green bonds[41].

It is encouraging to see continued progress in this process of convergence as part of broader international cooperation in the fight against climate change. While the similarities between the Chinese rules and the European Union (EU) Taxonomy have been increasing in the crucial areas of environmental financial objectives, for example, there have continued to be key differences. However, PBOC Governor YI Gang said in April 2021

---

38 Source: "China Corporates Snapshot — December 2020: China's green bond market to stay robust amid policy support", special report published on the website of Fitch Ratings, 23 December 2020.
39 Source: Ditto.
40 Source: "PBC, NDRC, and CSRC Release Green Bond Endorsed Projects Catalogue", published on the website of Moody's Analytics, 27 April 2021.
41 Source: "China's $113 billion green bonds caught in jumble of rules", *Bloomberg*, 22 June 2021.

that China was working with the EU to achieve greater convergence of sustainable finance taxonomies, with the aim of implementing a jointly recognised framework by the end of 2021[42].

Rest of Asia

The momentum behind the growth of sustainable bond markets is gathering across Asia. Japan has made its own ambitious commitments, with Prime Minister Yoshihide Suga declaring in October 2020 that Japan will become carbon-neutral by 2050. The country is also a leader in social bonds: its 40 transactions for a total of US$8.8 billion was the most by any country in 2020[43]. Furthermore, Japan's Government Pension Investment Fund (GPIF) partnered with the Inter-American Development Bank (IDB) in January 2020 to promote and develop socially responsible capital markets through investments in IDB social bonds[44].

In Southeast Asia, the Kingdom of Thailand took its first step in the sustainable finance markets with a nearly US$1 billion sustainability bond issued in August 2020, earmarking the proceeds for use on a government-owned mass rapid transit project and to partially fund the government's COVID-19 economic stimulus programme. The deal was structured to fall under Thailand's sustainable financing framework, which covers both green and social projects. From the financial sector, Bank of the Philippine Islands and Rizal Commercial Bank were among the earliest to tap the green market in Asia, issuing separate US$300m bonds in September 2019.[45]

Other initiatives from the region have gone beyond adding to the growing volume of sustainable bonds. The Asian Infrastructure Investment Bank (AIIB) announced in September 2020 that it had collaborated with European asset manager Amundi to develop a framework that ranks companies on how well their climate change objectives match up with those set out in the Paris Agreement. The framework divides issuers into different

---

42 Source: "China reveals cooperation with EU on green investment standards", *FT.com*, 7 April 2021.
43 Source: "More than 680 green bonds and 130 social bonds issued globally so far in 2020", published on the website of Linklaters, 17 December 2020.
44 Source: "Japan's government pension investment fund to support IDB social projects", news release on IDB's website, 15 January 2020.
45 Source: Securities and Exchange Commission of the Republic of the Philippines, "Sustainable finance market update", September 2020.

buckets based on how well they are performing[46]. Among the reasons to develop such a framework was the fact that investing in, for example, a green bond issuance without a broader assessment of the issuer's overall climate change commitments may present a distorted picture.

Innovation in Asia

As well as becoming active in all the established sustainable bond categories, Asian issuers have also taken the lead in two newer but no less important niches. The first was opened up with the HK$3 billion COVID-19 resilience bonds issued by Industrial Bank's Hong Kong branch in November 2020. The bank will use the proceeds from this issuance to finance or refinance loans to small and medium-sized enterprises, or loans intended to enable resilience against pandemics[47].

Asian issuers have also been at the forefront with blue bonds, a sub-category of green bonds in which proceeds are specifically invested in marine-related projects. The category was born with an October 2018 World Bank bond agreement to guarantee a portion of the Republic of Seychelles' debut US$15 million blue bond in exchange for a commitment by that country to use the proceeds for the building of sustainable fisheries. This transaction helped Seychelles reduce its sovereign debt burden, while also steering its economy towards sustainable development[48].

The first blue bond in Asia came from Bank of China Paris and Macau Branch, which issued a dual currency US$942.5 million bond in September 2020. This was also the first blue bond issued by a commercial bank globally, and only the fourth blue bond ever[49]. The proceeds were dedicated to financing eligible marine-related projects, such as renewable energy — including offshore wind power projects — as well as sustainable water and wastewater management in coastal cities[50].

---

46 Source: "AIIB and Amundi launch climate change investment framework to drive Asia's green recovery and transition", published on AIIB's website, 9 September 2020.

47 Source: "Industrial Bank Hong Kong Branch issues HK$3b COVID-19 bonds, US$450m blue bonds", published on the *S&P Global – Market Intelligence* website, 2 November 2020.

48 Source: "Blue Finance: A deeper shade of green", published on the website of BNP Paribas, 20 April 2018.

49 Source: "Case Study: Asia's first blue bonds to finance marine-related projects", published on the *STAGE* webpage on HKEX's website, December 2020.

50 Source: "Bank of China issues its first blue bond in offshore markets", news article on the website of Allen & Overy, 22 September 2020.

A second blue bond came from Industrial Bank's Hong Kong branch, which issued US$450 million of these bonds alongside its COVID-19 resilience notes in November 2020[51].

The Tropical Landscape Finance Facility (TLFF) in Indonesia merits a mention, too. The first such facility in the country was launched in 2016 with the support of various organisations, including UN Environment and the World Agroforestry Centre[52]. The facility aims to bring long-term finance to projects and companies that stimulate green growth and improve rural livelihoods. The TLFF is especially designed to support deforestation-free supply chains, sustainable agriculture and renewable energy initiatives through strict lending criteria, with the involvement of international capital. ADM Capital manages the TLFF lending platform, while BNP Paribas arranges commercially priced, long-term debt for individual projects.

As the last example to be quoted of innovation coming from the region, the Australian Climate Transition Index (ACT Index) has been launched as the first ever forward-looking index in the category. BNP Paribas issued an eight-year equity-linked green bond linked to the index in August 2020, which was the first financing to make use of the index[53]. The ACT Index uses five dynamic climate scenarios, set to be adjusted to reflect future regulatory, technology and social environmental changes. It includes companies likely to perform well in a world undergoing a 2°C transition and to continue to play a part of the Australian economy in a 2°C future.

Risk management tools

Of course, innovation in sustainable finance goes well beyond sustainable bonds. An increasingly broad range of risk management tools are available for corporates who want to reflect their strategic commitment to sustainability across the financial services they use.

This has significant impact on all types of sustainable bonds. According to International Swaps and Derivatives Association (ISDA), ESG-related derivatives channel more capital to sustainable investments, they help market participants hedge risk related to ESG

---

51 Source: "Industrial Bank Hong Kong branch issues HK$3B COVID-19 bonds, US$450M blue bonds", published on the *S&P Global — Market intelligence* website, 2 November 2020.
52 Source: The website of TLFF, viewed on 19 April 2021.
53 Source: "BNP Paribas issues A$140m green bond linked to newly launched Australian Climate Transition Index", press release on the website of BNP Baribas, 3 August 2020.

factors, and, importantly for the present discussion, they facilitate transparency, price discovery and market efficiency, all factors that can positively impact the appeal of the various types of sustainable bonds[54].

A wide variety of such risk management tools already exist, including the likes of sustainability-linked derivatives, ESG-related credit default swap (CDS) indices, exchange traded derivatives on listed ESG-related equity indices, emissions trading derivatives, renewable energy and renewable fuels derivatives, and finally catastrophe and weather derivatives.

According to a 2020 paper by the European Capital Markets Institute (ECMI), ESG derivatives can find their place as a risk management tool just like more traditional instruments in the category. The paper cites as an example "ESG foreign exchange derivatives" that can be used to hedge a company's foreign exchange exposure related to a wind farm construction project and commit the provider of the derivative to reinvest the premium it receives in a reforestation project, in line with the UN's SDGs[55].

At this stage, SDG-linked derivatives are primarily cross-currency swaps used to hedge against the potential exchange rate volatility and interest rate risk of the investment. But the ECMI also forecasts that investors could be using derivatives to hedge their investment against future ESG taxonomy indices, a taxonomy being a common classification system to define environmentally friendly investments[56], or to reduce transaction costs through performance swaps or total return swaps. For index-tracking or other types of passive investment managers in particular, ECMI expects the use of such derivatives to allow appropriate hedging strategies as well as boost the liquidity of the underlying ESG assets, whether in fixed income or equity.

One recent example from Asia involved real estate developer Hysan Development, which in October 2020 arranged the first sustainability-linked hedging solution in the Greater China region[57]. The near-15-year cross-currency swap with a notional value of US$125 million was embedded with five-year ESG features and contributions. The specifics of

---

54 Source: ISDA, "Overview of ESG-related derivatives products and transactions", January 2021.
55 Source: Lannoo, K. and A. Thomadakis. (2020) "Derivatives in Sustainable Finance", *CEPS-ECMI Study*, Centre for European Policy Studies.
56 Source: "EU taxonomy to provide investment benchmarks, transform environmental reporting", published on the *S&P Global – Market Intelligence* website, 3 January 2020.
57 Source: "Hysan announces the first-ever sustainability-linked derivative hedging solution", news release on the website of Hysan, 20 October 2020.

the issuance made it the longest ESG KPI commitment duration executed in Asia. Under the terms of the deal, Hysan committed to remain a constituent member of the Hang Seng Corporate Sustainability Benchmark Index from 2021 to 2024 and to reduce its electricity purchases by an average 20% by end-2024 compared with a 2005 baseline. Should Hysan fail to meet these KPIs, it will make financial contributions to impact-driven local projects or charities via BNP Paribas. HKEX noted that a sustainability-linked derivative hedging solution such as this one can incentivise companies in high carbon sectors such as real estate to reduce their carbon footprint and improve their overall ESG performance[58].

Global challenges and outlook

The continued rise of sustainable bonds looks assured given the growth drivers discussed in this chapter so far. However, there is one crucial link in the chain that requires careful consideration. That is the successful transition of sustainable bonds from a vehicle for policy-related issuance by government and international bodies to a self-sustaining and private sector-driven funding tool.

The expansion of demand for sustainable bonds appears inevitable. Investors and asset managers, from large institutions to young people investing for the first time, will increasingly expect that their capital is used for responsible and sustainable purposes.

That expectation will raise the bar for the standards that issuers of "labelled" sustainable bonds are expected to meet. Many sophisticated institutional ESG investors already look beyond labels and conduct their own analysis using a proprietary ESG lens. This will drive issuers to go beyond basic green labelling and broad adherence to standards like the Green Bond Principles to embrace more sector-specific and data-based principles that allow highly ESG-conscious investors to buy into their sustainable bonds with confidence.

This kind of data-driven approach has itself been a factor in the greater popularity of green bonds than other sustainable bonds so far. Metrics like reductions in greenhouse gas emissions or energy use are much more easily understood by investors than some social impact targets. This has served the key function of mitigating the risk of "greenwashing",

---

58 Source: "Case Study: First ESG-linked rates derivative in Asia", published on the *STAGE* webpage on HKEX's website, December 2020.

where a company misuses the "green" label to fund what are fundamentally non-sustainable initiatives.

The ability of other types of sustainable bond issuers to provide investors with clear, data-driven frameworks under which their issuance can be assessed will therefore be key to the continued growth of the market. Such frameworks can only be developed, though, as part of a holistic corporate sustainability strategy — which requires leadership from the very top of organisations.

At the same time, the development of the sustainable bond market will inevitably require more of global investors than simply demanding adherence to global principles and frameworks. Investors will be required to play a more active role in contributing to the development of standards in fast-growing markets like China, drawing on their international expertise and looking for convergence where possible, without necessarily expecting local standards to be a carbon copy of European or US norms.

The outlook for sustainable bonds is bright. Some 700 funds were launched in 2020 to capture the extraordinary influx of capital to sustainable assets[59]. The forecasts for sustainable bonds are positive for 2021 as well, with Moody's forecasting US$650 billion of issuance. This could be split between US$375 billion of green bonds, US$150 billion of social bonds and US$125 billion of sustainability bonds[60].

Overall, sustainable bonds could rise to some 8-10% of total global bond issuance in 2021[61]. That is an astonishing result for such a young market, but it could be argued that it is just the beginning if capital markets are going to play their part in delivering on the Paris targets, which would mean achieving net-zero emissions by mid-century — not to mention all the other SDG-related purposes that sustainable bonds are beginning to support. One day, perhaps, all bonds will be sustainable because all issuers and investors will be sustainable in their practices. Over the decades ahead, Asia and China — including Hong Kong as China's leading international financial centre — have the opportunity to lead the way in this transition.

---

59 Source: "German fund giant captures the investing zeitgeist", *Bloomberg*, 4 February 2021.
60 Source: "Record sustainable bonds issuance projected for 2021", *The Asset*, 5 February 2021.
61 Source: "Coca-Cola moves from plant-based bottles to recycled ones", *Bloomberg*, 9 February 2021.

第17章

定息市場：可持續債券
全球迅速發展

黃超妮
法國巴黎銀行
亞太區環球市場
可持續資本市場主管

摘要

綠色、社會和可持續融資現正迅速增長，對全球投資者和公司來說不無啟示和影響。本章嘗試討論可持續債券市場的一些主要發展。文中涵蓋可持續債券市場中各大分類（綠色債券、社會責任債券、可持續發展債券、轉型債券及可持續發展掛鈎債券）的定義和重大發展，我們特別着眼於亞太區（尤其是中國）的發展 —— 該地區佔全球綠色債券市場的份額最大。

本文嘗試闡述，中國在監管工作上的更趨協調統一和多項發展，對綠色債券之外的可持續債券市場將有極大的推動作用。多邊發展銀行和其他超國家機構也會陸續有進一步行動，在新冠病毒疫情影響下，市場在尋找融資去處理和應對一些本來就與綠色、社會及可持續發展相關的挑戰時，都有需要探索創新路徑。

可持續債券市場概覽

聯合國、世界銀行等環球多邊機構和全球大部分國家大都認同，轉型至可持續發展模式，以至最終達致碳中和目標已是迫在眉睫。當中涉及的資金需求固然極其龐大，對國際和本地資本市場而言都是前所未見的挑戰，但也同時是機遇所在。

當前，債券和貸款市場都反應積極，疊加切合環境、社會與管治（Environment、Social、Governance，簡稱 ESG）原則的融資和投資備受追捧，增長發展甚速，市場上新開發的綠色、社會責任和可持續發展（Green、Social、Sustainability，簡稱 GSS）融資產品百花齊放。本章集中討論可持續融資中的定息類產品，亦即一般統稱為可持續債券的部分。這類產品包括許多不同的工具，既有現已十分成熟的綠色債券，亦有新類目，如社會責任債券、可持續發展債券、轉型債券和可持續發展掛鈎債券等。

在本章中，可持續債券和可持續發展掛鈎債券均指按世界銀行所界定，其成果可配合聯合國於 2015 年訂立、並獲全部 195 個成員國採納的可持續發展目標（Sustainable Development Goal，簡稱 SDG）議程者 [1]。有關釋義的內容，下一節將有更深入的討論。

過去 15 年來，可持續債券市場一直沿用其他金融創新板塊的發展模式。扮演推手角色的往往是多邊發展銀行，先從政策目標做起（例如氣候金融和 SDG），到制定出商業上可行、市場參與者可廣為採納的發行架構，逐步地開展轉型。多邊發展銀行的創新有諸多方面：世界銀行在 2018 年發行了首隻區塊鏈債券，甚至於 2017 年便發行了首隻流行病債券，就頗有先見之明 [2]。

沒多久，銀行以至其他金融機構亦紛紛仿效、發行相關產品。之後，影響力不斷擴大，跨國公司和其他企業亦相繼加入這個行列。

首隻可視之為率先在資本市場推出氣候金融的綠色債券，由歐洲投資銀行於 2007 年發行，當時標榜為「氣候意識債券」，發行所得款項投放於可再生能源和能源效益項目 [3]。世界銀行於 2017 年 1 月公佈其「SDGs Everyone」計劃，同年 3 月發行了相關債券，為債券與

1　有關17個SDG的資料，請參閱聯合國網站（https://sdgs.un.org/goals）。

2　資料來源：〈世界銀行推出全球首隻區塊鏈債券〉（"World Bank launches world-first blockchain bond"），載於《路透社》，2018年8月23日；〈世界銀行推出首隻流行病債券，支援5億元流行病應急融資融通〉（"World Bank launches first-ever pandemic bonds to support $500 million pandemic emergency financing facility"），載於世界銀行網站上的新聞稿，2017年6月28日。

3　資料來源：國際金融公司〈推動私人氣候金融 —— 綠色債券及其他〉（"Mobilizing private climate finance —— Green bonds and beyond"），載於《EMCompass》第25號，2016年12月。

SDG 掛鈎踏出第一步[4]。2020 年 9 月，墨西哥發行 8.9 億美元的 SDG 債券，成為首個主權發行人[5]。

在綠色債券市場，亞洲主權國可算是走在前沿：印度尼西亞共和國是區內首個發行此類債券的主權國，債券是於 2018 年 3 月發行的五年期、規模達 125 億美元的伊斯蘭債券[6]。另外，香港特別行政區則於 2018 年 2 月成為少數設立綠色債券計劃的主權發行人之一，發行規模上限為 1,000 億港元（近 130 億美元）[7]。財政司司長陳茂波在 2021 至 2022 年度預算案演辭中，建議將上限提升一倍，讓未來五年可再發行 1,755 億港元（226 億美元）的綠色債券[8]。

圖 1 是國際資本市場協會（International Capital Market Association，簡稱 ICMA）分類下的可持續金融類別概覽。

圖 1：ICMA 的可持續金融分類

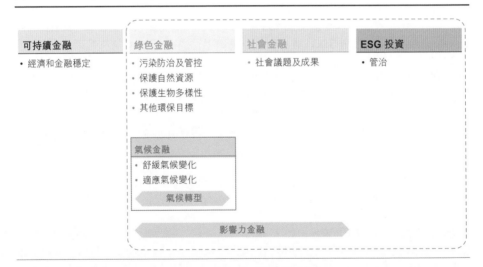

資料來源：ICMA〈綠色、社會和可持續債券：對可持續發展目標的簡要配對〉（"Green, Social and Sustainablility Bonds: A High-Level Mapping to the Sustainable Development Goals"），2020 年 6 月。

---

4   資料來源：〈世界銀行發行首隻聯合國可持續發展債券〉（"World Bank issues first UN sustainable development bond"），載於《路透社》，2017年3月9日。

5   資料來源：聯合國開發計劃署〈墨西哥歷史性發行8.9億元可持續發展目標債券〉（"Historic $890 million Sustainable Development Goals Bond issued by Mexico"），2020年9月14日。

6   資料來源：聯合國開發計劃署〈印尼的綠色伊斯蘭債券〉，2018年10月8日。

7   資料來源：中華人民共和國香港特別行政區政府〈政府綠色債券計劃〉，2018年11月15日。

8   資料來源：〈財政司司長陳茂波動議二讀「二零二一年撥款條例草案」的演辭〉，2021年2月24日。

現在，可持續債券市場已不再局限於從前的小眾投資，而是大小機構與散戶投資者均趨之若騖的熱捧市場。時至今日，發行可持續債券的所得款項用途涵蓋多項主題，由氣候至 17 個SDG 中任何一個目標，包括性別平等、脫貧、良好健康與福祉，以及可持續城市和社區等。

最近的調查顯示，全球散戶投資者在可持續金融方面累計投資了 7,150 億美元，其中資金配置最多的集中在能源和金融服務（不包括小額信貸），足見他們十分支持相關議程[9]。在亞洲，自 2018 年 12 月世界銀行在香港和新加坡推出 SDG 指數相關債券起，散戶投資者已可買賣 SDG 相關債券[10]。這些債券的回報與個別的股市指數掛鈎，這些股市指數追蹤那些被視為推動 SDG 發展的公司（包括在健康、性別平等和氣候相關領域營運）的業績表現。

全球可持續債券市場增長勢頭強勁，即使受疫情影響，2020 年的發行規模仍上升 29%（達7,321 億美元）。其中近五分之一是社會責任債券，近 700 億美元是可持續發展債券，綠色債券則升至 3,053 億美元的新高。單計氣候金融，從其 2007 年開始進入市場至 2020 年年底便累計發行了約 1 萬億美元[11]。

可持續債券在全球顯著增長，但只看歷史數字並未能完全反映其市場增長潛力，尤其是考慮到未來亞洲（特別是中國）可以擔當的角色。除了進一步優化支援可持續債券市場的基建和框架外，若能將其應用於對應和配合亞洲轉型至淨零排放過程中越來越大的資金需要，亦會是有關資產類別繼續增長和蓬勃發展的重要推手。

事實上，單是中國本身已是推動可持續債券發展的強大催化劑。2020 年，中國發行綠色債券總額為 376 億美元（從 2019 年的紀錄 555.8 億美元回落，主要是受新冠病毒疫情影響）[12]，是美國、德國及法國之後的全球第四大綠色債券發行國[13]。

只按中國國內綠色債券標準而發行的債券量為 153.3 億美元，佔總量 41%[14]。以下章節將會嘗試深入探討中國市場的各個相關監管機構。這裏值得一提的是，至 2021 年初為止，根據國家發展和改革委員會（簡稱「國家發改委」）定下的框架發行的國內綠色債券，與按國際標準發行的有一項主要分別，就是前者的發行人可將不多於一半的所得款項用於償還貸款或作為一般營運資金。然而，中國人民銀行、國家發改委與中國證券監督管理委員會於

9　資料來源：〈疫情下全球影響力投資市場仍暢旺—GIIN〉（"Global impact investment market going strong despite pandemic – GIIN"），載於 Pensions & Investments 的網站，2020 年 6 月 11 日。

10　資料來源：〈世界銀行向香港和新加坡散戶投資者推出可持續發展目標指數相關債券〉（"World Bank introduces sustainable development goals index-linked bonds for retail investors in Hong Kong and Singapore"），世界銀行網站上的新聞稿，2018年12月17日。

11　資料來源：〈社會債券推使2020年ESG發行規模創出7,320億元新高〉（"Social bonds propel ESG issuance to record $732 billion in 2020"），載於《彭博》，2021年1月11日。

12　資料來源：〈中國下一個能源轉型計劃勢推高2021年綠色債券發行量〉（"China's next energy transition plan set to boost green bond issuance in 2021"），載於《標普全球 —— 市場情報》網站，2021年1月28日。

13　資料來源：同上。

14　資料來源：同上。

2021 年 4 月共同發佈了綠色債券框架的更新版《綠色債券支持項目目錄（2021 年版）》（下稱「《綠色債券目錄》」），當中在合格使用所得款項的用途清單中剔除了化石燃料項目，被視為中國在與全球綠色債券標準融合接軌上向前踏出了一大步。[15]

不過，中國的環境政策可謂雄心勃勃，銳意進一步加快其可持續債券市場的發展。國家主席習近平於 2020 年 9 月聯合國大會期間宣佈，中國致力於 2060 年或之前達到碳中和。這對中國整體經濟勢將帶來深遠影響，推動市場大舉進行涉及龐大投資的變革。香港作為中國內地與全球資本市場的橋樑，亦能憑藉自身的可持續舉措擔當重要角色。這些舉措包括 2050 年淨零排放目標、率先推出主權綠色債券計劃，以及推出可持續及綠色交易所（Sustainable and Green Exchange，簡稱 STAGE）平台，羅列經香港聯合交易所完成發行的可持續債券的相關資訊，並將之分門別類。

中國身為全球第二大經濟體[16]、碳排放的最大源頭兼全球領先的可持續債券發行人之一，作出這樣的承擔還須有全球資金的支持。中國可持續債券市場的逐步全球化，將幫助這個資產類別現時仍是碎片化的全球標準逐漸協調統一。

可持續債券類別的定義

深入探討可持續債券市場的發展前，我們或可了解多一點細節，釐清不同類別的可持續債券之間的差異。正如上文所述，本章所討論的可持續債券涵蓋**綠色債券**、**社會責任債券**、**可持續發展債券**、**轉型債券**及**可持續發展掛鈎債券**。對於這幾類債券，多年來全球不同的諮詢和工作小組都曾先後探討研究，希望盡可能地完善相關指引，以協助那些尋求將融資目標與社會和環境議題聯繫上的公私營發行人。

要界定不同債券似乎頗為學術化，但我們很同意 ICMA 在 2020 年 5 月一份文件中的立場：將「氣候」、「綠色」和「可持續」等詞互換使用，或會降低推進特定政策目標的迫切性，不論是紓緩氣候影響或可持續增長的政策目標（有如巴黎協定或聯合國可持續發展目標所列）都會如此[17]。

15　資料來源：氣候債券倡議組織及中債登《中國綠色債券市場2019年報告》（China Green Bond Market 2019 Report）（由滙豐銀行支持）；〈地球高峰會2021：中國綠色債券排除化石燃料項目，向2060年達致全球標準邁進〉（"Earth Summit 2021: China excludes fossil fuel projects from green bonds, taking a step towards global standards on the path to 2060"），載於《南華早報》網站，2021年4月22日；〈《綠色債券支持項目目錄（2021年版）》發行通知〉（"Notice on Issuing the Green Bond Endorsed Projects Catalogue（2021 edition）"），載於氣候債券倡議組織網站上的非官方英譯本。
16　資料來源：世界銀行《本地生產總值2019》（"Gross Domestic Product 2019"）。
17　資料來源：ICMA《可持續金融：簡明釋義》（"Sustainable Finance: High-level Definitions"），2020年5月。

正如亞洲開發銀行在 2020 年的報告中所指，究竟綠色債券的具體組成有何元素，始終仍是眾説紛紜。例如本地定義通常較國際定義寬鬆，又例如對於投資於清潔煤是否符合某些特定資格、發債所得款項可作償還債務和一般企業用途的上限等，亦無共識 [18]。

先從綠色債券開始：按 ICMA 的《綠色債券原則》（2018 年 6 月發佈，2021 年 6 月更新），綠色債券的定義是：「其發行所得款項全部只用於部分或悉數融資或再融資新及 / 或合資格綠色項目，並符合《綠色債券原則》的四大核心的任何類型債券工具」（四大核心是指所得款項的用途、項目評估和甄選的程序、所得款項的管理以及匯報）[19]。

下一個是社會責任債券：社會債券專指一些為直接針對處理或紓緩特定社會問題及 / 或尋求取得正面社會成果（尤其是有（但不限於）目標羣眾者）的項目提供資金的債券 [20]。

同樣根據 ICMA 2018 年的定義，可持續發展債券是：「所得款項專用於對綠色及社會項目兩者作融資或再融資的債券。可持續發展債券符合《綠色債券原則》（相關綠色項目適用）和《社會責任債券原則》（相關社會項目適用）的四大核心」[21]。

2020 年 6 月，ICMA 明確了可持續發展掛鈎債券的定義。這類債券工具的金融及或結構特徵不盡相同，視乎發行人爭取達到的是可持續還是 ESG 方面的目標而定。可持續發展掛鈎債券的發行人均表明會在某段時間內改善可持續發展方面的成果。這是具前瞻性和以表現為本的工具，通過「主要績效指標」（Key Performance Indicator，簡稱 KPI）計量目標，並按「可持續表現目標」（Sustainability Performance Target，簡稱 SPT）作評估。[22]

轉型債券的定義較為寬泛。基於這類債券的目標有可能部分或全部屬於上文所界定的綠色債券、社會責任債券又或可持續發展債券的範圍，ICMA 就此提供的是一份手冊而非正式的原則文件 [23]。轉型債券手冊的主要目標對象，是那些碳排放甚高但沒有進行很多可持續項目的高碳公司。現在全球七成溫室氣體的排放均來約 100 家公司，因此，在市場能否廣泛採納可持續融資事宜上，這類高碳公司的影響很大。透過轉型債券，這些公司可以逐步減少其業務模式的碳排放，邁向巴黎協定的目標。如沒有這些主要排放源頭（受發債所得

18　資料來源：Hao Zhang〈規管中華人民共和國的綠色債券：定義分歧與對政策制定的影響〉（"Regulating green bonds in the People's Republic of China: Definitional divergence and implications for policy making"），亞洲開發銀行研究所工作報告1072號，2020年1月。

19　資料來源：ICMA《綠色債券原則：發行綠色債券的自願程序指引》（*Green Bond Principles: Voluntary Process Guidelines for Issuing Green Bonds*），2018年6月。

20　資料來源：ICMA《綠色、社會和可持續債券：對可持續發展目標的簡要配對》（*Green, Social and Sustainability Bonds: A High-Level Mapping to the Sustainable Development Goals*），2020年6月。

21　資料來源：ICMA《可持續發展債券指引》（*Sustainability Bond Guidelines*），2018年6月。

22　資料來源：ICMA《可持續發展掛鈎債券原則：自願程序指引》（*Sustainability-Linked Bond Principles: Voluntary Process Guidelines*），2020年6月。

23　資料來源：ICMA《氣候轉型融資手冊：相關問題》（*Climate Transition Finance Handbook: Related questions*），2020年12月9日。

款項用途所限，它們不能發行綠色債券）的參與，相信會很難達到 2015 年《巴黎協定》所定下的目標（把全球平均氣溫升幅控制在工業革命前水平以上不多於 2°C）[24]。

此外，ICMA 將上述四大債券類別與聯合國 17 個 SDG 配對，為發行人選擇合適類別提供進一步指引 [25]。

投資者的需求

《彭博行業研究》的預測反映了可持續投資的迅速增長。彭博預計到了 2025 年，ESG 資產管理總值將由 2018 年的 30.6 萬億美元增加到 53 萬億美元，佔預計屆時的資產管理總值超過三分之一 [26]。

國際貨幣基金組織（International Monetary Fund，簡稱 IMF）於 2020 年 10 月刊發的《全球金融穩定報告》指出，在全球疫情陰霾下，綠色融資仍能站穩陣腳，底氣十足 [27]。2020 年第一季，可持續和環境股權基金的資金流入放緩，但多年來的資金進賬趨勢仍力保不失，特別是固定收益基金，其他資產類別則錄得輕微跌幅（見圖 2）。

24　資料來源：〈氣候轉型融資手冊填補了高碳發行人的可持續融資缺口〉（"Climate Transition Finance Handbook bridges the sustainable finance gap for carbon-intensive issuers"），2020年12月17日。

25　參閱ICMA《綠色、社會和可持續債券：對可持續發展目標的簡要配對》（*Green, Social and Sustainablility Bonds: A High-Level Mapping to the Sustainable Development Goals*），2020年6月。

26　資料來源：〈2025 年ESG資產可達53萬億美元，佔全球管理資產總值三分之一〉（"ESG assets may hit $53 trillion by 2025, a third of global AUM"），載於《彭博行業研究》網站，2021年2月23日。

27　資料來源：《全球金融穩定報告：復甦之路》（*Global Financial Stability Report: Bridge to Recovery*），載於IMF的網站，2020年10月。

圖 2：可持續和環境資金流在基金總額中的佔比 —— 移動平均（2003 年第一季至 2020 年第一季）

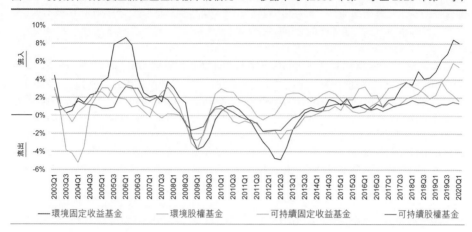

資料來源：IMF《全球金融穩定報告》，2020 年。

與此同時，ESG 交易所買賣基金勢將成為帶動相關升勢的主要產品之一，未來五年預計帶來高達 1 萬億美元的資金流入 [28]。

儘管新冠病毒疫情肆虐，投資者對各類可持續資產（尤其債券）仍需求殷切。如表 1 所示，2020 年上半年亞太地區發行人發行的美元可持續債券的超額認購率高達 6.35 倍，創下歷史新高，比去年同期升 29%。

表 1：亞太地區美元可持續債券的超額認購率（2019 年至 2020 年）

期間		可持續債券超額認購率（倍）
2019 年上半年		4.94
2019 年下半年		4.26
2020 年上半年		6.35
2020 年下半年		6.03
2019 年至 2020 年	全部	**5.33**
	投資級別	**4.96**

資料來源：法國巴黎銀行及彭博。

28　資料來源：〈2025 年ESG資產可達53萬億美元，佔全球管理資產總值三分之一〉（"ESG assets may hit $53 trillion by 2025, a third of global AUM"），載於《彭博行業研究》網站，2021年2月23日。

綠色債券續受追捧，我們有理由相信其他類型的可持續債券也將愈來愈受歡迎。例如，社會責任債券本來是小眾產品，但在疫情肆虐、市場關注氣候變化之餘也開始多考慮平等和社會公義等議題下，這類債券的發行量激增。

根據《氣候債券倡議組織》（Climate Bonds Initiative，簡稱 CBI）的資料，在 2019 年 4,000 億美元的可持續債券發行中，社會責任債券總額僅為 200 億美元 [29]。但是，2020 年情況明顯轉變，國際金融公司（International Finance Corporation）等發行人紛紛發行社會責任債券來籌措資金以支持疫情防控。非洲開發銀行（African Development Bank）於 2020 年 3 月更推出 30 億美元的「抗禦新冠疫情」社會責任債券 [30]，國際金融協會（Institute of International Finance）稱之為全球史上最大額的美元計價社會責任債券交易。2020 年 4 月，危地馬拉成為首個為了籌資以推出抗疫措施而發行社會責任債券的主權發行人，這債券的收益是用於改善衛生設施及糧食安全，以及支援預防性醫療護理服務。

可持續發展掛鈎債券的發行在 2020 年同樣勢頭日盛，其中一個重要的有利因素是同年 9 月歐洲中央銀行宣佈接受可持續發展掛鈎債券用作抵押品，其資產購買計劃亦開始購入這類債券 [31]。

交易所的角色

在可持續債券市場的發展路上，有助於推動當中進程的市場參與者種類不斷增多，證券交易所就是其中一個顯例。

例如，美國納斯達克在 2019 年底推出了「可持續債券網絡」。截至 2021 年 2 月底，網絡涵蓋 350 家發行人所發行的約 4,800 隻債券，佔全球合共約 7,000 隻可持續債券一半有多 [32]。該網絡並非用作此類債券的上市平台，而是旨在盡量向發行人收集有關可持續債券的各種資料，包括發行所得款項的用途、影響、框架和認證等，從而提供全面的資訊，方便投資者選取合適產品，豐富其投資組合。

29　資料來源：〈疫情帶動社會責任債券發行激增，反映可持續債務市場正在演變〉（"A pandemic-driven surge in social bond issuance shows the sustainable debt market is evolving"），載於標普全球評級的網站，2020 年 6月22日。

30　資料來源：〈非洲開發銀行推出破紀錄的30億美元「抗禦新冠疫情」社會責任債券〉（"African Development Bank launches record breaking $3 billion 'Fight COVID-19' Social Bond"），非洲開發銀行網站上的新聞稿，2020年3月27日。

31　資料來源：〈歐洲中央銀行接受可持續發展掛鈎債券用作抵押品〉（"ECB to accept sustainability-linked bonds as collateral"），載於歐洲中央銀行網站上的新聞稿，2020年9月22日。

32　資料來源：〈增加可持續債券市場的透明度〉（"Bringing transparency to the sustainable bond market"），載於 Environmental Finance 的網站，2021年2月22日。

亞洲地區也不遑多讓，相繼推出各項重要措施。2020 年 12 月，香港交易及結算所有限公司（簡稱「香港交易所」）推出 STAGE 平台，是亞洲首個多元資產類別可持續金融產品平台，主要涵蓋債券及交易所買賣產品。

STAGE 平台擔當可持續金融網上產品資訊庫的角色，於 2020 年 12 月推出時涵蓋 29 隻相關產品[33]。香港交易所表示，全球合共有超過 30 萬億美元投資於可持續資產，但來自亞洲的投資少於 1%[34]。截至 2020 年 12 月 31 日，通過 STAGE 平台載列的可持續發展、綠色、社會責任及轉型債券總值 287 億美元[35]。截至 2021 年 2 月底，STAGE 平台的資料顯示，在該平台載列的產品來自 21 家發行人，涉及貨幣有五種 —— 歐元、美元、港元、人民幣及澳門幣。

整體而言，亞洲市場有諸如 STAGE 這類的平台及類似措施，能將發行人和投資者連繫起來，亦促進資訊流通，有助於區內的可持續債券市場蓬勃發展。

亞洲可持續債券的發展前景

雖說本章並非要深入探討每個亞洲司法權區的可持續債券發展概況，但整個亞洲區（特別是中國）對可持續債券市場發展的重要角色不能不提。

中國

眾所周知，中國在可持續債券市場中的角色舉足輕重。根據惠譽評級，中國的綠色債券市場的發行規模在 2014 年年底尚未及 10 億美元，到了 2020 年 11 月底已增至 1,649 億美元[36]。對此，香港也有其貢獻：2020 年 1 月香港發行了 25 億美元的綠色債券，一年後再進行一宗金額相同的交易[37]。然而，雖然中國內地已陸續發行非綠色可持續債券標籤產品，例如中國國有和私營銀行所發行的「藍色債券」和抗疫債券，但這些產品尚未成氣候。

---

33 資料來源：〈香港交易所推出可持續及綠色交易所STAGE〉，載於香港交易所網站的新聞稿，2020年12月1日。

34 資料來源：同上。

35 資料來源：香港交易所網站的《STAGE》網頁，於2021年4月19日閱覽。

36 資料來源：〈中國企業概況 —— 2020 年12月：在政策支持下中國綠色債券市場保持強勁〉（"China Corporates Snapshot — December 2020: China's green bond market to stay robust amid policy support"），惠譽評級網站上的特別報告，2020年12月23日。

37 資料來源：〈香港特區政府發售綠色債券〉，香港金融管理局網站上的新聞稿，2021年1月27日。

中國的可持續債券發行主要仍是對內：按惠譽資料，中國 80% 以上的未償還綠色債券是在境內市場發行[38]。可是，全球投資者對中國債券的需求與日俱增，截至 2020 年年底，外資持有中國政府債券的比例已升至 10% 左右[39]。升勢背後的推動力包括內地和香港的監管機構和交易所不斷力拓投資渠道，例如連通香港與內地的「債券通」以及內地銀行間債券市場的直接入市計劃。

中國內地可持續債券市場的運作模式，長期以來均有別於國際同類市場的運作模式，故令部分國際投資者望而卻步，但中國內地新發佈的《綠色債券支持項目目錄》令人覺得兩者距離收窄。根據穆迪分析[40]，當中除了終止支持使用化石能源的高碳排放項目，也採用了更科學而精準的綠色項目界定標準，並首次統一了不同監管部門對綠色項目的界定標準，實現二級和三級目錄與國際主流綠色資產分類標準一致。

儘管如此，但國家發改委的指引仍容許交易收益的一半用於一般公司用途，正是這一點令有意投資 ESG 產品的國際投資者始終裹足不前，同時有違 CBI 與 ICMA 的方針（要求所有收益均用於可持續項目）。倘能繼續努力消弭分歧、促進劃一標準，相信會有助於增加全球對中國綠色債券的需求[41]。

隨着各國就對抗氣候變化通力合作，標準劃一指日可待。儘管中國的規則與歐盟的分類標準在環境金融目標的主要領域等方面漸趨一致，關鍵分歧仍然存在。中國人民銀行行長易綱於 2021 年 4 月表示，中國正與歐盟合作將可持續金融分類標準進一步劃一，務求在2021 年年底前制定出一個雙方認可的框架[42]。

亞洲其他地區

在亞洲各個地區，可持續債券市場的發展步伐也正在加快。日本首先定下了進取的目標，首相菅義偉在 2020 年 10 月誓言日本將在 2050 年實現碳中和。日本也在發行社會責任債券方面走在前沿，在 2020 年作出了 40 筆共計 88 億美元的交易，超越所有其他國家[43]。此

38 資料來源：〈中國企業概況──2020 年12月：在政策支持下中國綠色債券市場保持強勁〉（"China Corporates Snapshot — December 2020: China's green bond market to stay robust amid policy support"），惠譽評級網站上的特別報告，2020年12月23日。
39 資料來源：同上。
40 資料來源：〈中國人民銀行、國家發改委、中國證監會印發《綠色債券支持項目目錄》〉（"PBC, NDRC, and CSRC Release Green Bond Endorsed Projects Catalogue"），載於《穆迪分析》網站，2021年4月27日。
41 資料來源：〈中國的1,130億元綠色債券受困於混亂的規則〉（"China's $113 billion green bonds caught in jumble of rules"），載於《彭博》，2021年6月22日。
42 資料來源：〈中國與歐盟就綠色投資標準展開合作〉（"China reveals co-operation with EU on green investment standards"），載於《FT.com》，2021年4月7日。
43 資料來源：〈2020年至今全球已發行 680多隻綠色債券和130多隻社會責任債券〉（"More than 680 green bonds and 130 social bonds issued globally so far in 2020"），載於年利達律師事務所的網站，2020年12月17日。

外，日本年金積立金管理運用獨立行政法人於 2020 年 1 月與美洲開發銀行合作，通過投資美洲開發銀行的社會責任債券，來促進對社會有承擔的資本市場的發展[44]。

在東南亞，泰國於 2020 年 8 月在可持續金融市場邁出了第一步，發行了近 10 億美元的可持續債券，所得款項指定用於政府擁有的大眾捷運項目，另有部分用以資助政府的疫後經濟振興計劃。該交易屬於泰國的可持續融資框架的一部分，框架涵蓋綠色和社會項目。金融領域方面，菲律賓羣島銀行及中華銀行是最早參與亞洲綠色市場的銀行，各自於 2019 年 9 月發行了 3 億美元的債券。[45]

亞洲區內的其他舉措還不限於增加可持續債券的數量。亞洲基礎設施投資銀行於 2020 年 9 月宣佈與歐洲的東方匯理資產管理公司共建框架，評估各發行人公司所訂立的氣候變化目標有多符合《巴黎協定》所規定的目標，然後按各公司的表現將其排名分類[46]。制定這個框架的其中一個原因是，如無全面分析發行人的整體氣候變化應對措施，而單靠發行綠色債券這一點來對其作出評價，或未能反映實況。

亞洲區創新舉措

亞洲發行人除了積極發行現有各類別的可持續債券產品外，也率先推出兩款較新但不容忽視的特色產品。第一款是興業銀行香港分行於 2020 年 11 月發行的 30 億港元抗疫債券，發行所得款項用以為中小企業貸款又或旨在促進疫後業務復甦的貸款提供融資或再融資[47]。

亞洲發行人也在發行藍色債券方面走在最前。藍色債券是綠色債券的一個分類，收益專門投資於海洋相關項目。藍色債券起源自 2018 年 10 月世界銀行訂立債券協議，就塞舌爾共和國首次推出的 1,500 萬美元藍色債券之其中一部分提供擔保，換取塞舌爾承諾將發債所得款項用於建設可持續漁業。這筆交易既幫助塞舌爾減輕了主權債務負擔，也引導其發展可持續經濟[48]。

44　資料來源：〈日本年金積立金管理運用獨立行政法人支持美洲開發銀行社會項目〉（"Japan's government pension investment fund to support IDB social projects"），美洲開發銀行網站上的新聞稿，2020 年 1 月 15 日。

45　資料來源：菲律賓共和國證券交易委員會〈可持續金融市場動態〉（"Sustainable Finance Market Update"），2020 年 9 月。

46　資料來源：〈亞洲基礎設施投資銀行與東方匯理推出氣候變化投資框架，推動亞洲綠色經濟復甦及轉型〉（"AIIB and Amundi launch climate change investment framework to drive Asia's green recovery and transition"），載於亞洲基礎設施投資銀行的網站，2020 年 9 月 9 日。

47　資料來源：〈興業銀行香港分行發行 30 億港元抗疫債券及 4.5 億美元藍色債券〉（"Industrial Bank Hong Kong Branch issues HK$3b COVID-19 bonds, US$450m blue bonds"），載於《標普全球 —— 市場情報》網站，2020 年 11 月 2 日。

48　資料來源：〈藍色金融：比綠色更深的綠〉（"Blue Finance: A deeper shade of green"），載於法國巴黎銀行的網站，2018 年 4 月 20 日。

至於亞洲的首隻藍色債券，則是由中國銀行巴黎和澳門分行於 2020 年 9 月所發行，是 9.425 億美元的雙幣種債券。它亦是全球首隻由商業銀行發行的藍色債券，兼史上第四隻藍色債券 [49]。所得款項專門用於資助符合條件的海洋相關項目，例如可再生能源（包括海上風電項目）以及沿海城市的可持續水和廢水管理 [50]。

第二隻藍色債券由興業銀行香港分行於 2020 年 11 月發行，總值 4.5 億美元，與抗疫債券一同發行 [51]。

另外也不得不提印尼的《熱帶雨林景觀融資機制》。該國首個此類機制於 2016 年在聯合國環境署和世界農林業中心等機構的支持下啟動 [52]，旨在為刺激綠色增長和改善農村生計的項目和公司提供長期融資。《熱帶雨林景觀融資機制》冀能通過嚴格的貸款標準，拉動國際資本的參與，支持不伐林供應鏈、可持續農業和可再生能源倡議。機制的貸款平台由 ADM Capital 管理，法國巴黎銀行則為個別項目安排商業定價的長期債務。

最後可一提的亞洲區創新舉措，是澳洲氣候轉型指數（ACT 指數）的推出，成為首個前瞻性氣候轉型指數。法國巴黎銀行於 2020 年 8 月發行了與該指數掛鈎的八年期股票掛鈎綠色債券，是首次使用該指數的融資項目 [53]。ACT 指數使用五種動態氣候情景，情景將不時調整以反映未來的監管、技術和社會環境變化。指數涵蓋在全球升溫 2°C 的情況下仍可能表現良好並繼續在澳洲經濟中發揮作用的公司。

風險管理工具

當然，可持續金融的創新不僅限於可持續債券。市場上有越來越多不同類型的風險管理工具，公司企業可用以支持其可持續發展戰略的實施。

這對各類可持續債券都有很大影響。根據國際掉期及衍生工具協會（International Swaps and Derivatives Association，簡稱 ISDA），ESG 相關的衍生產品將更多資金導向可持續

49　資料來源：〈個案分析：亞洲首個為海洋相關項目融資而推出的藍色債券〉（"Case Study: Asia's first blue bonds to finance marine-related projects"），載於香港交易所網站的《STAGE》網頁，2020年12月。

50　資料來源：〈中國銀行在離岸市場發行首隻藍色債券〉（"Bank of China issues its first blue bond in offshore markets"），載於安理國際律師事務所網站上的新聞文章，2020年9月22日。

51　資料來源：〈興業銀行香港分行發行30億港元抗疫債券及4.5億美元藍色債券〉（"Industrial Bank Hong Kong Branch issues HK$3b COVID-19 bonds, US$450m blue bonds"），載於《標普全球——市場情報》網站，2020年11月2日。

52　資料來源：熱帶雨林景觀融資機制的網站，2021年4月19日閱覽。

53　資料來源：〈法國巴黎銀行發行1.4億澳元的綠色債券，與新推出的澳洲氣候轉型指數掛鈎〉（"BNP Paribas issues A$140m green bond linked to newly launched Australian Climate Transition Index"），載於法國巴黎銀行網站上的新聞稿，2020年8月3日。

投資，有助於市場參與者對沖 ESG 相關風險，更重要的是它們可協助提高透明度、便利價格發現和提升市場效率，令各類可持續債券更具吸引力[54]。

這些風險管理工具現時已然種類繁多，像與可持續發展掛鈎的衍生產品、ESG 相關信貸違約掉期指數、與上市 ESG 相關股市指數掛鈎的場內衍生產品、排放權交易衍生產品、再生能源及再生燃料衍生產品，以及災難和天氣衍生產品等。

根據歐洲資本市場研究所（European Capital Markets Institute，簡稱 ECMI）2020 年的報告，ESG 衍生產品也可以作為風險管理工具，正如一些較傳統的風險控制工具。該文以「ESG 外匯衍生產品」為例，這種衍生產品可用於對沖個別公司與某個建造風力發電場項目相關的外匯風險，產品的提供者承諾將所得溢價再投資於植樹造林項目，符合聯合國的可持續發展目標[55]。

現階段，與聯合國可持續發展目標掛鈎的衍生產品主要是跨貨幣掉期合約，用於對沖投資的潛在匯率波動和利率風險。不過，ECMI 亦預測投資者未來可利用與 ESG 分類標準有關的指數衍生產品（ESG 分類標準指界定環保投資的通用分類系統[56]）為其相關投資作對沖，或利用表現掉期或總回報掉期合約來減低交易成本。尤其是追蹤指數或其他類型被動式投資的管理人，對於這類投資者，ECMI 預期使用有關衍生產品可配合採取適當的對沖策略，同時提高相關 ESG 資產（不論是定息或股本）的流動性。

亞洲最近一個例子是地產發展商希慎興業於 2020 年 10 月推出大中華區首隻與可持續發展掛鈎的對沖解決方案[57]。這個為期約 15 年、名義價值 1.25 億美元的跨貨幣掉期合約內含前後五年的 ESG 特色和捐款，其 ESG 主要績效指標承諾年期是全亞洲最長。根據交易條款，希慎承諾於 2021 至 2024 年內保持其公司股票獲納入《恒生可持續發展企業指數》，並於 2024 年年底前將其用電量平均減少 20%（與 2005 年的水平相比）。如希慎未能符合這些主要績效指標，將通過法國巴黎銀行向對持續發展具影響力的本地項目或慈善機構捐款。香港交易所注意到，像這樣的與可持續發展掛鈎的衍生產品對沖解決方案，可推動房地產等高碳行業的公司減少碳足跡，提升其整體 ESG 表現[58]。

54　資料來源：ISDA〈ESG相關衍生產品及交易概覽〉（"Overview of ESG-related derivatives products and transactions"），2021年1月。

55　資料來源：K. Lannoo 與 A. Thomadakis（2020年）〈可持續金融的衍生產品〉（"Derivatives in Sustainable Finance"），載於《CEPS-ECMI Study》，歐洲政策研究中心（Centre for European Policy Studies）。

56　資料來源：〈歐盟分類標準提供投資基準，環境匯報一改面貌〉（"EU taxonomy to provide investment benchmarks, transform environmental reporting"），載於《標普環球 ── 市場情報》網站，2020年1月3日。

57　資料來源：〈希慎推出香港公司中首隻與可持續發展掛鈎的衍生工具對沖解決方案〉，載於希慎網站上的新聞稿，2020年10月20日。

58　資料來源：〈個案研究：亞洲首隻 ESG 掛鈎利率衍生產品〉（"Case Study: First ESG-linked rates derivative in Asia"），載於香港交易所網站的《STAGE》網頁，2020年12月。

環球挑戰與展望

基於上述各種增長動力，可持續債券的發展和升勢似乎未有稍歇。然而，有一點需特別注意，即可持續債券已由政府及國際機構的政策相關發行載體成功轉成為自我存續、由私營機構推動的融資工具。

可持續債券的需求上升似乎無可避免。投資者和資產管理人，不論來自大機構又或年輕投資新手，無不期望他們的投資會作負責任和可持續用途。

這些期望提高了要求發行人在發行「標籤」為可持續債券時所須符合的標準。許多成熟的 ESG 機構投資者已不單靠標籤，而是自行作其 ESG 分析，促使發行人除了符合基本綠色標籤和綠色債券原則等標準外，還要遵守更多針對個別行業和數據為本的原則，方可令極注重 ESG 元素的投資者有信心買入其可持續債券。

這類數據主導的投資方式本身亦是至今綠色債券會比其他可持續債券更受歡迎的因素之一。對投資者來說，何謂減少溫室氣體排放或能源使用，會比好些具「社會影響」的目標容易理解得多，因此有可減輕「漂綠」風險的重要功用（「漂綠」是指公司濫用「綠色」標籤，為基本上不屬可持續發展的舉措提供資金）。

所以，其他類型可持續債券的發行人能否提供清楚、數據主導的發行框架給投資者作出評估，將也是這個市場可否持續增長的關鍵，儘管要制定這些框架，必定是全面的企業可持續發展策略的其中一環，須由機構的最高層來領導。

與此同時，要可持續債券市場繼續發展，並不單純是依循全球原則和框架便可，還需要得到環球投資者的更大支持。投資者將要扮演更積極的角色，協助促進中國等增長迅速的市場制定相關標準，利用他們的國際經驗並盡可能相互接軌，而不一定要以歐洲或美國慣例作為本地標準的藍本。

可持續債券前景一片光明，2020 年就有約 700 隻新推出的基金來捕捉資金大量流入可持續資產這大趨勢 [59]。預期 2021 年可持續債券會延續強勢，按穆迪的預測，發行規模將達 6,500 億美元（綠色債券：3,750 億美元；社會責任債券：1,500 億美元；可持續發展債券：1,250 億美元）[60]。

---

59 資料來源：〈德國基金大戶順應投資思潮〉（"German fund giant captures the investing zeitgeist"），載於《彭博》，2021年2月4日。

60 資料來源：〈2021年可持續債券發行勢破紀錄〉（"Record sustainable bonds issuance projected for 2021"），載於《The Asset》，2021年2月5日。

整體而言，2021 年可持續債券佔全球債券發行總量的比率有機會升至 8% 至 10% 左右[61]。以這樣「年輕」的新興市場來說，這無疑是很了不起的成績。但也許我們亦可以說，即使我們設想資本市場完全投身於力求達到《巴黎協定》的目標（在世紀中前達至淨零排放），可持續債券市場的發展其實依然任重道遠，更不用說涉及聯合國可持續發展目標的可持續債券才剛剛起步。或許有一天，所有債券發行人和投資者都朝着可持續方向邁進，屆時所有債券都是可持續債券。未來數十年，亞洲和中國（包括香港這一中國領先的國際金融中心）都有機會在此進程中走在前沿，發揮引領作用。

61　資料來源：〈可口可樂棄用植物塑膠樽而改用回收塑膠樽〉（"Coca-Cola moves from plant-based bottles to recycled ones"），載於《彭博》，2021年2月9日。

Chapter 18

The role of carbon exchanges in green and sustainable finance

Chris LEEDS
Executive Director
Standard Chartered Bank

Summary

As the world looks to mitigate the risks of climate change, a broad range of policy tools have been discussed and implemented. Carbon markets, both mandatory compliance and voluntary can be a key enabler of necessary decarbonisation while minimising economic costs. Market-based carbon pricing policy, including cap-and-trade, carbon taxes and crediting schemes, all aim to make emitters internalise the external costs of their greenhouse gas (GHG) emissions — the principle of the "polluter pays". Most mandatory carbon markets use the "cap and trade" model, which puts limits on the amount of GHG that can be emitted within the economy and reduces them to net-zero over time. This of course is the goal. Emissions Trading Systems (ETS) using a cap-and-trade, quantity-based approach, enables a fair carbon market price to emerge while also ensuring that emissions are limited to a desired level. Voluntary Carbon Markets (VCM), on the other hand, are project-based and use of the principle of baseline and credit, where a project is put in place to reduce GHG emissions below a projected business-as-usual path of increasing emissions — referred to as a baseline. Reductions below the baseline earn carbon credits, which can be sold to other emitters whose costs of reducing emissions are higher. In this case there is no cap; so long as project emissions are below the baseline, overall emissions can keep rising. To ensure net emissions fall, it needs to be shown that these project credits are additional to what would have happened without the project and that the overall goal is to reduce emissions to net-zero. The VCMs should not be used as a way for higher cost emitters to do nothing.

Linking carbon markets, both mandatory national ETS and voluntary project-based ones, can magnify the gains from carbon trading but care needs to be taken to ensure integrity is not lost. A liquid, transparent and well supervised market for carbon supports innovation and investment in decarbonisation efforts but to get there will need standardised marketplaces, regulations and deep cooperation. This is where exchanges can contribute. The Paris Agreement offers the opportunity for market-based mechanisms to develop internationally but much work remains to be done to allow them to fully contribute to the goal of reducing net carbon emissions to zero by 2050. Defining the relationship between the mandatory and the voluntary carbon markets will be an important part of that. The emergence of ETS in several countries, including China, is an important step forward that will encourage others to follow. Exchanges can develop the rules, infrastructure and co-operative agreements to bring voluntary and compliance markets together internationally. Direct emissions reductions must be the priority, driven by mandatory carbon markets, complemented by project-based voluntary markets that will accelerate funding for climate mitigation action.

Ultimately the planet has set humanity a carbon cap — global emissions need to be reduced to net-zero by 2050 to avoid temperature increases exceeding 1.5°C.

Introduction

The Paris Agreement[1] was adopted by nearly every nation in 2015 to address climate change and its negative impacts. The deal replaced the Kyoto Protocol[2] and aims to substantially reduce global greenhouse gas (GHG) emissions to limit the global temperature increase in this century to 2 degrees Celsius (°C) above pre-industrial levels, while pursuing means to limit the increase to 1.5°C. But there is a long road between the pledges made by governments and the decisive action required to manage climate change.

By 2030, the world needs to cut emissions by 45% from 2010 levels[3]. Such a transition requires substantial scaling of market and policy mechanisms that incentivise decarbonisation and emissions reductions. Global carbon dioxide (CO_2) emissions fell by 6.4% (2.3 billion tonnes) in 2020 due to the pandemic but need to fall at least 7.6% annually for the next decade to avoid warming greater than 1.5°C[4]. The goal must be to reduce emissions in line with the science while at the same time allowing global economic growth that will support investment in new technology and allow for all nations and people to prosper. Effective carbon markets are a vital component of this transition, with exchanges at the epicentre. Emissions reductions anywhere make identical contributions to help alleviate the problem. The sheer number and variety of GHG emissions sources make it difficult to develop a comprehensive and effective command-and-control approach and magnifies the cost savings that could be achieved by enlisting the market to find the quickest and least costly abatement options.

As the world pushes for rapid decarbonisation, demand for carbon markets and pricing will expand. The United Kingdom (UK) and the European Union (EU) have vowed to be net-zero[5] by 2050, with interim targets of 68%[6] and 55%[7] by 2030 from a 1990 baseline

---

1   See "The Paris Agreement", webpage on the website of United Nations Framework Convention on Climate Change (UNFCCC).

2   See "What is the Kyoto Protocol?", webpage on UNFCCC's website.

3   See "Global warming of 1.5°C", special report published on the website of the Intergovernmental Panel on Climate Change (IPCC), 8 October 2018.

4   This analysis draws on the work of the IPCC by using a remaining carbon budget of 570 metric gigatonnes (Gt) CO_2 as of 1 January 2018. Remaining within this budget would equate to a 66% chance of limiting warming to 1.5°C.

5   Net-zero (carbon emissions) is a state where the anthropogenic emissions of GHG to the atmosphere are balanced by anthropogenic removals over a specified period.

6   Source: "UK sets ambitious new climate target ahead of UN Summit", press release of the UK Government on its website, 3 December 2020.

7   See "2030 climate & energy framework", webpage on the EU's website.

respectively. China is aiming to peak emissions by 2030 and for carbon neutrality by 2060[8]. In addition, voluntary net-zero pledges from corporates doubled within the course of just 12 months[9]. The Taskforce for Scaling the Voluntary Carbon Markets (TSVCM) estimated that voluntary carbon markets need to grow by more than 15-fold by 2030 in order to support the investment required to deliver the 1.5°C pathway[10].

Carbon markets can support new programmes to finance, structure, and deploy these critical solutions, so that in the future we can continue economic development in countries across the world, including those rapidly industrialising today.

There are a range of initiatives that are working towards scaling carbon markets, both in the voluntary and compliance space. The commitment to net-zero by 2050 has renewed corporate interest in carbon markets as a tool to support flexible pathways for decarbonisation, with huge potential to channel significant funding into additional mitigation, including emissions-reducing technologies and nature-based solutions.

While the voluntary carbon markets (VCMs) have come under scrutiny for potential "green-washing", the purchase of high-quality carbon credits is being employed as part of a credible pathway for companies to reach net-zero — through annual emissions reductions and compensation of unavoidable emissions as they make the transition. To ensure carbon credits are high quality they will have to be "VALID" — Verifiable, Additional to what would have happened anyway, free from Leakage of emissions elsewhere, Irreversible and do not Double-count.

Renewables, nature-based solutions and energy efficiency projects are all critical tools in reducing GHG and reaching net-zero emissions. But these alone will not be enough to support the global transition away from fossil fuels. There is the need to boost emerging technologies that can transform our economy — such as low carbon fuels for heavy transport, low carbon steel and cement, and better carbon removal technologies. Carbon markets can help channel the trillions of dollars of capital that will be needed to fund this transition.

---

8   Source: "China pledges to achieve CO2 emissions peak before 2030, carbon neutrality before 2060 — Xi", *Reuters*, 22 September 2020.
9   Source: "Commitments to net zero double in less than a year", press release on UNFCCC's website, 21 September 2020.
10 Source: "Taskforce on Scaling Voluntary Carbon Markets", webpage on the website of Institute of International Finance (IIF), viewed on 16 September 2021.

Carbon trading

Carbon trading began on a voluntary basis in 1989, before the first Conference of the Parties (COP) to the United Nations Framework Convention on Climate Change (UNFCCC). Early transactions mostly related to projects aimed at preventing deforestation. Several developments brought the use of carbon credits closer to mainstream practice. First, the adoption in 1997 of the Kyoto Protocol established several elements of a carbon-market infrastructure — including foundation for the international emissions trading and the Clean Development Mechanism (CDM)[11], which set standards for carbon-offsetting methodologies and laid the foundation for an official central registry of credits.

In 2003 came the launch of the first centralised cap-and-trade system, the voluntary but legally binding Chicago Climate Exchange (CCX) that also permitted the application of a limited percentage of verified credits to comply with the emissions reduction schedule. CCX was a self-regulated exchange, with oversight provided by the Commodity Futures Trading Commission and member baseline and reduction compliance audited annually by the National Association of Securities Dealers (NASD), which became the Financial Industry Regulatory Authority (FINRA), a self-regulatory organisation of the securities industry in the United States (US). CCX provided price discovery for emissions trading globally, and provided its 450 members, including major companies, universities, cities and states, a platform for making commitments to reduce emissions via standardised, legally binding contracts.

The tradeable instrument on CCX was the fungible CCX carbon financial instrument (CFI), equivalent to one tonne of CO_2. Members of CCX committed to directly reduce all Scope 1 emissions[12] from all North American operations on a specified reduction schedule and could apply credits on a limited basis to meet their compliance requirement. Members who achieved their reduction targets beyond their compliance requirements had surplus CFI allowances to sell or bank; those who did not meet the targets complied by purchasing additional CFIs from those with a surplus. Associate Members were Scope 2 emitters only and committed to reduce or offset their entire annual North American emissions by

---

11 See "Clean Development Mechanism (CDM)", webpage on UNFCCC's website.

12 Scope 1 covers direct emissions from entity owned or controlled sources. Scope 2 covers indirect emissions from the generation of purchased electricity, steam, heating and cooling consumed by the entity. Scope 3 includes all other indirect emissions that occur upstream or downstream in a company's value chain. See "Corporate Standard", webpage on the *Greenhouse Gas Protocol* website.

the purchase of CFIs from CCX members. By enabling members to achieve emissions reductions of 700 million tonnes (mt) of CO_2 equivalent (CO2e) over seven years, the CCX demonstrated that an exchange and trading platform could improve the transparency and liquidity of carbon markets, including integration of carbon credits. CCX also launched and co-owned China's first carbon market, the Tianjin Climate Exchange (TCX), and had affiliates worldwide, serving as a template for an eventual global market. The CCX ceased operations in 2010. This decline was partially triggered by unmet regulatory expectations, including the failure of the Wax-man-Markey bill in the US for a national cap-and-trade system to pass, as well as the breakdown in negotiations at Copenhagen in 2009, dashing hopes for global carbon markets taking off at that time.

In 2005 the European Union (EU) launched its emissions trading system (ETS) — the EU ETS[13], covering over 11,000 energy-intensive installations and airlines and approximately 45% of the EU's GHG emissions — primarily CO_2 but also nitrous oxide (N_2O) and perfluorocarbons (PFCs). The EU ETS operates in all EU countries as well as Iceland, Liechtenstein and Norway. In January 2020 it was linked to the Swiss ETS. The EU ETS is now in Phase 4, which runs from January 2021 to December 2030, with a target of 55% reductions from 1990 levels likely to be adopted. Companies receive or buy emissions allowances — European Union Allowances (EUAs), depending on which sector they belong to — companies in the power sector need to buy EUAs through regular auctions, whereas those in other sectors receive some free allocation. At the end of each year, companies must submit enough EUAs to cover all emissions for that year, keeping spare allowances for future use or for sale. The cost of non-compliance is €100/mt CO2e. In 2019, the EU introduced the Market Stability Reserve (MSR)[14] to address the surplus of allowances built up due to recession caused by the financial crisis of 2009, helping to support the stability of the market.

Compliance and voluntary carbon markets have been interlinked since their inception. One can observe correlated movements between compliance market, Certified Emissions Reductions (CERs) volumes generated from the CDM, and voluntary credit volumes traded. A critical development in compliance markets was the linking of the CDM to the EU ETS in 2008. This allowed companies to use CERs, which are carbon credits generated from CDM projects, to comply with EU emissions regulations. Several exchanges were set up to trade both EUAs and CERs, including the European Carbon Exchange (ECX — now part of ICE), Powernext and the European Energy Exchange (EEX). Between 2008 and

---

13 See "EU Emissions Trading System (EU ETS)", webpage on the EU's website.
14 See "Market Stability Reserve", webpage on the EU's website.

2016, the EU ETS reduced more than 1 billion tonnes of CO_2[15]. The connection between the CDM and the EU ETS also brought new attention to voluntary markets. Seeing that large industrial companies had to pay for the right to emit GHG, service providers like consulting and law firms anticipated that they might eventually face similar requirements and began purchasing voluntary credits. CER trading volumes dropped heavily after 2012, by which time covered entities of the EU ETS had purchased much of their allowed credits for the 2012 to 2020 phase and strict limits on their use were imposed by the EU[16]. Compliance schemes (e.g. EU ETS, the California Cap-and-Trade programme, the China ETS) are yet to finalise rules on accepting independent standard credits going forward, which may significantly impact overall demand for independent standard credits and drive further fungibility and liquidity across carbon markets. Compliance and voluntary markets can continue to be mutually reinforcing in the future.

According to the World Bank Group, over 70 market participants ranging from regional, national, and subnational entities participated in carbon pricing initiatives in 2019, covering nearly 22% of global GHG emissions[17]. They generated an excess of US$45 billion in carbon pricing revenues, a US$1 billion annual increase versus the previous year.

The origins of cap-and-trade

Cap-and-trade was developed at the United States Environmental Protection Agency (EPA) in the 1980s. At the time, heavy smog and acid rain plagued the northeast states due to sulphur dioxide (SO_2) and nitrogen dioxide (NO_2) emissions drifting eastwards from coal-fired plants based in Midwestern states. The proposed solution at the time was for the EPA to impose SO_2 reductions on the electricity suppliers but utilities claimed that compliance would be too costly and that cleaner technologies were not yet available. The cap-and-trade concept was conceived to add flexibility and spread costs of reducing SO_2 emissions among all emitters. As a result of the SO_2 cap-and-trade system introduced by the EPA, new scrubbing technologies came to market more quickly because of the need and demand of the over-emitters, costs of reductions were much lower than projected, and eventually the US smog and acid rain problems disappeared, with considerable health

---

15 Source: Bayer, P. and M. Aklin. (2020) "The European Union Emissions Trading System reduced CO2 emissions despite low prices", *Proceedings of the National Academy of Sciences*, Vol. 17, Issue 16, pp.8804-8812.
16 See "Use of international credits", webpage on the EU's website.
17 Source: World Bank Group. (2020). *State and Trends of Carbon Pricing 2020*. Washington, DC: World Bank.

and other benefits[18]. This success and the fact that GHG emissions are evenly distributed throughout the world's atmosphere means that cap-and-trade is well suited to addressing the problem of climate change.

Under a cap-and-trade scheme, a "cap" on carbon emissions from sectors of the economy (or the whole economy) would be imposed and allowances issued to match the cap. Without any restriction on emissions, a company does not have to consider the economic cost of emitting carbon dioxide. If, however, a cap is imposed on the amount of emissions that can be emitted, this changes the equation completely as the "right to pollute" becomes a scarce and therefore sought-after commodity. In order to generate environmental benefit, caps must be set in accordance with scientific limits, that is, how many tonnes of emissions need to be reduced by when in order to achieve notable environmental improvement — with CO_2 the goal is to reduce the cap to net-zero globally by 2050. The key to environmental progress through a cap-and-trade system is that the cap is progressively tightened, reducing allowable emissions and therefore tradable allowances. As supply shrinks, demand rises and allowance prices too. Emissions below that cap are allowable; emissions above the cap are not. Collective emissions must remain below the cap, and participants are issued or purchase allowances in proportion to their share of the allowable emissions pot.

The way these allowances are allocated, whether free or by auction, in theory makes no difference to the economic outcome[19]. In general, allowances should be auctioned rather than handed out for free, or "grandfathered", as auctioning makes sure that the rents linked to environmental policies goes to public authorities, instead of being captured by the existing polluters. Free allocations act as a subsidy and dull the incentive to make the emissions reductions, as the emitter is protected from the true costs of its emissions. While the EU ETS has moved to auction allowances for the power sector, free allocations remain for sectors, such as steel and cement, where international competition could lead to companies reducing activity within the EU to avoid the ETS costs, and increasing them in other countries without emissions restrictions; so called carbon "leakage".

Policy makers hope that by tightening the cap each year, prices will slowly rise so that everybody gets used to the higher costs being imposed on them, giving them time to

---

18 Source: Stavins, R., G. Chan, R. Stowe and R. Sweeney. "The US sulphur dioxide cap and trade programme and lessons for climate policy", published on *VoxEU.org* website, 12 August 2012.

19 See Stavins, R. "Two notable events prompt examination of an important property of cap-and-trade", published on *robertstavinsblog.org* website, 21 July 2012.

adapt. By making it more costly to buy allowances than to make reductions, it helps accelerate demand for new technologies and incentivises each emitting entity to transition to cleaner, more efficient processes.

For example, coal emits around 2.5 times the amount of CO_2 for the equivalent amount of power generation than natural gas. Some emitters may have already installed more efficient boilers or use natural gas instead of coal as a fuel. These participants can become sellers and are "long" in the market and may sell the allowances they do not use to participants who are in the opposite situation — having used up their annual allowances but still exceeding their annual limit. These "over-emitters" are short in the market, and if for whatever reason they cannot make further reductions directly, they must buy allowances from others who have a surplus so that, collectively, all participants remain below the common emissions cap. If they do not, they will pay a penalty at some compliance date in the future.

Brokers and commodity traders enter the market as well to buy, sell, hold and speculate on the price of a carbon allowance as on any other commodity, such as oil or metals. Futures and forward markets also evolve, bringing standardisation, transparency and liquidity, allowing the development of long-term carbon finance. Ideally, because of the public environmental purpose of such a market, transactions occur on regulated *bona fide* public exchanges, like stocks, so that trading prices are transparent and provide a constant open public market signal. In theory, this price equates to the cost of making a reduction of a tonne of CO_2. Also, each emitter will have a unique financial profile, which can influence borrowing and other costs that can in turn influence the overall cost of making direct reductions. It may be less expensive for an over-emitter to purchase allowances on the market than undertake the operational or strategic business changes necessary to make the reduction directly. As a result, prices can be as volatile as any commodity market and move in tandem with other related commodities such as coal and natural gas. In the EU ETS for example, where coal was the dominant source for electricity generation, the price where it became profitable to switch from coal to natural gas fired generation became the market price for a EUA.

Critics of cap-and-trade say emitters can simply buy their way out of reducing their own emissions but this misses the point — cap-and-trade encourages the least costly emissions reductions to occur first and forces others to act. It buys time for the economy to adjust, rather than forcing the change suddenly, which can cause unacceptable economic disruption. Sooner or later, all emitters also have to make direct reductions, since the cost of allowances will tend to rise as the cap is tightened and gradually the cost of actually making the reduction becomes financially irresistible as compared to the going price for allowances.

As the power sector has historically been the largest source of stationary emissions, and there are good cost-competitive alternatives to coal for generating electricity with lower emissions, such as natural gas and, more recently, renewables, most emissions trading schemes have the power sector at their core — the EU ETS, California ETS, the Regional Greenhouse Gas Initiative (RGGI) and now the China ETS. Of course, other sectors produce large volumes of carbon emissions but these tend to be in the so called "hard to abate" sectors such as steel, cement, aviation, marine or road transport. Efforts are being made to include them through schemes such as the Carbon Offsetting and Reduction Scheme for International Aviation (CORSIA) and by inclusion of aviation and shipping in the EU ETS but this is where offsets come in. Offsetting, under a "baseline and credit" system, allows companies in these sectors to invest in projects that will reduce emissions elsewhere — such as energy efficiency, forestry, agriculture or renewables. They are also encouraged to invest in the development of new technology in their value chain to support the reduction of emissions directly from their industry — technology such as direct air capture (DAC), carbon capture and storage (CCS) and sustainable aircraft fuels (SAF). Today these technologies are too expensive to be scaled commercially but by investing in them now we hope to be able to bring down their costs in the same way that investing in solar and wind has done over the last 20 years.

Absolute cap versus intensity-based caps

A variant on the absolute cap-and-trade system of emissions trading is a system where the cap is not absolute but relative. In such a system the ceiling is not measured in an absolute volume of emissions (e.g. tonnes of CO_2) but measured as a volume in relation to some level of activity (e.g. tonnes of CO_2 per unit of steel production). If a company produces cleaner than required by the relative standard, it can sell its "unused" pollution permits. The number of these permits is calculated as the difference between the actual emissions per unit of activity and the relative standard, multiplied by the size of the activity. As an example, suppose the relative standard is 1 tonne of CO_2 per megawatt-hour (MWh) of power production. If a company manages to emit only 0.9 tonnes of CO_2 per MWh of electricity and produces 1 million MWh of electricity in a year, it is allowed to sell 100,000 tonnes of CO_2 permits. Any company that cannot produce to the relative standard (or will not produce at this standard at the going market price of pollution permits) can buy pollution permits to make up for its deficit. Alternatively, demand for permits can come from other sectors that are, for example, faced with an absolute cap, or demand can come from abroad, where companies face the same performance standards but perform worse in terms of emissions per unit of output.

Producers often favour relative cap-and-trade because they fear that absolute cap-and-trade will effectively prevent them from expanding their production and output, even if they produce in the most environmentally friendly way. This latter argument is especially cogent if the company or industry operates on an international market where foreign competitors are not subject to the same level of environmental regulation. From an environmental perspective, the disadvantage is that the final level of pollution is not known in advance. The environmental effects depend on the relative standard but also on the level of activity specified by the standard (e.g. the level of output) that is not controlled by the environmental regulator. As stated previously, the ultimate goal is to reduce carbon emissions to net-zero, which intensity-based schemes alone could not achieve.

Voluntary Carbon Markets (VCM): Baseline and crediting

Baseline-and-credit is a type of emissions trading scheme where a project is put in place to reduce GHG emissions below a projected business-as-usual path of increasing emissions — typically referred to as a baseline. Any reduction below that future path earns carbon credits for the difference which can be sold to other emitters, whose cost of reducing emissions is higher. The Kyoto Protocol's CDM and Joint Implementation (JI) scheme were both examples of a baseline-and-credit model, as is the voluntary carbon market. The model is used when there is no cap on absolute emissions, to be able to measure the change in emissions from implementing an abatement project (e.g. a renewable energy project, energy efficiency project, avoided deforestation or reforestation) against a business-as-usual baseline. Carbon credits are then issued by an issuing body for the difference between what would have happened without the project and the actual emissions within the project boundary over a specific crediting period, say one year. Project developers need to put together a project plan, called a Project Design Document (PDD), which will apply an agreed emissions reduction, avoidance-or-removal methodology that is then validated by an independent auditor. To ensure the integrity of the project, the PDD must meet certain criteria, specifically, that it is additional to what would have happened in the business-as-usual scenario, reduces emissions permanently, is measurable and verifiable. When a project is implemented, at certain time intervals, possibly annually but not always so, another independent auditor will verify that the project followed the PDD and that the emissions reductions occurred. At this point the verifier will send its report to the standard setter, who will issue the carbon credits into its registry. Examples of standard setters include Verra[20], the Gold Standard[21], Plan Vivo[22], Climate Action Reserve[23] and American Carbon Registry[24].

Carbon taxes

While a carbon cap-and-trade scheme is one way of incentivising emissions reductions; subsidies and carbon taxes offer alternatives, which can complement carbon trading as they have different purposes. Subsidies are good if you want to focus on a specific technology. The problem here is that policy makers are being asked to "pick winners", which they are typically bad at doing. In addition, it is common for policy makers to change their minds about subsidies, which makes it difficult for investors to have certainty. Carbon taxes are essentially the other side of the policy coin to carbon trading. With a carbon tax, the cost is known upfront but the amount of emissions reductions is unknown. Setting a carbon tax at $10/mt will prompt only those with a marginal abatement cost below $10/mt CO_2e to cut their emissions. There are many sectors where the costs of abatement are much higher than $10/mt CO_2e and some well in excess of $100/mt CO_2e but a carbon tax that high can be politically unacceptable. It could also act as an unnecessary shock to the economic system as it raises costs for everyone at the same time, even those who can make reductions at much lower costs.

The atmosphere needs both carbon taxes and carbon trading, and they can be made to work together. Taxes have the virtue of simplicity, but the drawback of being too political and will not reduce emissions to zero. It is important to not to lock in a too-low price signal, which will then be difficult to raise, while avoiding making it too high, hence damaging viable businesses and undermining popular support.

Carbon taxes tend to be highly regressive, particularly when applied to activities such as home heating or cooling and rural transportation. In lower income groups the impacts of food costs can also be important. Carbon taxes can also lead to unequal outcome on jobs, with businesses migrating out of a higher taxed region, leading to no overall reduction of carbon.

---

20 See its website: www.verra.org.
21 See its website: www.goldstandard.org.
22 See its website: www.planvivo.org.
23 See its website: www.climateactionreserve.org.
24 See its website: www.americanregistry.org.

Proponents of carbon taxes will often say that such problems can be dealt with through a variety of additional measures such as side payments and border adjustments. While true in theory, in practice such strategies are hard to implement and have generally failed to work as hoped for. If the solutions for reducing carbon are not made widely accessible, such as development of new technologies, access to capital and government support, taxes may simply create even larger inherent advantages for the previously advantaged groups reducing competition and exacerbating income inequality. These distributional aspects mean that it matters how carbon taxes are structured and on whom and on what they are levied, which is quite different from normal economic assumptions, that the tax is perfectly applied on all activities everywhere.

Higher income individuals and stronger companies typically have greater ability to invest and to change consumption patterns and thus have greater ability to avoid paying taxes. Lower income individuals and weaker companies often cannot afford to invest in better technologies that would allow reduced consumption with little pain and are thus forced to choose between simply bearing the tax or painful changes in consumption patterns. When demand is elastic, small carbon taxes generate large changes in carbon emissions for relatively little tax and thus at low levels of redistribution and job loss. As the "easy" adjustments are made and more expensive changes in technology or more painful changes become necessary the demand curves become less elastic. This means that greater increases in taxes are needed to generate the same climate impact and distributional impacts and job losses grow. With carbon trading that process happens automatically — as supply (in the form of allowances) reduces, prices rise but at a pace that should allow the economy to adapt without these dislocations.

Benefits of emissions trading

Evidence from existing systems shows ETS (in particular emissions trading on exchanges) has driven emissions reductions, even when accounting for external factors. Estimates from the beginning of Phase II of the EU ETS (2008-2010) of emissions reductions by covered firms in Germany showed reductions of 25%-28% more than comparable non-covered firms[25]. For the RGGI states, modelling results indicate that emissions from covered entities would have been 24% higher in the absence of an ETS[26].

---

25 Source: Petrick, S. and U. J. Wagner, "The Impact of carbon trading on industry: Evidence from German manufacturing firms", 28 March 2014, available at SSRN.

26 Source: RGGI. (2017) *The Investment of RGGI Proceeds in 2015*, October 2019.

The quantity-based approach of ETS ensures emissions remain at or below the specified emissions cap across the covered sectors. An ETS should have progressively declining, credible caps in line with climate targets, providing a clear emissions reduction path over the mid- to long-term. This reduces uncertainty and helps companies adjust as appropriate.

ETS allows firms to choose where and when to reduce emissions. The cheapest abatement options are selected first. Moreover, participants can abate emissions when it is most cost-effective to do so. The price signal created through an ETS automatically adapts to changing economic conditions, making emissions reductions cheaper when the economy slows and more expensive during periods of growth. A high carbon price favours low-carbon production processes, products, and technologies.

Importantly ETS can help decouple emissions from economic growth. For example, the carbon intensity of California's economy has fallen 33% since it peaked in 2001, while during the same period the state's economy has grown by 37%[27]. From 2012-2015, emissions in the state steadily declined, while gross domestic product, population and employment grew.

Through auctioning allowances, ETS can generate an additional source of government revenue, which may then be used to invest in further climate action, lower other taxes, or compensate low-income households or adversely impacted groups.

Emissions trading and competitiveness

As has been shown, carbon markets provide an effective, flexible, and economically efficient approach to reducing GHGs. Combined with other policies, carbon markets can help accelerate and ensure a smooth transition to a low-carbon economy, by driving a shift away from high-emissions products to low-emissions products and processes. However, some firms that compete against these low-emissions substitutes may experience a loss of market share and reduced profits even as others adapt, increase their profitability and develop new business models.

---

27 Source: "New report shows California is reducing greenhouse gas emissions as economy continues to grow", news release on the website of California Air Resources Board, 7 June 2017.

Concerns exist that, due to differential carbon prices between jurisdictions, there is the potential risk that high-carbon economic activity may move to regions without, or with a lower, carbon price. This could result in decreased profits and job losses. It could also exacerbate political push-back and undermine the intended environmental outcome of reduced emissions. If this "carbon leakage" occurs, it would be a lose-lose situation: a loss of competitiveness or economic activity without an environmental gain.

There is little evidence to date that carbon pricing has resulted in the relocation of the production of goods and services or investment in these products to other countries. This outcome is consistent with the economic literature[28] assessing the competitive impact of environmental regulation more broadly. There may be several reasons for this, including the observation that carbon price levels have generally been moderate and existing programmes include protection for at-risk sectors, via free allocation of allowances for example. In addition, tax rates, labour availability, and infrastructure may be more significant to investment decisions regarding location of production than environmental regulations.

While competitiveness remains a key concern for policymakers considering a price on carbon, these concerns should not be overstated. Competitive risks exist primarily for highly emissions-intensive and trade-exposed sectors and jurisdictions that depend on such sectors. These risks can, and should, be addressed through locally tailored policy design choices intended to protect industry from unfair international competition even as they ensure that the incentive and support for low-carbon innovation remains. Options to address competitiveness include free allocation of emissions rights and border measures.

Greater ambition is likely to lead to higher carbon price levels, which could exacerbate competitiveness impacts on affected industries. Prices for EUAs on the ICE Futures Europe touched a high of €46.95/mt CO_2e on 22 April 2021[29], one of the highest prices for carbon in the world, leading for calls for the implementation of a Carbon Border Adjustment Mechanism (CBAM). However, having more countries adopt climate policies and develop linkages between carbon markets should help reduce the differences in carbon prices among countries and regions, alleviating competitiveness concerns. The more the linkage between markets, the more there will be equalisation of costs.

---

28 Aldy, J. E. (2016) "Mobilizing political action on behalf of future generations: The case of climate change policy", *The Future of Children*, Vol. 26, Issue 1, pp.157-178; Beale, E., D. Beugin, B. Dahlby, D. Drummond, N. Olewiler and C. Ragan, "Provincial carbon pricing and competitiveness pressures", published on the website of Canada's Ecofiscal Commission, November 2015; Cohen, M. A. and A. Tubb. (2018) "The impact of environmental regulation on firm and country competitiveness: A meta-analysis of the Porter hypothesis", *Journal of the Association of Environmental and Resource Economists*, Vol. 5, pp.371-399.

29 Source: "EUA Futures", webpage on ICE's website, viewed on 16 September 2021.

Concerns about competitiveness implications should not preclude carbon pricing or keep regions from increasing carbon prices or emissions targets over time to levels needed to implement the Paris Agreement.

Carbon pricing, along with complementary measures, can also drive innovation, investment and substantial growth in some sectors. The investment opportunities that arise from decarbonisation are considerable, as is the potential for the development of new industries and innovation within existing ones. Carbon pricing can also generate revenues to further national objectives and to support those who might be negatively impacted.

Innovation and investment, as well as stable and predictable policies, are crucial to the transition to a low-carbon economy. Policy clarity, with strong governmental commitment to meaningful policy which increases in stringency over time, can help ensure that companies and regions remain competitive in global markets. Furthermore, large mainstream investors are increasingly factoring in the development and implementation of low-carbon strategies when evaluating their portfolios[30].

Carbon financing

Transparent and liquid carbon markets will act in the way that any mature commodity market does to encourage financial institutions to provide finance. Companies will need to invest in low-carbon technology and energy efficiency. Supply chains will need green financing and companies will need to manage carbon price risk. A robust carbon market supported by financial institutions and exchanges will be essential. For example, a large oil company that needs to transition into a low-carbon energy producer will need huge amounts of finance to make the change. It is likely that carbon as a commodity will become a major part of the company's value chain: operating upstream to develop carbon reduction projects, midstream to trade carbon credits and downstream to supply its customers with carbon-neutral products. In the same way that a bank currently finances all parts of their oil upstream, midstream and downstream businesses, it will finance its carbon and clean energy businesses.

Banks and other supply chain financiers should provide lending facilities for project developers (both capital expenditures and working capital) collateralised by the right to

---

30 See Carbon Pricing Leadership Coalition, *Report of the High-Level Commission on Carbon Pricing and Competitiveness*, 23 September 2019.

generate carbon credits, subject to successful validation and verification. A liquid market in spot and futures contracts for carbon credits on exchanges would provide a great foundation for financing projects because it would provide clarity on pricing and facilitate risk transfer, improving the overall bankability of these projects. Financing could be provided based on expected cashflows from offtake agreements. This is an important way of bridging the gap between immediate investment needs and expected future cashflows. Until a liquid futures market develops, project developers will have to rely on physical offtake agreements provided by financially sound buyers, which financial intermediaries will be prepared to lend against. Offtakers could include oil companies, large corporates (technology companies, consumer goods, airlines, shipping, etc.) or governments.

Looking ahead, carbon finance is set to drive two main streams of financial innovation: (1) the decarbonisation of financial assets relating to the transition of carbon-intensive economic activities to low-carbon alternatives, in line with the science; and (2) the design and functioning of a sustainable financial system where economic growth is compatible with the socio-economic changes necessary to mitigate climate emergencies and enable a balanced cycle of production and consumption of natural resources.

While the harmonisation of international carbon pricing mechanisms is far from a global reality, carbon pricing will continue to be an essential policy lever in meeting climate targets. The future role of carbon finance ultimately depends on the incorporation of climate mitigation targets in the direct pricing of carbon risk causing the carbon price to rise significantly. Further standardisation of the contracts traded and the rise of liquid exchange-traded contracts will give greater certainty to market players, allowing financing to develop.

Growth drivers, challenges and outlook for the development of the carbon markets

Next steps for VCM — Exchange-traded reference contracts

The success of VCMs rests on building a market with both high-integrity and sufficient liquidity in selected reference contracts. Successful development of the carbon markets depends on building credibility and transparency. These issues have consistently plagued the voluntary markets as well as the CDM. For this reason, it's crucial to ensure the market has confidence in the reference contracts traded. To enable high-integrity voluntary market contracts that assure buyers and the wider ecosystem that genuine emissions reductions are made, we need to develop a set of "Core Carbon Principles" (CCPs) against which carbon credits and their underlying standard and methodology can be assessed. These will set out threshold quality criteria that an offset must adhere to.

Every offset project has somewhat different attributes, for example carbon removal vs. avoidance, geography, vintage[31] or project type, and every buyer has different attribute preferences. Some buyers look to purchase credits linked to their geography or supply chain or credits which offer particular Sustainable Development Goal (SDG)[32]-impacts or co-benefits. Matching each individual buyer with a corresponding supplier is a time-consuming and inefficient process. As a result, there are no "liquid" reference contracts, either spot or futures, with a daily, reliable price reference, which in turn makes price risk management almost impossible and serves as an impediment to the growth of supplier financing. In order to concentrate liquidity and unlock the benefits that come with it, there is a need for carbon reference contracts that can be traded on exchanges.

The first step toward reference contracts is to introduce a physical spot market reference contract based on high-quality projects. This contract bundles offset credits that satisfy these criteria from several suppliers into one contract. A buyer receives any of the eligible carbon offsets traded in the "core carbon contract" and, at delivery, a certificate for the underlying offset.

Development and listing of an exchange-traded spot core carbon contract, based on the CCPs, with physical delivery of offset certificates into the buyer's registry account, will allow development of a transparent, daily, market price. Exchanges could also develop reference contracts which combine the core carbon contract with additional attributes which are separately priced. For this to take off, key buyers need to become active in these reference contracts, to encourage the development of liquidity. After these reference contracts are developed, parties that continue making over-the-counter (OTC) trades can use the price of the core carbon contract as a starting point for negotiations and then negotiate pricing for additional attributes.

---

31 The vintage is the year in which the carbon emissions reduction project generates emissions reductions.
32 See "The 17 Goals", webpage on United Nation's website.

Several other markets with non-standardised products, for example corn, oil and other commodities, have successfully implemented reference contracts in the past to manage this "basis" risk. The Nordic Power markets have the Nordic System price as the core contract, and attributes, in this case the location of delivery, are traded as an add-on to the core contract. Many other commodity markets work according to similar principles and have succeeded in standardising and scaling contracts despite the vast complexity of the underlying physical substance, without compromising on integrity and quality.

In addition to the reference spot and futures contracts, if instead buyers wanted something more bespoke, and were willing to pay up for that, they could buy a project with specific additional attributes, such as the distinction between removal and reduction offsets, which can be woven into additional reference contracts. These are priced and traded as a "basis" or difference to the core carbon contracts — that way they would take delivery of a carbon credit that qualifies for the core carbon contract and in addition fulfils the desired additional attributes.

At delivery, a certificate for the underlying offset, related to that specific additional attribute, will be presented to buyers. Crucially, the number of permutations of these additional reference contracts should be kept to a minimum. The goal is to concentrate as much liquidity in as few contracts as possible. Therefore, the additional reference contracts should represent the most prevalent buyer preferences. It would be down to the seller to decide exactly what project met those criteria so the project type would not be entirely bespoke.

To do that a buyer would need to go back to the OTC markets but they would have a reference CCP price and a price for the additional attributes to help them negotiate an appropriate price.

As a result, OTC markets will continue to exist after the development of reference contracts on exchanges but will be tightly linked to them. When negotiating OTC contracts, both parties can use the price of the liquid core carbon contract as a starting point, negotiating only the pricing for the additional attributes, however complex they might be, for example unique combinations of offset type, location, vintage, SDG-impact and other co-benefits, etc.

The need for standardisation through carbon exchanges and related infrastructure

For a market to function, a core set of infrastructure components needs to be in place. These components must work together in a way that is resilient, flexible and able to handle large-scale trade volumes. To achieve this, market participants must build the required components while adhering to a set of trade and infrastructure principles.

While the voluntary carbon market has tended to be OTC historically, exchanges bring the necessary standardisation, transparency and safeguards that are needed to scale the market. Listing a contract on an exchange would mean making use of existing financial market infrastructure for pooling liquidity, which can involve the additional benefits of a regulated trading environment (e.g. market surveillance of trading activity, mandatory anti-money laundering or know-your-customer checks of participants). There are a number of benefits associated with an exchange market. Exchange-traded reference contracts can bundle suppliers' products and buyers' preferences to allow for significantly more efficient matching of buyers and suppliers. Buyers benefit from a simplified buyer journey and increased price transparency. Suppliers benefit from price risk management and improved access to financing, as well as a clear price signal to inform their investment decisions and an expansion of investor base. The market benefits from more efficient trading through a tighter bid-ask spread. The planet benefits due to increased climate action, financed by a scaled-up voluntary carbon market.

Clearing houses are needed to support a futures market and provide counterparty default protection.

Sophisticated and timely data is essential to all environmental and capital markets. In particular, data providers should offer transparent reference and market data, which is not readily available today, due to limited registry Application Programming Interface (API) access and an opaque OTC market. Data providers should also collect and offer historic project and developer performance as well as risk data to facilitate structured finance and the formulation of OTC contracts. New reporting and analytics services, spanning across registries, need to be developed for buyers and suppliers. Implementation could be supported by meta-registries, which collect and structure all openly accessible reference data. A critical enabler is that all registries offer reference data through open APIs. Furthermore, exchanges and clearinghouses should make aggregated market data available.

Benefits of linking systems

Market linkage is a popular topic, with many discussions underway, but progress has been slow. ETS allows for linking with systems in other countries, fostering international climate action. ETS policy enables distinct systems to be linked through the mutual recognition of emissions allowances. Linking reduces overall compliance costs, increases market liquidity, promotes market stability, and reduces the risk of leakage. Building on the existing EU ETS plus the emerging market in China, would increase the market from approximately 2Gt CO2e to 5Gt CO2e, giving far more scope for finding cost reductions across the different covered sectors.

As carbon markets continue to expand over time, coordination among jurisdictions using or considering carbon markets will be increasingly important to ensure environmental integrity and maximise cost-effectiveness. Market-based mechanisms and linked carbon markets attract investments where emissions reductions can occur at the lowest cost. The provisions in Article 6 of the Paris Agreement in relation to meeting NDC commitments[33], which sets out to establish an international carbon market, can help countries cooperate on carbon pricing in order to meet their mitigation commitments and increase their ambition over time.

Linkages and crediting mechanisms enable greater net emissions reductions than if governments attempt to achieve their targets in isolation. Access to markets could therefore enable countries to go beyond their NDC commitments, and at a lower cost. The provision for internationally transferrable mitigation outcomes (ITMOs) in Article 6 of the Paris Agreement will help drive deeper emissions reductions, quicker than would otherwise occur. Thus, an effective international carbon market coalition could achieve a greater outcome than the mere sum of the individual contributions.

The initial focus of such a coalition could be the development of common, credible standards or guidelines to ensure the integrity of carbon emissions units traded internationally, including through transparent monitoring, reporting and verification (MRV),

---

33 To achieve the Paris Agreement objectives, 186 countries — responsible for more than 90% of global emissions, submitted carbon reduction targets, known as "nationally determined contributions" (NDCs). These targets outlined each country's commitments for curbing emissions through 2025 or 2030. Article 6 of the Paris Agreement allows countries to reduce their emissions using international carbon markets. Countries that struggle to meet their emissions-reduction targets under their NDCs, or want to pursue less expensive emissions cuts, can purchase emissions reductions from other nations that have already cut their emissions more than the amount they had pledged, such as by transitioning to renewable energy.

as well as market oversight provisions and standards for environmental integrity. Over time, such standards and guidelines could provide the foundation for the development of a common market that jurisdictions could voluntarily link into. By promoting the development of standards for international emissions trading, that would build on and complement the guidelines for emissions accounting and reporting called for by the Paris Agreement, such a coalition would be fully compatible with the UNFCCC process.

A carbon market coalition could promote deep reductions in emissions by supporting the harmonisation of carbon markets across countries. As the coalition matured, members could establish harmonised or reciprocal standards for transparency, governance, and environmental integrity, create a shared market infrastructure to support the mutual recognition of emissions units, share experiences and cooperate in building institutional capacity, and work jointly to further the ability of these markets to promote domestic and cross-border investment in low-carbon technologies. One example of emerging linkage can be found in Europe where the EU and Switzerland signed an agreement to link their ETS in 2017, which came into force on 1 January 2020. The EU have also been exploring ways of linking with other markets such as China and Korea[34].

As greater participation and cooperation opens new avenues for more efficient emissions reductions, more ambition and action could be reflected at the international level. Over time, these linked carbon markets could catalyse the emergence of an international carbon price. The Paris Agreement provides a framework for cooperation among jurisdictions, but countries need to take the lead in implementing domestic carbon pricing policies and establishing links with others. Of the 90 countries which seek access to an international market mechanism as stated in their NDCs, many of them may decide it is technically easier and more cost-effective to join existing carbon markets or adopt similar policy architecture from existing markets.

International emissions trading and China

A number of countries are in the midst of formulating or ramping up their own ETS, with carbon exchanges being the main trading venues. South Korea, for example, has been successfully operating an ETS for the last six years. In keeping with Seoul's own net-zero target, South Korea is now planning to scale up its ETS to meet its 2050 pledge and

---

34 See "International carbon market", webpage on the EU's website.

ambitious interim targets. Japanese Prime Minister Yoshihide Suga has instructed his own ministries to draw up carbon pricing proposals. Indonesia and Vietnam are on track to introduce an ETS by 2022 and 2024 respectively, while Thailand and the Philippines are understood to be drawing up similar systems. For its part, Singapore already has a carbon tax and is working on plans to establish a regional VCM hub with Singapore at the centre.

According to the World Bank Group[35], 64 carbon pricing initiatives have been implemented or are scheduled for implementation, covering 46 national jurisdictions worldwide, mostly through cap-and-trade systems. These initiatives are gaining momentum, with China announcing the implementation of its own national ETS. This would be the world's largest national ETS, bringing a total of 12Gt CO2e of emissions (22.3% of the world's total GHG emissions in 2020) under some form of carbon pricing[36].

China's Ministry of Ecology and Environment hosted a media conference on 5 January 2021, confirming that the first compliance cycle of China's national ETS was effectively rolled out on 1 January 2021. Under the cycle, which will at first be limited to domestic thermal power generators, 2,225 companies in the industry have until 31 December 2021 to meet the requirements set by the government for carbon emissions[37]. It will allocate allowances based on the plant's generation output, with emissions benchmarks for each fuel and technology. In time China's ETS will expand to seven other sectors: aviation, non-ferrous metals, iron and steel, construction materials, chemicals, petrochemicals and paper manufacturing. Ultimately, benefits from China's national ETS will come from either surplus allowance for companies operating below the baseline threshold (e.g. "clean" coal utilities) or companies that are able to issue China Certified Emissions Reductions (CCERs), e.g. renewable operators. The latter could also drive demand for renewable projects, which could lead to growth in demand for renewable equipment, benefiting upstream players. Among coal operators, the suggested benchmark is likely to drive asymmetric risk exposure, with some potentially benefiting from the ETS. This view is based on the proposed thresholds and where industry intensity currently stands. The current proposed carbon emissions allowance baseline is 0.877-0.979 kilogram/kilowatt-hour (kg/kWh) for conventional coal units[38], depending on their installed capacity, which

35 Source: World Bank Group. (2020). *State and Trends of Carbon Pricing 2020*. Washington, DC: World Bank.

36 Source: "Carbon Pricing Dashboard", webpage on the World Bank's website, viewed on 5 May 2021.

37 Source: "Xinhua Commentary: China's resolute pursuit of reducing carbon emissions", *Xinhua*, 24 February 2021.

38 Source: *Implementation Plan on the Setting and Allocation of the Total National Quota of Carbon Emissions Allowance in 2019-2020 (Power Generation Industry)* (《2019-2020 年全國碳排放權交易配額總量設定與分配實施方案（發電行業）》), issued by the Ministry of Ecology and Environment (MEE), 30 December 2020.

will likely affect sub-critical coal plants as they have a lower thermal efficiency and a higher emissions intensity.

To support China's decarbonisation goals, it would make sense for the ETS to move to an absolute cap over time, which will also increase simplicity. It will be difficult for a market to understand what carbon intensity targets mean, for example growth increasing by 5% but emissions up only 4% should mean falling demand for allowances, even though emissions are still growing overall. Given China intends to peak emissions in 2030 then the sooner the move to an absolute cap within the ETS the better.

Outlook for China — Benefits and challenges

The emergence of the ETS and China's plan to dramatically reduce GHG emissions over the next four decades will mean banks and other financial institutions could benefit from rising demand for tens of billions of yuan of green financing to pay for sweeping changes throughout the economy. Achieving net-zero carbon emissions will require mobilising social capital through the financial system, bringing huge opportunities for green financing. However, the industry must learn to account for rising climate-change risks as they go about the business of underwriting credit. Assets invested in companies or projects that rely on traditional and dated technologies may risk becoming stranded or losing their value.

Chinese financial institutions need to develop knowledge of climate risks and the opportunities offered by carbon finance, which will require deeper internal talent pools and greater capacity for acquiring external data. In the past, China has relied more on administrative measures to prevent and control pollution. Now China will need to rely more on market and financial mechanisms, which could be a significant challenge to policymakers, financial and market regulators and market participants.

The transition to a zero-carbon economy is seen as a new round of the green industrial revolution. Carbon finance promises not only to create a new branch of green and sustainable finance but also to reshape the entire financial system's assets and investment and financing activities with a low-carbon approach.

An important foundation for reducing carbon emissions is the disclosure of consistent, high-quality climate information to measure existing emissions. One of biggest challenges is incomplete disclosure of environmental information by enterprises that banks are exposed to, with much of the data qualitative, not quantitative.

The People's Bank of China recently started an environmental information disclosure pilot programme involving 13 banks in the Guangdong-Hong Kong-Macao Greater Bay Area[39]. Under a guideline issued by the central bank, each pilot bank must formulate a working plan for environmental information disclosure and submit an annual report for by June each year. Starting in March 2022, pilot-programme banks will be required to submit an annual environmental information disclosure report for the previous year.

From a financial market perspective, a functioning cap-and-trade system relies heavily on competent financial regulatory authorities — in particular, the China Securities Regulatory Commission in the Mainland and the Securities and Futures Commission in Hong Kong.

A pro-competition, vibrant and pro-startup environment could support new product listing and innovation, leading to better price discovery and allow hedging by real-economy entities. Guangdong and Hubei have had large-scale spot carbon trading for 7-plus years now, but a regulated, transparent and functioning forward carbon price curve has yet to emerge.

Looking at China's energy market today, companies are facing two historical "transitions": one is planning to transition to market-based mechanisms, such as China's natural gas and power markets; the other is the transition from traditional energy sources to new low-carbon energy sources. Building an innovative derivatives market, serving China's successful energy transformation, and obtaining pricing power in the international energy market will have a major impact both domestically and internationally.

Chinese futures exchanges can learn from the successful experience of North American energy futures exchanges such as ICE and CME through OTC trading and centralised clearing to serve the development of China's future natural gas, electricity, carbon emissions, green certificate and other derivatives markets and contribute to the two energy "transitions" in China.

Exchanges can work together to jointly develop and list standard contracts to manage price risks and provide effective services for entities, making the management of these trading centres more professional and standardised. In addition, in terms of service product innovation, there are a wealth of internationally listed products. Successfully listed products can be listed directly in China to form an interconnection of international

---

39 Source: *UK-China Climate and Environmental Information Disclosure Pilot — 2019 Progress Report*, published on the website of the United Nations-supported Principles for Responsible Investment (PRI), 20 May 2020.

exchanges. They can also realise the localisation of international services and increase participation of companies.

In addition to providing traditional trading and settlement services, exchanges can also provide market-oriented services such as data, trading technology, delivery services, transportation and custody services, and consulting on the use of corporate derivatives. For example, ICE's main business has transitioned from a traditional futures exchange, based on transaction fees, to a business model based on big data and exchange technology supported connectivity, with income for the latter now exceeding transaction fees.

Shanghai-Hong Kong Stock Connect, Shenzhen-Hong Kong Stock Connect, Shanghai-London Stock Connect and Bond Connect have accelerated the internationalisation of China's capital markets and accumulated valuable practical experience and historical transaction data. Futures exchanges can work together with mainstream financial and energy institutions, in Hong Kong, Europe, and North America to list new futures contracts, embedding China's energy prices into Asian and international energy pricing chains. The limitations of traditional exchanges in serving the real economy are already visible. To build world-class exchanges, which can compete internationally for carbon and other ESG derivative products, requires separation of regulators and exchanges, free market competition in the exchange sector, robust information technology infrastructure, global selection of human talent, comprehensive planning, and regulations that balance the need for orderly market operation with an environment for innovation.

Conclusions

A global carbon market is needed such that a single price is put on carbon, sending the right signal to companies around the world to reduce emissions. Internationally set mandatory compliance markets are the best way to cap and reduce emissions. The preferred model would be for a global cap, tending to net-zero by 2050, with allocations shared equitably amongst nations. However, in the absence of global collaboration it is likely that a series of national or regional exchange-traded markets will emerge, with some linking between them. The voluntary carbon markets could play a role here, if countries allow companies to use carbon credits to meet compliance obligations, hence creating international arbitrage. Companies will be expected to commit to a credible net-zero pathway, reducing their carbon emissions first and foremost, which may increase costs in the short term. A guiding principle is that direct emissions reductions by corporates must be the priority, with appropriate offsetting playing an important complementary role to accelerate climate mitigation action. In order of priority, corporates should reduce, report and then offset. These principles outline the need for credible transition plans. Companies should publicly disclose commitments, detailed transition plans, and annual progress against these plans to decarbonise operations and value chains in line with science to limit warming to 1.5°C as per the Paris Agreement.

Clear rules and guidelines agreed upfront, exchanges and standardised contracts are the key ingredients for a successful carbon market. The main obstacles to scaling the VCM are a lack of standardisation, definition of quality and what quality looks like (i.e. how to monitor adherence to the quality criteria), good governance and lack of funding. Agreeing on how carbon credits can be used in a corporate net-zero claim is also a critical issue that needs to be resolved.

Financial institutions will bring the capital to reduce emissions by the volumes needed. Financial institutions can intermediate this market in the same way they do other commodity markets by providing finance across the value chain. In addition, financial institutions, and especially exchanges, can bring the duty of care they bring to other markets (retail banking, commodity trading, commodity finance) making them more transparent and safer places for organisations and individuals to participate. Development and listing of a standardised spot and futures core carbon contract with physical delivery of certificates will allow development of a transparent, daily market price. Exchanges should also develop reference contracts which will aid transparency, growth of liquidity and counterparty assurance.

Massive reductions in global emissions, far beyond the level of current ambition, will be required to achieve net-zero by 2050. If the world does not become net-zero by mid-century, the likelihood of global temperatures rising above 1.5°C increases significantly. Countries may take different pathways and have different end dates for net-zero targets, depending on equity and other considerations but the scale and urgency of emissions reductions needed, means that we are no longer looking to prioritise low-cost emissions reductions. Instead all emissions need to be reduced as quickly and efficiently as possible. There is now a "race to zero" in which all countries, sectors and companies need to participate. Investment needs to be made now in technologies that are currently not scalable and cost competitive. Carbon markets can support the commercialisation of such technologies by giving companies the opportunity to support the path to decarbonisation. Without finance for innovation now, it will be impossible to reach our decarbonisation goals before we run out of time. While carbon markets cannot deliver all of these goals alone, well-organised markets can create the right environment for everyone to reduce emissions so that we can continue to enjoy the benefits of economic development in countries across the world, including those rapidly industrialising today.

第18章

綠色及可持續金融 ——
碳交易所的角色

Chris LEEDS
渣打銀行　執行董事

摘要

隨着全球日益關注對緩解氣候轉變所帶來的風險，各地相關部門相繼開展了討論，並出台實施了一系列政策工具。脫碳勢在必行，不論強制性還是自願性碳交易市場都可以是推動這一進程的重要推手，同時實現最大限度地降低經濟成本。以市場為主導的碳定價政策，包括總量管制與交易、碳稅和信用計劃，皆遵循「污染者付費」的原則，旨在使排放者將其溫室氣體排放的外部成本內部化。大多數強制性碳市場採用「總量管制與交易」模式，該模式限制了經濟體可排放的溫室氣體數量，並隨着時間的推移逐漸將其淨排放減少到零，這當然是目標。「排放權交易機制」採用總量管制與交易的制度、利用數量化的方法，使碳市場能形成公允的市價，同時可確保將排放量限制在所需的水平。另一方面，「自願性碳交易市場」則以項目為基礎，遵循基線和信用原則；而相關項目實施的目的在於將溫室氣體排放量降至日常營運情況下所推算的排放水平（即基線）之下。低於基線的減排量可以獲得碳信用額度，這些碳信用額度可以出售給其他減排成本更高的排放者。在這種情況下不存在總量管制，只要項目排放量低於基線，總排放量還是會不斷上升。為了確保淨排放量下降，則須證明這些項目的碳信用確實是相比在沒有實施該項目下所額外產生的減排量，並且總體目標是將淨排放量減少到零。自願性碳交易市場不應被用來縱容成本較高排放者的不作為。

不管是強制性的國家排放權交易機制，還是以項目為本的自願性碳交易市場，連接不同的碳交易市場可以放大碳交易的得益，但我們必須努力保障市場的持正操作。一個流動性高、透明和受到良好監管的碳市場能支持脫碳工作的創新和投資，但要實現這一目標，還需要標準化的市場、法規和深度合作。這正是交易所可以作出貢獻的地方。《巴黎協定》為市場化機制在國際上的發展提供了機會，但為了使它們能夠在實現 2050 年淨零目標過程中充分發揮貢獻，我們仍然有許多工作要做。明確強制性和自願性碳交易市場之間的關係就將是其中的一項重要工作。排放權交易機制於一些國家（包括中國）的建立和興起是一項重大進展，這將鼓勵其他國家相繼效法。交易所可以制定規則、基礎設施和合作協議，將全球自願性和強制性的碳交易市場聯合在一起。直接減排必須作為優先事項，由強制性碳市場驅動，再輔以基於項目的自願性碳交易市場，加快為減緩氣候變化行動融資。

最終，地球為人類設定了碳排放上限：到 2050 年，全球淨排放量需要減到零，以避免溫度升高超過 1.5°C。

引言

2015 年，幾乎所有國家都通過了《巴黎協定》[1]，以應對氣候變化及其負面影響。該協議取代了《京都議定書》[2]，旨在大幅減少全球溫室氣體排放量，以將本世紀全球氣溫上升限制在比工業化前水平高出 2°C 之內，同時進一步尋求將上升幅度限制在 1.5°C 之內的方法。然而，在政府作出的承諾與管理氣候變化所需的果斷行動之間，還有很長的路要走。

到 2030 年，世界需要在 2010 年的水平上減少 45% 的排放量[3]。這種轉變需要大幅擴大市場和政策機制，以激勵脫碳和減排。受到疫情影響，全球二氧化碳排放量在 2020 年下降了 6.4%（23 億噸），但需要在未來十年內每年至少下降 7.6%，才可避免升溫超過 1.5°C[4]。減排目標必須基於科學，同時兼顧全球經濟增長，以支持新技術領域的投資，讓各國繁榮昌盛，人民安居樂業。有效的碳市場是這一轉變的重要組成部分，碳交易所處在其核心。不論哪個地方實現的減排都對緩解全球暖化問題作出相同的貢獻。溫室氣體排放源的數量和種類繁多使得制定全面有效的「指揮和控制」方針變得困難，通過召集調動市場來找到最快、成本最低的各種減排方案，即可放大成本節約效應。

隨着世界力爭快速脫碳，對碳交易市場和定價的需求將會擴大。英國和歐盟均已承諾在2050 年實現淨零[5]，其中期目標分別為於 2030 年之前實現相對於 1990 年的基線減少 68%[6]及 55%[7]。中國的目標是到 2030 年達到排放峰值，到 2060 年實現碳中和[8]。此外，在僅一年的時間內，自願以淨零為目標的公司承諾亦多了一倍[9]。擴大自願性碳交易市場工作組（Taskforce for Scaling the Voluntary Carbon Markets，簡稱 TSVCM）估計，自願性碳交易市場須在 2030 年實現增長 15 倍以上，以支持實現 1.5°C 路徑所需的投資[10]。

碳交易市場可以支持新的計劃來資助、構建和部署這些關鍵解決方案，以便在未來我們可以延續世界各國的經濟發展，包括今天快速工業化的國家。

1　參閱〈巴黎協定〉（"Paris Agreement"）聯合國氣候變化框架公約（United Nations Framework Convention on Climate Change，簡稱 UNFCCC）網站上的網頁。

2　參閱〈What is the Kyoto Protocol?〉，UNFCCC網站上的網頁。

3　參閱〈全球暖化1.5°C〉（"Global warming of 1.5°C"），政府間氣候變化專門委員會（Intergovernmental Panel on Climate Change，簡稱IPCC）網站上的特別報告，2018年10月8日。

4　有關分析借鑒了IPCC的工作，截至2018年1月1日使用了570兆噸的剩餘碳預算。若將餘下的預算換算為將氣候升幅限制於攝氏1.5度以下的機率，有關機率為66%。

5　在淨零（碳排放）的狀態下，大氣層中的溫室氣體人為排放可在指定期間透過人為清除達到平衡。

6　資料來源：〈英國於聯合國峰會前新訂遠大的氣候目標〉（"UK sets ambitious new climate target ahead of UN Summit"），載於英國政府網站的新聞稿，2020年12月3日。

7　參閱〈2030年氣候及能源框架〉（"2030 climate & energy framework"），歐盟網站上的網頁。

8　資料來源：〈習近平：中國承諾力爭二氧化碳排放於2030年前達到峰值，2060年前實現碳中和〉（"China pledges to achieve CO2 emissions peak before 2030, carbon neutrality before 2060"），載於《路透社》，2020年9月22日。

9　資料來源：〈清零計劃進展於一年內取得雙倍成果〉（"Commitments to net zero double in less than a year"），UNFCCC網站上的新聞稿，2020年9月21日。

10　資料來源：〈Taskforce for Scaling the Voluntary Carbon Markets〉，國際金融協會網站上的網頁，於2021年9月16日閱覽。

目前，在自願性和強制性的範疇均有一系列舉措，致力於擴大碳交易市場。到 2050 年實現淨零排放的承諾重新激發了企業對碳交易市場的興趣，因碳交易市場可作為支持靈活脫碳途徑的工具，能夠為更多氣候變化緩解措施引入大量資金，這些緩解措施包括減排技術及基於自然的解決方案。

雖然自願性碳交易市場因潛在的「漂綠」風險而受到審查，但購買高質量的碳信用額正被企業用作實現淨零排放的可靠途徑的一部分，即通過年度減排和對轉型過程中不可避免的排放進行補償。為了確保碳信用是高質量的，它們必須是「有效的」（英文簡稱「VALID」），即必須做到「可驗證」（Verifiable）、相較現行所產生的「額外性」（Additional）、無別處排放「泄漏」（Leakage）、「不可逆轉」（Irreversible），以及不「重複計算」（Double-count）。

可再生能源、基於自然的解決方案和能源效率項目都是減少溫室氣體和實現淨零排放的關鍵工具，但僅靠這些還不足以支持全球摒棄化石燃料而轉用其他能源。我們需要能夠實行經濟轉型的新興技術 —— 例如重型運輸的低碳燃料、低碳鋼和低碳水泥，以及更好的除碳技術。這類轉型需要的資金龐大，動輒萬億計，在這方面碳交易市場便可發揮其籌集引導資金的作用。

碳交易

1989 年，在聯合國氣候變化框架公約（United Nations Framework Convention on Climate Change，簡稱 UNFCCC）第一次締約方會議之前，碳交易在自願基礎上開始進行。早期交易大多與防止胡亂砍伐森林的項目有關。後來事態的發展使碳信用的使用漸成主流。首先，1997 年通過的《京都議定書》確立了碳交易市場基礎設施的幾個要素，包括國際排放交易的基礎和清潔發展機制（Clean Development Mechanism，簡稱 CDM）[11]，後者為碳抵銷方法設定了標準，亦為建立正式的中央碳信用登記處奠定了基礎。

2003 年推出了第一個中央化總量管制與交易系統，即自願但具有法律約束力的芝加哥氣候交易所（Chicago Climate Exchange，簡稱 CCX），該系統還允許應用有限百分比的經核實信用額度，以達到減排計劃符合時間表之要求。CCX 是一家自律監管的交易所，由美國商品期貨交易委員會（Commodity Futures Trading Commission）監督，並由全國證券交易商協會（National Association of Securities Dealers）每年對會員基線和減排合規性進行審計，該協會後來成為金融業監管局（Financial Industry Regulatory Authority，一家自律監管的美國證券業監管機構）。CCX 為全球排放權交易提供價格發現，並為其 450 個會員（包括主要的企業、大學、城市和州份）提供了一個平台，通過標準化、具有法律約束力的合約作出減排承諾。

---

11 參閱〈清潔發展機制〉("Clean Development Mechanism（CDM）")，UNFCCC網站上的網頁。

可於 CCX 交易的金融工具為可替代的碳金融工具（carbon financial instrument，簡稱
CFI），相當於一噸二氧化碳。CCX 的成員承諾按照指定的減排時間表直接減少所有北美
業務的所有範圍 1 的排放 [12]，並且可以在有限的基礎上使用碳信用以滿足其合規要求。超額
完成合規減排目標的成員有多餘的 CFI 配額可供出售或儲蓄；那些未能達到減排目標的成
員可通過從有盈餘的成員處購買 CFI 來達到合規要求。準成員只可以是範圍 2 排放者，並
承諾通過從 CCX 成員購買 CFI 來減少或抵銷其整個北美年度排放量。CCX 的成員於七年
內減少了 7 億噸的二氧化碳當量，證明交易所加上交易平台可提高碳市場的透明度及流動
性，包括碳排放信用額的應用。CCX 還發起並共同擁有中國第一個碳交易市場 —— 天津
排放權交易所，並在全球設有分支機構，作為最終全球市場的模板。CCX 於 2010 年停止
營運，造成這個結果的部分原因是監管目標未能達到，這包括美國擬建立全國性總量管制
與交易系統的《瓦克斯曼－馬基法案》（Wax-man-Markey bill）未能獲通過，以及 2009 年
哥本哈根談判破裂等，使當時全球碳交易市場起飛的希望破滅。

2005 年，歐盟啟動了其排放權交易機制（Emissions Trading System，簡稱 ETS）——
歐盟 ETS[13]，涵蓋超過 11,000 家能源密集型設施及航空公司，以及歐盟約 45% 的溫室氣
體排放，主要為二氧化碳，但也包括一氧化二氮和全氟化合物。歐盟 ETS 在所有歐盟國
家、冰島、列支敦斯登及挪威營運。2020 年 1 月，歐盟 ETS 與瑞士 ETS 連結。歐盟
ETS 目前處於第 4 階段營運，即 2021 年 1 月至 2030 年 12 月，可能會採用比 1990 年水
平減少 55% 的減排目標。各公司根據其所屬行業獲得或購買排放配額（European Union
Allowance，簡稱 EUA），電力行業的公司需要通過定期拍賣購買歐盟碳排放配額，而其
他行業的公司則獲得一些免費配額。每年年底，各公司必須提交足夠的 EUA 以涵蓋當年
的所有排放量，並保留備用配額以備將來使用或出售。每年年底，公司必須提交足夠的排
放配額以涵蓋當年的所有排放量，並保留備用配額以備日後使用或出售。不遵守有關規定
須按每公噸二氧化碳當量支付 100 歐元。2019 年，歐盟引入市場穩定儲備機制（Market
Stability Reserve）[14]，以應對 2009 年金融危機後經濟衰退導致的配額堆積過量的問題，有
助於支持市場穩定。

自成立以來，強制性和自願性碳交易市場便一直互有聯繫。人們可以觀察到強制性碳交易
市場、CDM 下產生的核證減排量（Certified Emissions Reductions，簡稱 CER）和自願
信用交易量之間的相關聯動。強制性市場的一項關鍵發展是 CDM 於 2008 年與歐盟 ETS
的聯通。這使企業能夠使用 CER，即 CDM 下項目產生的碳信用額，來遵守歐盟的排放
法規。歐洲碳交易所（European Carbon Exchange，現為洲際交易所（ICE）的一部分）、
Powernext 及歐洲能源交易所（European Energy Exchange）等先後成立，提供 EUA 和

12　範圍1涵蓋來自擁有或控制來源的實體的直接排放。範圍2涵蓋來自生產由實體購買的電力、蒸氣及冷暖調節的間接排放。
　　範圍3涵蓋所有其他於公司價值鏈上游或下游產生的間接排放。參閱〈企業標準〉（"Corporate Standard"）,《溫室氣體核
　　算體系》（*Greenhouse Gas Protocol*）網站上的網頁。
13　參閱〈歐盟ETS〉（"EU Emissions Trading System（EU ETS）"），歐盟網站上的網頁。
14　參閱〈市場穩定儲備機制〉（"Market Stability Reserve"），歐盟網站上的網頁。

CER 的交易。2008 至 2016 年間,歐盟 ETS 減少了逾 10 億噸二氧化碳[15]。CDM 與歐盟 ETS 之間的聯繫也為自願性碳交易市場帶來了新的關注。看到大型工業公司須付錢購買溫室氣體排放權,諮詢機構和律師事務所等服務供應商預計它們最終可能會面臨類似的要求,並開始購買自願信用額度。CER 交易量於 2012 年之後大幅下降,當時歐盟 ETS 所涵蓋的實體已經購買了大部分 2012 至 2020 階段允許的信用額度,並且歐盟對信用的使用施加了嚴格限制[16]。強制性合規計劃(例如歐盟 ETS、加州總量管制與交易機制、中國排放權交易機制)尚未最終確定關於未來接受獨立標準信用的規則,這可能會顯著影響對獨立標準信用的整體需求,並進一步提升碳市場之間的可替代性及流動性。展望未來,強制性與自願性碳交易市場可繼續相輔相成。

根據世界銀行集團的數據,在 2019 年,本身為區域性、國家級或次國家級實體的 70 多個市場參與者參與了碳定價計劃,涵蓋了全球近 22% 的溫室氣體排放量[17],它們以此創造了超過 450 億美元的碳定價收入,比上一年增加了 10 億美元。

「總量管制與交易」制度的源起

總量管制與交易制度由美國國家環境保護局(Environmental Protection Agency)於 20 世紀 80 年代制定。當時,美國中西部的燃煤發電廠排放的二氧化硫及二氧化氮向東飄散,使東北州份受嚴重霧霾及酸雨困擾。當時建議的解決方案是由國家環境保護局對電力供應商施加減少二氧化硫排放的規定,但公用設施公司紛紛表示遵守有關規定的成本太高,且當時亦未有較潔淨的技術。總量管制與交易的概念遂應運而生,旨在提升靈活性,並分散所有排放者減少二氧化硫排放的成本。國家環境保護局引入二氧化硫總量管制與交易制度後,在過量排放者的需要與需求的催逼下,新的清潔技術更快投入市場,而且減排成本遠低於預期,美國的霧霾及酸雨問題終於迎刃而解,還帶來許多健康及其他方面的好處[18]。這次的成功,加上溫室氣體的排放會於整個地球的大氣層平均分佈這一現實,反映了總量管制與交易制度能有效解決氣候變化的問題。

在總量管制與交易制度下,來自經濟體各行業(或整個經濟體)的碳排放會被封頂 —— 施加「總量管制」,同時因應有關總量限額而分發配額。在排放沒有任何限制的情況下,公司

---

15 資料來源:P. Bayer 與 M. Aklin(2020年)〈儘管價格偏低,歐盟排放權交易機制成功減少了二氧化碳排放〉("The European Union Emissions Trading System reduced CO2 emissions despite low prices"),《Proceedings of the National Academy of Sciences》,第117期,第16卷,8804-8812頁。

16 參閱〈國際排放信用額的用途〉("Use of international credits"),歐盟網站上的網頁。

17 資料來源:世界銀行集團(2020年)《2020年碳定價的狀態及趨勢》(State and Trends of Carbon Pricing 2020)。華盛頓哥倫比亞特區:世界銀行。

18 資料來源:R. Stavins、G. Chan、R. Stowe 與 R. Sweeney〈美國二氧化硫總額管制及交易計劃以及對氣候政策的啟示〉("The US sulphur dioxide cap and trade programme and lessons for climate policy"),載於《VoxEU.org》網站,2012年8月12日。

毋須考慮排放二氧化碳的經濟成本。然而，若排放量被封頂，整條公式便會徹底改變，因為「污染權」成了稀有而受追捧的商品。為產生環境效益，總量限額必須根據科學而設定，即若要達到顯著改善環境的效果便須於何時之前減去多少噸的排放量，就二氧化碳而言，目標是在 2050 年前將全球排放總量限額減至淨零。透過總量管制與交易制度改善環境的關鍵在於有關限額的逐步收緊，逐步減少允許的排放量以及可交易的配額。供應收縮時，需求增加，配額價格便會上升。總量限額以下的排放均獲允許，但超過該限額的排放即被禁止。集體排放必須維持在總量限額以下，參與者根據其在總允許排放量中的佔比，按比例獲分配或購買配額。

不論是免費配給還是透過拍賣獲得，有關配額的分配方法理論上對經濟結果的影響沒有分別[19]。一般而言，配額應透過拍賣獲得，而非免費配給或豁免而得，因為拍賣可確保與環境政策有關的得益都歸於公共當局，而非進了現有污染者的口袋。免費分配會作為一種補貼，減弱了減排的動力，因為排放者會因此受保護而免卻付出其排放的實質成本。儘管歐盟 ETS 已轉為讓電力業排放者透過拍賣獲得配額，但免費配給仍適用於鋼和水泥等行業，這些行業面對的國際競爭可能會驅使公司減少在歐盟的業務以規避因參與 ETS 所涉及的成本，而改為增加在其他沒有排放限制國家的業務，即所謂「碳泄漏」。

政策制定者希望透過每年收緊有關總量限額令價格慢慢上升，從而讓所有人有時間慢慢適應較高的成本。讓購買配額的成本比減排更高，有助於加速對新技術的需求，激勵所有排放實體向較潔淨和高效的營運方式轉型。

舉例而言，燃燒煤生產同等電量所排放的二氧化碳量約為天然氣的 2.5 倍。部分排放者可能已安裝高效能的鍋爐，或以天然氣取代煤作為燃料。這些參與者可以成為賣家並在市場上「做多」，並且可能將他們沒有使用的配額出售給處於相反情況的參與者，即已經用完他們的年度配額但其排放量仍然超過他們的年度限額的參與者。這些「過量排放者」在市場上是空頭的，如果由於某種原因他們不能直接進一步減排，他們必須從有盈餘的其他人那裏購買配額，以便所有參與者共同保持在排放總量限額以下。如果他們不這樣做，他們將在未來的某個合規日期支付罰款。

經紀及商品交易員亦會入市，購買、出售或持有碳配額，就其價格揣測炒作，就如石油或金屬等其他商品一樣。期貨及遠期市場亦由此衍生並不斷演變，漸漸帶來標準化、透明度及流動性，推動長期碳融資的發展。最理想的情況是，由於該市場旨在改善公眾環境，交易都在受規管的、善意公正的公眾交易所進行，因此交易價格能保持透明，並提供時刻公開的公眾市場信號，就如股票一樣。理論上，這個價格相當於減少一噸二氧化碳排放量的成本。此外，每名排放者的財務狀況都不同，會直接影響各自的借貸及其他成本，繼而影

---

[19] 參閱 R. Stavins〈兩項重大的活動促使對總量管制與交易制度的重要特性進行評估〉（"Two notable events prompt examination of an important property of cap-and-trade"），載於《robertstavinsblog.org》網站，2012年7月21日。

響直接減排的整體成本。相較於直接為減排而在營運或策略上作出所必要的變更，過量排放者在市場上購買配額的成本可能會更低。因此，相關價格可能會像任何商品市場般波動，並與其他相關大宗商品（例如煤及天然氣）聯動。以歐盟 ETS 為例，煤在歐盟是主要的發電燃料，因此，使從燃煤發電轉向天然氣發電得享盈利的價格便成為 EUA 的市場價格。

批評總量管制與交易制度的人會說，排放者要規避減排責任的話，付錢便可了事，但他們忽略了一個重點：總量管制與交易制度能鼓勵排放者最先使用成本最低的減排方法，並迫使其他排放者也採取行動。它為經濟體調整爭取了時間，而不是迫使突然改變，後者會令經濟出現不可接受的混亂。隨着配額收緊，配額的價格將逐漸上升，實際減排的成本逐漸變得比購買有關配額的現價更低，所有排放者早晚都會加入直接減排的行列。

由於電力行業過去一直是固定排放的最大來源，有其他價格較吸引且排放量低的發電燃料可取代煤（例如天然氣及較近期的可再生能源），大部分排放權交易計劃，如歐盟 ETS、加州 ETS、地區溫室氣體減排行動（Regional Greenhouse Gas Initiative，簡稱 RGGI）及已出台的中國 ETS，均以電力業為核心。當然，亦有其他碳排放量較大的行業，但它們大多都是一些所謂難以減排的行業，例如鋼、水泥、航空、航海及道路運輸等。正在努力通過國際航空碳抵銷和減排計劃（Carbon Offsetting and Reduction Scheme for International Aviation），以及將航空和航運納入歐盟 ETS 等計劃將這些行業包括在內，這就需要碳抵銷。在「基線和信用」系統下進行抵銷，允許這些行業的公司投資於在其他地方減少排放的項目，例如能源效益、林業、農業及可再生能源，還鼓勵他們投資開發其價值鏈中的新技術，以支持直接減少其行業的排放，如直接空氣捕獲、碳捕獲和儲存，以及可持續航空燃料等技術。今天，這些技術因太昂貴而無法進行商業規模化，但現在通過投資它們，我們希望能夠像過去 20 年投資太陽能和風能一樣可降低其成本。

絕對上限與按密集度計量的上限

排放權交易的絕對值總量管制與交易制度還有另一種形式，就是將限額由「絕對」值改為「相對」值。這樣，上限並非某個絕對排放量（例如二氧化碳噸數），而是以相對於其活動水平的排放量（例如生產每單位鋼所排放的二氧化碳噸數）來計算。若一家公司生產的排放較相對標準潔淨，公司便可出售其「未有使用」的污染許可。有關污染許可的數目是按每個活動單位的實際排放量與相對標準兩者之差乘以活動量來計算。舉例而言，假設相對標準是每兆瓦時發電量排放 1 噸二氧化碳，若一家公司能將排放量控制在每兆瓦時僅 0.9 噸二氧化碳，而一年內生產 100 萬兆瓦時的電力，其便可出售 100,000 噸二氧化碳排放權。任何未能按相對排放標準發電，或以當前的污染許可權的市價情況下不肯按有關排放標準發電的公司，可購買污染許可去填補有關差額。另外，對污染許可的需求亦可能來自其他行業，例如需要應對絕對限額的行業，又或有需求來自海外地區的相關公司，他們面對相同的排放標準，但其每產出單位的排放量表現卻未及標準。

生產商通常偏好採用相對值的總量管制與交易制度，因為擔心絕對值的總量管制與交易制度會導致其無法增加產能及產量，即使他們是以最環保的方式進行生產。若公司或行業的業務涉及國際市場，而海外競爭者毋須遵守同一水平的環境規例，這論點便尤其有力。只是從環保的角度看，一個棘手的問題就是最終的污染水平無法預先得知。有關對環境的影響除要看相對標準之外，亦取決於標準所指定但不受環境監管機構監控的活動水平（如生產水平）。如上文所述，最終目標是將碳排放達致淨零，而這目標僅依靠基於排放密集度的計劃是無法達到的。

自願性碳交易市場：基線與信用機制

基線與信用機制是排放權交易計劃的一種，在這機制下，參與者會實施專門項目來實現將溫室氣體排放量降至依如常營運路徑預計會增加的排放水平（基線）之下。凡將排放量減至低於該未來路徑水平時，即可就有關差額獲得碳信用額，有關碳信用額可售予其他減碳成本較高的排放者。《京都議定書》的清潔發展機制及聯合履約計劃都是基線與信用模式的例子，自願性碳交易市場亦是。當沒有絕對排放上限時使用該模式，能夠衡量實施減排計劃（例如可再生能源計劃、能源效益計劃、成功阻止的森林砍伐或重新造林）後排放量對比基線所產生的改變。碳信用額由發行機構發放，用於在沒有項目的情況下發生的情況與特定計入期內（例如一年）項目邊界內的實際排放量之間的差異。項目開發商須制定一個項目計劃，稱之為「項目設計文件」，計劃會採納經協定的減排量及「避免或移除」方式，其後由獨立核數師驗證。為確保項目的完整性，項目設計文件須符合若干條件，特別是：與一切如常下結果的區別所在，是額外所得的結果、可永久減排，以及減排量可計量及可驗證。項目實施後，每隔一段時間（如每年）就由另一獨立核數師驗證項目有否跟項目設計文件一致及減排情況有否發生。然後負責驗證的核數師會將報告送交標準制定者，由其發出碳信用並記入其登記冊。標準制定者的例子包括 Verra[20]、Gold Standard[21]、Plan Vivo[22]、氣候行動儲備（Climate Action Reserve）[23] 及美國碳登記處 [24]。

碳稅

碳總量管制與交易機制是一種激勵減排的方式，補貼和碳稅則提供了替代方案，可以補充碳交易，因為它們有不同的目的。如果你想專注於特定技術，有補貼就相當好。這裏的問

20　參閱其網站：www.verra.org。
21　參閱其網站：www.goldstandard.org。
22　參閱其網站：www.planvivo.org。
23　參閱其網站：www.climateactionreserve.org。
24　參閱其網站：www.americanregistry.org。

題是政策制定者被要求「挑選贏家」，而他們通常不擅長這樣做。此外，政策制定者改變對補貼的看法也很常見，這讓投資者很難掌握情況。碳稅本質上是碳交易政策硬幣的另一面。對於碳稅，成本是預先知道的，但減排量是未知的。將碳稅定為每公噸 10 美元，只會促使每公噸二氧化碳當量的邊際減排成本低於 10 美元的企業減少排放。許多行業的減排成本遠高於此，有些甚至超過 100 美元，但將碳稅設在如此高的水平在政治上是不可接受的。它也可能對經濟體系造成不必要的衝擊，因為它同時增加了每個人的成本，即使對於那些可以以低得多的成本進行減排的亦如是。

現時的氛圍是需要碳稅和碳交易，它們可以協同發揮作用。徵稅的優點是簡單，但缺點是過於政治化，不會將排放量減少到零。重要的是不要鎖定太低的價格信號，這將很難提高，同時亦須避免將其設置得太高，從而損害可行的業務並削弱民眾的支持。

碳稅往往具有高度累退性，特別是在應用於家庭供暖或製冷和農村交通等活動時。在低收入羣體中，食品成本的影響也很重要。碳稅還可能導致就業不平等，企業遷出稅收較高的地區，而碳總量並沒有減少。

支持碳稅的人士通常會說這些問題可透過配合一系列不同的額外措施來解決，例如附加費及邊界的調整。雖然這在理論上可行，但實際上有關策略卻難以施行，且通常無法達到預期的效果。若減碳解決方案不能被廣泛使用，例如開發新技術、取得資金及獲得政府支持，徵稅可能只會令本已受惠的羣體創造更大的固有利益，不僅會減少競爭，更會加深收入不均等的問題。這些分配方面的問題反映了碳稅的結構及其徵收對象均非常重要，而這與一般經濟上的假設 —— 即稅制完美地應用於所有地方的所有活動，頗為不同。

收入較高的人士及實力較強的公司一般較有能力投資及改變消費模式，因此亦較有能力規避稅項。收入較低的人士及實力較弱的公司一般無法投資可減少消費的優良技術，因此會被迫選擇直接負擔稅項或忍痛改變消費模式。若需求是有彈性的話，相對較低金額的碳稅可帶來較大的碳排放轉變，因此重新分配及失業的水平亦會較低。當較容易的改變調整已做完，而不得不求助於昂貴的技術變更或較痛苦複雜的轉變時，需求曲線的彈性將會減少。這意味着須進一步加稅，才可產生相同的氣候影響及分配性影響，且失業率也會有所上升。有了碳交易，這個過程將會自動進行：隨着配額供應減少，其價格會上升，但上升的速度仍可讓經濟有時間逐漸適應而不至於出現失調。

排放權交易的好處

從現有制度可見，即使已考慮外部因素，ETS 促進了減排的發生，尤其是於交易所進行的排放權交易。歐盟 ETS 第二階段 (2008 年至 2010 年) 開始時對有關涵蓋範圍內的德國公司減排估算顯示：有關公司的減排量較涵蓋範圍以外的可比公司多 25% 至 28%[25]。就 RGGI 涵蓋的國家而言，模擬結果顯示，若沒有 ETS，所涵蓋實體的排放量會多出 24%[26]。

ETS 基於數量的方法可確保排放量維持於各涵蓋行業的特定排放限額或以下。ETS 的限額應是循序漸進地降低的、合理可靠的、並與氣候目標一致的，為達到中長期的減排藍圖提供清晰的路徑。這可減少不確定因素，有助公司作出適當的調整。

ETS 的存在讓公司可選擇減排的地點及時間。排放者會首先選擇成本最低的減排選項。此外，參與者可於最具成本效益的時機進行減排。透過 ETS 發出的價格信號會自動適應不斷轉變的經濟環境，經濟較緩的時候減排成本較低，在經濟增長的時候則減排成本較高。碳價格在高水平有利於低碳的生產程序、產品及技術。

重要的是，ETS 有助於將排放問題從經濟增長中抽離出來。舉例而言，加州經濟的碳濃度已從 2001 年高位減少 33%，而同期加州經濟增長了 37%[27]。由 2012 年至 2015 年，加州排放量穩步減少，本地生產總值、人口及就業均呈現增長。

透過配額拍賣，ETS 可帶來額外的政府收入，可用於投資進一步的氣候行動、降低其他稅項，或為低收入家庭或受不利影響的羣體提供補償。

排放權交易及競爭力

如資料所示，碳市場可就減少溫室氣體提供高效、靈活及具有經濟效益的方法。碳市場結合其他政策，可推動市場從高排放產品向低排放產品及程序轉移，加快並確保順利過渡至低碳經濟。然而，縱使有公司正不斷適應變化、提升盈利能力，並開發新業務模式，但仍有部分本身為低排放替代品競爭對手的公司可能要面臨市佔率縮小、盈利減少的問題。

有人擔心，由於不同司法權區的碳價格各有不同，高碳經濟活動可能會移向沒有碳價格或碳價格較低的地區。這可能會造成盈利減少及失業的問題，並可能會加劇政治方面的反對力度，無法達到減排的預期環境效益。若出現這樣的「碳泄漏」，便只換來「雙輸」局面：既失去經濟競爭力或經濟活動，亦無益於環境。

25　資料來源：S. Petrick 與 U. J. Wagner〈碳交易對行業的影響：德國製造業公司提供的證據〉（"The Impact of carbon trading on industry: Evidence from German manufacturing firms"），2014年3月28日，載於SSRN。

26　資料來源：RGGI（2017年）《2015年RGGI所得款項的投資》（*The Investment of RGGI Proceeds in 2015*），2019年10月。

27　資料來源：〈最新報告顯示加州在經濟繼續增長的同時正在減少溫室氣體排放〉（"New report shows California is reducing greenhouse gas emissions as economy continues to grow"），加州空氣資源局（California Air Resources Board）網站上的新聞稿，2017年6月7日。

目前尚沒有太多證據顯示碳定價使商品及服務的生產或對有關產品的投資轉移至其他國家。這與評估環境法規對競爭力的影響的經濟文獻[28]結論一致。其中可能有數個原因，包括根據觀察，碳價格水平普遍不高，現行計劃對承受風險的行業有保障措施（例如免費配給配額）等。此外，就選擇生產基地的投資決策而言，稅率、勞動力供應及基礎設施可能較環境法規更為重要。

儘管競爭力仍為政策制定者在審視對碳定價時的主要考慮因素之一，但這些因素的重要程度不應被過度放大。此競爭風險主要存在於排放密集度高以及與貿易相關的行業，以及很依賴此類行業的地區。有關風險可以並應該透過制定本地專屬政策來保障行業免受不公平國際競爭，同時確保仍具有激勵及支持低碳創新項目的政策。解決競爭力問題的方法包括免費配給排放權及邊界的措施。

目標定得愈高，碳價格水平便可能愈高，這可能會加劇對受影響行業競爭力的衝擊。洲際歐洲期貨交易所（ICE Futures Europe）的 EUA 價格於 2021 年 4 月 22 日達到每公噸二氧化碳當量 46.95 歐元的高位[29]（全球最高碳價格之一），要求實施歐盟碳邊境調節機制（Carbon Border Adjustment Mechanism）的呼聲隨之而來。然而，讓更多國家採納氣候政策並建立碳市場之間的聯繫，會有助於減少各國和地區之間碳價格的差異，減輕競爭力方面的顧慮。市場之間的聯繫愈多，成本便愈趨同。

有關競爭力的顧慮不應妨礙碳的定價，以及有關地區隨着時間提升碳價格或減排目標以符合《巴黎協定》要求的相關水平。碳定價結合補充措施亦可促進一些行業的創新、投資及重大增長。脫碳可帶來龐大的投資機遇，以及提升新行業的發展及現有行業的創新潛力。碳定價亦可產生收入，進一步實現國家目標，並支援可能受到負面影響的人士。

創新和投資，以及穩定而可預測的政策，對於向低碳經濟轉型至關重要。政策的明確性加上政府履行有意義且逐漸收緊政策的堅定承諾，有助於確保公司及地區在全球市場保持競爭力。再者，大型的主流投資者在評估其投資組合時越來越趨向考慮及採用低碳策略[30]。

28 J. E. Aldy（2016年）〈為下一代實施政策行動：氣候變化政策〉（"Mobilizing political action on behalf of future generations: The case of climate change policy"）；E. Beale、D. Beugin、B. Dahlby、D. Drummond、N. Olewiler 與 C. Ragan〈省級碳定價及競爭壓力〉（"Provincial carbon pricing and competitiveness pressures"），載於加拿大的Ecofiscal Commission的網站，2015年11月；M. A. Cohen 與 A. Tubb（2018年）〈環境規例對公司及國家競爭力的影響：有關波特假說的統合分析〉（"The impact of environmental regulation on firm and country competitiveness: A meta-analysis of the Porter hypothesis"），《Journal of the Association of Environmental and Resource Economists》，第5期，317-399頁。
29 資料來源：《EUA期貨》（"EUA Futures"），ICE網站上的網頁，於2021年9月16日閱覽。
30 參閱碳定價領導聯盟（Carbon Pricing Leadership Coalition）《碳定價及競爭力高級委員會報告》（*Report of the High-Level Commission on Carbon Pricing and Competitiveness*），2019年9月23日。

碳融資

一如所有成熟的商品市場，透明度和流動性高的碳市場同樣會吸引金融機構提供融資服務。企業需要投資低碳技術及能源效益。供應鏈需要綠色融資，而公司亦需要管理碳價格風險。穩健的碳市場背後有金融機構及交易所的支持便很重要。舉例而言，大型石油公司若要轉型為低碳能源生產商，將需要大量資金方可成事。碳作為商品很可能會成為該公司價值鏈上的重要一環：上游的須開發減碳項目，中游的須買賣碳信用，下游的則向客戶供應碳中和產品。所以，就如銀行現時會為公司石油業務的上中下游所有部分提供資金一樣，銀行亦會為其碳及潔淨能源業務提供資金。

銀行和其他供應鏈融資方應為項目開發商提供貸款便利（作其資本支出和營運資金），以產生碳信用額的權利為抵押，前提是成功驗證和核實碳信用。流動性高的交易所碳信用現貨和期貨合約市場將為項目融資提供良好的基礎，因為它們將提供清晰的定價並促進風險轉移，提高這些項目的整體融資能力，可以根據承購協議的預期現金流提供融資。這是彌合當前投資需求與預期未來現金流量之間差距的重要方式。在發展出一個流動性高的期貨市場之前，項目開發商將不得不依賴財務狀況良好的買家提供的實物承購協議，金融中介機構將就此準備向其提供貸款。承購方可能包括石油公司、大型企業（科技公司、消費品、航空公司、航運等）或政府。

展望將來，碳融資將促進金融創新的兩大主流：(1) 將與科學契合的碳密集型經濟活動向低碳替代品轉型相關的金融資產脫碳；(2) 可持續金融體系的設計和運作 —— 在有關系統下，經濟增長和緩解氣候緊急狀況而必要作出的社會經濟轉變相協調，亦讓天然資源的生產與耗用有平衡的週期。

儘管現行國際碳定價機制距離實現全球一體化甚遠，但碳定價仍是達到氣候目標的必要政策槓桿。碳融資未來的角色最終將取決於如何在碳風險的直接定價中加入氣候緩和目標的考量（而令碳價大幅提升）。若再加上成交合約的進一步標準化，以及越來越多流動性高的場內買賣合約，令市場參與者有更大的確定性，融資方面的發展當可再進一步。

碳市場發展的推動因素、挑戰及前景

自願性碳交易市場的下一步 —— 場內參考合約

自願性碳交易市場的成功取決於為選定的參考合約建立一個高度健全並具有充足流動性的市場。要成功發展碳交易市場，須建立可信度及透明度。這些問題也一直困擾着自願性碳交易市場及清潔發展機制。因此，確保市場對所買賣的參考合約有信心就至關重要。為了實現高度誠信的自願市場合約，向買家和更廣泛的生態系統保證真正的減排，我們需要制定一套「核心碳原則」（Core Carbon Principles，簡稱 CCPs），根據這些原則可以評估碳信用及其背後的標準和方法。這些將規定相抵銷的碳量所必須遵守的質量標準門檻。

每個抵銷項目在某程度上都有不同的特質，例如除碳／避碳、地理、收成期[31] 或項目類型，而每名買方對於這些特質都有不同的偏好。有些買方專門尋找並購買與其地理或供應鏈有關的碳信用，或對特定的可持續發展目標（Sustainable Development Goal，簡稱 SDG）[32] 有影響或協同利益的碳信用。將每一名買方與相應的供應商配對是一個非常費時、低效率的過程。因此，無論現貨或期貨，均沒有任何包括可靠的每日參考價格及「流動性高」的參考合約，這使價格風險管理幾近無法進行，也阻礙供應商融資的增長。為集中流動性並且發揮出其優勢，市場就需要有可於交易所場內交易的碳參考合約。

邁向參考合約的第一步是引入基於優質項目的實物現貨市場參考合約。該現貨市場參考合約可以將來自多個供應商、滿足這些標準的抵銷信用捆綁到一份合約中。買方會收到「碳核心合約」下所交易的任何合格碳抵銷，交收時將會獲得相關抵銷的證明書。

市場若發展出基於 CCP 的場內現貨核心碳合約，並將其上市交易，以及將實物抵銷證明書存入買方的註冊賬戶，這將有助於建立透明的每日市價。交易所亦可開發參考合約，將核心碳合約與另外單獨定價的附加屬性結合起來。要做到這點，主要的買方須積極參與有關參考合約的交易，以鼓勵流動性的建立。在開出這些參考合約後，繼續進行場外交易的各方可以以核心碳合約的價格作為談判的起點，然後再為附加屬性談判定價。

其他幾個擁有非標準化產品的市場，例如玉米、石油和其他商品，過去均已成功實施參考合約來管理這種「基差」風險。北歐電力市場將「北歐系統」價格作為核心合約，將屬性（交付地點）作為核心合約的附加項進行交易。許多其他商品市場根據類似的原則運作，儘管標的物實際涉及的物質極其複雜，但仍在不影響完整性和質量的情況下，成功地實現合約的標準化及規模化。

除現貨及期貨的參考合約外，若買方想要更加度身訂造的方案並願意為此支付價格，他們可以購買具有特定附加屬性的項目，例如除碳與減碳抵銷之間的差別，將其編入附加的參考合約。這些附加屬性會作為核心碳合約的「基差」或差異進行定價及交易。那樣，他們會獲得合格納入核心碳合約的碳信用，同時也獲得其想要的附加屬性特質。

在交付時，買方將獲得與該特定附加屬性相關的基礎抵銷證書。至關重要的是，這些不同附加參考合約的數量應保持在最低限度。目標是將儘可能多的流動性集中在儘可能少的

31　收成期即減碳項目成功減排的年份。

32　參閱〈17個目標〉（"The 17 Goals"），聯合國網站上的網頁。

合約中。因此，各附加的參考合約應代表最普遍的買方偏好。最後由賣方決定究竟哪個項目符合這些標準，因此項目類型不會是完全定制的。要做到完全定制這一點，買家需要回到場外市場，但他們會有在 CCP 下的參考價格和附加屬性的價格，幫助他們協商合適的價格。

因此，在交易所參考合約開發完成後，場外市場將繼續存在，但將會與交易所市場緊密相連。在談判場外合約時，雙方可將具有流動性的核心碳合約的價格作為起點，只談判附加屬性的定價，無論屬性有多複雜，例如作抵銷的類型、位置、年份、對 SDG 的影響和其他協同利益等之間的獨特組合。

標準化的需要：碳交易所及相關基礎設施

要使市場發揮作用，需要具備一組核心基礎設施組件。這些組件必須以一種有彈性、靈活且能夠處理大規模交易量的方式協同工作。為實現這一目標，市場參與者必須構建所需的組件，同時遵守一套交易和基礎設施原則。

雖然歷史上自願性碳交易市場往往是場外交易，但交易所帶來了擴大市場規模所需的必要標準化、透明度和保障措施。在交易所上市合約意味着可利用現有的金融市場基礎設施來匯集流動性，這可以獲得受監管的交易環境帶來的額外好處，例如對交易活動的市場監督、強制性反洗黑錢或對市場參與者進行「了解客戶」的檢查等。交易市場有眾多益處：在交易所交易的參考合約可以將供應商的產品和買家的偏好捆綁在一起，從而顯著提高買家和供應商的匹配效率；買家受益於簡化的買家行程和更高的價格透明度；供應商受益於價格風險管理，融資渠道的改善，投資者基礎的擴大，以及明確的價格信號來幫助他們作出正確的投資決策；市場受益於通過縮小買賣價差進行更有效的交易；通過大規模自願性碳交易市場提供資金的氣候行動將會增加，整個地球亦會因此受益。

為支持期貨市場並提供交易對手違約保護，我們需要清算所。成熟而及時的數據提供對於所有環境和資本市場都是必不可少的。數據供應商應提供透明的參考數據和市場數據，但是由於註冊系統的應用程式介面（Application Programming Interface，簡稱 API）的訪問受限和場外市場不透明，這在今天並不容易獲得。數據供應商還應收集並提供歷史項目和開發商的績效以及風險數據，以促進結構性融資和場外市場合約的制定；亦需要為買家和供應商提供跨註冊機構的新的報告和分析服務，在這方面，元註冊系統可收集和構建所有可公開訪問的參考數據，用來支持實施新的報告和分析服務。一個關鍵的推動因素是所有註冊系統都通過開放的 API 提供參考數據。此外，交易所和清算所應提供匯總的市場數據。

連結不同系統的好處

現在市場聯動是一項熱門議題，相關討論不少，但進展緩慢。ETS 能讓國與國之間的系統得以連結，有利推動國際氣候行動。ETS 政策可讓不同系統透過對排放配額的相互認可而連結起來。連結可減低整體合規成本、提升市場流動性、促進市場穩定並減低泄漏風險。以現有歐盟 ETS 與中國新興市場為基礎，聯動使整個市場大概可由約 2 兆噸二氧化碳當量增加至 5 兆噸二氧化碳當量，為所涵蓋的各個行業尋求減低成本提供更大的空間。

碳市場會隨着時間不斷擴大，使用或考慮碳交易市場的司法權區之間的協調合作對於保護環境和最大限度地提高成本效益將變得越來越重要。市場機制和聯動的碳交易市場可吸引投資，以最低成本實現減排。《巴黎協定》第 6 條關於履行國家自主貢獻目標承諾[33] 的條文，旨在建立一個國際碳交易市場，可以幫助各國在碳定價方面進行合作，以實現其減排承諾並隨着時間增強其雄心。

與各國政府試圖孤立地實現其目標相比，碳交易市場的聯動和信用機制的實施能夠實現更大的淨減排量。市場准入可以使各國以更低的成本達到超越其國家自主貢獻目標承諾。《巴黎協定》第 6 條中對可國際轉讓的減排成果的規定將有助於推動更深入的減排，相比其他做法更快。因此，一個有效的國際碳市場聯盟可以比簡單地將單一個體的貢獻加總獲得更大的成就。

這種聯盟的最初重點可能是制定共同的、可信的標準或指引，通過透明度高的監測、報告和驗證，以及市場監督的規定和環境保護的標準，以確保國際交易的碳排放單位的可靠完整性。假以時日，這些標準和指引可以為發展出一個各司法權區都可以自願連結的共同市場奠定基礎。國際排放交易標準以《巴黎協定》要求的排放核算和報告準則為基礎，並加以補充，聯盟推動發展這些標準，將與 UNFCCC 進程完全兼容。

碳交易市場聯盟可以通過支持各國碳交易市場的趨同來促進深度減排。隨着聯盟的成熟，成員可以在透明度、治理和環境保護方面建立協調或互認的標準，創建一套共享的市場基礎設施來支持排放單位的相互認可，在機構能力建設方面分享經驗和合作，共同努力提升這些市場促進國內和跨境低碳技術投資的能力。在歐洲可以找到一個新興的聯繫例子，歐盟和瑞士於 2017 年簽署了一項協議將各自的 ETS 聯繫起來，該協議於 2020 年 1 月 1 日生效。歐盟也一直在探索與中國和韓國等其他市場聯繫的方法[34]。

---

33 為實現《巴黎協定》的目標，186個國家(全球90%以上排放量的來源)提交了減碳目標(稱為「國家自主貢獻」)。有關目標概述了各國於2025年或2030年控制排放的承諾 。《巴黎協定》第6條允許各國利用國際碳市場減少排放 。難以按其國家自主貢獻達到減排目標或追求成本較低的減排方案的國家， 可向其他減排量已超出其承諾(例如透過轉型至可再生能源)的國家購買減排權。

34 參閱〈國際碳市場〉("International carbon market")，歐盟網站上的網頁。

由於更多的參與和合作為提升減排效率打開了新的渠道,國際層面可以看到更大的宏圖和行動。假以時日,這些互相連結的碳市場可催化國際碳價格的誕生。《巴黎協定》為不同司法權區之間的合作提供了框架,但各國還須主動實施國內碳定價政策,並與其他國家建立連結。在其國家自主貢獻目標承諾中表示有意加入國際市場機制的 90 個國家之中,許多國家可能認為加入現有碳交易市場或採用現有市場的類似政策架構在技術上更容易,且更具成本效益。

國際排放權交易與中國

許多國家正在制定或加強自己的 ETS,其中碳交易所是主要的交易場所。例如,韓國在過去六年中一直成功運行其 ETS。為了與首爾的淨零排放目標保持一致,韓國現在正計劃擴大其 ETS 規模,以實現其 2050 年的承諾和雄心勃勃的中期目標。日本首相菅義偉已指示他自己的部委制定碳定價建議書。印尼和越南有望分別在 2022 年和 2024 年引入 ETS,而據了解,泰國和菲律賓正在制定類似的系統。新加坡已經開始徵收碳稅,現正計劃建立以新加坡為中心的地區自願性碳市場樞紐。

據世界銀行集團稱[35],已經實施或計劃實施的碳定價舉措已有 64 項,覆蓋全球 46 個國家司法權區,主要是通過總量管制與交易系統。這些舉措正在不斷快速發展,而中國亦已宣佈實施自己的國家 ETS,這將是世界上最大的國家 ETS,會將總計 12 兆噸的二氧化碳排放當量歸入某種形式的碳定價系統下,佔 2020 年世界溫室氣體排放總量的 22.3%[36]。

中國生態環境部於 2021 年 1 月 5 日召開媒體發佈會,確認中國國家 ETS 首個合規週期已於 2021 年 1 月 1 日有效落地。這一週期首先只涵蓋內地火力發電廠,業內 2,225 家公司最遲須於 2021 年 12 月 31 日符合政府設定的減碳規定[37]。它將根據工廠的發電量分配配額,並為每種燃料和技術制定排放基準。中國的 ETS 將按時擴展到其他七個領域:航空、有色金屬、鋼鐵、建築材料、化工、石化和造紙。最終,中國國家 ETS 的收益將來自於營運低於基線的公司的剩餘配額(例如「清潔」煤炭公用事業公司)或能夠發出中國核證減排量(China Certified Emissions Reduction,簡稱 CCER)的公司,例如可再生能源營運商。後者還可能推動對可再生能源項目的需求,這可能帶來再生能源設備的需求增長,從而使上游企業受益。在煤炭營運商中,建議的基準可能會推動不對稱風險敞口,其中一些營運商可能從 ETS 中受益,這觀點是基於所建議的閾值和當前行業排放密集度的情況。目前所

35　資料來源:世界銀行集團(2020年)《2020年碳定價的狀態及趨勢》(*State and Trends of Carbon Pricing 2020*)。華盛頓哥倫比亞特區:世界銀行。

36　資料來源:〈碳定價儀錶板〉("Carbon Pricing Dashboard"),世界銀行網站上的網頁,於2021年5月5日閱覽。

37　資料來源:〈中國堅決追求減少碳排放〉("Xinhua Commentary: China's resolute pursuit of reducing carbon emissions"),載於《新華社》,2021年2月24日。

建議的傳統煤單位的碳排放配額基線為每千瓦時 0.877-0.979 千克 [38]，取決於其裝機容量，這可能會影響次要燃煤電廠，因為它們的熱效率較低，排放密集度較高。

為了支持中國的脫碳目標，ETS 應隨着時間逐漸轉向採用絕對值總量限額，這也將事情變得更簡單。市場很難理解碳排放密集度目標的含義，即使排放量總體上仍在增長，例如有 5% 的增長但僅有 4% 的排放量增幅應該意味着對配額的需求下降。鑒於中國打算在 2030 年達到排放峰值，那麼 ETS 越早轉向採用絕對值總量限額就越好。

中國展望 —— 裨益與挑戰

ETS 的興起，加上中國計劃未來 40 年大幅減少溫室氣體排放，整體經濟將見大幅改革和變動，市場綠色融資需求當會上升，涉及金額百億元計，意味着銀行及其他金融機構可能會從中受惠。碳排放要達到淨零，將需要透過金融體系調動社會資本，這會為綠色融資帶來大量機遇。然而，業界在探索信用擔保業務時，必須學會考慮到越來越高的氣候轉變風險。資產若投資於依賴傳統及過時技術的公司或項目，或會面臨「擱淺」甚或失去價值的風險。

中國的金融機構需要掌握有關氣候風險及碳金融帶來的機遇的知識，而這需要有專業的內部人才庫和更大的能力以獲取外部數據。中國過往傾向依賴行政措施去預防及控制污染情況，現在將要更多依靠市場及金融機制，而這對政策制定者、金融及市場監管機構以至市場參與者而言，都可能是重大的挑戰。

向零碳經濟轉型被視為新一輪綠色工業革命。碳金融不僅有望開創綠色可持續金融的新分支，而且還將以低碳的方式重塑整個金融體系的資產和投融資活動。

減少碳排放的一個重要基礎是披露一致的、高質量的氣候信息來衡量現有的排放量。最大的挑戰之一是銀行所接觸的企業對環境信息的披露不完整，大部分數據是定性的，而不是定量的。

中國人民銀行最近開展一項環境信息披露試點計劃，當中涉及粵港澳大灣區的 13 家銀行 [39]。按中國人民銀行發出的指引，每家試點銀行均須就環境信息披露制定工作計劃，並於每年 6 月前提交年度報告。由 2022 年 3 月起，試點銀行將須提交前一年度的環境信息披露報告。

---

38 資料來源：《2019-2020年全國碳排放權交易配額總量設定與分配實施方案（發電行業）》，中華人民共和國生態環境部發佈，2020年12月30日。

39 資料來源：《中英氣候及環境資料披露試點計劃 —— 2019年進展報告》（*UK-China Climate and Environmental Information Disclosure Pilot — 2019 Progress Report*），載於聯合國支持的責任投資原則組織（Principles for Responsible Investment，簡稱PRI）的網站，2020年5月20日。

從金融市場的角度來看，一個有效的總量管制與交易系統在很大程度上依賴於有能力的金融監管機構，包括內地的中國證券監督管理委員會和香港的證券及期貨事務監察委員會。

鼓勵競爭、充滿活力和支持創業的環境有助於新產品上市及創新，從而改善價格發現、使實體經濟中的各方可以對沖風險。廣東及湖北兩省的大規模現貨碳交易至今已逾 7 年，但尚未形成規範、透明、有效的遠期碳價格曲線。

綜觀中國現時的能源市場，各企業正面臨兩項歷史「轉型」：一是計劃向市場化機制轉型，如中國的天然氣和電力市場；二是傳統能源向低碳新能源轉型。打造創新衍生品市場，服務中國能源成功轉型，在國際能源市場上獲得定價權，這些都將在國內外產生重大影響。

中國的期貨交易所大可學習北美的能源期貨交易所（例如 ICE 及芝加哥商品交易所（Chicago Mercantile Exchange，簡稱 CME））的成功經驗，透過場外交易及中央結算協助中國未來發展天然氣、電力、碳排放、綠色證書及其他衍生產品市場，促進中國的兩項能源「轉型」。

各交易所可合作共同制訂標準合約及相關上市安排以管理價格風險，並為經濟實體提供高效的服務，讓這些交易場所的管理更專業和標準化。此外，就服務產品創新而言，國際市場上上市的產品繁多。成功上市的產品可於中國直接上市，實現全球各交易所之間的互聯，同時亦可實現國際服務本地化，提升公司的參與度。

除提供傳統交易及結算服務外，交易所亦可提供以市場為本的服務，例如數據、交易技術、交收服務、運輸及託管服務，以及有關使用企業衍生產品的諮詢服務等。舉例來說，ICE 的主營業務已經從收取交易費的傳統期貨交易，轉向基於大數據和交易所技術支持互聯互通的商業模式，後者的創新收入現在已經超過了交易徵費。

「滬港通」、「深港通」、「滬倫通」、「債券通」等加速了中國資本市場的國際化進程，積累了寶貴的實踐經驗和歷史交易數據。在香港、歐洲和北美的期貨交易所可以與主流的金融和能源機構合作，推出新的期貨合約，將中國的能源價格嵌入亞洲和國際能源定價鏈。傳統交易所服務實體經濟的局限性已經顯現。建設有國際競爭力的碳和 ESG 衍生產品交易所，需做到監管者和交易所的分離、交易所領域的自由市場競爭、穩健的資訊科技基礎設施、全球專業人才的儲備、全面規劃，以及兼顧市場運作秩序與創新環境的監管規則。

總結

我們需要一個全球碳市場，以便對碳實行單一定價，從而向世界各地的公司發出減少排放的正確信號。設立具國際標準的強制合規市場是限制及減少排放的最佳方法。最理想的模式是為了於 2050 年趨於淨零排放而設定全球總量管制,再在各國之間公平分攤。然而,在沒有全球合作的情況下,或許會出現一系列國家或地區性的交易所市場,這些市場之間可能會有某些連結。如果各國允許公司使用碳信用來履行合規義務從而造成國際套利,那自願性碳交易市場可以在這裏發揮作用。預計企業將致力於可靠的淨零排放途徑,首先減少碳排放,這可能會在短期內增加成本。一個指導性的原則是企業的直接減排必須是優先事項,適當的碳排放抵銷對加快氣候應對行動會起到重要的補充作用。企業應按優先順序減量、申報、抵銷。這些原則列出了制定可靠過渡計劃的必要性。企業應公開披露其承諾與詳細的過渡計劃,以及按照這些計劃的年度進展,科學地將營運和價值鏈脫碳,以協助根據《巴黎協定》將氣溫上升限制在 1.5°C。

預先協定的明確規則及指引、交易所及標準化合約是碳交易市場成功的關鍵因素。拓展自願性碳交易市場的主要障礙是缺乏標準、質素的定義及面貌(即如何監察質素準則有否達到)、缺少良好的管治以及缺少資金。就碳信用如何在企業淨零聲明中的使用達成一致,也是一個需要解決的關鍵問題。

金融機構將為減少所需的排放量提供資金。像為其他商品市場整體價值鏈提供融資一樣,金融機構也可以相同的方式作為碳交易市場的市場中介。此外,金融機構,尤其是交易所,可以為此市場履行其謹慎責任,就像於其他市場(如零售銀行、商品交易、商品金融)履行的一樣,使市場成為更透明和更安全的場所,讓各組織和個人參與。標準化的現貨和期貨核心碳合約的開發和上市,並有實物證書交割,將可產生透明的每日市場價格。交易所還應制定參考合同,這將有助於提高透明度、增加流動性,並增強對交易對手的保證。

到 2050 年實現淨零排放,全球排放量需要大幅減少,程度須遠遠超出當前的目標水平。如果到本世紀中葉世界還未實現淨零排放,全球氣溫升至 1.5°C 以上的可能性將顯著增加。各國可能會採取不同的途徑,對達到淨零排放目標日期也不一樣,這會取決於公平性和其他因素的考量,但所需減排的規模和緊迫性意味着我們不再尋求優先考慮低成本減排。相反,我們需要儘可能快速及有效地減少所有排放。現在有一場所有國家、部門和企業都需要參與的「歸零競賽」。現在就有需要對目前尚無法規模化和成本不具有競爭力的技術進行投資。碳交易市場可以通過給與企業支持脫碳道路的機會,來支持此類技術的商業化。如果現在沒有為此類創新提供資金,就不可能在時間耗盡之前實現我們的脫碳目標。雖然單靠碳交易市場不能實現所有這些目標,但組織良好的市場可以為每個人創造合適的環境來減少排放,這樣我們就可以繼續享受世界各國(包括當今快速工業化的國家)的經濟發展所帶來的好處。

註:本文原稿是英文,另以中文譯本出版。如本文的中文本的字義或詞義與英文本有所出入,概以英文本為準。

Chapter 19

The role of exchange platforms in growing the investment product ecosystem and driving green and sustainable finance

Chief China Economist's Office
Hong Kong Exchanges and Clearing Limited

Summary

Exchanges can play a unique role as centralised and regulated marketplaces that provide listing, trading, and related services for products that incorporate environmental, social and governance (ESG) factors and connect issuers, investors, and other market participants to support sustainable finance and investment.

More specifically, exchanges can drive green and sustainable finance (GSF) by offering fund-raising and exit channels, supporting product and service innovation, providing a standardised and regulated environment, and promoting enhanced disclosure.

Global initiatives like the Paris Agreement and the United Nations' 2030 Agenda for Sustainable Development are driving demand for GSF. To meet this demand, exchanges worldwide have developed a number of initiatives to accelerate GSF and ESG investment.

Such initiatives include innovations across different asset classes and products such as equities, bonds, exchange traded funds, real estate investment trusts, and derivatives. In addition, exchanges have introduced dedicated service platforms to connect issuers and investors.

While exchanges have made much progress in promoting and facilitating GSF, there are many opportunities to accelerate this. Possible measures include harmonising classification standards for ESG product labelling, providing incentives and a comprehensive policy framework, improving the availability and quality of data, increasing the spectrum and liquidity of ESG products, and driving inter-exchange cooperation.

By taking such steps, we believe that exchange platforms will continue to play a pivotal role in connecting different market participants in the global ecosystem of sustainable finance and investment and driving the development of products and services for the transition to a sustainable global economy.

The role of exchange platforms in supporting green and sustainable finance

Exchange platforms provide companies with access to a deep pool of capital, enable price discovery, spread risk, help wealth creation, and promote transparency and corporate governance standards.

Exchange platforms are also centralised and regulated marketplaces that can provide listing, trading, and related services for environment, social, and governance (ESG) products and connect issuers, investors, and other market participants to support sustainable finance and investment.

In light of the growing need for capital to finance sustainable development, many exchange platforms now offer products and services that support green and sustainable finance (GSF) and offer investments incorporating ESG factors (broadly referred to as ESG investment or sustainable investment) to mobilise capital and promote good governance[1].

Global initiatives like the Paris Agreement and the United Nations' 2030 Agenda for Sustainable Development are driving demand for GSF — and the sums required are substantial.

In 2014, the United Nations Conference on Trade and Development (UNCTAD) estimated that between US$5 trillion to US$7 trillion of annual global investments are needed through 2030 to meet the United Nations Sustainable Development Goals (UNSDGs)[2]. The sums required may become even larger after the COVID-19 outbreak in 2020[3].

GSF grew remarkably between 2018 and 2020 (see Figure 1). New issuance of equities and bonds grew fastest, increasing by 590% and 307%, respectively, in CAGR (compound annual growth rate) terms during the period, according to Refinitiv data.

---

1   See World Federation of Exchanges and United Nations Conference on Trade and Development (UNCTAD), "The role of stock exchanges in fostering economic growth and sustainable development", published on UNCTAD's website, 7 September 2017.

2   See UNCTAD, "World investment report 2014 — Investing in the SDGs: An action plan", published on UNCTAD's website, 24 June 2014.

3   Source: "Mobilising institutional capital for renewable energy", published on the website of International Renewable Energy Agency (IRENA), November 2020.

Figure 1. Global GSF fund flows (2018 – 2020)

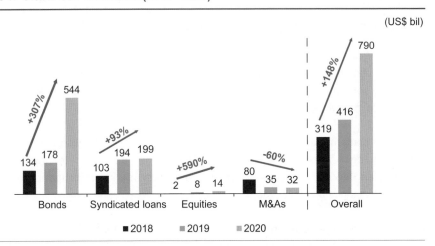

(US$ bil)

Note: The fund flows of GSF are those classified as "sustainable finance" by Refinitiv.

Source: "Refinitiv Sustainable Finance Review — Full Year 2020", published on Refinitiv's website, 2 February 2021.

In 2020, assets under management (AUM) in sustainable investment strategies amounted to US$35.3 trillion — almost double the US$18.3 trillion registered in 2014, and about 36% of total global AUM, according to Global Sustainable Investment Alliance[4] (see Figure 2).

---

4   The sustainable investment assets refer to the AUM adopting ESG factors into investment processes based on the seven approaches defined by Global Sustainable Investment Alliance. See "Global sustainable investment review", 2020 issue, published on Global Sustainable Investment Alliance's website.

**Figure 2. Total AUM of global sustainable investments and other investments
(2014 – 2020)**

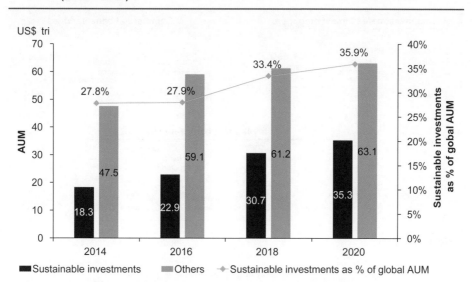

Source: Global total AUM and AUM of sustainable investments (except the data in 2014) are obtained from "Global
sustainable investment review", 2016, 2018 and 2020 issues, published on Global Sustainable Investment
Alliance's website. The data of global total AUM in 2014 is obtained from "Global asset management 2021:
The $100 trillion machine", Boston Consulting Group's website, July 2021.

Figure 3. Illustration of the core support offered by an exchange platform

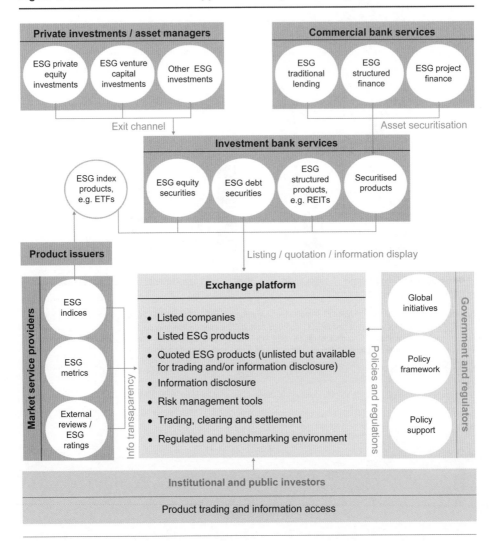

Looking in more detail, as depicted in Figure 3, exchange platforms can support sustainable finance and investment in four specific ways:

(1) Offering fund-raising and exit channels for sustainability-related investments

Private investment vehicles, asset managers, commercial banks and investment banks all play prominent roles in the fund-raising and exiting process.

Commercial bank lending has been a significant source of GSF for the transition to a sustainable economy. Banks can securitise loan assets into asset-backed securities (ABS), which can then be issued and listed through exchange platforms, thus freeing up capital and allowing banks to increase GSF support.

Apart from bank lending, private equity and venture capital may also fund small-scale, sustainability-related projects or start-up companies. Exchange platforms thus serve as both an exit channel for private investments and a continuous funding channel.

(2) Developing ESG investment products to widen funding sources

Investment banks help list various ESG investment products (e.g. equities, debt securities, structured products, ABSs) on exchanges.

Market service providers assess various sources of ESG information, including companies' related disclosures on exchanges, and transform them into metrics, ratings, and scores that help classify and label ESG products.

Index providers also formulate ESG indices on various asset classes to facilitate the development of ESG index products.

Product issuers launch index-related products, including exchange traded funds (ETFs) that cover ESG indices or themes.

The exchange platform will make these products available to institutional and retail investors and establish a secondary market.

In addition, exchange platforms continuously develop and offer related derivative products, such as futures and options, as portfolio management and risk management tools for ESG investments.

(3) Providing a regulated environment of recognised standards

Government and regulators formulate initiatives, policies, and regulations to promote and support the development of sustainable finance and investment.

Compared to off-exchange ESG products, exchange platforms usually provide more clarity on applicable rules, regulations, and classification criteria stipulated in, for example, related guidelines and best practices for listed ESG products.

Exchanges may refine the governance and disclosure framework for GSF and ESG products from time to time according to their engagements with relevant regulators and various service providers on the latest market developments.

Exchanges are often also responsible for monitoring both initial and ongoing compliance with applicable rules and regulations and classification criteria for listed ESG products.

(4) Enhancing ESG information disclosure

Disclosing more detailed information and making ESG products more identifiable can increase investor participation by meeting investors' needs for insights, raising awareness of ESG issues, and reducing information asymmetry between GSF issuers and ESG investors.

Global exchanges' product and service initiatives to promote GSF and ESG investment

Exchange platforms have developed several initiatives to drive GSF and ESG investment.

The United Nations Sustainable Stock Exchanges Initiative (SSEI) and the World Federation of Exchanges (WFE)[5] have recommended that exchange platforms promote green products and services, green financial markets by imposing sustainability standards and labelling, strengthen ESG information disclosure, and grow dialogue about GSF among stakeholders.

Between 2019 and 2020, world exchanges increased the amount and widened the range of green products and services available to investors, according to annual WFE surveys (see Figure 4).

---

5   See "How stock exchanges can grow green finance" and "How derivatives exchanges can promote sustainable development", published on SSEI's website, 16 November 2017 and 5 May 2021 respectively; "WFE sustainability principles" and "The World Federation of Exchanges: Sustainability and commodity derivatives white paper", published on WFE's website, 4 October 2018 and 20 August 2019 respectively.

The most popular green products listed across exchanges at the end of 2020 were equity indices and bonds, with 27 out of 39 surveyed exchanges offering sustainability indices and 30 offering green bonds, according to a 2021 WFE survey.

In terms of geography, exchanges in Europe and the US have developed more green products and services, but exchanges in Asia, particularly in China, are quickly advancing[6].

Many global exchanges have also proactively supported ESG product development with a range of measures, such as enhancing ESG disclosure requirements, building capacity amongst market participants, and connecting issuers and investors via dedicated service platforms, like Hong Kong Exchanges and Clearing Limited (HKEX)'s Sustainable and Green Exchange (STAGE).

Figure 4. Number of exchanges offering ESG products by product type (2019 & 2020)

Product type	2020	2019
Green bonds	30	27
Sustainability indices	27	25
Sustainability/Social bonds	22	17
ESG ETFs	20	13
ESG ranking or rating	9	6
Carbon trading platform	5	6
ESG derivatives	10	6
Sustainability-linked bonds	10	
Others	10	11

**Total number of surveyed exchanges:
36 (2019); 39 (2020)**

■ 2020   ■ 2019

Note: The product categories are more granular in the 2020 survey where social bonds and sustainability bonds are separate categories and sustainability-linked bonds is a new category. Green bonds, social bonds, sustainability bonds and sustainability-linked bonds are classified according to recognised international standards, such as those of the International Capital Market Association.

Source: *The WFE's 6th Annual Sustainability Survey* and *The WFE's 7th Annual Sustainability Survey,* published on WFE's website, 15 July 2020 and 14 July 2021, respectively.

6   See *WFE Sustainability Survey April 2017* and *The WFE's 7th Annual Sustainability Survey*, published on WFE's website, April 2017 and 14 July 2021 respectively; "Sustainable finance: A global overview of ESG regulatory developments", published on Cleary Gottlieb's website, 22 October 2020; "China to see significant growth in responsible and ESG-themed investment", Invesco's website, 22 March 2021; "ESG in Asia: Accelerating momentum", Barings' website, May 2021.

The following sub-sections take a more detailed look into new products and services developed by exchanges across the world to promote GSF and ESG investment.

ESG investment products

ESG product innovation continues growing to meet the different needs of issuers and investors.

Issuers can choose to issue an ESG product on their companies, projects, or underlying assets to generate financing.

Investors can choose ESG products that align with their ESG investment strategies and their preferred risk-return profiles.

We discuss below global exchanges' experience of developing ESG products for equities, bonds, and indices, as well as structured products, like real estate investment trusts (REITs).

Equities

Equities can be classified as "green" if they meet certain ESG criteria. For example, service providers could base their criteria on a company's sector[7], ESG ratings[8], revenue sources, or business activities[9].

Although classification is not part of the initial public offering (IPO) listing process on exchanges, listing rules may require the company to make an ESG disclosure.

While major standard setters for ESG reporting are still in the process of harmonising their standards[10], some exchanges may set out recommended reporting frameworks to facilitate

---

7 See for example "Refinitiv Sustainable Finance Review — Full Year 2020", published on Refinitiv's website, 2 February 2021.
8 See "MSCI ESG ratings", published on the website of MSCI, viewed on 18 Mar 2021.
9 For example, the London Stock Exchange's list of companies/funds with "Green Economy Mark". See "London Stock Exchange launches Green Economy Mark and Sustainable Bond Market", news release published on the LSE's website, 11 October 2019; "Green Economy Mark", published on the website of London Stock Exchange Group, October 2020.
10 See "Global sustainability and integrated reporting organisations launch prototype climate-related financial disclosure standard", published on Climate Disclosure Standards Board's website, 18 December 2020.

the comparison of performance over time, possibly versus a comparable company in the same sector[11].

Such information is useful for investment analysis and may also shed light on management strength and the long-term prospects of the company.

An increasing number of listed companies across the world are required to disclose their ESG information. The number of stock exchanges with mandatory ESG reporting in their listing requirements has increased from two in 2010 to 24 in 2020 (see Figure 5).

These 24 stock exchanges had 16,359 listed companies with a total market capitalisation of US$18.2 trillion as of 17 March 2021. Those listed companies accounted for 30.7% of total listed companies and 20.7% of the market capitalisation in a sample of 105 stock exchanges[12].

In Asia, HKEX was one of the first in the region to require listed companies to make ESG disclosures in 2016, and markets in Mainland China are expected to start mandatory ESG reporting in 2021[13].

---

11 An exchange may accept the ESG reporting of listed companies based on one set or multiple sets of international standards, e.g. Global Reporting Initiative (GRI), Sustainability Accounting Standards Board (SASB), Task Force on Climate-Related Financial Disclosure (TCFD), etc.
12 Calculated based on the data on the number of listed companies and market capitalisation from "Stock exchange database", SSEI's website, viewed on 17 March 2021.
13 See Zembrowski, P., M. Leung and K. Schacht, "ESG disclosures in Asia Pacific: A review of ESG disclosure regimes for listed companies in selected markets", published on the website of CFA Institute, 21 July 2019; "A green wave of ESG is poised to break over China", published on the website of World Economic Forum (WEF), 4 December 2020.

Figure 5. Number of stock exchanges with mandatory ESG reporting as listing requirements (2000 – 2020)

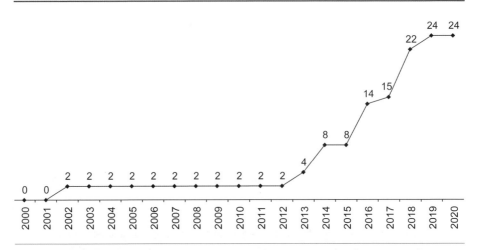

Source: "United Nations SSE initiative: 10 Years of Impact and Progress", published on the website of SSEI (26 September 2019) for the data in 2000-2019; "Stock exchange database", SSEI's website (viewed on 17 March 2021) for the data in 2020.

Bonds

Green, social, and sustainability (GSS) bonds, and more recently transition bonds and sustainability-linked bonds, support specific areas of sustainable development and are classified according to recognised international standards, like those from the International Capital Market Association (ICMA)[14]. These bonds usually follow a similar listing process to other bonds but ESG disclosures are required.

Listing GSS bonds on exchanges is rather popular for issuers. Take green bonds as an example, during the first three quarters of 2020, about 69% of newly issued green bonds were traded on global stock exchanges, while the remaining 31% were traded on over-the-counter (OTC) markets (including the China Interbank Bond Market (CIBM) in Mainland China) (see Figure 6). In this respect, GSS bonds are different from non-GSS bonds, which are usually only traded in OTC markets.

---

14 See *Green Bond Principles, Social Bond Principles, Sustainability Bond Guidelines, Sustainability-Linked Bond Principles and Climate Transition Finance Handbook*, published on ICMA's website, viewed on 18 March 2021.

European exchanges, including the Luxembourg Stock Exchange (LuxSE), Euronext exchanges, German exchanges, and the London Stock Exchange (LSE), issued most of the green bonds in value terms in the first three quarters of 2020. In Asia, HKEX issued the largest amount of green bonds.

Figure 6. Share of green bonds listed on exchanges in terms of year-to-date global issue amount (2018Q4 – 2020Q3)

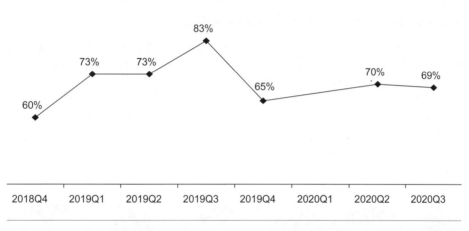

Note: Climate Bonds Initiative (CBI) did not publish the quarterly report for 2020Q1 and data is therefore not available for 2020Q1.

Source: "Green bond market summary", issues from 2018Q4 to 2020Q3, published on the website of CBI.

In Mainland China, exchanges have supported the development of green ABS. The number of ABSs issued and the total amount raised has grown rapidly in recent years, with the majority issued and traded on exchanges[15].

In the US, agency mortgage-backed securities (MBS) have dominated green ABS issuance. For example, Fannie Mae, one of the largest agency MBS issuers, was the world's largest green bond issuer in 2020, with a total of US$13 billion (about 5% of total global green bond issuance)[16]. ABSs in the US are liquid but are mainly traded in the OTC market[17].

---

15 See HKEX research report, "The burgeoning Mainland Green ABS market and the potential support from the Hong Kong market", published on HKEX's website, 3 May 2021.

16 Source: "Green securitisation: Unlocking finance for small-scale low carbon projects", published on CBI's website, March 2018; "Record $269.5bn green issuance for 2020: Late surge sees pandemic year pip 2019 total by $3bn", published on CBI's website, 24 January 2021.

17 Source: "Fixed Income Market Structure: Treasuries vs. Agency MBS", FEDS Notes published on the Federal Reserves' website, 25 August 2020.

In Europe, only eight green and other ESG-related ABSs were issued in 2020, reportedly because of a lack of green collateral and standardisation[18].

Exchanges also support product innovations in the GSS bond market, such as standardised bond repurchase transactions (repo) dedicated for green bonds to provide short-term financing to bondholders. The first standardised repos for individual green bonds, or for a basket of green bonds, were made available on Eurex in 2020[19].

Indices, investment funds and index products

ESG index products such as exchange traded products (ETPs) are becoming more popular as ESG investment tools. From 2018 to 2020, the AUM of ESG ETPs grew much faster than for other ETPs (see Figure 7).

An increasing number of ESG indices have been introduced in recent years. Currently, ESG indices mainly cover equities in the US, Europe, Asia Pacific, China and other emerging markets, and their coverage has expanded to also include GSS bonds in major markets.

18 Source: "ESG-labelled ABS: a (very) brief history of the market", published on *bondvigilantes.com, 3 March 2021*.
19 "Repo goes green", published on Eurex's website, 10 November 2020; "Repo market" and "Repo baskets" webpages on Eurex's website, viewed on 19 March 2021.

Figure 7. Total AUM of ESG ETPs and other ETPs in the global market (2018 – 2020)

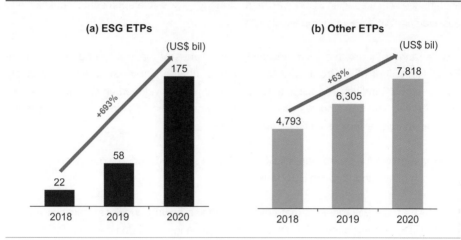

Note: AUM of other ETPs is calculated as the total AUM of all ETPs minus that of ESG ETPs.

Source: Data in 2018 and 2019 for ESG ETPs are from "ETF reports assets invested in ESG (environmental, social, and governance) ETFs and ETPs listed globally reached a new record of 88 billion US dollars at the end of June 2020", *ETFGI.com*, 22 July 2020; data in 2020 for ESG ETPs are from "ESG observatory" webpage on *Trackinsight.com*, viewed on 29 March 2021; aggregate data for all ETPs are from "ETFGI reports assets invested in ETFs and ETPs listed globally reach a new milestone of US$7.99 trillion at the end of December 2020", *ETFGI.com*, 14 January 2021.

To facilitate the development of ESG indices, index providers use their own assessment frameworks to measure an issuers' ESG performance[20]. However, different providers use different methodologies, so assessments between providers may not be fully compatible.

Listed companies' ESG disclosures are one key source of information on which index providers compile ESG scores or ratings. As listed companies' disclosures usually follow the same or similar reporting framework, disclosures are more comparable, and therefore the development of ESG indices is relatively faster for equities than for fixed-income securities.

---

20 See "MSCI ESG ratings methodology: Executive summary", published on MSCI's website, December 2020; "ESG ratings and data model: Integrating ESG into investment", published on FTSE Russell's website, viewed on 29 March 2021; "ESG evaluation", webpage on S&P Global's website, viewed on 29 March 2021.

An ESG index is usually constructed from a broad market index (the parent index) in accordance with a specific ESG investment strategy — possible approaches could include positive/negative screening and weight tilts[21].

A wide range of index providers, including subsidiaries of major exchange groups (e.g. FTSE Russell of LSE Group and Qontigo of Deutsche Börse Group), have actively developed ESG indices. As such, these providers have developed an increasing number of ESG equity and bond indices which have home-market benchmark indices and popular regional and global indices as their parent indices.

As exchange platforms are where ESG ETFs are listed and traded, so they are pivotal in promoting investment through ESG indices.

ESG ETFs track ESG indices that cover companies having business practices aligned with UNSDGs and/or good ESG performance. Exchange platforms can also facilitate the secondary market liquidity of ESG ETFs.

In the US, the share of on-exchange trading of ESG equity and fixed income ETFs in 2020 was lower than the share for all equity ETFs and all fixed-income ETFs (see Figure 8). This indicates that the liquidity of ESG ETFs on exchanges still has room to grow, and may be boosted by incentives and supportive market mechanisms such as market making.

Independent labelling agencies grant labels to ESG funds and exchanges and provide platforms with label recognition and identification of labelled products for investment decisions. For instance, LuxSE recognises the various ESG labels in the European markets for investment funds (including ETFs) listed on its exchange platform and requires on-going disclosure of the accreditation of these labels.

---

21 See "An evolution in ESG indexing", published on BlackRock iShares' website, viewed on 29 March 2021.

Figure 8. Distribution of ETF turnover in the US by trading venue (2020)

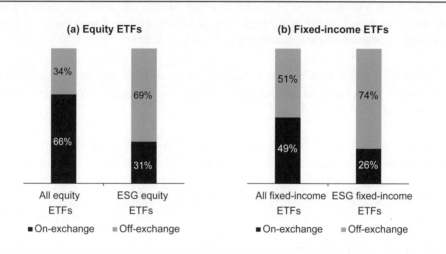

Note: The total turnover includes on-exchange trades and off-exchange creation and redemption activities and block trades.

Source: "ESG ETF liquidity continues to warm alongside demand", published on *ETFDB.com*, 18 March 2021.

REITs

Exchanges can contribute to the classification of green REITs through enhanced transparency. In the US, which was the largest REIT market in 2020[22], the share of the top 100 largest REITs with ESG disclosure increased from 78% of total in 2018 to 98% in 2020[23].

Certain REITs may make disclosures according to the specific standards for real estate industry (e.g. Global ESG Benchmark for Real Assets (GRESB)). This information helps identify green REITs in accordance with their classification criteria, e.g. the certifications of green building in their portfolios.

---

22 The US market accounted for 69% of the global total, compared to 21% for Asia-Pacific markets as of end-2020. (Source: "Global real estate total markets table Q4-2020", published on European Public Real Estate Association's website, January 2021.)

23 Source: "REIT industry ESG report", 2020 and 2021 issues, published on Nareit's website.

However, similar to equities, there are no universal standards for classification and no specific rules and regulations yet for listing green REITs. REITs can be classified into green REITs in accordance with certain "green" criteria such as how portfolio buildings measure against industry standards for sustainable real estate.

A green REIT must be a REIT with holdings in green buildings but the certification schemes of green buildings vary across the world[24] and the proportion of certified green buildings held vary across REITs.

In Europe, ESG fund labels have different thresholds on the share of green buildings for the classification of green REITs (e.g. 75% of AUM for LuxFLAG in Luxembourg and 90% of AUM for Greenfin fund label in France)[25]. Certain fund labels are recognised by exchanges for classification as ESG ETFs/funds (see above).

In addition, a number of green REIT indices are constructed from their respective parent REIT indices to track the performance of green REITs in global, regional and local markets like the US and Japan[26]. The availability of green REIT indices can facilitate the development of related index products. The first ETF covering green REITs was issued in the US in April 2021[27]. The first ESG REIT index futures on Nikkei ESG-REIT Index futures started trading on the Singapore Exchange (SGX) in June 2021[28].

---

24 These include Leadership in Energy and Environmental Design (LEED) and Energy Star in the US, Building Research Establishment Environmental Assessment Method (BREEAM) in the UK, Haute qualité environnementale (HQE) in France, Green Star in Australia and New Zealand. See "Green building rating systems", published on International Facility Management Association's website, viewed on 19 July 2021.

25 See "Eligibility criteria", webpage on LuxFLAG's website, viewed on 19 July 2021 and "Greenfin label: Criteria guidelines", published on the website of French Ministry for Ecology and Inclusive Transition, April 2019.

26 See "MSCI Global Green Building Index factsheet", published on MSCI's website, viewed on 19 July 2021; "Dow Jones select green real estate securities indices methodology", published on S&P Dow Jones Indices' website, April 2021; "FTSE EPRA Nareit green index series", published on FTSE Russell, April 2021; "Nikkei ESG-REIT Index monthly factsheet", published on Nikkei Indexes' website, 30 June 2021; "Index guideline: Solactive CarbonCare Asia Pacific green REIT Index PR", published on Solactive's website, viewed on 19 July 2021.

27 See "Invesco launches first 'green building' ETF", *Financial Times*, 22 April 2021.

28 See "SGX launches the world's first ESG REIT derivatives", press release on SGX's website, 14 June 2021.

ESG derivative products

ESG derivatives are useful to facilitate ESG investment and manage associated risks.

The wide spectrum of ESG derivatives includes ESG index derivatives, carbon emissions derivatives, sustainability-linked derivatives, renewable energy and renewable fuels derivatives and catastrophe and weather derivatives (see Table 1), according to a study[29] conducted by the International Swaps and Derivatives Association (ISDA) in 2021 (referred to as the "2021 ISDA Study") and another study[30] conducted by the Futures Industry Association (FIA) in 2020 (referred to as the "2020 FIA Study").   Exchanges offer the trading platform for many of these products.

Table 1. Illustrative product suite of ESG-related derivatives in the global market

Trading venue	On-exchange	Off-exchange
ESG index derivatives	• ESG equity index futures and options	• ESG-related credit default swap (CDS) indices

Carbon emissions trading and derivatives	• Emissions caps and allowances
	  - Spot bilateral transactions
	• Futures and options
		• Emissions caps and allowances
		  - Spot bilateral transactions
		  - Forwards

Sustainability-linked derivatives	Not identified	• Interest rate derivatives • Foreign exchange derivatives (with an ESG pricing component)
Others	• Commodity futures and options (product design and encompassing sustainability factors in physical delivery) • Renewable energy and renewable fuels derivatives - Futures and options on credits of renewable energy and fuels and wind index • Weather derivatives • Temperature-based index futures and options	• Catastrophe and weather derivatives • Catastrophe swap

Source: Compiled from the 2020 FIA Study and the 2021 ISDA Study.

---

29 "Overview of ESG-related derivatives products and transactions", published on ISDA's website, January 2021.
30 "How derivatives markets are helping the world fight climate change", published on FIA's website, September 2020.

Exchanges possess a number of advantages over the OTC market to support the development of ESG derivatives[31].

For ESG derivatives, global exchanges' initiatives include widening the product spectrum to meet risk management needs, introducing market-making incentives to support secondary liquidity, and applying sustainability elements to pricing and physical delivery.

ESG index derivatives

Global exchanges offer a range of ESG index derivatives to meet the growing demand for ESG investment and risk management, and particularly for equity index futures[32].

According to the 2020 FIA Study, as of September 2020, there were 18 futures and options products on major local, regional and global ESG equity indices traded on CME, Eurex, Euronext, Intercontinental Exchange (ICE) US, NASDAQ and Taiwan Futures Exchange.

Apart from trading, exchanges can also offer central clearing services for transactions in ESG index derivatives through their associated clearing houses.

Investor demand and exchanges' market-making incentives have increased the liquidity of ESG index derivatives traded on exchanges. After the first ESG equity index futures product was launched in October 2018[33], the trading volume of major ESG equity index futures has grown steadily to reach a record high in March 2021, with European exchanges seeing the highest amount of trading volume (see Figure 9).

31 See Nystedt, J. (2004) "Derivative market competition: OTC markets versus organised derivative exchanges", *International Monetary Fund Working Paper*, WP/04/61.

32 See HKEX research paper, "ESG equity index futures: Meeting the increasing needs for ESG investment", published on HKEX's website, 12 April 2021.

33 The world's first ESG futures was NASDAQ's futures on OMX Stockholm 30 ESG Responsible Index launched in October 2018. See "The world's first ESG future — The result of a successful collaboration", published on NASDAQ's website, 7 June 2021.

**Figure 9. Monthly trading volume of futures on major ESG equity indices
(Oct 2018 – Mar 2021)**

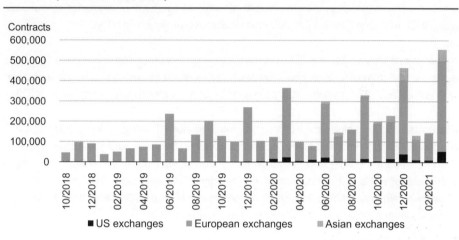

Note: US exchanges comprise CME and ICE US; European exchanges comprise Eurex, Euronext and NASDAQ
Stockholm; Asian exchanges comprise Singapore Exchange and Taiwan Futures Exchange. The list of
ESG equity index futures follows that in the HKEX research paper, "ESG equity index futures: Meeting the
increasing needs for ESG investment", published on HKEX's website, 12 April 2021, and is not exhaustive.

Source: Calculated based on daily trading volume of individual index futures from Bloomberg.

However, the number of ESG index derivatives traded off-exchange was still limited,
according to the 2021 ISDA Study. One example are derivatives on the first ESG-related
CDS index — iTraxx MSCI ESG Screened Europe Index — launched by IHS Markit in
May 2020[34].

Nevertheless, the liquidity of ESG equity index futures is still relatively low compared to the
futures of their parent index[35]. To support the liquidity of ESG index futures, exchanges
may need to offer incentives to help grow market making activities[36].

---

34 See "iTraxx MSCI ESG Screened Europe Index: Provisional methodology", published on IHS Markit's website, viewed
on 14 April 2021; "Markit Credit Indices — The market standard for credit derivatives", published on IHS Markit's
website, viewed on 14 April 2021.

35 See example of Stoxx Europe 600 ESG-X Index futures on Eurex ("ESG Futures — How is the industry tracking in the
ESG transition?", published on Qontigo's website, 9 December 2020).

36 See, for example, Eurex's initiative — "Product specific supplement for futures on STOXX® and DAX® ESG indices",
issued by Eurex, 22 March 2021.

Carbon emissions trading and derivatives

Under the Paris Agreement, countries can set their own reduction targets for greenhouse gas (GHG) emissions, which can be achieved through emissions trading.

An emissions trading system (ETS) covers a defined scope of companies and facilitates the creation and trading of carbon allowances between those who pollute more and those who pollute less. The trading unit is usually one tonne of carbon dioxide equivalent (CO2e).

Examples of ETSs include the European Union Emissions Trading Scheme (EU ETS), the national ETSs in Korea and New Zealand, regional ETSs in US and Canada — Western Climate Initiative (WCI) and Regional Greenhouse Gas Initiative (RGGI), and eight Chinese pilot ETSs in Beijing, Shanghai, Chongqing, Hubei, Fujian, Tianjin, Guangzhou, Shenzhen. Notably, China has recently launched its national ETS in July 2021, initially run by the Shanghai Environment and Energy Exchange (SEEE).

In terms of trading volumes and values, the EU ETS dominated the global market from 2017 to 2020, followed by regional markets in North America and Asia Pacific[37].

In terms of the scale of emissions covered, China's national ETS covers the largest amount of emissions — exceeding 4 billion tonnes of CO2e, about 40% of total emissions in the Mainland (similar to the level in the EU)[38]. On its commencement day of 16 July 2021, more than 4 million tonnes of CO2e were traded.

Exchanges can also provide platforms for auctions of newly created carbon allowances and secondary trading of carbon allowances.

---

37 Source: "Carbon market year in review: Record high value of carbon markets in 2019" and "Carbon market year in review 2020: Blooming carbon markets on raised climate ambition", published on Refinitiv's website, 22 January 2020 and 26 January 2021 respectively.

38 Source: "Xinhua Headlines: World's largest carbon trading market opens in Shanghai", *Xinhua*, 17 July 2021; "China National ETS", published on International Carbon Action Partnership's website, 9 August 2021; "EU Emissions Trading System (EU ETS)", webpage on European Commission's website, viewed on 16 September 2021.

Take EU Allowances (EUAs) of EU ETS as an example:

- The number of EUAs are created by governments of nations in Europe in accordance with EU regulations[39].

- There is a central registry (the Union Registry) of EUAs to guarantee accurate accounting for all allowances issued under the EU ETS. Some EUAs are allocated to companies free of charge, while others are allocated through auctions conducted on designated exchange platforms.

- European Energy Exchange (EEX) is the EUA auction platform for all participating countries of EU-ETS[40], and Deutsche Börse (DB) owns a majority interest in the platform.

- Secondary trading of EUAs is conducted either through bilateral spot trading transactions on the OTC market, or spot futures contracts on exchanges. Futures and options of EUAs with longer tenors are traded on exchanges.

- The majority of secondary trading of EUAs is conducted via exchanges, including ICE Futures Europe, EEX, CME, and NASDAQ OMX.

- Trading of futures and options on EUAs on exchanges reached EUR 181.6 billion and accounted for about 90% of total trading value in 2020 (see Figure 10).

- The European Commission has reported that most secondary transactions of EUAs, including both on-exchange and off-exchange transactions, were centrally cleared through exchanges' associated clearing houses[41].

---

39 See the details of creation, allocation, trading and clearing of EUAs at "Emissions Trading System", webpage on European Commission's website, and "Interplay between EU ETS registry and post trade infrastructure", published on European Commission's website, January 2015.

40 Source: "Auctioning of allowances" webpage on EU's website and "EU ETS auctions" webpage on EEX's website. ICE offers auctions of EUAs in the UK before Brexit (see "Emissions auctions", webpage on ICE Europe's website, viewed on 15 September 2021).

41 See "Interplay between EU ETS registry and post trade infrastructure", published on European Commission's website, January 2015.

Figure 10. Trading value of EUAs by venue (2017 – 2020)

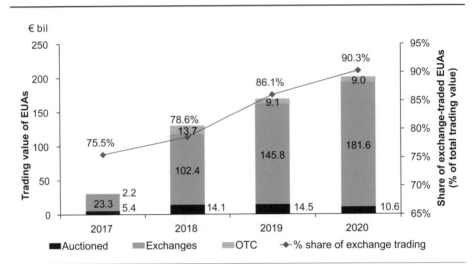

Source: "Carbon market year in review: Record high value of carbon markets in 2019" and "Carbon market year in review 2020: Blooming carbon markets on raised climate ambition", published on Refinitiv's website, 22 January 2020 and 26 January 2021 respectively.

Exchange platforms have facilitated the development of the carbon market in the EU and other major economies[42].

In Europe, the UK is in the process of setting up its UK ETS after Brexit and the first auction was held through ICE Europe on 19 May 2021.

In Mainland China, it was reported that the national ETS will pave the way for launching the first carbon emissions futures product on the Guangzhou Futures Exchange.

In North America, futures and options on regional carbon credits have been actively traded on ICE US and Nodal Exchange. However, in the US, there has been no consensus to set up a national ETS yet, but it was reported that major financial trade groups have called for carbon pricing.

---

42 See "Expanding carbon markets show big potential in 2021", published on the website of FIA, 12 March 2021; "Top finance trade groups join calls for U.S. carbon pricing", published on *Reuters.com*, 18 February 2021; "Participating in the UK ETS" webpage on the UK Government's website; "China to launch national carbon emissions trading scheme on Feb 1", published on S&P Global's website, 6 January 2021.

Sustainability-linked derivatives

Sustainability-linked derivatives are conventional derivatives (e.g. interest rate swaps, cross-currency swaps or forwards) with the addition of an ESG pricing component. These derivatives are highly customised for specific issuers and use various key performance indicators (KPIs)[43] to determine the sustainability goals to be achieved by their issuers.

As the contract terms of sustainability-linked derivatives is difficult to standardise, exchanges only support the listing of certain types of these derivatives. The transactions of these derivatives may be conducted in the OTC market and there is no secondary market and central clearing for these transactions yet. For example, a number of sustainability-linked derivatives are listed in the form of "certificates with sustainability focus" on Börse Frankfurt (FWB) and the trading of which are redirected and conducted through banks and brokers[44].

Commodity derivatives

Commodity futures traded on exchanges are a crucial element in global supply chains[45] in the real economy. Therefore, exchanges can support a sustainable economy by imposing sustainability factors on the trading of their commodity products.

Major commodity exchanges recently began incorporating sustainability standards on the sourcing of commodities for physical delivery:

- In 2015, crude palm oil futures on Bursa Malaysia, one of the world's most active palm oil futures markets, began to require that sellers fill out a document with information on the mill used to produce the oil. This requirement gives buyers more information on whether the oil was produced responsibly and supplements the national certification scheme for the Malaysian Sustainable Palm Oil (MSPO) standards[46].

- In 2015, COMEX of CME Group required that gold producers for its gold futures comply with the London Bullion Market Association (LBMA) Responsible Gold Guidance for the physical delivery of gold[47].

---

43 See "Sustainability-linked derivatives: KPI guidelines", published on ISDA's website, September 2021.
44 See "Certificates with sustainability focus", webpage on Börse Frankfurt's website.
45 See HKEX research paper, "Global experience of commodity futures serving the real economy", published on HKEX's website, 21 April 2020.
46 The physical delivery of certified palm oil started in 2018. See "Supply chain documentation helps indicate sourcing", published on FIA's website, 27 November 2018; "How derivatives exchanges can promote sustainable development", published on SSEI's website, 5 May 2021.
47 Source: "Amendment to gold produce requirements", notice issued on CME Group's website, 24 March 2015.

- In 2019, London Metal Exchange (LME) (wholly owned by HKEX) published its requirements for the responsible sourcing of all LME-listed brands of metals. In 2020, LME published a discussion paper[48] to explore how to expand its sustainability strategies, including the potential launch of LMEpassport, a digital register to enhance disclosure of sourcing information further. In July 2021, it launched six new cash-settled metals futures (including lithium hydroxide, steel scrap, and aluminium scrap) to support the transition to electric vehicles (EVs) and the sustainable economy[49].

Other ESG derivatives

US exchanges offer derivatives on renewable energy and renewable fuels, which help hedge against risks associated with fluctuations in renewable energy production and encourage more capital to be directed to sustainable projects. These products include futures and options on renewable energy certificates (RECs)[50] traded on ICE US, NASDAQ Commodities, New York Mercantile Exchange and Nodal Exchange.

Additionally, futures on credits for compliance with the renewable fuel standard (RFS) programme in the US (i.e. renewable identification numbers) and the low carbon fuel standard (LCFS) programme in California are traded on CME, ICE US and Nodal Exchange. A number of these derivatives are settled with physical delivery, which support the needs of the real economy.

ESG-related service platforms

Exchanges set standards for and require ESG information disclosure to develop ESG metrics. Such metrics evaluate underlying issuers and projects and can help drive innovation in ESG investment products and derivatives.

Since 2010, an increasing number of exchanges have set mandatory ESG reporting as part of their listing requirements (see above). To provide a starting reference point to help exchanges develop their ESG reporting regimes, WFE introduced ESG guidance and

---

48 See "LME sustainability: Discussion paper", published on LME's website, August 2020.
49 Source: "LME progresses sustainability agenda with launch of new lithium and scrap cash-settled futures", press release on LME's website, 19 July 2021.
50 An REC is issued when one megawatt hour of electricity is generated and delivered to the electricity grid from a renewable energy resource. See the 2021 ISDA Study.

metrics in 2015, which were updated in 2018[51].

Compliance with listing requirements regarding ESG disclosures and metrics by listed companies can facilitate communication between issuers and investors on how listed companies deal with different ESG issues and can potentially lower issuers' financing costs.

Some exchanges have also introduced different initiatives to promote ESG disclosure. In Hong Kong, for example, HKEX has promoted corporate governance and ESG disclosures and implementation. ESG reporting helps improve transparency and enhance stakeholders' understanding of listed companies' ESG practices.

Exchanges may also contribute to the classification (or labelling) of ESG investment products. One way to facilitate the labelling of listed products is for exchanges to develop their own classification methodology which is complementary to external reviews versus recognised international standards. In Europe, the LSE introduced its Green Economy Mark to identify listed green issuers (see above)[52]. In addition to the classification based on the international standards for green bonds, social bonds, sustainability bonds, and sustainability-linked bonds, the LSE also labels a bond issued by an LSE-listed company as a "Green Revenues" bond if at least 90% of the company's revenues are green revenues.

Another way to support the labelling of listed ESG investment products is to accept a broad range of recognised international standards. LSE and LuxSE explicitly specified the standards for the classification of GSS bonds (e.g. the ICMA's standards and also those standards specifically for EU and Mainland China)[53]. For the classification of investment funds, LuxSE accepted not only the recognised standards in Luxembourg, but also those in Germany, France, Austria and Nordic markets.

However, the classification of listed products is often considered prudentially on a case-by-case basis to avoid the risk of labelling based on misleading ESG information (i.e. "greenwashing").

---

51 See WFE Sustainability Working Group, "Exchange guidance and recommendations — October 2015", published on WFE's website, October 2015; "WFE ESG guidance and metrics (Revised June 2018)", published on WFE's website, 27 June 2018.

52 See "A comprehensive guide: Navigating the green finance landscape", published on LSE's website, January 2021.

53 See "Sustainable bond market (SBM)", published on LSE's website, 18 June 2020; "Sustainability standards and labels", published on LuxSE's website, viewed on 26 April 2021.

Certain major global exchanges have also launched dedicated ESG information platforms. These include FWB's webpage on sustainable investment, Euronext's webpage on ESG bonds, HKEX's STAGE, JPX's webpage on ESG-related products, LSE's Global Sustainable Investment Centre, LuxSE's Luxembourg Green Exchange (LGX), NASDAQ's NASDAQ Sustainable Bond Network (NSBN), SGX's Future in Reshaping Sustainability Together (FIRST) and the Shanghai Stock Exchange (SSE)'s Green Securities.

These dedicated information platforms are one-stop, web-based portals offered by exchanges to better serve ESG communication between issuers and investors on (1) classification and labelling of ESG investment products, (2) enhanced disclosure of these products, and (3) capacity building and market education (see Table 2).

Table 2. Dedicated information platforms of selected exchanges

Exchange	Dedicated information platform	Geographical focus	Free access to the list of individual products	Labelled product types by asset class	Types of enhanced disclosure	Resources for capacity building
DB	FWB's Sustainable Investment webpage	Europe	Yes	Indices, green bonds, ETFs, mutual funds, sustainability-linked derivatives	• Price and trading information of products	Not found
Euronext	ESG bonds; ESG ETFs	Europe	Yes	Bonds, ETFs	• Bonds: External review • ETFs: Names of underlying indices	Not found
HKEX	STAGE	Asia	Yes	Bonds, ETPs	• Bonds: External review • ETPs: Investment strategy	Guidance materials (e.g. international standards), case studies, webinar and research papers
JPX	Sustainability webpage	Japan	Yes	Indices, ETPs, Infrastructure funds, green and social bonds	• Bonds: External review • ETPs: Names of underlying indices • ETPs: Methodologies of indices	Practical handbook for ESG disclosure

(continued)

Exchange	Dedicated information platform	Geographical focus	Free access to the list of individual products	Labelled product types by asset class	Types of enhanced disclosure	Resources for capacity building
LSE	Global Sustainable Investment Centre	Global, mainly Europe	No	Bonds, ETFs	• List of green companies • List of bonds and external reviews (not publicly available)	Comprehensive guide for listing by types of ESG products on LSE
LuSE	LGX	Mainly Europe, Mainland China	Yes (except ESG metrics)	Bonds, funds	• Bonds and funds: External review • Price and trading information • ESG metrics of issuers (not publicly available)	Guidance materials (e.g. international standards), online courses, webinars, industry reports
NASDAQ	NSBN	Global, mainly Europe and US	No	Bonds	• List of bonds (as well as external reviews) and ESG metrics of issuers (not publicly available)	Factsheets of the platform
SGX	FIRST	Asia	Yes	Bond, equities (and index derivatives), commodities, indices	• Bonds: External review • ESG ratings of issuers • Factsheets of indices and index derivatives	Market reports and research papers
SSE	Green securities	Mainland China only	Yes	Indices, bonds (incl. ABSs), ETFs	• List of indices, bonds, ABSs and ETFs	Rules and guidelines for issuance, research papers

Note: The table is compiled based on information on the public websites of selected exchanges and may not be complete.

Source: Respective exchanges' websites, viewed on 4 May 2021.

What other measures are needed to unleash sustainable finance and investment through exchange platforms?

Since financial markets are a crucial source of the required funding to propel the world economy to its sustainability goals, exchange platforms with a wide range of products and services are indispensable.

Looking to the future, with the support of exchange platforms, measures that could accelerate GSF include:

1. **Harmonising classification standards for labelling ESG products.** Exchanges offer transparency on the classification criteria of ESG products, but they may have different market practices for classification. For example, global exchanges adopt different sets of classification standards for GSS bonds[54] and some of them (e.g. European exchanges) require external reviews for GSS bonds to confirm their alignment with the core components of the standards while others do not (e.g. exchanges in Mainland China)[55]. In Mainland China, green bonds issued and listed on exchanges are required to follow the relevant official guidelines of specific bond types, which include the classification criteria of green bonds[56]. The underlying classification standards of ESG products in China, including green bonds, are in the process of being harmonised with European markets. The International Platform on Sustainable Finance (IPSF) has developed the "Common Ground Taxonomy"

---

54 See "Sustainability standards and labels", webpage on the website of LuxSE; "Euronext ESG bonds process", published on Euronext's website; "Segment for green bonds", webpage on FWB's website; "Factsheet: Sustainable bond market", published on LSEG's website; "Inclusion criteria: Nasdaq Sustainable Bond Network (NSBN)", published on NASDAQ's website.

55 See "Guidelines for green, social and sustainability bonds external reviews", published on ICMA's website, June 2020.

56 See *Green Bonds Endorsed Project Catalogue (2015 Edition)*《綠色債券支持項目目錄 (2015 年版)》, issued by the People's Bank of China (PBOC)'s China Green Finance Committee, 22 December 2015; *Notice on the Publication of Green Bonds Endorsed Project Catalogue (2021 Edition)* (〈關於印發《綠色債券支持項目目錄 (2021 年版)》的通知〉), issued by the PBOC, the National Development and Reform Commission (NDRC) and the China Securities Regulatory Commission (CSRC), 22 April 2021; *SSE Guidelines on Review and Approval of Corporate Bond Issuance and Listing No. 2 — Specific Types of Corporate Bond* (《上海證券交易所公司債券發行上市審核規則適用指引第 2 號 —— 特定品種公司債券》), issued by the SSE, 27 November 2020; *SZSE Business Guidelines on Innovative Types of Corporate Bond No. 1 — Green Corporate Bonds* (《深圳證券交易所公司債券創新品種業務指引第 1 號 —— 綠色公司債券》), issued by the Shenzhen Stock Exchange (SZSE), 27 November 2020.

(an initiative led by China and the EU) and released in 2021[57], which attempts to enhance transparency for all investors and companies by constituting common references for labelling green products.

2. **Providing a comprehensive policy framework and incentives to promote GSF and ESG products**. Governments and regulators can formulate tailor-made comprehensive policy frameworks to suit their local market circumstances for promoting GSF and ESG products. Such policy frameworks can enhance ESG disclosure and provide guidance on classification (e.g. Sustainable Finance Disclosure Regulation) to give clarity to both issuers and investors on ESG products. These efforts can facilitate the issuance and investment of ESG products and may also reduce the risk of "greenwashing" — e.g. conveying a false impression or providing misleading information about how a company's products are environmentally friendly. Complementary to providing a comprehensive policy framework, issuers can be given incentives (e.g. subsidies for external reviews of GSS bonds) to issue ESG products for financing purposes. Similarly, cost incentives in addition to education efforts can also motivate investors to take up and increase ESG investment.

3. **Improving both the availability and quality of ESG data.** Depending on the commitment of the issuer, ESG data disclosed by issuers may not be sufficient. ESG data may also be sourced from alternative sources like media reports, governments and non-government organisations[58]. Market data service providers, in collaboration with other market participants, may offer support in this regard. Standardisation of market practices may also help improve the assessment processes of ESG data.

4. **Widening the spectrum and supporting the liquidity of ESG products to meet demand.** To meet investors' diversified demands, ESG product innovations should be encouraged to cover different asset classes and themes (e.g. UNSDG-aligned themes). These products can be made available to investors through listing on the exchange platform. As ESG investment products become increasingly popular,

---

57 See "The European Green Deal", "International platform on sustainable finance: Annual report 2020", "Annex to the Communication 'Strategy for financing the transition to a sustainable economy'" and "IPSF Common Ground Taxonomy Instruction Report", published on European Commission's website, 11 December 2019, 16 October 2020, 6 July 2021 and 4 November 2021 respectively; "EU taxonomy for sustainable activities" and "International Platform on Sustainable Finance" webpage on European Commission's website; *Notice on the Publication of Green Industry Guidance Catalogue (2019 Edition)* (〈關於印發《綠色產業指導目錄 (2019 年版)》的通知〉), issued by NDRC, Ministry of Industry and Information Technology, Ministry of Natural Resources, Ministry of Ecology and Environment, Ministry of Housing and Urban-Rural Development, PBOC and National Energy Administration; *Notice on the publication of Green Bonds Endorsed Project Catalogue (2021 Edition)* (〈關於印發《綠色債券支持項目目錄 (2021 年版)》的通知〉), issued by PBOC, NDRC and CSRC, 22 April 2021.

58 See the example of MSCI ESG rating, "MSCI ESG ratings methodology: Executive summary", published on MSCI's website, November 2020.

demand for ESG risk management products, including futures and options on ESG indices and carbon emissions, is expected to increase. To support this, the on-exchange liquidity of ESG products and their derivatives needs to grow and exchange platforms may provide incentives for this.

5. **Further inter-exchange cooperation.** Areas of exchange cooperation may include joint initiatives and enhancement of ESG-related products and services. These include cross- or dual-listing of ESG products[59] to widen product spectrum and mutual market access between exchange platforms[60] to support the liquidity. In addition, there are some exchange partnerships on information display for foreign GSS bonds on dedicated information platforms of local exchanges[61].

In China, further inter-exchange cooperation between the Mainland and Hong Kong can be expanded into ESG-related products and services. The Hong Kong market has been the most effective gateway connecting the Mainland market and the rest of the world, exemplified by its status as the largest offshore equity and bond financing centre for Mainland enterprises[62] and the success of the Stock and Bond Connect schemes[63]. Policies on mutual market development have recently been extended to GSF initiatives in the Guangdong-Hong Kong-Macao Greater Bay Area (GBA)[64]. Specific steps include the inter-exchange cooperation agreement signed in August 2021 between Guangzhou Futures Exchange and HKEX to promote sustainability and develop the GBA[65].

---

59 See the example of the dual-listing initiative of Indian green bonds on India International Exchange (India INX) and LuxSE ("LuxSE takes first important steps into Indian market", news release on LuxSE's website, 19 November 2020).

60 See the example of cross membership for trading on LuxSE and Euronext ("Luxembourg Green Exchange: The world's leading platform for sustainable securities", published on LuxSE's website, January 2021; "LuxSE and our partnership with Euronext", webpage on LuxSE's website).

61 Examples include the Mainland green bonds traded on the CIBM, SSE and SZSE being displayed on the LuxSE's LGX and the GSS bonds traded on SGX being displayed on NASDAQ's NSBN. See "Chinese domestic Green Bond Channel", webpage on LuxSE's website; "SGX strengthens commitment to sustainability with S$20 million plan", news release on SGX's website, 15 December 2021.

62 See HKEX research paper, "Hong Kong's role in supporting the fund-raising of Mainland private enterprises", published on HKEX's website, 13 June 2019.

63 For example, the trading value through Northbound Stock Connect accounted for 7% of A shares' average daily turnover in March 2021 (up from 2.8% in 2018) and the trading value through Northbound Bond Connect accounted for 51% of total trading values of overseas investors on CIBM cash bonds during the first quarter of 2021 (up from 28% in 2018). Source: HKEX.

64 See *Outline of Development Plan for the Guangdong-Hong Kong-Macao Greater Bay Area* (《粵港澳大灣區發展規劃綱要》), issued by the State Council, 18 February 2019 and *Guiding Opinions on Supporting the Financial Development of Guangdong-Hong Kong-Macao Greater Bay Area* (《關於金融支持粵港澳大灣區建設的意見》), jointly issued by the PBOC, the China Banking and Insurance Regulatory Commission, the China Securities Regulatory Commission and SAFE, 24 April 2020.

65 See "HKEX signs MOU with Guangzhou Futures Exchange", news release on HKEX's website, 27 August 2021.

Conclusion

Exchanges can play a unique role in the financial system as a central marketplace for issuers, investors, and other stakeholders.

Exchange platforms with a wide range of products and services can also play a crucial role in developing GSF and ESG investment by offering fund-raising and exit channels, supporting product innovation, providing a standardised and regulated environment, and promoting enhanced disclosure.

In recent years, many exchanges have increased the number and widened the range of green products and services available to investors. Exchanges in Europe and the US are taking the lead in delivering GSF and ESG investment products and services, but exchanges in Asia, particularly China, are advancing.

The most popular green products listed across exchanges at the end of 2020 were equity indices and bonds. However, product and service innovation is speeding up in other areas, such as ESG-related ETPs, REITs, and derivatives.

In the future, exchange platforms will continue to play a pivotal role in connecting different market participants in the global ecosystem of sustainable finance and investment. With the support of exchange platforms, GSF may be accelerated by harmonising classification standards for ESG product labelling, providing incentives and a comprehensive policy framework, improving the availability and quality of ESG data, increasing the spectrum and liquidity of ESG products, and driving inter-exchange cooperation.

第19章

交易所平台在
促進投資產品生態圈成長
與助推綠色及可持續金融
的角色

香港交易所
首席中國經濟學家辦公室

摘要

交易所作為受監管的中央市場，扮演着獨特角色，為包含環境、社會及管治（environment、social、governance，簡稱 ESG）元素的產品提供上市、交易及相關服務，並連結發行人、投資者與其他市場參與者，以支持可持續金融與投資。

交易所可支持綠色及可持續金融（green and sustainable finance，簡稱 GSF）的發展。具體而言，交易所提供融資或退出渠道、支持開發各種投資產品與服務、提供標準化的受監管環境，以及促進 ESG 披露質素及透明度的提升。

《巴黎協定》（Paris Agreement）及聯合國《2030 年可持續發展議程》（2030 Agenda for Sustainable Development）等全球倡議一直推動着對 GSF 需求的增長。為滿足這需求，全球多家交易所已推出多項舉措，積極推動 GSF 及 ESG 投資的發展。

這些舉措包括不同資產類別的 ESG 產品，涉及股票、債券、交易所買賣基金、結構性產品，以及衍生產品等。此外，還有各種特別為連接發行人與投資者而專設的交易所服務平台。

交易所於推動及便利 GSF 方面雖然已有長足進展，但仍有大量空間進一步發揮這方面的潛力。可能的措施包括：統一 ESG 產品標籤分類標準、提供全面的政策框架及激勵措施、改善 ESG 數據的可得性及質量、擴大 ESG 產品的覆蓋範圍及其流動性，並進一步促進交易所同業之間的合作。

通過這些措施，我們相信，不論在連接全球可持續金融及投資生態圈中的不同市場參與者，抑或是在推動惠及全球可持續經濟轉型的產品及服務的進一步發展方面，交易所平台均將繼續發揮關鍵作用。

支持綠色及可持續金融的交易所平台

交易所平台可為公司企業提供源源不絕的資本、促成價格發現、分散風險、協助財富創造，以及提升透明度及企業管治水平。

交易所平台都是中央化和受規管的市場，為包含環境、社會及管治（environment、social、governance，簡稱 ESG）元素的產品提供上市、交易及相關服務，並連結發行人、投資者與其他市場參與者，以支持可持續金融與投資。

鑒於為了可持續發展的資金需求不斷增長，許多交易所平台已推出各種產品和服務，以支持綠色及可持續金融（green and sustainable finance，簡稱 GSF），以及兼顧 ESG 因素的投資（統稱為「ESG 投資」或「可持續投資」），促進資金的投入及良好管治[1]。

《巴黎協定》（Paris Agreement）及聯合國《2030 年可持續發展議程》（2030 Agenda for Sustainable Development）等全球倡議，一直推動着對 GSF 需求的增長，當中涉及的投資金額相當巨大。

於 2014 年，為實現聯合國可持續發展目標所需的全球投資額，直至 2030 年為止估計為每年 5 萬億美元至 7 萬億美元[2]。2020 年爆發新冠肺炎疫情後，有關投資需求可能變得更大[3]。

全球市場的 GSF 於 2018 年至 2020 年的增長相當顯著（見圖 1）。根據 Refinitiv 的數據，新發行債券及股票於期內的三年複合年均增長率最高 —— 債券為 307%，股票為 590%。

1　參閱國際證券交易所聯會（World Federation of Exchanges）及聯合國貿易與發展會議（United Nations Conference on Trade and Development，簡稱UNCTAD）〈證券交易所促進經濟增長及可持續發展的角色〉（"The role of stock exchanges in fostering economic growth and sustainable development"），載於UNCTAD的網站，2017年9月7日。

2　參閱UNCTAD〈世界投資報告 2014 —— 投資SDG：行動計劃〉（World investment report 2014 — Investing in the SDGs: An action plan），載於UNCTAD的網站，2014年6月24日。

3　資料來源：〈動員可再生能源機構資本〉（Mobilising institutional capital for renewable energy），載於國際可再生能源署（International Renewable Energy Agency）的網站，2020年11月。

圖 1：全球市場的綠色可持續金融的資金流總額（2018 年至 2020 年）

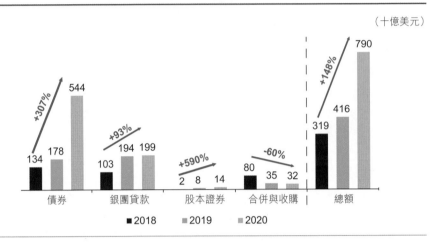

（十億美元）

註：綠色可持續金融的資金流金額按路孚特的「可持續金融」分類。

資料來源：〈Refinitiv 可持續金融回顧——2020 年全年〉（"Refinitiv Sustainable Finance Review — Full Year 2020"），載於 Refinitiv 的網站，2021 年 2 月 2 日。

根據全球永續投資聯盟（Global Sustainable Investment Alliance），2020 年可持續投資的資產管理規模[4] 達 35.3 萬億美元，差不多是 2014 年 18.3 萬億美元的兩倍，佔全球總資產管理規模約 36%（見圖 2）。

4　可持續投資的資產是指根據全球永續投資聯盟所界定的七個方法將ESG因素納入投資過程的資產管理規模。參閱〈全球可持續投資回顧〉（"Global sustainable investment review"），2020年期，載於全球永續投資聯盟的網站。

圖 2：全球可持續投資與其他投資的資產管理規模總額（2014 年至 2020 年）

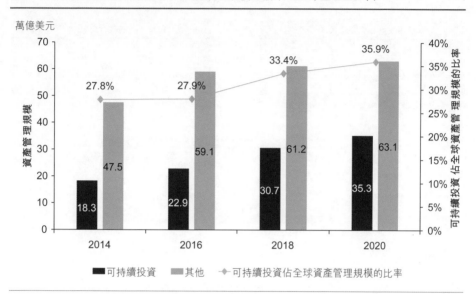

資料來源：全球資產管理規模總額及可持續投資的管理規模（2014 年的數據除外）來自 2016 年、2018 年及 2020 年期的〈Global sustainable investment review〉，載於 Global Sustainable Investment Alliance 的網站。2014 年的全球資產管理規模總額來自〈Global asset management 2021: The $100 trillion machine〉，載於 Boston Consulting Group 的網站，2021 年 7 月。

圖 3：交易所平台所提供的核心支持

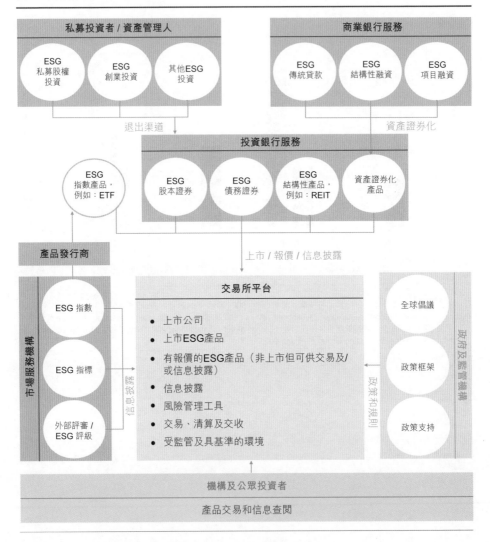

在支持可持續金融及投資方面，如圖 3 顯示，交易所平台的功能分為四個主要範疇：

(1) 為可持續發展相關投資提供集資及退出渠道

支持這功能的主要參與者包括私募投資公司及資產管理人、商業銀行以及投資銀行。

商業銀行的貸款一直是 GSF 的主要資金來源，用於協助過渡至可持續經濟。這類貸款資產可以被證券化成為「資產支持證券」，然後通過交易所平台發行並上市，之後，商業銀行便可騰出資金，對 GSF 作更多的支持。

除銀行貸款外，私募股權及風險投資亦為小型可持續發展相關項目或初創公司提供資金。在交易所平台上市，為這些私人投資提供退出渠道或持續的融資渠道。

(2) 開發 ESG 投資產品以拓寬資金來源

投資銀行的服務用於協助各類 ESG 投資產品（如股本證券、債務證券、結構性產品、資產支持證券等）在交易所上市。

市場服務供應商會評估不同的 ESG 信息來源（包括公司於交易所的相關信息披露），再將之轉為各類指標、評級及評分，協助將 ESG 產品分類並附以標籤。

指數公司亦就不同資產類別制定 ESG 指數，推動 ESG 指數產品的發展。

產品發行人則推出涉及 ESG 指數或主題的指數相關產品，包括交易所買賣基金（exchange traded funds，簡稱 ETF）。

交易所平台的存在令不同的機構及散戶投資者都可以買賣這些產品，為產品建立一個交易市場。

此外，交易所平台會持續開發並提供相關的衍生產品（如期貨及期權），作為 ESG 投資的投資組合管理及風險管理工具。

(3) 提供受規管的、具備認可標準的環境

政府及監管機構會制定倡議、政策及法規，促進及支持可持續金融及投資的發展。

與場外 ESG 產品相比，交易所平台對於其上市的 ESG 產品通常會有較清晰的適用規則及法規，以及在相關指引和最佳常規中提供清楚說明的分類標準。

交易所可因應其與相關監管機構和不同服務供應商就最新市場發展進行的溝通，不時完善其 GSF 及 ESG 產品的管治及信息披露框架。

此外，交易所一般會負責監督上市 ESG 產品於初上市時及上市後持續遵守適用規則及法規、以及相關分類標準的情況。

(4) 加強 ESG 相關的信息披露

投資者要進行 ESG 投資，自然需要有關 ESG 因素的額外信息披露。就相關信息作更詳盡的披露，以及使 ESG 產品更容易被識別，可滿足投資者的需求、加深他們對 ESG 方面事宜的認知，並減少 GSF 發行人與 ESG 投資者兩邊信息不對稱的情況。

全球交易所推動 GSF 及 ESG 投資的產品及服務舉措

交易所平台已推出多項舉措，推動 GSF 及 ESG 投資的發展。

聯合國可持續證券交易所倡議（United Nations Sustainable Stock Exchanges Initiative，簡稱 SSEI）及國際證券交易所聯會（World Federation of Exchanges，簡稱 WFE）提出建議[5]，強調交易所可推動綠色產品及服務，通過實施綠色標準及標籤來綠化金融市場，加強 ESG 信息披露，以及增加持份者之間的綠色對話。

根據 WFE 的年度調查，全球交易所所提供的綠色投資產品及服務的數量及種類，於 2019 年至 2020 年間呈現增長（見圖 4）。

根據 WFE 2021 年的一項調查，截至 2020 年年底，股票指數及債券的綠色產品較受歡迎 —— 在 39 家受訪交易所中，有 27 家提供可持續發展指數，有 30 家提供綠色債券。

5　參閱〈證券交易如何發展綠色金融〉（"How stock exchanges can grow green finance"）（2017年11月16日）及〈衍生品交易所如何促進可持續發展〉（"How derivatives exchanges can promote sustainable development"）（2021年5月5日），載於SSEI網站；〈WFE可持續發展原則〉（"WFE sustainability principles"）（2018年10月4日）及〈國際證券交易所聯會：可持續發展及商品衍生白皮書〉（"The World Federation of Exchanges: Sustainability and commodity derivatives white paper"）（2019年8月20日），載於WFE的網站。

按地區分佈看，綠色產品和服務的發展於歐美的交易所較為顯著，但於亞洲（尤其是中國）的交易所亦見快速進展 [6]。

許多全球交易所一直都積極支持 ESG 產品的開發，推出各種舉措例如加強產品的 ESG 披露要求，以及培訓市場參與者在這方面的能力。此外，還有各種特別為連接發行人與投資者而專設的交易所服務平台，例如香港交易及結算所（簡稱「香港交易所」）的「可持續及綠色交易所」（Sustainable and Green Exchange，簡稱 STAGE）。

圖 4：提供 ESG 產品的交易所數目（按產品類別）（2019 年及 2020 年）

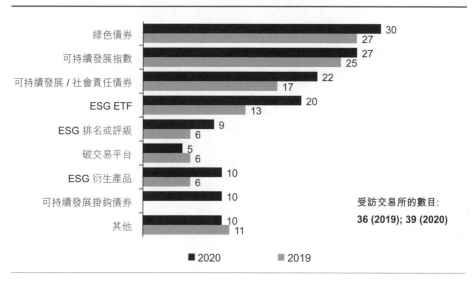

註：2020 年調查的產品分類更細緻，當中社會責任債券和可持續債券是兩個不同的類別，而可持續發展掛鈎債券是新增的類別。

資料來源：《WFE 第 6 屆可持續發展年度調查》（*The WFE's 6th Annual Sustainability Survey*）（2020 年 7 月 15 日）和《WFE 第 7 屆可持續發展年度調查》（*The WFE's 7th Annual Sustainability Survey*）（2021 年 7 月 14 日），載於 WFE 的網站。

以下分節將較詳細地討論全球交易所為推動 GSF 及 ESG 投資所開發的新產品及服務。

6　參閱《WFE 2017年4月可持續發展調查》（*WFE Sustainability Survey April 2017*）（2017年4月）及《WFE第七屆年度可持續發展調查》（*The WFE's 7th Annual Sustainability Survey*）（2021年7月14日），載於WFE的網站；〈可持續金融：ESG監管發展的全球概覽〉（"Sustainable finance: A global overview of ESG regulatory developments"），載於Cleary Gottlieb的網站，2020年10月22日；〈中國負責任的、以及以環境、社會及管治為主題的投資顯著增長〉（"China to see significant growth in responsible and ESG-themed investment"），載於Invesco的網站，2021年3月22日；〈亞洲ESG：加速勢頭〉（"ESG in Asia: Accelerating momentum"），載於Barings的網站，2021年5月。

ESG 投資產品

因應發行人及投資者的不同需要，ESG 產品持續創新。

從發行人的角度而言，他們可選擇就其公司、特定項目或相關資產發行 ESG 產品，以進行融資。

從投資者的角度而言，他們可從芸芸的 ESG 產品中選擇與其 ESG 投資策略及風險回報偏好一致的產品。

以下討論全球交易所在支持股票、債券、指數產品及結構性產品（如房地產投資信託）各資產類別中的 ESG 產品開發方面的經驗。

股票

股票若符合若干 ESG 準則，市場參與者便可將其歸類為「綠色」。例如，服務供應商採納的相關準則可能建基於公司的行業性質[7]、ESG 評級[8]、收益來源或業務活動[9]。

雖然將產品分類並非於交易所進行首次公開發售（initial public offering，簡稱 IPO）上市程序的一部分，但上市規則可能會要求上市公司進行 ESG 信息披露。

儘管 ESG 匯報的主要標準制定者還在協調各自的標準[10]，但有些交易所可能會制定建議匯報框架，以協助對照、比較不同時間的表現（並可能與同一行業的可比公司作對照[11]）。

這些資料有助於投資分析，亦有助於展示「公司的管理實力及長遠前景」[12]。

---

7   參閱〈Refinitiv可持續金融回顧——2020年全年〉（"Refinitiv Sustainable Finance Review — Full Year 2020"），載於 Refinitiv的網站，2021年2月2日。

8   參閱〈MSCI ESG評級〉（"MSCI ESG ratings"），載於MSCI的網站，於2021年3月18日閱覽。

9   例如倫敦證券交易所的〈綠色經濟標誌〉公司／基金名單。參閱〈倫敦證券交易所推出綠色經濟標誌及可持續債券市場〉（"London Stock Exchange launches Green Economy Mark and Sustainable Bond Market"），倫敦證券交易所網站上的新聞稿，2019年10月11日；〈綠色經濟標誌〉（Green Economy Mark），載於London Stock Exchange Group的網站，2020年10月。

10 參閱〈全球可持續發展及綜合報告機構發佈與氣候相關的財務披露標準原型〉（"Global sustainability and integrated reporting organisations launch prototype climate-related financial disclosure standard"），載於氣候披露標準委員會（Climate Disclosure Standards Board）的網站，2020年12月18日。

11 交易所可接受上市公司基於某一套或多套國際標準所做的ESG報告，這些國際標準的例子有來自全球報告倡議組織（Global Reporting Initiative）、永續會計準則委員會（Sustainability Accounting Standards Board）、氣候相關財務信息披露工作組（Task Force on Climate-Related Financial Disclosure）等。

12 參閱〈有關檢討《環境、社會及管治報告指引》的諮詢文件〉，載於香港交易所的網站，2015年7月。

環顧全球，越來越多上市公司都被要求披露其 ESG 信息。在上市規則中加入強制性 ESG
匯報規定的證券交易所數目，由 2010 年的 2 家增至 2020 年的 24 家（見圖 5）。

於 2021 年 3 月 17 日，這 24 家證券交易所涉及的上市公司共 16,359 家，總市值達 18.2
萬億美元，於作為樣本的 105 家證券交易所當中按數目計佔 30.7%，而按市值計則佔
20.7%[13]。

亞洲方面，香港市場自 2016 年起便規定上市公司須實行 ESG 信息披露，是最早有此規定
的亞洲市場之一，預期中國內地市場於 2021 年亦開始實施強制性的 ESG 匯報規定 [14]。

圖 5：以強制性 ESG 匯報規定作為上市要求的交易所數目（2000 年至 2020 年）

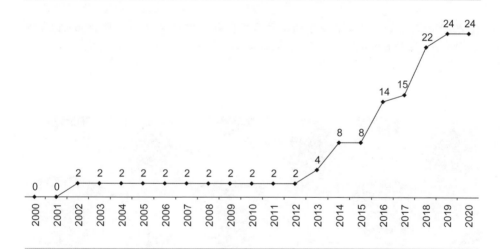

資料來源：2000 年至 2019 年的數據來自〈United Nations SSE initiative: 10 Years of Impact and Progress〉，載於
SSEI 的網站，2019 年 9 月 26 日；2020 年的數據來自 SSEI 網站上的〈Stock exchange database〉，於
2021 年 3 月 17 日閱覽。

13　按〈證券交易所數據庫〉（Stock exchange database）（載於SSEI的網站，於2021年3月17日閱覽）中有關上市公司數目及
市值的數據來計算。

14　參閱Zembrowski, P.、M. Leung與K. Schacht〈ESG disclosures in Asia Pacific: A review of ESG disclosure regimes
for listed companies in selected markets〉，載於特許金融分析師協會（CFA Institute）的網站，2019年7月21日；〈中
國將迎來ESG的一波綠色浪潮〉（"A green wave of ESG is poised to break over China"），載於全球經濟論壇（World
Economic Forum，簡稱WEF）的網站，2020年12月4日。

債券

支持特定的可持續發展範疇的債券類型包括綠色、社會責任及可持續發展（green、social、sustainability，簡稱 GSS）債券，以及較近期的過渡債券和可持續發展掛鈎債券，都是參考國際資本市場協會（International Capital Market Association，簡稱 ICMA）等認可的國際標準進行分類[15]。這些債券的上市程序通常與其他債券類似，惟須遵守 ESG 信息披露規定。

將 GSS 債券於交易所上市是相當受發行人歡迎的做法。以綠色債券為例，於 2020 年首三季，全球新發行的綠色債券約有 **69%** 於證券交易所上市，其餘的 **31%** 只於場外市場（包括中國內地的中國銀行間債券市場）買賣（見圖 6）。這有別於非 GSS 債券，非 GSS 債券通常都不在交易所上市，而僅於場外市場買賣。

於 2020 年首三季，歐洲的交易所 —— 包括盧森堡證券交易所（Luxembourg Stock Exchange，簡稱 LuxSE）、泛歐交易所（Euronext）、德國交易所及倫敦證券交易所 —— 在上市綠色債券發行金額方面佔主導地位；其次是香港交易所，其上市綠色債券的發行金額位列亞洲第一。

---

15 參閱《綠色債券原則》（*Green Bond Principles*）、《社會責任債券原則》（*Social Bond Principles*）、《可持續發展債券指引》（*Sustainability Bond Guidelines*）、《可持續發展掛鈎債券原則》（*Sustainability-Linked Bond Principles*）及《氣候轉型融資手冊》（*Climate Transition Finance Handbook*），載於ICMA的網站，於2021年3月18日閱覽。

圖 6：於交易所上市的綠色債券佔當年至該季的全球綠色債券發行金額的百分比
（2018 年第 4 季至 2020 年第 3 季）

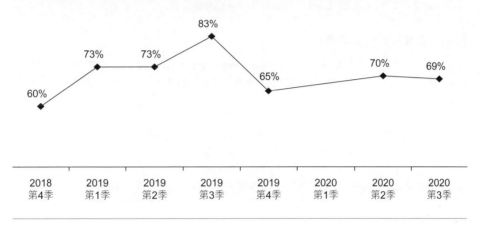

註：氣候債券倡議組織（Climate Bonds Initiative，簡稱 CBI）沒有發佈 2020 年第 1 季的季度報告，所以數據不包括 2020 年第 1 季的數字。

資料來源：〈綠色債券市場摘要〉（"Green bond market summary"），2018 第 4 季至 2020 年第 3 季的期數，載於 CBI 的網站。

在中國內地，交易所一直都很支持綠色資產支持證券的發展。近年，綠色資產支持證券的數目及發行量快速增長，大多數均於交易所發行及交易[16]。

在美國，綠色資產支持證券都是以代理按揭支持證券（mortgage-backed securities，簡稱 MBS）為主導 —— Fannie Mae 是代理 MBS 最大的發行人之一，也是 2020 年全球最大的綠色債券發行人，當年的發行金額達 130 億美元（佔全球綠色債券發行總額約 5%）[17]。美國的這些資產支持證券流動性高，但主要於場外市場（如財資市場）買賣[18]。

歐洲方面，據報由於缺乏綠色抵押品及規範，歐洲市場至今僅發行過 8 隻綠色及其他 ESG 相關的資產支持證券[19]。

---

16 參閱香港交易所研究報告 〈蓬勃發展中的內地綠色資產支持證券市場與香港市場的潛在助推力〉，載於香港交易所的網站，2021年5月3日。

17 資料來源：〈綠色證券化：解鎖小型低碳項目融資〉（"Green securitisation: Unlocking finance for small-scale low carbon projects"），載於CBI的網站，2018年3月；〈2020年綠色發行金額創2,695億美元新高：較2019疫年總金額升30億美元〉（"Record $269.5bn green issuance for 2020: Late surge sees pandemic year pip 2019 total by $3bn"），載於CBI的網站，2021年1月24日。

18 資料來源：〈固定收益市場結構：國債與機構MBS的比較〉（"Fixed Income Market Structure: Treasuries vs. Agency MBS"），載於聯邦儲備局網站上的《聯儲局備忘錄》（FEDS Notes），2020年8月25日。

19 資料來源：〈ESG貼標ABS：（非常）概括的市場簡史〉（"ESG-labelled ABS: a (very) brief history of the market"），載於 *bondvigilantes.com*，2021年3月3日。

交易所亦支持 GSS 債券市場的產品創新,其中包括專為綠色債券而設的標準化債券回購交易,為債券持有人提供短期融資。首批涉及個別綠色債券或一籃子綠色債券的標準化回購產品是歐洲期貨交易所(Eurex)於 2020 年推出的產品 [20]。

指數、投資基金及指數產品

作為 ESG 投資工具,交易所買賣產品(exchange traded product,簡稱 ETP)等 ESG 指數產品越來越受歡迎。於 2018 年至 2020 年間,ESG ETP 的資產管理規模增長遠高於其他 ETP(見圖 7)。

近年推出的 ESG 指數日益增加。目前,ESG 指數主要涵蓋美國、歐洲、亞太區、中國及其他新興市場的股票,並已擴展至包括主要市場的 GSS 債券。

圖 7:全球市場 ESG ETP 及其他 ETP 的資產管理規模總額(2018 年至 2020 年)

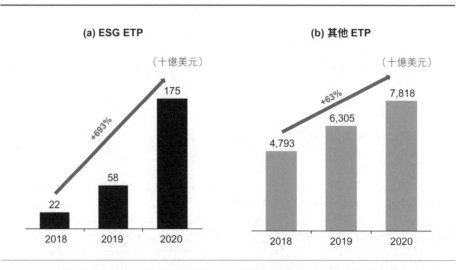

註:其他 ETP 的資產管理規模是按所有 ETP 的資產管理規模減去 ESG ETP 的數字來計算。

資料來源:2018 年和 2019 年 ESG ETP 的數據來自〈ETF reports assets invested in ESG (environmental, social, and governance) ETFs and ETPs listed globally reached a new record of 88 billion US dollars at end of June 2020〉,載於 *ETFGI.com* 網站,2020 年 7 月 22 日;2020 年 ESG ETP 的數據來自 *Trackinsight. com* 網站上的〈ESG observatory〉網頁,於 2021 年 3 月 29 日閱覽;所有 ETP 的總體數據來自〈ETFGI reports assets invested in ETFs and ETPs listed globally reach a new milestone of US$7.99 trillion at the end of December 2020〉,載於 *ETFGI.com* 網站,2021 年 1 月 14 日。

---

20 〈綠色回購〉("Repo goes green"),載於歐洲期貨交易所的網站,2020年11月10日;歐洲期貨交易所網站上的〈回購市場〉("Repo market")及〈回購籃子〉("Repo baskets")網頁。

為便利編製 ESG 指數，指數公司對發行人的 ESG 表現都有其自身的評估框架[21]，而因為各指數公司採用不同方法論，故其所作的評估彼此未必完全兼容。

上市公司的 ESG 信息披露是編備 ESG 評分或評級時所依據的主要資料來源之一。由於上市公司這類披露通常都是遵循相同或類似的匯報框架，披露的信息會更具可比性，因此股票的 ESG 指數發展比固定收益證券的 ESG 指數發展更快。

ESG 指數通常是按特定的 ESG 投資策略，從個別的廣泛市場指數（母指數）中建構出來 —— 可用的方法包括正面 / 負面篩選及權重傾斜[22]。

許多不同類型的指數公司 —— 包括主要交易所集團的附屬公司（如 LSE 集團的富時羅素、德國交易所集團的 Qontigo）—— 一直積極開發 ESG 指數。這些指數公司推出越來越多 ESG 股票及債券指數，其母指數為本地市場基準指數，以及熱門的地區和全球指數。

交易所平台對推動 ESG 指數投資至關重要，因為那是 ESG ETF 上市和交易的地方。

ESG ETF 是追蹤 ESG 指數的 ETF，涵蓋的公司在營商實踐上與聯合國可持續發展目標一致，及 / 或有良好 ESG 表現。交易所平台有助於提升 ESG ETF 的二級市場流動性。

在美國，ESG 股票 ETF 和 ESG 固定收益 ETF 於 2020 年的場內成交於其場內場外總交易金額中的佔比，低於所有股票 ETF 及所有固定收益 ETF 場內成交的相應佔比（見圖 8）。這說明場內 ESG ETF 的流動性可有進一步的增長空間，可以引入激勵措施及配套的市場機制（如提供莊家作價買賣）來推動。

市場上有獨立的標籤機構授予 ESG 基金各種標籤，而交易所就為認可標籤及識別貼標產品提供平台以助投資決策。例如，LuxSE 認可在其交易所平台上市的投資基金（包括 ETF）在歐洲市場的多個 ESG 標籤，並要求持續披露該等標籤的認證。

21　參閱〈MSCI ESG評級方法：概要〉（"MSCI ESG ratings methodology: Executive summary"），載於MSCI的網站，2020年12月；〈ESG評級及數據模型：將ESG融入投資〉（"ESG ratings and data model: Integrating ESG into investment"），載於富時羅素的網站，2021年3月29日；〈ESG評估〉（"ESG evaluation"），S&P Global網站上的網頁。

22　參閱〈ESG指數的演變〉（"An evolution in ESG indexing"），載於BlackRock iShares的網站。

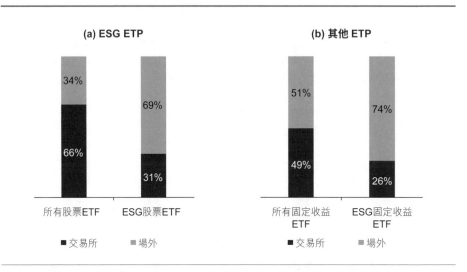

| (a) ESG ETP | (b) 其他 ETP |

註：交易金額的總額包括交易所的交易和場外的申購與贖回活動，以及大宗交易。

資料來源：〈ESG ETF liquidity continues to warm alongside demand〉，載於 *ETFDB.com* 網站，2021 年 3 月 18 日。

房地產投資信託（real estate investment trust，簡稱 REIT）

交易所可透過提高透明度協助綠色 REIT 的分類。美國作為 2020 年最大的 REIT 市場[23]，首 100 家最大的 REIT 中有 ESG 披露的佔比由 2018 年的 78% 增加至 2020 年的 98%[24]。

若干 REIT 可能是根據房地產行業的特定標準 —— 例如全球房地產資產的 ESG 基準 （Global ESG Benchmark for Real Assets，簡稱 GRESB）—— 作出信息披露。這些資料 有助於根據分類準則（例如其投資組合中的綠色建築認證）識別綠色 REIT。

然而，與股票類似，綠色 REIT 亦還未有通用的分類標準或上市的特定規則及規例。REIT 可根據若干綠色準則 —— 例如其所持樓宇根據可持續房地產的行業標準所作的評估 —— 來分類為綠色 REIT。

23　截至2020年年底，美國市場佔全球總額的69%，亞太區市場則佔21%。（資料來源：〈2020年第四季全球房地產市場 總表〉（"Global real estate total markets table Q4-2020"），載於歐洲公共房地產協會（European Public Real Estate Association）的網站，2021年1月。

24　資料來源：〈房地產投資信託行業ESG報告〉（"REIT industry ESG report"），2020年及2021年期，載於Nareit的網站。

綠色 REIT 必須是持有綠色建築的 REIT，但全球綠色建築認證計劃各有不同 [25]，而各 REIT 持有的認可綠色建築比例亦有所不同。

歐洲的 ESG 基金標籤為綠色 REIT 作分類的綠色建築比重要求有不同門檻（例如盧森堡的 LuxFLAG 與法國的 Greenfin 基金標籤分別要求其佔資產管理規模的 75% 與 90%）[26]。有些基金標籤獲交易所認可，可為 ESG ETF / 基金作分類（見上文）。

此外，有多個綠色 REIT 指數乃根據其各自的 REIT 母指數編製，以追蹤全球、地區及本地市場（如美國及日本市場）綠色 REIT 的表現 [27]。增加綠色 REIT 指數的可得性可促進相關指數產品的發展。首隻涵蓋綠色 REIT 的 ETF 於 2021 年 4 月在美國發行 [28]。首隻 ESG REIT 指數期貨 —— 日經 ESG-REIT 指數（Nikkei ESG-REIT Index），於 2021 年 6 月開始在新加坡交易所（簡稱「新交所」）買賣 [29]。

ESG 衍生產品

ESG 衍生產品有助於促進 ESG 投資及管理相關風險。

根據國際掉期及衍生工具協會（International Swaps and Derivatives Association，簡稱 ISDA）於 2021 年進行的研究 [30]（簡稱為《2021 年 ISDA 研究》）和美國期貨業協會（Futures Industry Association，簡稱 FIA）於 2020 年進行的另一項研究 [31]（簡稱為

25　其中包括美國的《能源與環境設計先鋒》（Leadership in Energy and Environmental Design）及《能源之星》（Energy Star）、英國的《建築研究機構環境評估法》（Building Research Establishment Environmental Assessment Method）、法國的《華特合資格環境評估法》（Haute qualité environnementale），以及澳洲與紐西蘭的《綠色之星》（Green Star）。參閱〈綠色建築評級系統〉（"Green building rating systems"），載於國際設施管理協會（International Facility Management Association）的網站，2021年7月19日。

26　參閱〈資格標準〉（"Eligibility criteria"），LuxFLAG網站上的網頁，於2021年7月19日閱覽，以及〈綠色金融標籤：標準指引〉（"Greenfin label: Criteria guidelines"），載於法國生態轉型部（French Ministry for Ecology and Inclusive Transition）的網站，2019年4月。

27　參閱〈MSCI全球綠色建築市場概覽〉（"MSCI Global Green Building Index factsheet"），載於MSCI的網站；〈道瓊斯選擇綠色房地產證券指數方法〉（"Dow Jones select green real estate securities indices methodology"），載於標準普爾道瓊斯指數的網站；〈富時EPRA Nareit綠色指數系列〉（"FTSE EPRA Nareit green index series"），載於富時羅素的網站；〈日經ESG-REIT指數月度資料表〉（"Nikkei ESG-REIT Index monthly factsheet"），載於日經指數的網站；〈指數指南：Solactive低碳亞洲綠色REIT指數PR〉（"Index guideline: Solactive CarbonCare Asia Pacific green REIT Index PR"），載於Solactive的網站。

28　參閱〈Invesco推出首個「綠色建築」ETF〉（"Invesco launches first 'green building' ETF"），載於《金融時報》，2021年4月22日。

29　參閱〈新交所推出全球首個ESG REIT衍生工具〉（"SGX launches the world's first ESG REIT derivatives"），新交所網站上的新聞稿，2021年6月14日。

30　〈ESG相關衍生產品及交易概覽〉（Overview of ESG-related derivatives products and transactions），載於ISDA的網站，2021年1月。

31　〈衍生產品市場如何協助全球應對氣候變化〉（How derivatives markets are helping the world fight climate change），載於FIA的網站，2020年9月。

《2020 年 FIA 研究》），ESG 衍生產品範圍廣泛，包括 ESG 指數衍生產品、碳排放權衍生產品、可持續發展掛鈎衍生產品、可再生能源與可再生燃料衍生產品，以及巨災和天氣衍生產品（見表 1）。上述這些產品當中，許多都能在交易所進行交易。

表 1：全球市場的 ESG 相關衍生產品範例

交易場所	交易所	場外
ESG 指標衍生產品	• ESG 股票指數期貨及期權	• ESG 相關信用違約掉期（credit default swap，簡稱 CDS）指數
碳排放權交易及衍生產品	• 排放上限和配額 - 現貨的雙邊交易 • 期貨及期權	• 排放上限和配額 - 現貨的雙邊交易 - 遠期
可持續發展掛鈎衍生產品	未有發現	• 利率衍生產品 • 外匯衍生產品（包含 ESG 定價元素）
其他	• 大宗商品期貨及期權（產品設計及於實物交收中採納可持續發展因素） • 可再生能源與可再生燃料衍生產品 - 基於可再生能源及燃料信用額度以及風能指數的期貨及期權 • 天氣衍生產品 • 基於溫度的指數期貨及期權	• 巨災和天氣衍生產品 • 巨災掉期

資料來源：按《2020 年 FIA 研究》和《2021 年 ISDA 研究》編製。

交易所比場外市場有較多優勢去支持 ESG 衍生產品的發展[32]。

具體就 ESG 衍生產品而言，全球交易所的舉措包括：擴大產品範圍以切合風險管理需要、提供市場作價買賣（莊家）獎勵以支持二級市場流動性，以及於定價和實物交付程序中加入可持續發展元素。

ESG 指數衍生產品

全球交易所提供一系列 ESG 指數衍生產品（尤其是股票指數期貨），切合對 ESG 投資及風險管理日益增長的需求[33]。

---

[32] 參閱Nystedt, J.(2004年)〈衍生產品市場競爭：場外市場與有組織的衍生產品交易所〉("Derivative market competition: OTC markets versus organised derivative exchanges")，《國際貨幣基金組織工作文件》(*International Monetary Fund Working Paper*)，WP/04/61。

[33] 參閱香港交易所研究報告〈ESG股票指數期貨：迎合愈益殷切的ESG投資需求〉，載於香港交易所的網站，2021年4月12日。

根據《2020 年 FIA 研究》，截至 2020 年 9 月，全球市場有 18 種主要本地、地區及全球 ESG 股票指數的期貨及期權產品在芝加哥商品交易所（Chicago Mercantile Exchange，簡稱 CME）、Eurex、Euronext、洲際交易所（Intercontinental Exchange，簡稱 ICE）（美國）、納斯達克證券交易所（NASDAQ，簡稱「納斯達克」）及台灣期貨交易所的市場上交易。

除交易外，交易所亦會通過其相關結算所為 ESG 指數衍生產品交易提供中央結算服務。

投資者的強勁需求及交易所提供的莊家獎勵，推動着於交易所交易的 ESG 指數衍生產品的流動性增長。自 2018 年 10 月首隻 ESG 股票指數期貨產品推出以來 [34]，主要 ESG 股票指數期貨的成交量一直穩步增長，於 2021 年 3 月更創歷史新高，而以歐洲的交易所的相關產品成交量佔比最高（見圖 9）。

圖 9：主要 ESG 股票指數的期貨產品的月度交易數量（2018 年 10 月至 2021 年 3 月）

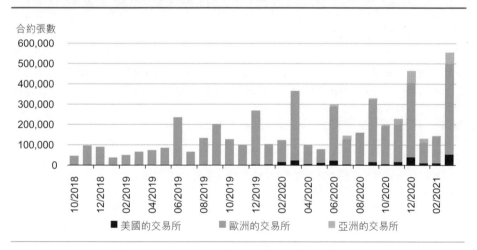

註： 美國的交易所涵蓋 CME 和洲際交易所（美國）（ICE US）；歐洲的交易所涵蓋歐洲期貨交易所、泛歐交易所，以及 NASDAQ 斯德哥爾摩證券交易所；亞洲的交易所涵蓋新加坡交易所和台灣期貨交易所。ESG 股票指數期貨的清單來自香港交易所研究報告〈ESG 股票指數期貨：迎合愈益殷切的 ESG 投資需求〉，載於香港交易所的網站，2021 年 4 月 12 日，清單並非整全。

資料來源： 按彭博的個別指數期貨的每日成交數量來計算。

---

34 全球首隻ESG期貨是納斯達克於2018年10月推出的OMX斯德哥爾摩30 ESG責任指數期貨。參閱〈全球首隻ESG期貨 —— 合作成果〉（"The world's first ESG future — The result of a successful collaboration"），載於納斯達克的網站，2021年6月7日。

相較之下，根據《2021 年 ISDA 研究》，場外交易的 ESG 指數衍生產品數目仍然不多。IHS Markit 於 2020 年 5 月推出的首隻 ESG 相關 CDS 指數 —— iTraxx MSCI ESG Screened Europe Index —— 的衍生產品便是一例 [35]。

然而，與母指數的期貨相比，ESG 股票指數期貨的流動性仍相對較低 [36]。要支持 ESG 指數期貨的流動性，交易所可為莊家活動提供激勵措施 [37]。

碳排放權交易及衍生產品

根據《巴黎協定》，各國可以為減少溫室氣體排放定下各自的減排目標，並通過排放權交易來實踐。

排放權交易機制（emissions trading system，簡稱 ETS）涵蓋既定範圍的公司，方便建立碳排放配額並推動污染較多與污染較少國家之間進行碳排放配額交易。交易單位通常為一噸二氧化碳當量。

ETS 的例子包括歐盟排放權交易計劃（歐盟 ETS）、韓國及紐西蘭的全國 ETS、美國及加拿大的地區性 ETS —— 西方氣候倡議（Western Climate Initiative，簡稱 WCI）及地區溫室氣體減排行動（Regional Greenhouse Gas Initiative，簡稱 RGGI），還有北京、上海、重慶、湖北、福建、天津、廣州、深圳等八個中國試點 ETS。值得注意的是，中國最近於 2021 年 7 月推出其全國 ETS（全國碳排放權交易市場），最先負責營運的是上海環境和能源交易所。

就交易量和金額而言，於 2017 年至 2020 年間，歐盟 ETS 主導全球市場，其次為北美及亞太區的地區性市場 [38]。

---

35 參閱〈iTraxx MSCI ESG Screened Europe Index：臨時方法〉（"iTraxx MSCI ESG Screened Europe Index: Provisional methodology"），載於IHS Markit的網站；〈Markit信用指數 —— 信用衍生產品的市場標準〉（"Markit Credit Indices — the market standard for credit derivatives"），載於IHS Markit的網站。

36 參閱Eurex的Stoxx歐洲600 ESG-X指數期貨的例子：〈ESG期貨 —— ESG過渡中的行業追蹤如何？〉（"ESG Futures — How is the industry tracking in the ESG transition?"），載於Qontigo的網站，2020年12月9日。

37 參閱例如Eurex的倡議：〈STOXX®與DAX®ESG指數期貨產品特定補充資料〉（"Product specific supplement for futures on STOXX® and DAX® ESG indices"），Eurex發佈，2021年3月22日。

38 資料來源：〈碳市場年度回顧：2019年碳市場價值創新高〉（"Carbon market year in review: Record high value of carbon markets in 2019"）（2020年1月22日）及〈2020年碳市場年度回顧：在氣候抱負方面蓬勃發展的碳市場〉（"Carbon market year in review 2020: Blooming carbon markets on raised climate ambition"）（2021年1月26日），載於Refinitiv的網站。

就涵蓋的排放規模而言，中國的全國 ETS 涵蓋全球最多的排放量 —— 超過 40 億噸二氧化碳當量，約佔中國內地總排放量的 40%（比率與歐盟相近）[39]。於 2021 年 7 月 16 日開始營業之日當天，中國的全國 ETS 所交易的二氧化碳當量超過 400 萬噸。

交易所亦可為新設定的碳排放配額的拍賣和二級市場交易提供平台。

以歐盟 ETS 的歐盟碳排放配額（EU Allowance，簡稱 EUA）為例：

- EUA 的數目由歐洲各國政府根據歐盟法規設定[40]。

- EUA 設有中央登記處（Union Registry），以確保為歐盟 ETS 之下分配的所有 EUA 進行準確的會計處理。部分 EUA 是免費分配予各公司的，而其他 EUA 則是通過於指定交易所平台進行的拍賣進行分配。

- 歐洲能源交易所（European Energy Exchange，簡稱 EEX，其大部分權益由德國交易所擁有）是所有歐盟 ETS 參與國的 EUA 拍賣平台[41]。EUA 的二級市場交易主要是即期交易（以場外市場的雙邊交易或交易所的即期期貨合約形式進行），以及於交易所買賣年期較長的 EUA 期貨及期權。

- EUA 的大部分二級市場交易是通過交易所（包括 ICE（歐洲）、EEX、CME 及納斯達克 OMX）進行的。EUA 期貨及期權於交易所的交易金額達 1,816 億歐元，佔 2020 年交易總額約 90%（見圖 10）。

- 此外，據歐盟所報導，大部分 EUA 的二級市場交易（包括場內及場外交易）都是通過交易所的相關結算所作中央結算[42]。

交易所平台不僅促進了歐盟地區的碳市場發展，在其他主要經濟體的情況也一樣[43]。

39　資料來源：〈新華頭條：上海設全球最大的碳交易市場〉（"Xinhua Headlines: World's largest carbon trading market opens in Shanghai"），載於《新華社》，2021年7月17日；〈中國的全國ETS〉（"China National ETS"），載於國際碳行動夥伴（International Carbon Action Partnership）的網站，2021年8月9日；〈歐盟排放權交易系統〉（"EU Emissions Trading System (EU ETS)"），歐洲委員會（European Commission）網站上的網頁，於2021年9月16日閱覽。

40　參閱載於歐洲委員會網站〈歐盟排放權交易系統〉網頁上有關EUA的創建、分配、交易及結算詳情；及〈歐盟ETS登記處與交易後基礎設施之間的相互作用〉（"Interplay between EU ETS Registry and Post Trade Infrastructure"），載於歐洲委員會的網站，2015年1月。

41　資料來源：歐盟網站上的〈排放配額拍賣〉（"Auctioning of allowances"）網頁與EEX網站上的〈歐盟ETS拍賣〉（"EU ETS auctions"）網頁。ICE在英國脫歐前於英國提供EUA的拍賣服務（參閱〈排放配額拍賣〉（"Emissions auctions"），ICE Europe網站上的網頁，於2021年9月15日閱覽）。

42　參閱〈歐盟ETS登記處與交易後基礎設施之間的相互作用〉（"Interplay between EU ETS registry and post trade infrastructure"），載於歐盟委員會的網站，2015年1月。

43　參閱〈2021年碳市場的拓展方面顯現巨大潛力〉（"Expanding carbon markets show big potential in 2021"），載於FIA的網站，2021年3月12日；〈頂級金融交易集團響應呼籲進行美國碳定價〉（"Top finance trade groups join calls for U.S. carbon pricing"），載於Reuters.com，2021年2月18日；〈參與英國ETS〉（"Participating in the UK ETS"），英國政府網站上的網頁；〈中國於2月1日推出全國碳排放權交易計劃〉（"China to launch national carbon emissions trading scheme on Feb 1"），載於S&P Global的網站，2021年1月6日。

圖 10：EUA 於各交易場所的交易金額（2017 年至 2020 年）

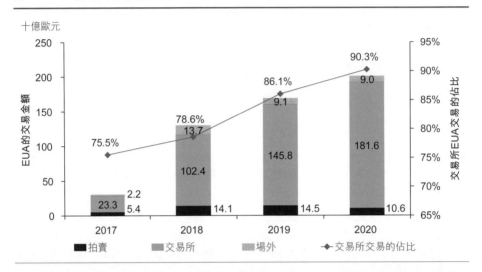

資料來源：〈Carbon market year in review: Record high value of carbon markets in 2019〉（2020 年 1 月 22 日）和〈Carbon market year in review 2020: Blooming carbon markets on raised climate ambition〉（2021 年 1 月 26 日），載於 Refinitiv 的網站。

歐洲方面，英國於脫歐後正在建立其英國 ETS，首次拍賣於 2021 年 5 月 19 日通過 ICE（歐洲）的平台上進行。

中國內地方面，據報導，全國 ETS 將為廣州期貨交易所推出首個碳排放權期貨產品舖路。

北美方面，於 ICE（美國）及 Nodal 交易所買賣的區域碳信用額的期貨及期權交投活躍。然而，美國尚未就建立全國 ETS 達成共識，但據報主要金融交易團體已要求提供碳定價。

可持續發展掛鈎衍生產品

可持續發展掛鈎衍生產品是加入了 ESG 定價元素的傳統衍生產品（如利率掉期、交叉貨幣掉期或遠期）。這些衍生產品為發行人量身定製，使用多項不同的關鍵績效指標[44] 來釐定發行人要實現的可持續發展目標。

44　參閱〈可持續發展掛鈎衍生產品：關鍵績效指標指引〉（"Sustainability-linked derivatives: KPI guidelines"），載於ISDA的網站，2021年9月。

由於可持續發展掛鈎衍生產品的合約條款難以標準化，交易所僅支持當中某幾類產品的上市。這些衍生產品可於場外市場交易，而這些交易尚未有二級市場或中央結算。例如，多項可持續發展相關衍生產品以「可持續發展證書」形式於法蘭克福交易所 (Börse Frankfurt，簡稱 FWB) 上市，主要經由銀行及經紀轉介並進行交易 [45]。

大宗商品衍生產品

於交易所買賣的大宗商品期貨是實體經濟中全球供應鏈的重要一環 [46]。因此，交易所在大宗商品產品交易中加入可持續因素，可大力支持可持續經濟。

主要商品交易所最近已在用作實物交付的大宗商品方面開始加入可持續發展的標準：

- 於 2015 年，馬來西亞交易所 (全球最活躍的棕櫚油期貨市場之一) 的棕櫚油期貨開始要求賣方提交的文件中，要載有用於生產棕櫚原油的磨機資料。此舉為買家提供更多有關棕櫚油是否以負責任方式生產的資料，以及有關馬來西亞棕櫚油可持續發展 (Malaysia Sustainable Palm Oil) 標準的國家認證計劃的資料 [47]。

- 同年，CME 集團的紐約商品交易所 (COMEX) 要求黃金生產商就其黃金期貨遵守倫敦金銀市場協會 (London Bullion Market Association) 有關黃金實物交割的《責任黃金指引》[48]。

- 2019 年，倫敦金屬交易所 (London Metal Exchange，簡稱 LME) (由香港交易所全資擁有) 公佈其對所有於 LME 掛牌的金屬品牌關於責任採購方面的規定，並於 2020 年刊發討論文件 [49]，探討如何擴大其可持續發展策略，包括可能推出數碼登記冊 LMEpassport，以進一步加強披露採購資料。2021 年 7 月，LME 推出六隻以現金結算的金屬期貨 (包括氫氧化鋰、廢鋼和廢鋁)，以支持轉型至電動車及可持續經濟 [50]。

其他 ESG 衍生產品

美國的交易所均有提供可再生能源及可再生燃料的衍生產品，有助於對沖與可再生能源生產的波動有關的風險，並鼓勵於可持續項目投放更多資金。有關產品包括於 ICE 美國、納

45 參閱〈可持續發展證書〉("Certificates with sustainability focus")，FWB網站上的網頁。

46 參閱香港交易所研究報告〈大宗商品期貨服務實體經濟的國際經驗〉，載於香港交易所的網站，2020年4月21日。

47 經認證的棕櫚油的實物交付於2018年開始 。參閱〈供應鏈文件有助於採購證明〉("Supply chain documentation helps indicate sourcing")，載於FIA的網站，2018年11月27日；〈衍生品交易所如何促進可持續發展〉("How derivatives exchanges can promote sustainable development")，載於SSEI的網站，2021年5月5日。

48 資料來源：〈修訂黃金生產規定〉("Amendment to gold produce requirements")，CME集團網站上的通告，2015年3月24日。

49 參閱〈LME可持續發展：討論文件〉("LME sustainability: Discussion paper")，載於LME的網站，2020年8月。

50 資料來源：〈LME推行可持續發展議程，推出新的以現金結算的鋰及廢料期貨〉("LME progresses sustainability agenda with launch of new lithium and scrap cash-settled futures")，LME網站上的新聞稿，2021年7月19日。

斯達克商品（NASDAQ Commodities）、紐約商品交易所（New York Mercantile Exchange）
和 Nodal 交易所買賣的可再生能源證明書期貨及期權[51]。

另外，於 CME、ICE 美國及 Nodal 交易所買賣的衍生產品，有符合美國可再生能源標準
計劃（可再生能源識別號碼）及加州低碳燃料標準計劃的信用期貨。當中若干產品是實物
交割，切合實體經濟的需要。

ESG 相關服務平台

交易所制定了 ESG 信息披露的標準和要求，方便 ESG 指標的制定。這些指標用於對相關
發行人及項目作評估，以及幫助推動 ESG 投資產品和衍生產品的創新。

自 2010 年以來，越來越多交易所於其上市規則中加入強制性 ESG 匯報規定（見上文）。
為了協助交易所建立其 ESG 匯報制度時有所參照，WFE 於 2015 年發佈 ESG 指引及指
標，其後於 2018 年進行更新[52]。

有關上市公司須遵守 ESG 披露及指標的上市規定，可促進發行人與投資者之間有關上市
公司如何處理不同 ESG 議題的溝通，有機會降低發行人的融資成本。

有些交易所亦推出不同措施推動 ESG 信息披露。例如在香港，香港交易所一直積極推動
企業管治以及 ESG 的信息披露和實施。交易所的 ESG 匯報規定將有助於提高透明度及加
強持份者對上市公司 ESG 實踐的了解。

此外，交易所亦可為 ESG 投資產品的分類（或貼標）作出貢獻。要促進上市產品貼標，方
法之一便是自行開發自身的分類方式，這與對照認可國際標準作外部審查相輔相成。

歐洲方面，倫敦證券交易所推出「綠色經濟標誌」，以識別上市綠色發行人（見上文）[53]。除根
據綠色債券、社會責任債券、可持續發展債券及可持續發展掛鈎債券的國際標準進行分類
外，於其上市的公司倘有至少 90% 的收益為綠色收益，倫敦證券交易所亦會將該公司發行
的債券列為「綠色收益」債券。

---

51 「可再生能源證明書」是當以可再生能源的方式發電一兆瓦並傳送至電網時才會發出。參閱《2021年ISDA研究》。
52 參閱WFE可持續小組（WFE Sustainability Working Group）〈交易所指引及建議 —— 2015年10月〉（"Exchange guidance
   and recommendations — October 2015"），載於WFE的網站，2015年10月；〈WFE ESG指引及指標（2018年6月修訂）〉
   （"WFE ESG guidance and metrics (Revised June 2018)"），載於WFE的網站，2018年6月27日。
53 參閱〈全面指引：綠色金融格局的導航〉（"A comprehensive guide: Navigating the green finance landscape"），載於倫
   敦證券交易所的網站，2021年1月。

支持上市 ESG 投資產品貼標的另一種方式，是接受獲認可的多種國際標準。倫敦證券交易所及 LuxSE 明確訂明 GSS 債券的分類標準（例如 ICMA 的標準及特別針對歐盟與中國內地的標準）[54]。就投資基金分類而言，LuxSE 不僅接納盧森堡的認可標準，亦接納德國、法國、奧地利及北歐市場的認可標準。

然而，上市產品的分類通常要按個別情況謹慎處理，以避免根據具誤導性的 ESG 信息貼標（即「漂綠」）。

若干主要全球交易所亦已推出 ESG 專屬信息平台，包括 FWB 的可持續投資網頁、Euronext 有關 ESG 債券的網頁、香港交易所的 STAGE、JPX 有關 ESG 產品的網頁、倫敦證券交易所的「全球可持續投資中心」（Global Sustainable Investment Centre）、LuxSE 的「盧森堡綠色交易所」（Luxembourg Green Exchange，簡稱 LGX）、納斯達克的「可持續債券網絡」（NASDAQ Sustainable Bond Network，簡稱 NSBN）、新交所的「可持續金融創新平台」（Future in Reshaping Sustainability Together，簡稱 FIRST）及上海證券交易所（簡稱「上交所」）的「綠色證券」。

這些專屬信息平台是交易所提供的一站式門戶網站，於以下各方面進一步協助發行人與投資者之間的 ESG 溝通：（1）ESG 投資產品的分類及貼標；（2）有關產品的增強披露；及（3）能力建設與市場教育（見表 2）。

54　參閱〈可持續債券市場（SBM）〉（"Sustainable bond market (SBM)"），載於倫敦證券交易所的網站，2020年6月18日；〈可持續發展標準及標籤〉（"Sustainability standards and labels"），載於LuxSE的網站，2021年4月26日。

表 2：某些交易所的專屬信息平台

交易所	專屬 信息平台	主要 涵蓋地區	個別產品的 清單可供 免費查閱	貼標產品種類 （按資產類別）	增強信息披露的種類	培訓資源
德意志 交易所	法蘭克福 證券 交易所的 可持續投資 網頁	歐洲	有	指數、綠色 債券、ETF、 互惠基金和 可持續發展 掛鈎衍生產品	• 產品的價格和交易 　信息	未有發現
泛歐交易所	ESG 債券； ESG ETFs	歐洲	有	債券和 ETF	• 債券：外部評審 • ETF：相關指數名稱	未有發現
香港交易所	可持續及綠色 交易所 （STAGE）	亞洲	有	債券和 ETP	• 債券：外部評審 • ETP：投資策略	指引材料（如 國際標準）、 個案研究、 網上研討會 和研究報告
日本交易所 集團	可持續發展 的網頁	日本	有	指數、ETP、 基建基金、 綠色債券和 社會債券	• 債券：外部評審 • ETP：相關指數名稱 • ETP：指數的編制 　方法	ESG 信息 披露的 實務手冊
倫敦證券 交易所	全球可持續 投資中心 （Global Sustainable Investment Centre）	全球， 主要是 歐洲	無	債券和 ETF	• 綠色公司的名單 • 債券名單與外部 　評審 　（沒有對外公開）	不同種類的 ESG 產品於倫交所 上市的全面性 指引
盧森堡 證券交易所	盧森堡綠色 交易所 （LGX）	主要是 歐洲 和中國 內地	有 （ESG 指標 除外）	債券和基金	• 債券和基金：外部 　評審 • 價格和交易信息 • 發行人的 ESG 指標 　（沒有對外公開）	指引材料（如 國際標準）、 網上課程、 網上研討會 和行業報告
納斯達克	可持續債券 網絡（NSBN）	全球， 主要是 歐洲和 美國	無	債券	• 債券名單（以及外部 　評審）和發行人的 　ESG 指標（沒有對 　外公開）	平台的 資料頁
新加坡 交易所	可持續金融 創新平台 （FIRST）	亞洲	有	債券、股票 （及指數衍生 產品）、大宗 商品、指數	• 債券：外部評審 • 發行人的 ESG 評級 • 指數及指數衍生 　產品的資料頁	市場報告和 研究報告

（續）

交易所	專屬信息平台	主要涵蓋地區	個別產品的清單可供免費查閱	貼標產品種類（按資產類別）	增強信息披露的種類	培訓資源
上海證券交易所	綠色證券	只限中國內地	有	指數、債券（包括資產支持證券）和 ETF	• 指數、債券、資產支持證券和 ETF 的名單	發行的規則和指引、研究報告

註：本表按這些交易所公開網站上的資料編製，資料可能並不整全。

資料來源：相關交易所的網站，於 2021 年 5 月 4 日閱覽。

有何其他措施使交易所平台能充分發揮可持續金融及投資的潛力？

由於推動全球經濟實現可持續發展目標所需的資金來源取決於金融市場，擁有廣泛產品及服務的交易所平台可說不可或缺。

展望將來，在交易所平台的支持下，讓綠色及可持續金融有飛躍式發展的措施包括：

1. **統一 ESG 產品標籤分類標準。**交易所提供 ESG 產品分類標準的透明度，但其分類的市場實踐或各有不同。例如，全球交易所對 GSS 債券採用不同的分類標準[55]，其中某些交易所（例如歐洲的交易所）要求對 GSS 債券進行外部審查，以確認其與標準的核心組成部分一致，而其他標準則沒有這個要求（例如中國內地的交易所）[56]。中國內地方面，於內地交易所發行並上市的綠色債券須遵守特定債券類別的相關官方指引，包括綠色債券的分類準則[57]。中國正將其 ESG 產品（包括綠色債券）的分類標準與歐洲市場的分類標準協調。可持續金融國際平台（International Platform on Sustainable Finance）於 2021 年完成制訂並發佈《共通綠色分類目錄》計劃（由中國及歐盟牽

---

[55] 參閱〈可持續發展標準及標籤〉（"Sustainability standards and labels"），載於LuxSE的網站；〈Euronext ESG債券程序〉（"Euronext ESG bonds process"），載於Euronext的網站；〈綠色債券板塊〉（"Segment for green bonds"），FWB網站上的網頁；〈市場概覽：可持續債券市場〉（"Factsheet: Sustainable bond market"），載於倫敦證券交易所集團的網站；〈納入標準：納斯達克可持續債券網絡（NSBN）〉（"Inclusion criteria: Nasdaq Sustainable Bond Network (NSBN)"），載於納斯達克的網站。

[56] 參閱〈綠色、社會及可持續發展債券外部評審指引〉（"Guidelines for green, social and sustainability bonds external reviews"），載於ICMA的網站，2020年6月。

[57] 參閱《綠色債券支持項目目錄(2015年版)》，中國人民銀行中國綠色金融委員會發佈，2015年12月22日；〈關於印發《綠色債券支持項目目錄(2021年版)》的通知〉，中國人民銀行、國家發展和改革委員會（簡稱「國家發改委」）及中國證券監督管理委員會（簡稱「中國證監會」）發佈，2021年4月22日；《上海證券交易所公司債券發行上市審核規則適用指引第2號——特定品種公司債券》，上交所發佈，2020年11月27日；《深圳證券交易所公司債券創新品種業務指引第 1 號——綠色公司債券》，深圳證券交易所（簡稱「深交所」）發佈，2020年11月27日。

頭）[58]，旨在構建於綠色產品標籤的共同參考標準，提高透明度以惠及所有投資者與公司。

2. **提供全面的政策框架及激勵措施，以推廣 GSF 及 ESG 產品。**政府及監管機構可制定符合本地市場情況的全面政策框架，以推廣 GSF 及 ESG 產品。有關政策框架可加強 ESG 信息披露及提供分類指引（例如《永續金融披露規範》），讓發行人與投資者清晰了解 ESG 產品。有關工作可促進 ESG 產品的發行及投資，並或會減低「漂綠」的風險（例如通過傳達虛假印象或提供有關公司的產品如何促進環保的誤導性資料）。除提供全面的政策框架外，發行人可被激勵發行 ESG 產品作融資用途（例如對 GSS 債券的外部評審提供補貼）。同樣，除教育工作外，成本方面的激勵措施亦能鼓勵投資者接受及增加 ESG 投資。

3. **改善 ESG 數據的可得性及質量。**視乎發行人的承擔有多大，發行人所發放的 ESG 數據可能不足。ESG 數據亦可取自其他來源，如媒體報導與政府及非政府組織[59]。市場數據服務供應商與其他市場參與者合作，可在這方面提供支持。此外，市場實踐的標準化亦將有助於改善 ESG 數據的評估流程。

4. **擴大 ESG 產品的覆蓋範圍及支持其流動性以滿足需求。**為滿足投資者的多元化需求，應鼓勵 ESG 產品創新，以涵蓋不同資產類別及主題（例如與聯合國可持續發展目標一致的主題）。這類產品在交易所平台上市，投資者便可參與買賣。隨着 ESG 投資產品日益普及，預期對 ESG 風險管理工具（包括 ESG 指數的期貨及期權，以及碳排放權）的需求將會增加。ESG 產品及其衍生品的場內流動性需要進一步發展，交易所平台可在這方面提供激勵措施。

---

58 參閱〈歐洲綠色協議〉（"The European Green Deal"）（2019年12月11日）、〈可持續金融國際平台：2020年年報〉（"International Platform on Sustainable Finance: Annual report 2020"）（2020年10月16日）、〈通信附件「向可持續經濟過渡提供資金的策略」〉（"Annex to the Communication 'Strategy for financing the transition to a sustainable economy'"）（2021年7月6日）及〈可持續金融國際平台共通綠色分類目錄指示報告〉（"IPSF Common Ground Taxonomy Instruction Report"）（2021年11月4日），載於盟委員會的網站；〈可持續發展活動的歐盟分類標準〉（"EU taxonomy for sustainable activities"）及〈可持續金融國際平台〉（"International Platform on Sustainable Finance"），歐盟委員會網站上的網頁；〈關於印發《綠色產業指導目錄(2019年版)》的通知〉，國家發改委、工業和信息化部、自然資源部、生態環境部、住房和城鄉建設部、中國人民銀行及國家能源局發佈；〈關於印發《綠色債券支持項目目錄(2021年版)》的通知〉，中國人民銀行、國家發改委及中國證監會發佈，2021年4月22日。

59 參閱MSCI ESG評級的例子：〈MSCI ESG評級方法：概要〉（"MSCI ESG ratings methodology: Executive summary"），載於MSCI的網站，2020年11月。

5. **交易所之間的進一步合作**。交易所之間的合作範疇可包括與 ESG 相關產品及服務有關的共同倡議及優化計劃。這包括 ESG 產品的交叉或雙重上市 [60]，擴大產品範圍及交易所平台之間的相互市場准入 [61]，從而支持流動性。此外，交易所之間亦會建立合作夥伴關係，在本地交易所的 專屬信息平台上展示外國 GSS 債券的信息 [62]。

在中國，內地與香港交易所之間的進一步交流合作可擴展至 ESG 相關產品及服務範疇。香港市場一直是連接內地市場與世界其他地區的最有效的門戶，這從香港作為內地企業最大的離岸股票及債券融資中心 [63]，以及「滬深港通」和「債券通」計劃的成功可見一斑 [64]。有關共同市場發展的政策近期更擴展至粵港澳大灣區（大灣區）有關 GSF 的倡議 [65]。具體舉措包括廣州期貨交易所與香港交易所於 2021 年 8 月就促進大灣區可持續發展的戰略合作簽署了合作協議 [66]。

總結

交易所在金融體系中扮演着獨特的角色，是發行人、投資者及其他持份者的中央市場。

有豐富產品及服務的交易所平台可提供融資或退出渠道、支持開發各種投資產品與服務、提供標準化的受監管環境，以及促進 ESG 披露質素及透明度的提升，故能在發展 GSF 及 ESG 投資方面扮演着關鍵角色。

近年來，多家交易所已然向投資者提供更多數量及更多元化的綠色產品與服務。雖然歐洲的交易所在 GSF 及 ESG 投資的產品及服務方面處於領先地位，但亞洲（尤其是中國）的交易所也有長足進展。

---

60 參閱印度綠色債券於印度國際交易所(India INX)及LuxSE雙重上市計劃的例子：〈LuxSE進軍印度市場的第一步〉("LuxSE takes first important steps into Indian market")，LuxSE網站上的新聞稿，2020年11月19日。

61 參閱LuxSE及Euronext的交叉會員交易例子：〈盧森堡綠色交易所：全球領先的可持續證券平台〉("Luxembourg Green Exchange: The world's leading platform for sustainable securities")，載於LuxSE的網站，2021年1月；〈 LuxSE及我們與Euronext的合作〉("LuxSE and our partnership with Euronext")，LuxSE網站上的網頁。

62 例子包括於中國銀行間債券市場、上交所及深交所買賣的內地綠色債券於LuxSE的LGX展示，而於新交所買賣的GSS債券於納斯達克的NSBN展示。參閱〈中國國內綠色債券頻道〉("Chinese domestic Green Bond Channel")，LuxSE網站上的網頁；〈新交所以2,000萬新加坡元計劃加強對可持續發展的承諾〉("SGX strengthens commitment to sustainability with S\$20 million plan")，新交所網站上的新聞稿，2021年12月15日。

63 參閱香港交易所研究報告〈香港支持內地民營企業集資的角色〉，載於香港交易所的網站，2019年6月13日。

64 見證例子：於2021年3月，通過北向「滬深港通」的交易金額佔A股平均每日成交額的7%（高於2018年的2.8%），而於2021年第一季，通過北向「債券通」的交易金額佔中國銀行間債券市場現貨債券海外投資者交易金額的51%（高於2018年的28%）。資料來源：香港交易所。

65 參閱〈粵港澳大灣區發展規劃綱要〉，國務院發佈，2019年2月18日；及《關於金融支持粵港澳大灣區建設的意見》，中國人民銀行、中國銀行保險監督管理委員會、中國證監會及國家外匯管理局發佈，2020年4月24日。

66 參閱〈香港交易所與廣州期貨交易所簽署諒解備忘錄〉，香港交易所網站上的新聞稿，2021年8月27日。

截至 2020 年年底，股票指數與債券在云云綠色產品中較受歡迎。然而，在其他方面的產品及服務創新已急起直追，例如與 ESG 相關的交易所買賣產品、REIT 及 ESG 衍生產品。

展望未來，不論在連接全球可持續金融及投資生態圈中的不同市場參與者，抑或是推動惠及全球可持續經濟轉型的產品及服務的進一步發展方面，交易所平台均將繼續發揮關鍵作用。在交易所平台的支持下，可以通過一系列舉措來加速推動 GSF，這些舉措包括統一 ESG 產品標籤分類標準、提供全面的政策框架及激勵措施、改善 ESG 數據的可得性及質量、擴大 ESG 產品的覆蓋範圍及流動性，並進一步促進交易所同業之間的合作。

Capital markets, the net-zero transition, and Hong Kong's role as a change agent

At least USD 90 trillion is required to drive the transition to a net-zero global economy, and capital markets have a key role to play, according to the United Nations (UN).

And we need global action now. An August 2021 report by the Intergovernmental Panel on Climate Change (IPCC) detailing the current pace of global warming was described as a "code red for humanity" by Antonio Guterres, the Secretary-General of the UN.

The IPCC report shows that global greenhouse gas emissions will only fall 1% by 2030 based on current commitments. According to the UN Net Zero Coalition, we need at least a 45% reduction by 2030 to limit global warming to 1.5°C and there is no shortcut to reaching our sustainability goals.

Related large-scale investments are required; and this book sets out some broad analysis of the various roles that exchanges and various parties can play in mobilising green and sustainable finance (GSF) to drive the world's net-zero transition.

The book has examined the global GSF ecosystem and used China as a case-study to take an in-depth look at how it is developing GSF to achieve its climate goals, what opportunities exist in China's green and sustainable investment market, and how the Hong Kong Special Administrative Region (HKSAR) can grow as a sustainable finance hub.

The book also charted the rise of green and sustainable financial instruments, as well as exploring advances in financial technology that measures issuers' environment, social and governance (ESG) performance; and the role of exchanges in developing and strengthening the broader GSF ecosystem.

Sitting at the heart of Asia's capital markets, Hong Kong Exchanges and Clearing Limited (HKEX) sees itself as a change agent and has a critical role to play in this sustainability journey as a regulator, market operator, and corporate. As part of the Green & Sustainable Finance Cross-Agency Steering Group, HKEX also works closely with the HKSAR government and financial regulators to accelerate the growth of sustainable finance in Hong Kong and the Guangdong-Hong Kong-Macao Greater Bay Area.

New GSF products and asset classes have emerged in the past few years, and we will undoubtedly see more in the future. New policies and market initiatives are being released nearly every day to ensure that GSF and ESG investments contribute to our planet. This book provides a variety of perspectives on GSF that are certainly not exhaustive and we welcome your feedback.

I would like to thank my HKEX colleagues across all departments for their support in creating this book. My thanks also go to our publisher, The Commercial Press (H.K.) Limited, and the various sustainable associations and professionals from market institutions for their notable contributions.

The rich array of content in this book shows that capital markets are fast-evolving and that GSF is mainstreaming. It is now up to us, as individuals, businesses, and investors, to invest in the right projects for ourselves, and for the planet.

Grace HUI
Managing Director, Head of Green and Sustainable Finance, Markets Division
Hong Kong Exchanges and Clearing Limited

November 2021

後 記

資本市場、淨零轉型及
香港市場推動變革的角色

根據聯合國的資料，推動全球轉型至淨零經濟至少需要 90 萬億美元，故資本市場能發揮關鍵作用。

我們現在就需要全球一起採取行動。政府間氣候變化專門委員會（Intergovernmental Panel on Climate Change，簡稱 IPCC）於 2021 年 8 月發表了報告，詳述當前全球暖化的步伐，聯合國秘書長古特雷斯稱這步伐為「人類的紅色警報」。

根據 IPCC 的這份報告，按照目前各國所作的承諾，全球溫室氣體排放量到 2030 年才將僅下降 1%。然而，根據聯合國淨零聯盟，我們需要於 2030 年前至少減少 45% 的排放量，方有望將全球暖化限制在攝氏 1.5 度，而我們要達致可持續發展目標，實在別無捷徑。

相關的大規模投資自不可少。就此，本書嘗試對交易所及各方在推動綠色及可持續金融來達至全球淨零轉型上可以發揮的各種作用作出廣泛分析。

本書檢視了全球綠色及可持續金融的生態圈，並以中國作為個案研究，細看中國如何發展綠色及可持續金融以實現其氣候目標、中國的綠色及可持續投資市場有何機遇，以及香港特別行政區可如何發展為可持續金融樞紐。

書中亦展示綠色及可持續金融工具冒起的趨勢，又探索金融科技的進步，用以衡量發行人的環境、社會及管治（Environment、Social、Governance，簡稱 ESG）方面的表現；以及交易所在發展並強化更廣泛的綠色及可持續金融生態圈方面的角色。

香港交易及結算所有限公司（香港交易所）置身於亞洲資本市場的中心，以推動變革為定位，並同時作為監管機構、市場營運者的一家企業，一直致力協助推動可持續發展的進程。作為「綠色和可持續金融跨機構督導小組」的成員，香港交易所亦與香港特別行政區政府及各金融監管機構緊密合作，協力加快推進香港及粵港澳大灣區可持續金融的發展。

過去幾年，市場漸漸出現不少新的綠色及可持續金融產品和資產類別，相信未來還會陸續出現更多。全球各地幾乎每天都有新的政策和市場舉措出台，以確保綠色及可持續金融與 ESG 投資對地球的環境生態有所貢獻。本書嘗試羅列關於綠色及可持續金融的各種觀點，雖不能詳盡無遺，但還望拋磚引玉，聽取你的寶貴意見。

在此感謝香港交易所各科部同事對本書出版的支持，亦感謝出版商商務印書館（香港）有限公司，以及多個可持續發展協會與市場機構的各位專家，對本書所作出的貢獻。

本書的豐富內容從多角度告訴我們：在迅速演變的資本市場中，綠色及可持續金融已漸成主流。我們不論作為個人、企業還是投資者，現在都是時候細加思索，為自己、為地球作出正確的投資。

許淑嫻
香港交易所
市場科董事總經理
綠色及可持續發展金融主管

2021 年 11 月